WATER WISDOM

WATER WISDOM

Preparing the Groundwork for Cooperative and Sustainable Water Management in the Middle East

EDITED BY ALON TAL AND
ALFRED ABED RABBO

RUTGERS UNIVERSITY PRESS
New Brunswick, New Jersey, and London

Library of Congress Cataloging-in-Publication Data

Water wisdom : preparing the groundwork for cooperative and sustainable water management in the Middle East / edited by Alon Tal and Alfred Abed Rabbo.

    p. cm.

  Includes bibliographical references and index.

  ISBN 978-0-8135-4770-1 (hardcover : alk. paper) — ISBN 978-0-8135-4771-8 (pbk. : alk. paper)

  1. Water resources development—Middle East—Planning. 2. Water resources development—Government policy—Middle East. 3. Water resources development—Environmental aspects—Middle East. 4. Water-supply—Middle East—International cooperation. I. Tal, Alon, 1960– II. Abed Rabbo, Alfred.

  HD1698.M53W388 2010

  333.9100956—dc22

                                     2009048301

A British Cataloging-in-Publication record for this book is available from the British Library.

Visit our Web site: http://rutgerspress.rutgers.edu

Manufactured in the United States of America

Contents

List of Illustrations — ix
Preface — xiii
Acknowledgments — xvii
Abbreviations — xix

Introduction
ALON TAL AND ALFRED ABED RABBO — 1

Part 1   **Characterizing Water Resources**

Water Resources: The Palestinian Perspective
AMJAD ALIEWI — 13

Water Resources: The Israeli Perspective
ALON TAL — 26

Editors' Summary — 37

Part 2   **Past Water Agreements and Their Implementation**

The Oslo II Accords in Retrospect: Implementation of the
Water Provisions in the Israeli and Palestinian Interim
Peace Agreements
ANAN JAYOUSI — 43

Article 40: An Israeli Retrospective
DORIT KERRET — 49

Editors' Summary — 62

Part 3   **The Water Culture of Israelis and Palestinians**

Water Culture in Palestine
ZIAD ABDEEN — 67

Water Culture in Israel
CLIVE LIPCHIN — 71

Editors' Summary — 76

Part 4   Water Legislation

The Palestinian Legal Regime for Water Quality Protection
HIBA I. HUSSEINI — 81

Legal Framework for Allocation of Water and for Protection
of Water Quality in Israel
MARCIA GELPE — 90

Editors' Summary — 98

Part 5   Groundwater Management

Shared Groundwater Resources: Environmental Hazards
and Technical Solutions in Palestine
KAREN ASSAF — 103

The Mountain Aquifer: Shared Groundwater Resources,
Environmental Hazards, and Technical Solutions
DROR AVISAR — 117

Editors' Summary — 122

Part 6   Stream Restoration

The Condition of Streams and Prospects for Restoration
in Palestine
NADER EL-KHATEEB — 127

Stream Restoration under Conditions of Water Scarcity:
Insight from the Israeli Experience
AVITAL GASITH AND YARON HERSHKOVITZ — 136

Editors' Summary — 148

Part 7   Drinking-Water Standards

Drinking-Water Quality and Standards: The Palestinian
Perspective
ALFRED ABED RABBO — 153

Israeli Drinking-Water Resources and Supply
RAMY HALPERIN — 162

Editors' Summary — 170

Part 8   Sewage Treatment

Sewage Treatment in Gaza and the Quest to Upgrade
Infrastructure
KHALIL TUBAIL — 175

Wastewater Treatment and Reuse in Israel
YOSSI INBAR — 183

Editors' Summary — 189

Part 9   Agriculture and Water

Sustainable Water Supply for Agriculture in Palestine
SAID A. ASSAF — 195

Sustainable Water Supply for Agriculture in Israel
ALON BEN-GAL — 211

Editors' Summary — 224

Part 10   Desalination

The Coming Age of Desalination for Gaza: Visions, Illusions, and Reality
NAHED GHBN — 229

Desalination in Israel: Status, Prospects, and Contexts
YAAKOV GARB — 238

Editors' Summary — 246

Part 11   The Jordan River Basin

Managing the Jordan River Basin: A Palestinian Perspective
NANCY RUMMAN — 251

Managing the Jordan River Basin: An Israeli Perspective
RICHARD LASTER AND DAN LIVNEY — 258

Editors' Summary — 264

Part 12   Gaza's Water Situation

The Gaza Water Crisis
YOUSEF ABU-MAYLA AND EILON M. ADAR — 267

Editors' Summary — 278

Part 13   Citizen Involvement

The Role of Civil Society in Addressing Transboundary Water Issues in the Israeli-Palestinian Context
IYAD ABURDEINEH, GIDON BROMBERG, LUCY MICHAELS, AND NA'AMA TESCHNER — 283

Editors' Summary — 293

Part 14   **The Role of Third Parties in Conflict Resolution**

The Role of Third Parties in Helping to Resolve the Conflicts over Water Issues in Israel and Palestine
ROBIN TWITE — 297

Editors' Summary — 308

Part 15   **Cooperative Water Management Strategies**

Joint Aquifer Management: Institutional Options
MARWAN HADDAD AND ERAN FEITELSON — 313

Editors' Summary — 321

List of Contributors — 323
Index — 327

Illustrations

FIGURES

1.1   Location map showing Palestinian aquifers — 14

1.2   The complex picture of water use in the West Bank — 16

1.3   Water supply-demand gap in Palestine — 18

1.4   Distribution of groundwater chloride, nitrate, sulfate, and total dissolved solids (TDS) across the West Bank — 23

1.5   Average groundwater salinity (Cl) and nitrate concentration (NO_3) of the Coastal Aquifer for year 2004 in the Gaza Strip — 24

1.6   Israeli and Palestinian average rain gradient — 27

1.7   Israeli and Palestinian freshwater resources — 27

1.8   Water levels in Lake Kinneret — 29

1.9   Average nitrate and chloride concentrations in wells along Israel's Coastal Aquifer, 1960–2007 — 30

1.10   Pumping rates in the Coastal Aquifer over 12 years — 31

1.11   Development of seawater desalination plants in Israel — 34

5.1   Shared and non-shared groundwater aquifers — 105

5.2   Shared and non shared surface water catchments — 106

5.3   The Jordan River, Dead Sea, and Wadi Arava catchment area — 107

5.4   The western part of the Mountain Aquifer, the Yarkon-Taninim Basin — 118

9.1   Quality index of agricultural production, crops, and livestock — 212

9.2   Size distribution of active farms among Israeli moshavim — 213

9.3   Breakdown of agricultural output by branch, 2004 — 214

9.4   Breakdown of agricultural crop areas, 2003 — 215

9.5   Extent of irrigated land since the establishment of the State of Israel — 216

9.6   Agricultural production, 1986–2006 — 216

9.7   Number of people employed in agriculture, 1960–2010 — 216

9.8   Wastewater reuse as part of the overall water balance (drought years excluded) — 219

10.1   Location map of the Gaza Strip and the desalination plants — 234

12.1   Generalized cross-section plain for the Gaza Strip Coastal Aquifer — 270

12.2   Groundwater flow directions in the Gaza Strip Coastal Aquifer — 270

12.3   Groundwater level in the Gaza Strip Coastal Aquifer, 2005 — 271

12.4 Average groundwater level in selected wells across the
      Gaza Strip — 272

12.5 Present and future water demand for agricultural
      versus municipal and industrial use in the Gaza Strip — 273

12.6 Chloride and nitrate concentrations in drinking wells — 274

15.1 Issues raised by separate management — 315

15.2 Recharge zones in the West Bank — 316

TABLES

1.1   Palestinian aquifer recharge rates — 13

1.2   Estimated municipal and industrial total water use in Palestine — 15

1.3   Estimated total water supply for irrigation in Palestine — 15

1.4   Estimated total water supply in Palestine — 15

1.5   Projected municipal water needs — 16

1.6   Projected industrial water needs — 17

1.7   Projected agricultural water needs — 17

1.8   Estimated total water needs in Palestine — 17

1.9   Estimated gap between water supply and needs in Palestine — 17

1.10 Summary of Palestinian water rights — 19

1.11 Water supply and demand in Israel, 1998–2020 — 32

1.12 Water pricing in Israel, 2008 — 35

3.1   Potable water consumption by purpose — 73

3.2   Water production in agriculture by type — 73

5.1   Natural water recharge of the aquifer basins — 108

5.2   Water usage cycle — 110

6.1   Selected geophysical characteristics of Israel — 138

6.2   Maximum and average values of readily degradable organic
      matter in selected streams in Israel — 140

6.3   Maximum and average values of total suspended solids in
      selected streams in Israel — 141

7.1   Summary of the existing Israeli drinking-water standards — 166

8.1   Wastewater treatment plants existing in Gaza governorates — 176

8.2   Current effluent quality (chemical and biological) of the
      Gaza wastewater treatment plant — 177

8.3   Classification of effluent quality (PS 742/2003) — 178

8.4   Comparison of expected effluent quality from Central Gaza
      WWTP with local quality standards — 178

8.5   Criteria recommended by PWA for effluent standards in the
      Gaza Strip — 180

8.6   Proposed new Israeli standards for effluent — 186

9.1   Land use in the West Bank and Gaza Strip in 2005 — 197

9.2   Key crops in the West Bank and Gaza Strip in 2006
       (crops with highest ton production) —— 198

9.3   Cultivated land in the West Bank and Gaza Strip before and after
       the Israeli occupation —— 199

9.4   Type of agricultural crops cultivated before and after occupation
       in the West Bank —— 200

9.5   Olive and olive oil production in the West Bank —— 200

9.6   Changes in the cultivated area of wheat, barley, and sesame
       in the West Bank, 1964–2006 —— 201

9.7   Irrigation water sources and amounts used —— 202

9.8   Area of protected cultivation in the West Bank —— 203

9.9   Feasible irrigatable land areas and the amount of irrigation
       water required —— 204

9.10   Trees grown in the Jordan River Basin and their water sources —— 205

9.11   Field crops grown in the Jordan River Basin and their
       water requirements —— 206

9.12   Salt-tolerant crops and maximum salinity for cultivation —— 206

9.13   Water requirements of some vegetable crops under greenhouse
       and open-field cultivation —— 207

9.14   Water needs and productivity of jojoba and almond trees —— 207

9.15   Agricultural use of land in Israel —— 214

9.16   Cultivated area, major crops, and irrigation water use, 1996 and
       predicted for 2020 —— 218

9.17   Supply of water to agriculture —— 218

9.18   Agricultural water prices —— 220

10.1   Brackish and seawater desalination plants in the Gaza Strip —— 233

10.2   Environmental impact assessment of desalination plants —— 235

11.1   Potential for future development of water resources in the
       Jordan Valley —— 256

12.1   Water balance in the Gaza Strip, 2007 —— 273

Preface

For too long the professional literature characterizing the conflicts between Israelis and Palestinians over water issues has suffered from the twin transgressions of excessive generalization and alarmism. Books and articles did not engage experts on the two sides and encourage them to systematically identify those areas about which they agree and disagree. There has been an unfortunate shortage of focused academic frameworks in which to explore pragmatic solutions to overcome existing controversies. Only when differences are clearly mapped can they can be addressed. Indeed, sometimes, when the two positions are laid side by side, there is less discord than originally anticipated. At the same time, there has been no shortage of academics, politicians, and diplomats who broadcast disquieting and defeatist scenarios about the conflicts that emerge from the region's growing water scarcity. "The next Middle East war will be fought over water" is a commonly heard platitude. But we believe this perspective to be simplistic and detached from the actual dynamics in the field. As friends and colleagues who have worked together in the field of water science and policy for over a decade, we are more optimistic.

The Palestinian and Israeli experts who join us in this book were selected based on their experience, expertise, and positive approach toward a coordinated water policy for the region. Each agreed to increase the level of resolution regarding the water management challenges that they face. Each of the central areas that make up the heart of the "water conflict" is addressed in an essay by an authority from each side or in a joint presentation. These dispassionate "twin" analyses, with a Palestinian perspective followed by an Israeli view, enable us (and readers) to better consider the specific areas of dispute and agreement. Our work as editors and mediators who seek to say something constructive and new was made much easier after we convened a gathering of the authors in Amman Jordan in May 2008.

Draft essays were presented, and an informal but intense practical discussion ensued about the implications of the two positions. Based on the dialogue and the ideas which arose, we offer a series of summaries on each subject that constitute a consensus about the present situation and what a comprehensive accord needs to contain so that water might constitute a catalyst for cooperation rather than conflict. In the final essays, common visions of cooperative institutional and management frameworks are set forth by Palestinian and Israeli experts in single essays about the role of NGOs (nongovernmental organizations) in resolving water conflicts and joint management frameworks. Given their longtime involvement in the field, discussions in Amman especially benefited from the individual perspectives of retired British diplomat Robin Twite and Hillel Shuval, who has been a leading expert in local water quality issues for sixty years in Israel, exploring models for Israeli-Palestinian cooperation for over twenty years.

An underlying theme of all essays in this book is that while there are many acute hydrological problems, solutions are at hand. Technological alternatives, models for joint water management, and public policies exist. There is no reason why an adequate supply of high quality water cannot be available to both Israelis and Palestinians. This book offers a blueprint for cooperation, pragmatism, and, ultimately, sustainable water management. From stream restoration to groundwater management, from the Jordan River to the aquifer in Gaza, from desalination to wastewater reuse—this book provides an update of where we are and where we might go.

Resolving existing Palestinian-Israeli tensions over water issues must begin with a focus on water allocation and supply. Although there have been modest improvements, the average per capita consumption of water (suitable for drinking purposes) in the West Bank and Gaza remains below World Health Organization standards. This chronic scarcity is unacceptable and places constant pressure on the stability of the socioeconomic future of the Palestinians. Without a sufficient and safe supply of water it will be difficult to ensure a stable future for the emerging Palestinian state.

Finding additional water sources constitutes a core political issue in the final status negotiations for Palestinians, and Israel is highly aware of this. Indeed, the Oslo Accords established only an interim arrangement for water allocations, leaving ultimate division of shared water resources as an issue for negotiations in the final accord. This was reiterated at the 2007 Annapolis peace talks. Palestinians have consistently held that water rights should be resolved according to principles of international law, which presumably would guarantee sufficient quantities and grant sovereignty to Palestinians to utilize and control their water resources. Given the amorphous nature of existing international principles—and such concepts as the "reasonable and equitable share of water resources" or its "beneficial uses"—it is not clear whether international legal instruments provide sufficiently clear direction for the kind of resolution that a final agreement will need to provide. As they did in the peace accord between Israel and Jordan, negotiators will need to take a more pragmatic approach to water quantities and qualities and ensure that a final settlement accounts for the "just" water rights and needs of Palestinians and Israelis.

The gap between the supply and needs of Palestinian communities makes additional conventional and non-conventional water resources essential. The availability of low-cost desalination changes the "zero-sum game" dynamics that characterized discussions in the past. The 1995 agreement on water between Israel and Palestine was made before desalination became a central part of Israeli water supply strategy. But the change constitutes a historic opportunity. Effluent reuse, water conservation, and efficiency measures are already part of present accepted practices and must be expanded.

Water quality issues are likely to be less divisive as the sides seek a final accord. The lack of sanitation services, poor management of sewage and solid waste, overzealous application of fertilizers and pesticides along with the over-extraction of water contribute to the polluting of the springs, streams, and aquifers of both parties. This chronic pollution has led to the decommissioning of many wells and has taken its toll on the limited water resources in Israel and Palestine. The environmental damage serves to exacerbate existing gaps between water supply and demands. Accordingly, joint management frameworks constitute a win-win dynamic and offer an opportunity to enhance the sustainable development and protection of water resources on both sides of the border.

Of paramount interest for both sides is the matter of sewage and infrastructure. Wastewater treatment is an essential element in alleviating pollution to Palestinian water resources, improving their quality of life, and expanding the available water for irrigation and stream restoration. But sewage treatment not only is a technical/engineering challenge, but also needs to be addressed in a holistic approach that takes into consideration the institutionalization of wastewater treatment, technologies and system maintenance, and reuse strategies for agriculture, along with promulgation and implementation of regulations. In Israel, beyond continued progress in reducing discharges from factories and municipal sewage systems, non-point sources of pollution, especially from agricultural and urban storm runoff, have not been systematically addressed heretofore. Gas stations have also emerged as a major source of groundwater contamination.

In short, there is the full menu of water issues that are addressed in the essays of this book. We have tried to put together a volume that is both scientifically precise and accessible to readers who are not hydrologists or scientists working in the field. The importance of cooperation is not uniform for all issues. Some hydrological challenges require complex and politically charged joint management strategies, while for others, coordination in a general sense is sufficient. Yet, none of the Palestinian and Israeli water problems are insurmountable. Political commitment, economic resources, creativity, flexibility, and goodwill are required.

Alon Tal
Alfred Abed Rabbo
April 2010

Acknowledgments

The authors would like to express their gratitude to the many people who assisted in the preparation and production of this volume. Na'ama Teschner was a superb administrator during the initial stages of the project and oversaw much of the logistics for the workshop in Amman. Omar Khassawneh, made all the arrangements in Amman and was of invaluable help in organizing the workshop there. Lucy Michaels provided additional appreciated support for these activities. Cochy Abuharon graciously assisted with establishing the project's Web site. For the past year, Liat Oshry's ongoing and diligent assistance in correcting the different drafts of the manuscript and preparing the figures, as well as communicating with the diverse team of authors was invaluable. This book reflects her hard work and competence.

At Rutgers University Press, Audra Wolfe and Doreen Valentine were editors who shepherded the book through the initial and interim phases of the publishing process. They showed great patience with the sundry delays and challenges of putting out a book of this nature. Suzanne Kellam was very helpful in the final production stages. Karen Johnson was an extraordinary copy editor whose thoughtful corrections and suggestions are greatly valued. We appreciate their professional acumen and thank them all for their efforts. The editors also thank Tamsin Arnold for her precise and expeditious work in compiling the book's index.

Finally, there are the thirty-three Palestinian and Israeli authors, all experts and very busy people who found the time to write chapters for this volume. This book indeed is ultimately an expression of their collective wisdom and hope for a better day in our troubled region. We are grateful for their confidence and involvement in this publishing project. Of course we thank our families for their constant support in our work.

Abbreviations

ARIJ   Land Research Centre and Applied Research Institute Jerusalem
BOD   biological oxygen demand (a measure of organic loadings
           into a stream)
BOT   build/operate/transfer
CMWU   Coastal Municipalities Water Utility
dS/m   desi Semins per meter
EC   electrical conductivity
EU   European Union
FAO   United Nations Food and Agriculture Organization
FOEME   Friends of the Earth Middle East
HWE   House of Water and Environment
IPCRI   Israeli-Palestinian Centre for Research and Information
JSETs   Joint Supervision and Enforcement Teams
JWC   Joint Water Committee
l/c/d   liter per capita per day
mcm   million cubic meters (billions of liters)
MO   Military Order
NGO   nongovernmental organization
NSU   negotiation support unit
PARC   Palestinian Agricultural Relief Committees
PCBS   Palestinian Central Bureau of Statistics
PHG   Palestine Hydrology Group
ppm   parts per million
PWA   Palestine Water Authority
RO   reverse osmosis (desalination technology)
SPNI   Society for the Protection of Nature in Israel
SUSMAQ   Sustainable Management of the West Bank and Gaza Aquifers
TDS   total dissolved solids
TSS   total suspended solids (a measure of water turbidity)
UN   United Nations
USAID   United States Agency for International Development
U.S. EPA   United States Environmental Protection Agency
WHO   World Health Organization
WSERU   Water and Soil Environmental Research Unit at Bethlehem
           University
WWTP   wastewater treatment plant

WATER WISDOM

Introduction

This book offers considerable details about a range of water issues. The systematic and symmetrical enumeration of key controversies surrounding Israeli-Palestinian water resources by experts on both sides offers a unique contribution to this wide-ranging literature. Each subject has its own nuances which need to be considered. Specificity, indeed, is critical for resolving what often appears to be a litany of disagreements. Yet this book demonstrates that hydrological matters about which Israelis and Palestinians already agree are, in fact, far greater than the areas of disagreement. It is also encouraging that many common themes emerge from the disparate chapters. These should be stated at the outset, to create a conceptual context within which to consider the political and hydrological issues that need to be addressed in a permanent accord.

Statistically, five successive years of drought suggest that historic assumptions about Palestinian and Israeli water supply were optimistic. Climatic impacts on precipitation that were thought to be part of future scenarios, thus allowing time for adaptation measures, may very well already be the region's new reality. If, in the past, water shortages were expected to be acute, the more severe hydrological projections now demand new ways of addressing the growing scarcity and more serious formats for cooperation. Water quality concerns can no longer be put off as a luxury but, in fact, hold greater economic and humanitarian ramifications than ever before.

Accordingly, this book's underlying message is that there are many issues and assumptions about which Israeli and Palestinian water experts agree and which provide a basis for moving expeditiously toward a lasting peace. Among them are these:

- In light of the geometric population growth, Israel's past and existing water policies in the West Bank have left Palestinians with inadequate water resources.
- Whether or not providing additional Palestinian water to the Palestinian communities and economy is perceived as a fundamental political right or simply a more "reasonable and equitable sharing of water resources," there is a consensus that a final peace agreement must expand Palestinian water resources.
- Palestinians and Israelis must agree on a safe level of extraction from water resources and share a commitment to prevent extraction below these redlines.
- Desalination, reuse of effluents, and reduction of leakages in water delivery are all part of a comprehensive strategy that will be needed to expand the overall water resources in the region.

- More stringent measures to improve water quality are needed, with sewage infrastructure being the highest immediate priority for investment.
- Water is not just a commodity or a resource to be produced or mined, but holds a special spiritual and religious role for both sides in the conflict. Similarities in Israeli and Palestinian heritage suggest that water need not be a source of division but can be leveraged to produce greater cooperation and commitment to sustainable management.

At the same time, there are many areas where traditional disputes and competing claims have not been resolved. The following points summarize the most fundamental historic disagreements:

- Controversy remains as to whether Palestinians enjoy rights to the entire Mountain Aquifer or not. Israel argues that the water in the aquifer was almost entirely utilized prior to 1967. While water sharing is possible, in no way does Israel concede its historic rights to this resource. Palestinians hold that as the aquifer is recharged largely by rainfall in the West Bank, the water should be theirs. Disagreements also exist with regards to utilization of waters from the Jordan River by Israel, which Israel sees as a right consistent with past agreements and its historic rights.
- Palestinians are unwilling to accept desalinized water in lieu of water resources drawn from the Mountain Aquifer. This position relies not only on assumptions regarding their hydrological independence, but also on what they believe is a more logical, geographically driven, management and supply scheme.
- Palestinians reject the legitimacy of Israeli settlements in the West Bank, with the implication being that any water usage by these settlements is by definition illegitimate.
- Israel argues that Palestinian administrative capacity remains insufficient to guarantee sustainable yields and oversight of pumping and accessing waters. Moreover, it is dissatisfied with Palestinian commitment to reducing discharge of poorly treated effluents which ultimately contribute to contamination of shared resources.

The ideas put forward in this book seek to trump some of the traditional impasses about regional water management. By increasing the level of resolution, solutions emerge. When ideology is replaced by hydrology and engineering, most of the water conflicts appear surmountable, with alternatives appearing increasingly feasible.

Water Rights

The specific allocation of water remains a threshold issue which will need to be addressed in a final accord. It is axiomatic among Palestinians of all political denominations that the hydrological narrative of the region is dominated by the ongoing violation of their basic national rights of access to water. Any final accord, in their view, must first and foremost rectify the situation. There appears to be no real argument over the inadequacy of present water allocations by the two sides. Yet, most Israelis contest the Palestinian position regarding water rights, and the resulting deadlock has done little to serve Palestinian or Israeli interests.

While many Israelis have argued that progress can be made through a changed focus in the discourse from "rights" to "needs," Palestinians are uncomfortable with this approach and believe that recognition of their legitimate rights under international law should be the basis for a formal understanding and agreement. In this context, for over 50 years the position of international law under Helsinki Rules has recognized the validity of claims to a "reasonable and equitable share in the beneficial uses of the waters in an international drainage basin." Quantifying the specific volume of an equitable share ultimately requires a climate-specific characterization of human and economic needs—as well as those of ecosystems.

This technical exercise can be done transparently either jointly or by an authorized third party. The results should lead to a clearer definition and recognition of Palestinians' rights to an equitable share, in the spirit of international law, of the waters of the mountain aquifer, the coastal aquifer in Gaza, the Jordan River, and the Dead Sea. A parallel and concomitant effort should also recognize the legitimacy of Israeli claims to these water resources and clearly set forward the water deficit, allowing for intensive efforts through international assistance and private-sector investment, to eliminate it.

Specific allocation quantities will need to be defined in a final accord on this basis, with the assumption that basic human needs should be guaranteed before alternative uses are approved. The increasingly dominant role of wastewater reuse and the adoption of drought-resistant crop types among local farmers suggest that agriculture on both sides need not be a victim of water provisions in a final accord. The ultimate agreement should define projected development goals for each side, enabling them to articulate a clear list of hydrological development projects to potential donors as part of the investment needed to facilitate a final resolution of the conflict.

Desalination

Until recently, debates regarding water rights involved "zero-sum game" dynamics, based on assumptions that supply is static or shrinking. New technological advances allow for future discussions about water needs to take place in a totally different context. The present and potential contribution of desalination for resolving water scarcity dynamics, in general, and in conflict regions, in particular, offers a source of optimism.

Already the Israeli water system has seen critical benefits from the additional 15% of water supply that is presently received from its new coastal water factories. Within a decade this amount should triple, making water resources from the sea far greater than even those provided by the contested Jordan River Basin. Given the mixing of water sources by Israeli utilities, Palestinians, in fact, for several years have also enjoyed this ultra-clean, new source of water. It is time for the region's pervasive political hydro-conflict to begin to benefit from what desalination can offer.

Beyond the actual quantities, desalination for the first time has also introduced a significant private-sector presence into local water management—substantially in Israel and much more modestly in Gaza. Thus far, Israeli experience suggests that due to the highly regulated nature of local water supply, the pitfalls associated with privatized water supply have not been a problem. Palestinian leadership remains skeptical about desalination's role in long-term Palestinian water supply due to its high costs for farmers, the finite life span of plants, and implicit concessions on Palestinian claims to the mountain aquifer. Yet, Palestinian experts also recognize that their citizens continue to pay exorbitant prices for bottled and privately supplied water while a centralized desalination strategy, which takes advantage of economies of scale and proven new technological advances, could provide more water, at higher quality, more cheaply.

With confidence constituting the scarcest resource of all in the region, it is probably too early to advocate a bilateral or multilateral water market for the region. But given the charged climate of the Middle East, the fact that desalinated water suppliers are consortiums and corporations, with headquarters dispersed around the world, whose economic interests are fundamentally apolitical, should be seen as an advantage. Their pursuits need not clash with those of local governments, and the steady advance of privatized desalination facilities constitutes a quiet step in the right direction.

Desalination surely makes discussion about the creation of a regional water market more possible. By commoditizing water through major production facilities, there is an implicit depoliticization of water resources. While environmental ethicists can and should raise legitimate concerns about the moral implications of private water supply, given the overall dynamics of controversy, the overall effect may be propitious.

The international community can surely play a role in expediting massive new quantities of water through international aid to support Palestinian desalination. The Israeli government has already agreed to the establishment of Palestinian desalination facilities on Israeli coastal lands. Plans for major Gazan desalination facilities have been collecting dust for more than a decade. It would be morally wrong and politically foolish to ignore Palestinian reservations about receiving a gift of desalination capacity. Yet, Palestinian commitment to the symbolic significance of groundwater resources can still be reflected in a final agreement in which groundwater rights are granted in return for transfer of operational control of Palestinian desalination facilities.

Concerns about desalination's environmental impacts are both global (via the greenhouse gas emissions associated with energy sources) and local (via the cumulative impact of antiscalant discharge, loss of coastal habitats, etc.). Now is the time to highlight these concerns and insist on adoption of specific (and available) solutions. Especially given the anticipated role of the private sector, clear expectations regarding environmental performance and tough oversight for desalination facilities can and should be part of a final water agreement. Already, Sydney and

Perth, Australia, have mandated clean energy as part of their desalination programs. A comprehensive peace agreement offers an opportunity to ensure that one environmental asset does not come at the expense of other environmental values and that desalinated water not only will be ultra-clean, but also will in no way harm the marine environment and the atmosphere.

Protecting Water Quality

Both Israeli and Palestinian experts for some time have recognized the win-win dynamics associated with coordinated efforts to protect water quality. The considerable expense of replacing scarce water resources contaminated by pollution with desalinized alternatives is a practical reminder that there is a clear common interest in pollution prevention and control.

A recurring theme in this book is that upgrading sewage treatment in Palestinian communities (and several Israeli ones as well) constitutes the single most immediate task facing the two entities. This is particularly true with regards to stream restoration as well as protection of groundwater in the region. An immediate, "emergency" initiative must be initiated to collect and treat all untreated sewage in the Palestinian sector, phasing out existing cesspool systems so that wastewater connects to these centralized facilities.

Typically, water quality standards drive water development activities, and coordinated prescriptions and criteria for Palestinians and Israelis in a final agreement are essential. Assuming that the economies (as well as the drinking-water supply) of the two entities will remain connected, asymmetrical regulatory expectations create unfair competitive advantage for polluters.

Israel traditionally has taken a position which expects the Palestinians to meet its environmental criteria. Israeli standards over time are increasingly close to those required in Europe. It would seem, however, that for the immediate future, environmental expectations must be adjusted to meet existing Palestinian capacity and available resources.

The role of donor nations in providing the necessary resources for achieving water quality objectives will be critical. During the past 15 years, the Palestinian economy has fallen behind; and it will take some time until a sufficient tax base exists to maintain, much less construct, the necessary environmental infrastructure. Not withstanding its own economic challenges, Israel is in a position to help. An interesting model is that provided by the United States and Mexico, which have for many years proven the benefits of cooperation in restoring shared water resources. Given compelling American interests in environmental improvement, the United States demanded higher levels of performance but was willing to participate in the associated investment within Mexico.

After infrastructure development, the next regulatory challenge involves implementation and compliance monitoring. The pervasive use of raw sewage by some Palestinian farmers and the frequent violations associated with polluted discharges of effluents by industrial and municipal facilities in Israel are examples of the gap that exists between theory and practice for water quality.

It is important to emphasize that unilateral efforts are unlikely to solve the region's environmental problems. For instance, Israeli efforts at the border to capture and treat sewage and wastes that flow from the Palestinian Authority into the Alexander and Beer Sheva streams in Israel may be justified as a short-term exigency given the present collapse of cooperative efforts. But this constitutes a dubious long-term strategy. Recent research suggests that roughly half of the wastewater percolates from the waste stream into the ground during its route into Israel, leaving real concerns about groundwater contamination. International assistance along with clear Palestinian performance standards must treat pollution at the source and, in the case of industry, promote pollution prevention measures.

Institutional Cooperation

After 15 years, the institutional framework that was adopted under Article 40 of the interim agreements, the Joint Water Committee (JWC), is no longer sufficient. As successive Israeli governments preferred to maintain water as a core issue that should be resolved in the overall negotiations over a final peace accord, the temporary arrangement became entrenched. Unfortunately, the JWC and the veto power held by its Israeli representatives perpetuate the inherent asymmetry between Israeli and Palestinian influence and engender resentment about what has been called hydrological hegemony.

While there is agreement that the very survival and stamina of the JWC are worthy of praise, there also seems to be an agreement that it could benefit from expansion. For instance, it should include independent professional experts as well as qualified NGO (nongovernmental organization) representatives (at least as observers) from both sides. There is a strong case to be made for permanent international presence on the committee by representatives of the European Union, the United States, or the United Nations. Such participation is especially compelling when the key role envisioned for international assistance in providing the infrastructure necessary to reach water quality objectives is considered.

Experience from around the world suggests that the most stable and effective management frameworks of common water resources are based on the empowering of independent professionals and isolating political consideration and personalities. A shift in the makeup of the JWC and adoption of an approach such as that existing between the United and Mexico regarding the utilization of waters of the Colorado and Tijuana rivers and of the Rio Grande could both return the faith among Palestinians about the fairness of the Committee's decisions as well as expedite progress in meeting the sides' shared interest in expanding water supply to Palestinians and protecting water quality.

Ironically, discontinuation of the most important component of the interim agreement, from the perspective of Israel's hydrological interest, the Joint Supervision and Enforcement Teams, rarely is the subject of discussion. The interim agreement empowered these teams of Israelis and Palestinians to enjoin activities that can produce transboundary contamination or extraction of water in violation of quantitative agreements. Unfortunately, political turbulence prevented the launching of these enforcement units. Israel may want to consider making concessions in the makeup of the JWC, to ensure a more balanced and less-politicized discussion among equals there. But at the same time, there is also room to link such reform to a firmer political commitment by both parties to return to the coordinated enforcement program, even as it may not enjoy immediate public popularity.

Legal Coordination

While both Israeli and Palestinian laws contain sufficient basic statutes and regulations to address domestic challenges to water quality, there are many areas in the realm of transboundary contamination that require clarification and harmonization. Present normative provisions may be inadequate for cases where discharged wastewater crosses the border and reaches surface or groundwater sources or where dispersion of leachate from solid waste facilities and discharges from new development produce transboundary pollution. While measures to allow for such coordination will ultimately need to be integrated into each country's statutes and regulations, rather than leaving the matter to chance, the substantive strategy should be driven by very clear provisions in a bilateral peace accord.

Coordination of water quality standards will also be essential. Israel traditionally has taken a position which expects the Palestinians to meet Israeli requirements, even as Israel's own compliance with environmental standards is frequently deficient. Environmental expectations must be adjusted to meet available capacity. Overcoming the inherent asymmetry between the two sides' infrastructure, resources and capacity may involve the gradual phasing in of increasingly stringent performance standards through realistic timetables for compliance. Just as East German industries were allotted several years to meet the higher West German environmental expectations after unification, Israelis and Palestinians will need to agree that Palestinians enjoy a grace period to allow for the improvement of both their physical infrastructure and human capacity. While it will be hard for Israeli environmentalists to swallow, it is prudent to temporarily accept somewhat less stringent water quality standards in the interest of ensuring high compliance levels. The alternative may be creating a fiction about water quality performance along with a pattern of "lip service" regarding environmental compliance and alienation from shared environmental commitments for years to come.

For example, drinking-water standards for Palestinian communities may, in the short term, need to be less stringent than those in Israel. Designing standards with "recommended" and "maximum" contaminant levels offers the public a clearer sense of what compromises are being made in drinking-water quality so that individual decisions can be made with regard to purchase of mineral or bottled water.

Public Participation

"Encouraging public involvement" has become such a frequently employed slogan in discourses involving environmental policies that it often has come to mean very little. In the present context, the challenge is hardly trivial. Actually engaging Israelis and Palestinians in domestic—much less joint—efforts to protect water resources surely is no simple task given the range of other economic, social, and security concerns which compete on the national agendas. Yet, it is clear that no water management strategy will be sustainable without substantial backing from local citizens. Because conflicts of interests may arise between agricultural and environmental uses of water, or when zoning imposes limitations in a watershed protection scheme, it is important that decision-makers enjoy public support. Water conservation efforts, almost by definition, require the engagement of the public. It is also important that managers be able to leverage enthusiasm—or at the very least a reasonable commitment to the peace process in their efforts to ensure sustainable utilization of water resources.

River restoration offers a particularly promising opportunity for public education programs that can engender a greater zeal for environmental and natural resource protection objectives. Even as the Palestinian public has seen little real utility to date from stream restoration projects, surveys suggest that there is especially keen interest in restoring local streams. This may be a result of the general paucity of parks and the total absence of beach front in the West Bank. Water agreements should include commitments for expanding recreational access of citizens to stream banks, with international assistance not limited to treatment technologies but to the public spaces and parks that can take advantage of upgraded water quality.

Israel's Water Authority has recently begun to promote a policy where surface water and effluents are no longer tapped for agricultural use at stream heads, but rather only after they have completed their flow downstream. Pumping water to farmers upstream often requires additional energy and infrastructure but provides two uses from one stream flow. Such an approach increases the likelihood of support for stream restoration by farmers and those urban communities that can benefit from restored water ways.

A Message of Hope

There are many reasons why the overall context of future negotiations of shared Palestinian and Israeli water resources should be one of optimism. Today, it is possible to make water at a relatively modest price, unlike land. Efforts to protect water quality offer real opportunities for cooperation with shared benefits for both the Israeli and Palestinian economies. Expanded tourism remains one of the greatest dividends which a peace process can produce. Clean water resources surely make visits to the region more attractive and expand the menu of natural and religious sites.

From time to time, foreboding admonitions are heard from academic experts and even leading international spokespeople, such as former U.N. Secretary-General Boutros Boutros-Ghali, who warn that the next war in the Middle East will be over water. The present study and cooperative exercise flies in the face of such pessimistic doomsday visions. Even a modest level of dispassionate analysis will lead to practical solutions and compromises. Left to their own devices, neither Israeli nor Palestinian historic management of water resources has been impressive. As a final peace accord forces the two rivals to reach verifiable common commitments, ironically, it is possible that the region's tensions can be channeled to ensure better collective performance.

Water can wash away a lot of past problems. When professionals sit together from both sides, solutions appear. There is no reason why politicians cannot reach similar results.

PART 1

CHARACTERIZING WATER RESOURCES

While Israeli and Palestinian management of water resources can constitute a politically charged issue, there are some objective facts about which the sides generally agree. A brief overview of the water resources available to each side and the major environmental threats facing them offers an important foundation for any analysis about the full range of transboundary water issues considered in this book. The opening two chapters offer a brief description of the hydrological reality shared by Israelis and Palestinians as well as several salient disparities. It will attempt to characterize the basic quantities and qualities of water resources; past, present, and future plans to develop resources; and the competing claims of sovereignty held by each side. This background is important for understanding subsequent discussion of specific issues associated with coordinated water management. This introductory section opens with a description of Palestinian water resources, continues with a description of Israeli water resources, and then concludes with a summary of the areas of agreement and disagreement between the two sides. Disparities between the objective quantities and quality cited in the chapters are minimal, allowing for a common basis for the future consideration of management challenges.

Water Resources

THE PALESTINIAN PERSPECTIVE

AMJAD ALIEWI

Palestinian Water Resources: Quantities and Use in the West Bank

Current Status

This essay considers the water resources available both in the West Bank and in the Gaza Strip. First, review of the quantities is provided along with Palestinian claims and expectations for expanded resources. The essay then considers the associated water qualities, the sources of contamination, and challenges for environmental protection.

The existing Palestinian water resources in the West Bank are primarily derived from four aquifer basins (table 1.1 and figure 1.1) as well as a series of springs that emanate from the groundwater. Other sources of water are the Jordan River and wadi runoffs.

Tables 1.2, 1.3, and 1.4 represent the water use in Palestine for different purposes (Aliewi 2005) and show a generic picture that varies from year to year. In this volume, water will be presented metrically by cubic meters or m³—the equivalent of 1,000 liters. Hence, 100 million meters or mcm, the fundamental unit of accounting, is actually 100 billion liters of water.

Figure 1.2 shows the complex picture of the water use and control in the West Bank for the year 2005. The Palestinians attribute these complicated dynamics to several factors, particularly the presence of the Israeli settlements inside the West

Table 1.1 Palestinian aquifer recharge rates

Aquifer basin	Recharge rates (mcm/yr)
Eastern	100–172
Northeastern	130–200
Western	335–450
Gaza coastal	55–65
Total	620–887

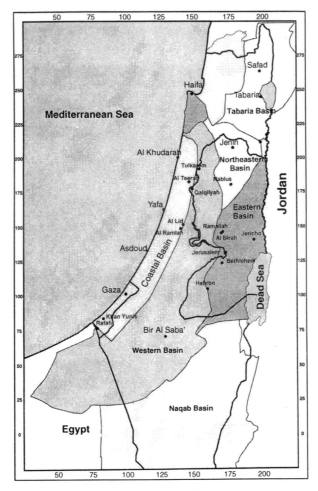

Figure 1.1 Location map showing Palestinian aquifers.
Courtesy of the House of Water and Environment (HWE) Database.

Bank. These settlements consume some 35 mcm/yr from wells drilled in the West
Bank and controlled by Israel, plus a mixed source of water supplied to these settlements by the West Bank Water Department (WBWD). This mixed source is
based largely on Palestinian wells that are operated by the WBWD. Relatively little
water used by Israeli West Bank settlements is delivered from Israeli wells outside
the 1967 West Bank borders. While Palestinians consume their water from water
resources under their control in the West Bank, they also purchase some
25 mcm/yr of water from Israeli sources outside the West Bank as well as some
22 mcm/yr from the WBWD.

   The ownership of WBWD wells has yet to be settled in negotiations.
Accordingly, it is difficult to consider these wells to be fully within Palestinian
sovereignty. According to the 1996 Oslo II agreement, the responsibilities and

Table 1.2 Estimated municipal and industrial total water use in Palestine (mcm/yr)

Region	Wells	Springs	Total
West Bank	55[a]	4	59
Gaza Strip	53[b]	—	53
Total	108	4	112

Source: Data based on several recent studies conducted by the Palestinian Water Authority (PWA) and the House of Water and Environment (HWE).
[a] 22 mcm/yr are purchased from Israeli sources.
[b] 48 mcm/yr are abstracted from wells in the Gaza aquifer and 5 mcm/yr are supplied from the Mekorot Israeli water company.

Table 1.3 Estimated total water supply for irrigation in Palestine (incm/yr)

Region	Wells	Brackish wells	Springs	Total
West Bank	40	0	49	89
Gaza Strip	43	42	0	85
Total	83	42	49	174

Source: Data based on several recent studies conducted by the PWA.

Table 1.4 Estimated total water supply in Palestine (mcm/yr)

Region	Wells	Springs	Total
West Bank	95	53	148
Gaza Strip	138	0	138
Total	233	53	286

Source: Data based on several recent studies conducted by the PWA and HWE.

authorities over the WBWD should have been transferred to the Palestinian Water Authority, but this did not take place. This complex system is not limited to sources of Palestinian water but is also true for the water supply system.

Water Needs and Gap

Municipal, industrial, and agricultural water needs are presented in tables 1.5 to 1.8. The gap between available water resources and needs is presented in table 1.9 and figure 1.3.

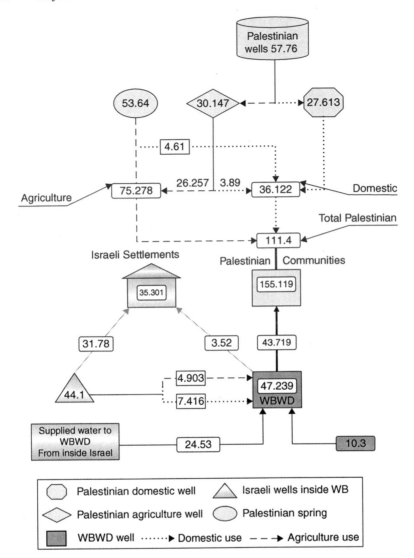

Figure 1.2 The complex picture of water use in the West Bank.

Table 1.5 Projected municipal water needs (mcm/yr)

Year	2000	2005	2010
West Bank	127	159	187
Gaza Strip	77	96	115
Total	204	255	302

Note: Assumption of 100–150 l/c/d, physical losses 8%–12%.

Table 1.6 Projected industrial water needs (mcm/yr)

Year	2000	2005	2010
West Bank	5	25	30
Gaza Strip	3	16	18
Total	8	41	48

Note: Assumption of 8%–16% of total municipal needs.

Table 1.7 Projected agricultural water needs (mcm/yr)

Year	2000	2005	2010
West Bank	177	205	233
Gaza Strip	102	121	140
Total	279	326	373

Table 1.8 Estimated total water needs in Palestine (mcm/yr)

	Municipal			Industrial			Agricultural			Total		
Region Year	2000	2005	2010	2000	2005	2010	2000	2005	2010	2000	2005	2010
West Bank	127	159	187	5	25	30	177	205	233	309	389	450
Gaza Strip	77	96	115	3	16	18	102	121	140	182	233	273
Total	204	255	302	8	41	48	279	326	373	491	622	723

Table 1.9 Estimated gap between water supply and needs in Palestine (mcm/yr)

	Supply			Needs			Gap		
Region Year	2000	2005	2010	2000	2005	2010	2000	2005	2010
West Bank	148	148	148	309	389	450	161	241	302
Gaza Strip	138	138	138	182	233	273	44	95	135
Total	286	286	286	491	622	723	205	336	437

Note: The gap is estimated on the basis that the water supply of 2000 remains the same until 2010.

Estimated Present per Capita Current Water Use

The overall per capita supply rate (including losses) for urban domestic purposes in the West Bank was estimated to vary between 30 l/c/d (liter per capita per day) and

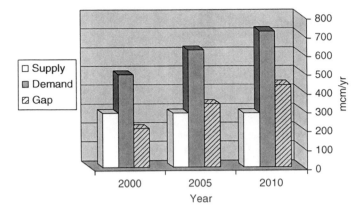

Figure 1.3 Water supply-demand gap in Palestine.

70 l/c/d with an average of about 50 l/c/d. These estimated domestic water consumption rates are substantially lower than the WHO minimum value of 150 l/c/d due to the Israeli restrictions on water usage by the Palestinians. In the Gaza Strip, of the total water supplied to the domestic sector only some 8.9 mcm/yr may be considered of acceptable quality (based on health considerations). This 8.9 mcm/yr corresponds to only 18% of the water supplied by municipal wells and translates to a more acceptable per capita supply rate for domestic use of only about 13 l/c/d—less than the 150 l/c/d WHO-recommended levels.

Water Quantities: Competing Claims

The average per capita consumption of 50 liters per day in the West Bank and the shortfall of some 350 mcm/yr to the Palestinians in the West Bank and Gaza place a constant pressure on the stability of the socioeconomic future of the Palestinians. At present, the Palestinian citizens pay about $1.25/1 m³ of water, which is a high cost compared to the average income of the Palestinian citizen. At a minimum, Palestinians argue that Palestinian citizens should be entitled to receive a basic quantity of water (basic human right to water) amounting to at least 100 liters per day at an affordable cost. This water should be safe, acceptable, and physically accessible.

The specific quantities that should be allocated to the Palestinians constitute a core political matter in the final status negotiations. But even so, a sustainable solution to the Palestinian water crisis will require effective management, development, and planning of the resources. A consensus in this regard among Palestinians includes the following points:

- Palestinian water rights should be solved according to international legal principles which will guarantee sufficient quantities and grant sovereignty to Palestinians to utilize and control their water resources.
- Palestinian water rights should extend to their indigenous and shared groundwater aquifers as well as surface water, including the Jordan River.

Table 1.10 Summary of Palestinian water rights

Source	Quantity mcm/yr	Shared or indigenous	Possible Palestinian share[a]
Eastern Aquifer Basin	172	indigenous	172 (100%)
Northeastern Aquifer Basin	150	shared	90 (60%)
Western Aquifer Basin	443	shared	266 (60%)
Gaza Coastal Aquifer	65	indigenous in Gaza	65 (100%)
Jordan River including eastern wadis	1,500	shared	165 (11%)
Western wadis	72	shared	72 (100%)
Dead Sea wadis	17	shared	17 (100%)
Wadi Gaza	25	shared	25 (100%)

[a] The figures here are based on assumptions and studies conducted by Palestinians (e.g., Mimi and Aliewi 2006).

- Final agreements will have to ensure removal of any obstacles in Palestinian lands that limit water to the Palestinians (e.g., access to wells currently controlled by Israel inside the West Bank, the separation-wall constraints imposed by Israeli settlements, etc.).
- Bilateral and multilateral cooperation remains the key element in any final status negotiations over Palestinian water rights.

Beyond groundwater, the Jordan River and the surface runoff constitute the other sources of Palestinian water resources. Table 1.10 shows Palestinian claims for water rights that reach a total of 880 mcm/yr. This quantity needs to be available in order to meet future Palestinians water needs, though the actual figures will be decided and agreed upon in the final status negotiations.

Improving Water Resources and Demand Management

The growing gap between water supply and the needs of the Palestinian population makes the utilization of additional conventional and non-conventional water resources essential in the future. Moreover, it is important that Palestinian water policies be based on a sustainability assessment of water resources, taking into consideration socioeconomic, governance, and environmental issues. Palestinian water resources need to be managed in a way that integrates laws, regulations, tariff structure, regulatory procedures, and a comprehensive wastewater strategy. This integrated water resources management should take into consideration structural and non-structural measures that should be adopted for the sustainable development of the water sector. It is important to adjust unsustainable consumption (e.g., agricultural use) of water and support the promotion of reforms in which water institutions are strengthened with integrated approaches and improved governance.

The following are important actions to reduce the gap between water supply and water needs in Palestine.

- Demand management. Rehabilitation of networks and reduction of physical losses: This includes internal household plumbing and use of water-saving and efficient fixtures; metering and tariffs; irrigation efficiency; restrictions on water demand for different purposes.
- Wastewater reuse. Having been collected, wastewater should be treated to acceptable standards for reuse or for recharge of the aquifer. The challenge is to make use of this water for agriculture while minimizing the health risk. All wastewater in the Gaza Strip should be made available for direct irrigation as needed or for recharge into the aquifer during the off-season. During the winter seasons the reclaimed water will need to be stored in the aquifer through infiltration basins and later reused by agriculture through recovery wells, particularly during the dry seasons.
- Changes to water use policy. No increase of freshwater supply to the agricultural sector should be considered beyond currents levels. Any water saving due to upgrading the agricultural water supply system, to modification of agricultural practices, techniques, or cropping patterns, will ultimately need to be reallocated to the domestic/industrial sector. Wells and springs in the West Bank need to be prioritized to meet domestic/industrial water demand because the groundwater aquifer system offers the best level of water quality.
- Groundwater supply development. New water supplies should be introduced into the Palestinian water sector as soon as possible. The Palestinian water supply system can be increased from development in all Palestinian aquifer basins except the Gaza Coastal aquifer since this aquifer is already over pumped. This program should include rehabilitation of existing wells, springs development, converting Israel's Mekorot-operated wells located on Palestinian lands to the PWA, artificial recharge, and exploitation of finite-thickness of fresh groundwater lenses in Gaza. Finally, development of the Palestinian share in Jordan River should be an important component of supply.
- Desalination. The PWA is planning to have four large-scale seawater desalination plants in Gaza, creating a total desalination capacity of about 45 mcm/yr by 2010. Small-scale desalination plants, desalination of brackish groundwater, and household treatment plants are also recommended for future plans.
- Administrative and institutional management. The sustainable development of the Palestinian water resources will require improving the institutional, administrative, and legislative capabilities within the water sector.

- Rainwater harvesting. The farmers will participate in the process of reducing the gap between water supply and demand by using the harvested rainwater to water their animals and partially irrigate their farms and gardens.
- Environmental protection/conservation. It is important to bring an end to the flow of raw municipal sewage as well as to other types of wastes (industrial waste, solid waste, etc.) into the natural environment through implementation of collection and treatment works in Palestine.

Water Quality in the West Bank

Protecting water quality is critical for ensuring the sustainable supply of water from West Bank groundwater resources. Water management strategies must provide solutions to the associated risks of pollution.

For many years, raw sewage from the Palestinian cities and localities and from Israeli settlements in the West Bank has been discharged into the wadis of the area. Moreover, leachate from dumping sites, zebar from olive mills, industrial wastes, agricultural returns rich with agrochemicals, and hazardous wastes, in addition to overpumping of aquifers, have caused groundwater quality of Palestinian aquifers to deteriorate. Since the carbonate aquifers of the West Bank have pronounced mature karst features, both above and below the water table, these aquifers show high potential for extensive and rapid spread of pollution.

A recent report considered the quality records available from some 490 wells and springs in the PWA database of the West Bank for major ion analyses (Ca, Mg, Na, K, HCO_3, Cl, SO_4, and NO_3) (SUSMAQ 2003). The results suggest that there is ample cause for concern. In particular, chloride concentrations were found to range from 25 to 1,000 mg/l. The highest levels of salinity (showing chloride concentration values of 600 to 2,578 mg/l) were observed in 58 wells. These are found in the aquifers that extend as a narrow strip along the Jordan Valley, located close to the Jordan River in the Jericho District (figure 1.4). Due to heavy pumping in the Jordan Valley, a considerable decline in water table levels has also been observed with profound implications for salinity.

It was also noticed that much lower chloride concentrations exist in the areas near wadis as they are considered as sources of groundwater recharge in the West Bank aquifers. The Palestinian standard for chloride in drinking water is set as a recommended maximum concentration of 250 mg/l, which is increased to 600 mg/l when no alternative source is available. Chloride concentrations increase gradually from recharge areas in the eastern highland to the Jordan Valley in the east and from the south of the city of Nablus to the El Jalemeh area in the north. The chloride concentration in groundwater located close to cities like Jerusalem, Bethlehem, Ramallah, Nablus, and Jenin is far better, ranging from 50 to 100 mg/l (SUSMAQ 2003).

The salination of groundwater is caused mainly by saline upconing in the Jordan Valley of the West Bank. The steep dipping of the aquifers along the Jordan Valley has caused deep circulation of the recharging groundwater, bringing it into contact with the contaminated salty formations that originate at greater depths. Recent drillings in the Jordan Valley show that salinity increases with depth. Salinity data obtained from one well in Jericho indicates that the chloride content increased from 380 mg/l at 30 m depth to over 2,000 mg/l at a depth of 162 m. Increased salinity levels can also be a result of the flushing of soluble salts from the soil zone by excess irrigation water.

Nitrate concentration in groundwater is naturally low but can reach high levels as a result of agricultural runoff, runoff from garbage dumps, or contamination from human or animal wastes. The toxicity of nitrate to humans is mainly attributable to its reduction to nitrite, with young infants being the most susceptible population. The PWA has adopted the World Health Organization's upper limit of 50 mg/l as (NO_3) with 70 mg/l deemed acceptable to PWA in the absence of any better quality water source. The nitrate standards are designed to prevent health risks from methemoglobinemia (blue baby syndrome), which in acute cases can cause premature death and disability. Nitrate concentrations in West Bank water sources have at time reached problematic concentrations (e.g., greater than 50 mg/l) especially in newly urbanized areas. High levels have been measured in Qalqilia, Tulkarem, Jenin, and Nablus in the north, Ramallah and Jericho in the center, and the Beit Jala-Hebron region in the south. However, these hotspots appear to be comparatively localized and water in the vicinity is generally of better quality (SUSMAQ 2003).

Total dissolved solids (TDS) can have an important effect on the taste of drinking water. The palatability of water with a TDS level of less than 600 mg/l is generally considered to be good; drinking water becomes increasingly unpalatable at TDS levels greater than 1,200 mg/l. The presence of high levels of TDS may also be objectionable to consumers owing to excessive scaling in water pipes, heaters, boilers, and household appliances. The PWA acceptable limit is 1,000 mg/l, while up to 1,500 mg/l is acceptable in the absence of any better source. Problem levels tend to be encountered only toward the boundaries of the West Bank, in other words, down-dip within each of the West Bank aquifer basins. This suggests that while urbanization plays a part in the creation of high TDS concentrations, down-dip water-rock interaction must also be a contributory cause (SUSMAQ 2003).

Sulfate is not a serious problem anywhere in the West Bank. All water resources except for one are below the "taste" level of 250 mg/l. Yet, trends suggest that there may be reason for concern, as there are some sites where SO_4 concentrations are now higher than in the past. These findings might simply be anomalous analytical artifacts, but they may well be the result of changes in pumping regimes (for example, where groundwater is strongly layered in terms of quality) or simply the flushing over time of pockets of poor-quality water in gypsiferous strata. Figure 1.4 shows maps for chloride, nitrate, sulfate, and TDS values across the West Bank, respectively.

In the northern part of the West Bank, recent deep drilling of wells penetrating very thick layers of Senonian chalk reveals processes of ion exchange between bituminous shale and limestone, serving to increase the concentration of fluoride and

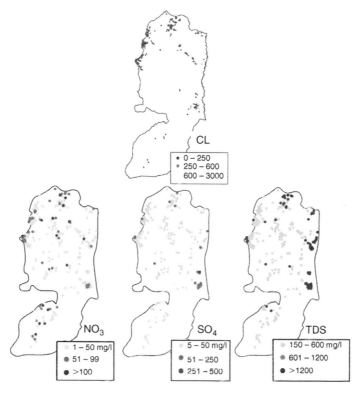

Figure 1.4 Distribution of groundwater chloride, nitrate, sulfate, and total dissolved solids (TDS) across the West Bank.
From Sustainable Management of the West Bank and Gaza Aquifers (SUSMAQ) 2003.

decrease the levels of calcium and magnesium. The high level of fluoride constitutes a major health risk.

Water Quality in the Gaza Coastal Aquifer

Groundwater in the Gaza segment of the coastal aquifer is generally of poor quality, characterized by medium to high salinity levels. Very few parts of this aquifer still have high water quality. These few reasonable segments of the aquifer are located along the extreme north and extreme south of the Gaza Strip (figure 1.5). In the whole of the coastal region, aquifer quality remains a critical issue as the values of nitrates and chlorides are frequently extremely high.

Chloride (salinity) affects usability for irrigation and water supply. Intensive exploitation of groundwater in the Gaza Strip during the past 30 to 40 years has disturbed the natural equilibrium between fresh and saline waters and has resulted in increased salinity in most areas. In Gaza City, chloride values in several wells are increasing at rates up to 10 mg/l per year. Sources of chloride that can be documented or inferred within the Gaza Strip are seawater intrusion, lateral inflow of brackish water from Israel in the middle and southern areas of the Gaza Strip (chloride concentration varying from 800 to 2,000 mg/l), as well as the presence of

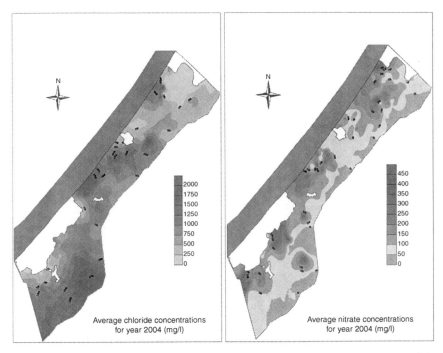

Figure 1.5 Average groundwater salinity (Cl) and nitrate concentration (NO_3) of the Coastal Aquifer for year 2004 in the Gaza Strip.
From Al-Banna et al. 2006.

deep brines at the base of the coastal aquifer with chloride concentrations of 40,000 to 60,000 mg/l. Figure 1.5 shows the distribution of chloride levels in Gaza Strip in the year 2004.

Nitrate concentrations are also increasing rapidly in the urban centers with concentrations rising as much as 10 mg/l per year (PWA 2000). The main sources of nitrates are fertilizers and domestic sewage effluent. The quantities of sewage that infiltrate through cesspits and septic tanks to the water table on an annual basis are significant and are estimated to be about 12 mcm/yr. In contrast to salinity, groundwater flowing from the east has relatively low nitrate levels. This is reflected in the maps shown in figure 1.5. Nitrate concentration of hundreds of mg/l is common, however, in the groundwater of the Gaza Strip (PWA 2000). Nitrate levels, in particular, those found in the water used for drinking purposes in certain parts of the region, are well above WHO standards. In some extreme cases this can lead to premature death and disability.

Conclusions

The average per capita consumption of 50 liters per day in the West Bank and the 13 liters per day per capita (suitable for drinking purposes) in Gaza put a constant pressure on the stability of any socioeconomic future of the Palestinians. Without a sufficient and safe supply of water it will be difficult to ensure a stable future for the emerging Palestinian state. The existence of additional water sources will make Palestinians perceive the quantities of water allocated to the new state as a core political issue in the final status negotiations. Such issues must be resolved before moving on to the problem of sustainable management, development, and planning. Palestinian water rights should be resolved according to international law principles which will guarantee sufficient quantities and grant sovereignty to Palestinians to utilize and control their water resources.

The growing gap between the water supply and the needs of Palestinian communities makes additional conventional and non-conventional water resources essential. Moreover, putting in place water policies based on a sustainability assessment of the water resource, taking into consideration socioeconomic, governance, and environmental issues, will be an important stage in the move toward sustainability.

In the West Bank, the sources of pollution continue to cause severe damage to the mature karst aquifers. The poor sanitation services, poor management of sewage and solid waste, the over application of fertilizers and pesticides in the agricultural sector, as well as the over-extraction and reduction in storage volumes have produced substantial pollution levels in the Palestinian aquifers. During all the years of occupation, the Israeli civil administration never built a wastewater treatment plant in the West Bank, although Israeli settlements contributed to the pollution of the West Bank aquifers. Contamination of water will minimize the already limited quantities of water resources in Palestine, i.e., enlarging the gap between water supply and needs. Hence, there is a critical challenge to sustainable development of the Palestinian water resources. Wastewater treatment is an essential element in alleviating pollution to the Palestinian water resources. This matter needs to be addressed as part of a holistic approach that takes into consideration the institutionalization of wastewater treatment and reuse for agriculture, regulations and laws, and wastewater treatment technologies and strategies.

REFERENCES

Al-Banna, M., Z. Abu Heen, M. Al-Baba, A. Aliewi, Kh. Qahman, and M. Kishta. 2006. *Optimal management of groundwater resources: Rafah, Gaza Strip.* Final technical report, Gaza, Palestinian Water Authority.

Aliewi, A. S. 2005. Sustainable development of the Palestinian water sector under arid/semi-arid conditions. *Proceedings of the workshop on arid/semi-arid groundwater governance and management, April 3–7.* Cairo, Egypt.

Mimi, Z. A., and A. Aliewi. 2006. Management of shared aquifer systems using multi-criteria decision tool: Palestinian-Israeli mountain aquifer as case study. *Arabian Journal for Engineering and Science.* Saudi Arabia.

Palestinian Water Authority (PWA). 2000. *Gaza coastal aquifer management program.* Vol. 1 of *Integrated aquifer management plan* (Task 3). Palestinian Water Authority.

Sustainable Management of the West Bank and Gaza Aquifers (SUSMAQ). 2003. *Hydrogeochemistry of the aquifers of the West Bank: Review and interpretation of the available data with regard to recharge, water quality, and groundwater flow.* Ramallah: Palestinian Water Authority.

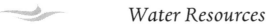

Water Resources

THE ISRAELI PERSPECTIVE

ALON TAL

Water Resources—the Israeli Perspective

Precipitation

Climatically, Israel and its neighbors are located in areas that are identified as water scarce regions. Figure 1.6 shows the enormous variation in rainfall that characterizes the relatively modest distance of 300 km from Israel's northern tip near the Lebanese and Syrian border to its southern most point, at the Gulf of Aqaba. Some 20% of the water potential lies in the south of the country with 80% of the precipitation occurring in the north. Accordingly, most of the country can be classified as "drylands" by international standards (under 500 mm rainfall per year). The general scarcity of rain and its spatial imbalance is exacerbated by its temporal asymmetry—with virtually no precipitation occurring during a dry season that runs over half the year, between May and October.

Like many Mediterranean climates, Israel has always been subject to drought cycles, but this may be growing worse. The United Nations' International Panel on Climate Change has projected general drops in rainfall for the region in the years ahead. Yet, during the past 16 years, average precipitation has already dropped from 1,350 to 1,175 mcm (million cubic meters) a year, suggesting that climate change may already be exacerbating water scarcity. Indeed, in 2008 Israel's Water Authority reported that the probability of four consecutive extreme drought years occurring as they have since 2005 is only 2%.

When Israel received its independence in 1948, water managers working for the government mistakenly overestimated that the available renewable resources would reach 3,500 mcm/yr. Israel's governmental Hydrological Service for many years set the figure for rain-supplied renewable water sources in Israel, the West Bank, and Gaza at less than half of that (some 1,355 mcm). Recently, however, it has issued new estimates reflecting the climatic change as reported in figure 1.7. A full 95% of this amount is utilized for agricultural, industrial, domestic, and well-supporting ecological systems. This figure does not include an additional 350 mcm that is recycled as wastewater reuse or over 300 mcm that now enters the system as desalinized water for consumption and irrigation. By the end of 2013, the volume of desalinized water produced should reach 550 mcm. At the same time, a growing number of wells have been classified as too contaminated for use of any kind.

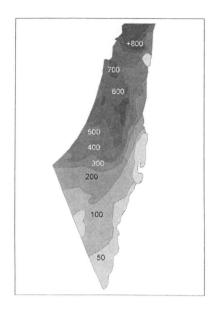

Figure 1.6 Israeli and Palestinian average rain gradient (in mm rain/yr).
Courtesy of the Israel Hydrological Service.

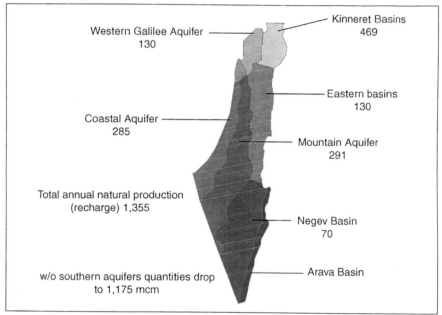

Figure 1.7 Israeli and Palestinian freshwater resources in million cubic meters (mcm).
Courtesy of the Israel Water Authority, 2008.

Figure 1.7 maps out the main freshwater resources which might be utilized by the two sides. These include three primary water bodies: Lake Kinneret (or the Jordan River watershed), the Coastal Aquifer, and the Mountain Aquifer, which is, in fact, a series of connected groundwater systems. Each one of these bodies will be characterized in greater detail in future chapters and will only be described in a cursory fashion in the present context. In addition, there are several smaller regional resources of variable qualities located in the Upper Galilee, Western Galilee, Beit Shean Valley, Jordan Valley, the Dead Sea Rift, the Negev, and the Arava. Israel's two "seas" (the Mediterranean and the Red Sea) increasingly provide water for desalination while the Dead Sea remains largely a recreational and historic resource.

Lake Kinneret (the Sea of Galilee)

Lake Kinneret is the only natural surface reservoir in the region and holds the distinction of being the lowest freshwater lake in the world. Known to Christians throughout the world as the Sea of Galilee, much of the evangelical activities ascribed to Jesus in the New Testament took place around the Kinneret, and it is the area of many important religious sites for Jews as well. Hence, the lake is not only a hydrological resource, but also a critical recreational and spiritual one. The Kinneret itself is not exceptionally large, with a width of only 22 km and a total surface area of only 168 km². At its deepest point Kinneret reaches 43 m and only has an average depth of 24 m. The lake for decades was a productive fishing ground, providing a range of catch, most notably the indigenous "St. Peter's fish" and a variety of bass. Sadly, due to dramatic drops in fish populations, Israel's Ministry of Agriculture recently issued a moratorium on fishing in the Kinneret to allow for recovery.

For some 40 years now, Lake Kinneret has served as Israel's national "reservoir," but only a fraction of its potential volume of 4.3 billion m³s can be utilized during any given year as excessive drawdown makes the lake vulnerable to salination from underlying saline flows. Accordingly, a maximum extraction level has been established in the lake, whereby water cannot be pumped when the lake falls below 215.5 m below sea level. (This is a relatively new "minimum" water level; the older, more stringent 213 m "red line" level was amended in a controversial decision during a recent drought.)

Lake Kinneret lies at the bottom of a catchment area that includes not only Galilee and the Golan Heights, but also Lebanon and Syria. Some 800 mcm of water naturally flows into the lake, primarily via the Jordan River or its tributaries. A substantial portion of these waters (roughly 300 mcm) is lost to evaporation. Recent changes in precipitation are already reflected in the Kinneret's water supply. While the lake used to provide 500 mcm to Israel's water network during the 1960s, as of late the average amount utilized is closer to 320 mcm. Figure 1.8 shows the flux in water levels and the general tendency of government water managers to avoid pumping below the red lines, below which it is thought that hydrological damage from salinization begins.

The precipitous drop in the water levels in the lake that has followed the recent drought has pushed the water beyond these red lines. During the spring of 2008 a national campaign was launched to encourage water conservation, lest water levels fall below the "black lines," where hydrological damage is expected to be irreversible.

In some respects, the water quality in the lake has improved during the past 40 years due to the diversion of most of the local saline streams which historically brought the salinity of the lake to average concentrations of 389 milligrams of

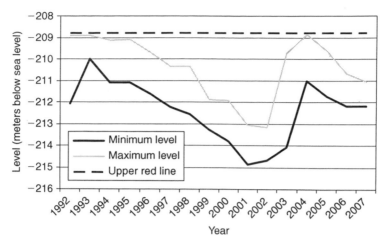

Figure 1.8 Water levels in Lake Kinneret.
Courtesy of the Kinneret Administration, 2008.

chloride per liter. Today, chloride levels are almost half that, holding steady at 200 mg/l. Yet, due to the drainage of wetlands upstream in the Huleh Valley and intensified economic activities in the watershed, there is also a steady increase in nutrient loadings, raising the specter of eutrophication in the lake. In recent years, the rate of point and nonpoint source discharges has been reduced due to the intervention of the Kinneret Authority, which catalyzes a variety of pollution prevention and enforcement activities.

The Mountain Aquifer

With a recharge area that largely lies in Palestinian territories and wellheads that are for the most part located inside of Israel, the Mountain Aquifer is undoubtedly the most contested of the water resources shared by Israelis and Palestinians. Geologically, the aquifer is dominated by karstic limestone formations, and hydrologically it is characterized by great depth (averaging 250 m) and relatively rapid flow. In fact, the Mountain Aquifer is something of a misnomer; the term refers to three separate but contiguous basins: the Yarkon Taninim Aquifer, the Eastern Aquifer, and the Northeastern Aquifer. The Yarkon Taninim contains about half of the total water in the aquifer, which flows from the eastern Judaean/Sumarian foothills to the coast. This aquifer provides about a fifth of Israel's freshwater, typically at a very high quality. The Eastern Aquifer discharges in the Beit Shean Springs. It lies almost completely in the West Bank and naturally contains somewhat more saline waters. The Northeastern Aquifer, where natural replenishment reaches some 130 mcm of water, is about half brackish.

The Coastal Aquifer

The Coastal Aquifer runs the length of the Mediterranean, from the Haifa "Carmel" region all the way down through the Gaza Strip (see figure 1.7). With the water table lying a mere 30 m below an unsaturated zone of sandy soils, the aquifer

(a)

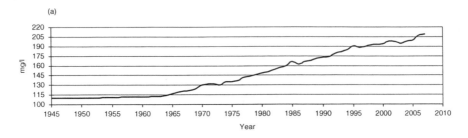

(b)

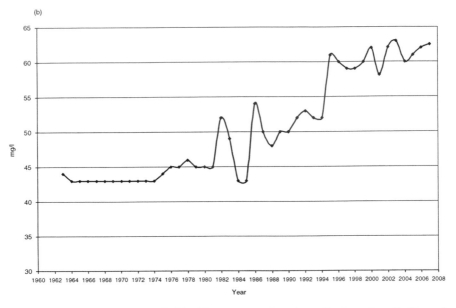

Figure 1.9 Average nitrate and chloride concentrations in wells along Israel's Coastal Aquifer, 1960–2007 (in mg/l).
Courtesy of the Israel Hydrological Service.

serves as an excellent storage facility. Moreover, the filtration provided by the sands tends to contain the spread of pollution, making most contamination a localized phenomenon. Typically, natural recharge is set at 250 mcm, although recent figures are slightly lower (233 mcm). This figure, however, does not include waters from the National Water Carrier and advanced, treated effluents that are intentionally injected into the aquifer as well as irrigation return flows, which together make up a volume of almost equal size.

Testing done during the 1930s suggested that the aquifer originally enjoyed extremely high quality water (50 to 100 mg/l of chlorides and less than 10 mg/l of nitrates). Figure 1.9 shows just how dramatically this profile has changed. Today, the coastal aquifer reflects the cumulative impact of decades of environmental insults, exhibiting continuous deterioration during the past 50 years. In many sections of the aquifer, it takes roughly a year for pollutants to seep down a distance of 1 m, linking today's contamination with activities that took place during the 1970s.

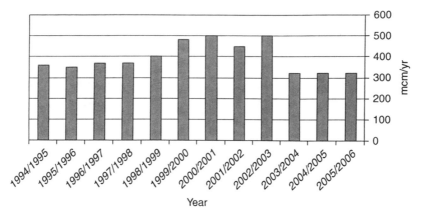

Figure 1.10 Pumping rates in the Coastal Aquifer over 12 years.
Courtesy of the Israel Hydrological Service, 2002, and the Israel Ministry of Environmental Protection, 2006.

The steady rise in nitrates produced by sewage, fertilizers, and industrial wastes reflects this process. Indeed, without appropriate pretreatment and wastewater infrastructures Israel's extensive municipal effluent recycling is responsible for contamination by a range of industrial solvents, including benzene and toluene as well as metals.

Yet, the most prominent problem historically has been that of overpumping. The safe yield of the aquifer has been set at around 275 mcm, depending on the condition of the aquifer. As shown in figure 1.10, pumping rates were typically higher, and sometimes far higher. This lowered the level of the water table, in some places by as much as 6 to 10 m. The resulting vacuum is filled by seawater. Moreover, the original flow of water to the sea, which naturally flushes out salts and minerals from the aquifer, is interrupted. By the mid-1950s Tel Aviv's wells had already grown too salty for drinking, and over the years over 10% of wells along the coast have been decommissioned. Since the 1950s, average chloride concentrations increased to roughly 200 mg/l, reflecting average annual increases of 2.4 mg/l. In some areas, such as the Gaza Strip, concentrations are far higher.

This twin pathology of increased nitrates and salinity levels is not limited to the Coastal Aquifer and can be found in many of the other smaller groundwater systems, such as those in the Jezereal Valley, the Arava, and Western Galilee.

Additional Water Sources: Israel's Water Management Strategy

The history of Israel's water management is best characterized as a relentless pursuit of expanded resources. With the steady, geometric growth in population, per capita water availability by definition faced continuous decline. Efforts to reduce demand through improving efficiency in agriculture or water conservation promotion ameliorated the problem. But the centerpiece of Israel's management strategy was aggressive and creative policies to develop new sources of water. This is as true

Table 1.11 Water supply and demand in Israel, 1998–2020 (mcm/yr)

Year	Population (million)	Surface water	Groundwater	Brackish water	Treated effluents	Desalination	Total
1998	6.0	640	1,050	140	260	10	2,100
2010	7.4	645	1,050	165	470	100	2,430
2020	8.6	660	1,075	180	565	200	2,680

today as it was during the 1950s. Table 1.11 contains projections by Israel's Water Commission regarding anticipated water demand in Israel alone.

THE NATIONAL WATER CARRIER

The initial challenge involved bridging the disparity of almost two orders of magnitude in rainfall between the water-rich Galilee in the north and the water-poor Negev in the south. Almost from the advent of Jewish settlement in Palestine, establishing a "carrier" to transfer water to arid regions was an amorphous but important part of the Zionist vision. In the 1950s, the new nation made a prodigious investment in the National Water Carrier, which since 1964 brings water from the Kinneret Lake in the north to the south of Israel as part of a national grid.

WASTEWATER REUSE

By that time, water managers had already approved an ambitious strategy of wastewater reuse. Israel was among the first countries to recognize the potential of recycled municipal effluents as a source of water for its citizens. As the country's population grew exponentially, the amount of sewage produced began to exceed the carrying capacity of the existing infrastructure. Until the 1950s, it had been based largely on septic tanks, with relatively few central sewage collection systems and practically no treatment facilities. The resulting contamination of water resources, the sea, and the attendant mosquito infestation created a "push" to compliment the "pull" of creating an additional source of water for agriculture.

As early as 1956, it was estimated that 150 mcm of wastewater would be recycled for agricultural usage. Within 6 years, 50 projects connecting Israeli farms to municipal sewage treatment centers were up and running. By 1972, the number had climbed to some 120 projects, using 20% of all urban sewage. Today Israel recycles some 77% of its sewage, a rate far higher than in other countries. (For example, the United States only recycled 2.4% of its municipal wastes.) The 350 mcm of recycled sewage contributes roughly a fifth of Israel's total water supply. For irrigated agriculture, effluents constitute roughly half of the available water sources, and crop strategies increasingly take this into consideration.

By far, the country's largest treatment scheme is the Dan Region Wastewater Reclamation Project (Shafdan). Originally financed by a loan to the Israeli government from the World Bank during the 1970s, the plant today treats most of the sewage in the Tel Aviv metropolitan area at a high tertiary level. Some 130 mcm of near-drinking-water quality are produced each year, most of it utilized by farmers in the Negev desert after it is injected into the coastal aquifer, where it undergoes an additional filtration process. There are several other large-scale wastewater treatment plants that provide agriculture with water of varying degrees, notably the Jerusalem, Haifa, Netanya, and Beer Sheva facilities.

From the start of wastewater reuse in Israel, there were questions raised about the quality of the recycled effluents. By 1953 the Ministry of Health recommended some of the first wastewater irrigation standards in the world, disqualifying raw sewage as an irrigation source and limiting the crops that could be grown with effluents to cotton, fodder, and produce that is not consumed raw. Subsequent epidemiological studies did not reveal any statistically significant disparities in health indicators among farmers who worked with effluents and those who did not.

Recently, two major developments in wastewater reuse policy are contributing to a general upgrade in the field. These can be characterized as both quantitative and qualitative in nature. First, in response to 3 years of consecutive droughts, in 2000 Israel's government decided to increase wastewater reuse to 500 mcm by 2010 (with the present total percentage recycled being 77%). The attendant investment in sewage treatment and delivery infrastructure will expedite reductions in freshwater allocation to irrigation while preserving the scope of agriculture. It is expected that as a result of this investment, the amount of effluents available to farmers will soon provide the majority of the water utilized by agriculture.

Second, to minimize environmental health risk from the increase in wastewater reuse, in 2001 the Ministry of the Environment proposed to upgrade the water quality standards for both agricultural use of treated wastewater and its discharge into streams and rivers. The more stringent and expanded standard was approved by the government in 2005 and will be phased in through upgraded facilities. Recent studies suggest that greater efforts will be required to remove biologically active antibiotics and endocrine disrupting chemicals present in the treated effluent.

DESALINATION

At the instigation of Israel's first prime minister, David Ben Gurion, by the 1960s water managers were exploring the feasibility of large-scale desalination. Waters from the National Water Carrier did not reach the southern port city of Eilat and the neighboring Arava farming communities. Desalination proved to be the most feasible solution for local drinking-water needs. Initially, it was only brackish groundwater that was desalinized. With time, Eilat's Sabha facility was expanded and a seawater section was built that could treat 24,000 m³ a day for the cost of 90¢/m³.

Recently, Israel's government decided to build a series of five new desalination plants that are projected to produce over 500 mcm of desalinized water. The policy change reflects the substantial improvement in membrane technologies and innovations in energy efficiency. The attendant drop in prices for desalinized water reinforced a growing recognition that traditional water resources are inadequate.

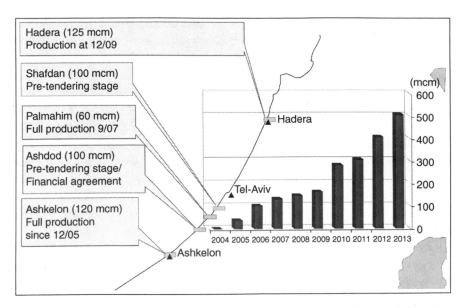

Figure 1.11 Development of seawater desalination plants in Israel (in million cubic meters).
Courtesy of the Israel Water Authority, 2008.

The first desalination plant to open was in Ashkelon. A privately financed BOT (build/operate/transfer) water development, it produces some 120 million mcm of desalinized water per year at a cost of 52¢/m³. Figure 1.11 depicts the present trend in anticipated desalination facilities. A facility at the Palmachim beach financed by an Israeli consortium began operations soon thereafter and, most recently, the Hadera desalination plant was opened.

Conclusion: Toward Economic and Environmental Sustainability

For many years, Israeli efforts to reduce water demand focused on technology diffusion, in particular, in the field of drip irrigation. Government pricing policies through the provision of artificially low-cost water, especially to the agricultural sector, did little to encourage efficiency. The ability to produce water coincided with general government policy trends which began to phase out the traditional subsidies for agricultural users. Indeed, the country today is at the end of a major reform in water pricing. Table 1.12 shows present prices for water in Israel. Households in Israel pay according to a sliding scale, where costs increase with the amounts utilized. While basic needs are supplied at relatively low costs, families that are water intensive pay higher rates for watering their gardens and additional usage. The lower agricultural price tag reflects the actual reduced costs associated with supplying water to the farming sector, which requires less treatment, quality control, etc.

Beyond utilization of pricing, Israel for several years has encouraged conservation of water through regulation of municipalities (fines for leakages and daytime

Table 1.12. Water pricing in Israel, 2008

	Domestic	Agricultural	Wastewater	Public institutions
1st price	0.72 €	0.24 €	0.11 €	1.08 €
2nd price	0.88 €	0.29 €	—	—
3rd price	1.41 €	0.38 €	—	—

Source: Israel Water Authority, 2008.

sprinkler use), standards for public toilets, and technical assistance programs. During the summer of 2009, water consumption in Israel dropped 13.5% as the public responded to a high-profile public relations campaign and an appeal by the Water Authority that clearly presented the severity of the current water shortages. There is a growing recognition that while water supply must continue to grow, conservation must be part of the solution as well.

From its inception, the story of Israel's water management has been unique internationally. As a developing country, many of Israel's hydrological achievements have been impressive. But there has been an environmental price paid for the aggressive expansion of water supply. Today, Israeli water resources face the twin challenges of negative trends in precipitation along with contamination of natural resources. To this can be added the challenge of learning to share management responsibilities and allocation of water with its neighbors. If the country's historic ideological zeal to develop water resources can be harnessed as part of an economically rational, technologically sophisticated policy orientation, there is reason to believe that present challenges can be overcome.

REFERENCES

Avnimelech, Y. 1993. Irrigation with sewage effluents: The Israeli experience. *Environmental Science and Technology* 27:7.

Dreizin, Y. 2004. The impact of desalination: Israel and the Palestinian Authority. Paper presented in the 2nd Israeli-Palestinian International Conference on Water for Life in the Middle East. Antalya, Turkey.

Fattal, B., and H. Shuval. 1981. Historical prospective epidemiological study of wastewater utilization in Kibbutzim in Israel, 1974–1977. In *Developments in arid zone ecology and environmental quality*, ed. H. Shuval, 333–343. Philadelphia, PA: Balaban.

Israel Ministry of Foreign Affairs. 2002. Spotlight on Israel: Israel's chronic water problem. http://www.mfa.gov.il/mfa/facts%20about%20israel/land/israels%20chronic%20water%20problem (accessed November 8, 2009).

Kroneneberg, G. 2004. The largest SWRO plant in the world: Ashkelon 100 million m³/y BOT project. *Desalination* 166:457–463.

Rassas, D. 2007. Seawater desalination in Israel: A stakeholders' view of agriculture and environmental implications. Master's thesis, Ben Gurion University.

Shuval, H. 1962. Waste water utilization in Israel. *Proceedings of an international seminar on soil and water utilization.* Brookings, SD.

Tal, A. 2002. *Pollution in a promised land*. Berkeley: University of California Press.

———. 2006. Seeking sustainability: Israel's evolving water management strategy. *Science* 313:1081–1084.

Tal, A., A. Ben-Gal, P. Lawhon, and D. Rassas. 2005. *Sustainable water management in the drylands: Recent Israeli experience*. Jerusalem: Israel Ministry of Foreign Affairs.

Wachs, A. M. 1971. The outlook for wastewater utilization in Israel. In *Developments in water quality research*, ed. H. Shuval, 109–111. Ann Arbor, MI: Ann Arbor Science Publishers.

Editors' Summary

There appears to be little substantive differences between Israeli and Palestinian assessments of available water resources and their condition. For the most part, the sides are no longer arguing about facts or data, but rather water rights, allocation, and policy. There are, of course, clear objective disparities in the hydrological circumstances of the two populations which inform each party's positions.

The average per capita consumption of 50 l/day in the West Bank and the 13 l/day per capita (suitable for drinking purposes) in Gaza place constant pressure on the stability and socioeconomic conditions of a future Palestinian state. Without a sufficient and safe supply of water, Palestinians believe that it will be difficult to ensure a sustainable future. Especially during a period of consecutive drought years, Israel, particularly its agricultural sector, also has legitimate concerns about hydrological sustainability. Israel's economy and political interests are, however, far less vulnerable to present and projected levels of water scarcity. Moreover, its negotiators have never denied the importance for Israel of ensuring that a Palestinian state not be a thirsty one, or ensuring that it is a country with an advanced sanitary infrastructure. Hence, reaching a future agreement in the water realm need not involve the traditional "zero-sum game" approaches that characterized past negotiations.

The Palestinians perceive the quantities of water allocated to them as a core political issue in the final status negotiations. Because of past sensitivities and the historic dynamics of occupation, they prefer to view the issue in terms of "rights." Indeed, Palestinians have always held that their water rights should extend to their "indigenous and shared groundwater aquifers" as well as to surface waters that run through their jurisdiction, in particular, the Jordan River. It should, however, be emphasized that never have the Palestinians demanded "equal" quantities of water—but rather only what they believe to be their fair share. While Palestinians would like water quantity issues resolved before moving on to the problems of sustainable management, development, and planning to protect water quality, it is likely that they will agree that the two topics be considered in tandem.

Israel has always seen the resolution of conflict over water as part of a broader package of peace issues. Given the new affordability of desalinated water and the relatively modest role of agriculture in Israel's economy, it is likely to be one of the core issues about which it will be easier for Israel to be flexible. At the same time, Israel realizes that coordinated efforts to protect water resources are critical for a long-term strategy. Just as the provisions regulating water were among the most detailed and ambitious of the interim agreements between the two parties, a future agreement from Israel's perspective should go far beyond allocations accounting and include management, policy, standards, and enforcement.

Palestinians insist that water rights be resolved according to principles of international law, which they believe will guarantee them sufficient quantities and the sovereignty to utilize and control their water resources. The basic axiom of international water law, though, is rather vague, requiring only that all sides receive a reasonable and equitable share. This should not be deemed problematic as the principle is sufficiently amorphous and given to sufficiently flexible interpretations to allow Israel to agree to have it as a basis for resolving the existing disputes. To be sure, the two sides do not agree about the legality of past water developments for Israeli settlements, nor to the legitimacy of Israel's "historic rights" to water resources that originate in the West Bank. Yet, resolving the clashing interpretations of international legal principles ultimately belongs to the tit-for-tat bickering of the past. Such theoretical controversies should not stand in the way of a pragmatic approach that can reach accommodation about water rights, water distribution, management, and common efforts to improve water quality.

There are some differences in the data that the two sides will bring to the table, particularly in the area of potential aquifer recharge and present and future needs. It is possible that climate change and dwindling precipitation are at the heart of the gap in perceptions. Such disparities can be clarified and resolved either through joint scientific commissions or the utilization of third-party arbiters. Ultimately, these differences are not excessive, and were any of the remaining disagreements about available water resources to be quantified, the volume probably would be no greater than the water production in a single large desalination plant.

While in the past Palestinians insisted on focusing on water rights rather than on expanding available sources, the steady rise in population over the past decade appears to have extended their position to cover water quantity and water quality within the overall context of Palestinian sovereignty over their water resources. Both sides agree that the growing gap between the supply and the needs of Palestinian communities makes additional conventional and non-conventional water resources essential. Moreover, putting in place water policies based on a sustainability assessment of the water resources, taking into consideration socioeconomic, governance, and environmental issues, is considered to be an important stage in the move toward sustainability.

There is also broad acknowledgment of the importance of significant upgrades in waste treatment and environmental infrastructure. This is not a concession on the part of Palestinians, but a clearer recognition of the consequences of continued neglect in this field. Poor sanitation services, poor management of sewage and solid waste, over application of fertilizers and pesticides in the agricultural sector, as well as over-extraction and reduction in storage volumes have caused pollution to the Palestinian aquifers, and this harms their quality of life far more acutely than Israel's. Contamination of water will also minimize the already limited quantities of water resources in Palestine, exacerbating Palestinian shortages, even after future Israeli concessions.

While Palestinians correctly point out that occupying Israeli forces never built a wastewater treatment plant in the West Bank during all the years of occupation, they also realize that relieving themselves of any historic blame will do little to improve their future quality of life. The peace process brings with it rare opportunities to receive considerable funds to jump start a Palestinian waste treatment system that is based on tertiary treatment that can supply high quality water to Palestinian agriculture. There is a growing recognition that most Palestinian farmers will be hard pressed to receive any freshwater as the Palestinian population continues to grow and quality of life improves.

In short, the present quantity and quality of the water resources on both sides are well understood. It is clear that regardless of the ultimate allocation, present supply is insufficient for the population that will be living in the region in the near future. The steady contamination of these resources exacerbates the situation significantly. Yet, there are reasons for optimism, including the following:

- the feasibility of expanded water production via desalination;
- greater Palestinian commitment to expanded water supply from waste water reuse (and desalination);
- the increasing commitment on both sides to environmental protection;
- the proven interest of donor nations in establishing water infrastructure.

All these point to water as a source of future cooperation rather than conflict.

PART 2

PAST WATER AGREEMENTS AND THEIR IMPLEMENTATION

As the focus of this book is the potential for reaching a comprehensive final agreement for allocation and management of water resources, it is important to consider relevant past accords between the parties, their achievements and failures. These two essays provide a review of the provisions in the interim peace agreement with regards to water, for the first time considering their actual implementation. Not surprisingly, Palestinian and Israeli perceptions are dissimilar.

The Oslo II Accords in Retrospect

IMPLEMENTATION OF THE WATER
PROVISIONS IN THE ISRAELI AND
PALESTINIAN INTERIM PEACE
AGREEMENTS

ANAN JAYOUSI

Background

Article 40 of the Oslo II agreement between the Israelis and Palestinians forms the normative basis for cooperation in the water and sewage sector during the interim period as identified in the agreement for the West Bank and Gaza Strip. In this essay we will highlight the main issues addressed through a brief review of the expectations of the Palestinian side versus what it perceives as has actually happened on the ground.

The main principles that cover Article 40 can be summarized as follows:

- Israel recognizes the Palestinian water rights in the West Bank;
- both sides recognize the necessity of developing additional water for various uses;
- both sides agree to coordinate the management of water and sewage resources and systems;
- additional quantities of water need to be made available to Palestinians during the interim period for different uses; and
- there is a need to establish a permanent Joint Water Committee (JWC) for the interim period.

The Palestinian Expectations

In general, the expectations from the outcomes of the Oslo II agreement in September 1995, directly after the signing of the agreement, were very high. In the fields of drinking water and wastewater, like other sectors, it was assumed that the sides would fully implement the agreement within the proposed time frame of the interim period. The main outcomes that Palestinians expected from Article 40 can be summarized through review of the following five issues: additional water quantities, upgrading of water networks, data and information systems, the Joint Water Committee, and cooperation.

Additional Water Quantities

As agreed under Article 40, Palestinians were to receive the additional quantity of 28.6 mcm/yr for domestic purposes as immediate needs according to a program detailing where, how, and whose responsibility it was to develop these additional quantities. This 28.6 mcm/yr was considered to be part of the 70 to 80 mcm/yr that forms the Palestinian future water needs for the different sectors. It is worth noting that according to the agreement, the above mentioned quantities were not in any way to prejudice the provision of additional water in the ultimate negotiations that would determine final Palestinian water rights in the West Bank.

Upgrading of Water Networks

The Palestinian water and wastewater infrastructure in the West Bank and Gaza Strip in 1995 was fragmented, insufficient, and deteriorating. More than 68% of the Palestinian communities in the West Bank did not have a water supply network. Only nine municipalities had wastewater collection systems, and these were hardly comprehensive. Two or three inadequate wastewater treatment plants existed. The Palestinians hoped that with the signing of this agreement and the help of the donor community, during the interim period they would be able to construct, upgrade, and rehabilitate most of their water and wastewater systems.

Data and Information Systems

Data availability is an important element in any water resources management and planning effort. All the data related to water during the occupation period were in the hands of the Israeli authorities. It was expected that this data would be provided after the signing of the agreement. According to Article 40, both sides are to cooperate in the exchange of available relevant water and sewage data. According to Article 40, the data regarding hydrological resources was to include measurements and maps related to water resources and uses; reports, plans, studies, research, and project documents related to water and sewage; and data concerning the existing extractions, utilization, and estimated potential of the Eastern, Northeastern and Western aquifer systems.

The Joint Water Committee (JWC)

The establishment of the Joint Water Committee (JWC) was seen as one of the positive outcomes of Article 40. The main function of the JWC is to address all water- and sewage-related issues in the West Bank and Gaza Strip, including generating additional data and facilitating an information exchange. Its primary mandate was to include coordination of management of water resources; coordination of management of water and sewage systems; protection of water resources and water and sewage systems; oversight of the operation of the joint supervision and enforcement mechanism; resolution of water and sewage related disputes; cooperation in the field of water and sewage, as detailed in Article 40; establishment of arrangements for supplying water between the two sides; and the setup of monitoring systems.

Cooperation

Article 40 encourages cooperation in the water and sewage sector. The expectations for such cooperation were high from the Palestinian perspective. In light of the agreement, Palestinians expected cooperation with the Israelis concerning regional development programs; water production- and development-related projects agreed upon by the JWC within the framework of the joint Israeli-Palestinian-American Committee; promotion and development of other agreed-to water- and sewage-related joint projects, in existing or future multilateral forums; expedited water-related technology transfer, research and development, training, and setting of standards; and development of mechanisms for dealing with water-related and sewage-related natural and man-made emergencies and extreme conditions.

Status of Implementation

In general, the status of the implementation of Article 40 has not met Palestinian expectations. Reviewing the same five major issues mentioned above, the following section tries to summarize implementation and what has actually happened and been implemented regarding the agreed-upon actions mandated by Article 40.

Additional Water Quantities

According to Article 40, the total agreed-upon quantity of water supplied to the Palestinians was to range between 70 to 80 mcm/yr. Of this, 28.6 mcm/yr were to be provided to meet the immediate needs of domestic use; an amount of 29.4 mcm/yr was approved by the JWC. The actual quantity of water supplied from the approved amount, however, has only been 19.7 mcm/yr. This is because the 5 mcm/yr approved for distribution in the Gaza Strip has not yet been implemented and the 24.4 mcm/yr approved for pumping in the West Bank had an actual yield of 19.7 mcm/yr. Here it should be mentioned that the Israeli commitment of 4.5 mcm/yr of the 28.6 mcm/yr has been met while the Israeli commitment of five mcm/yr to the Gaza Strip has not been fulfilled.

The remaining quantity of 40.6 to 50.6 mcm/yr over the 29.4 mcm/yr was also not implemented. A first component of 19.1 mcm/yr was to have come from seventeen wells approved by the JWC: three drilled wells of 4.1 mcm/yr in Hebron and Bethlehem area and 15.0 mcm/yr from the remaining fourteen wells. Of these, three wells of 5 mcm/yr have reached the stage of tenders and the remaining eleven wells of 10 mcm/yr are being developed or in need of funding. A second component of 21.5 to 31.5 mcm/yr from wells was submitted for approval to JWC.

The above numbers show that the quantities of water agreed upon according to Article 40 have not been implemented. The shortfall can be attributed to lack of funding or delayed approval by the Israeli representatives at the JWC.

Water and Sewerage Networks

During the past 15 years and since the signing of the Oslo Agreement, different water and sewerage projects have been implemented. According to Article 40, any water or sewerage projects must receive approval from the JWC. During the last 12 years, the Palestinian side submitted 384 projects to the JWC. While 232 projects were approved, 53 were not. Approval for some 99 projects is still pending.

This suggests that roughly 65% of the submitted projects were approved. Yet of the 232 approved projects, only 138 projects were actually implemented while 79 projects were not (25 projects are partially implemented and 11 projects are in different stages of completion). Ultimately, this means that only 40% of the submitted projects were actually implemented.

The situation regarding the progress of sewerage projects is even worse. While 16 sewerage projects were submitted to the JWC for approval, only 8 of the submitted projects were approved and 8 were not approved. Out of the 8 approved projects, only 1 project is implemented and 2 projects are under implementation.

To conclude, it can be said that due to the steady efforts of the Palestinian Water Authority, the water sector has improved in many areas of the West Bank, especially in areas where new water supply systems were installed. In the Gaza Strip, the lack of the additional supply of 5 mcm/yr by the Israelis and the poor condition of the Gaza groundwater aquifer has made it impossible to see improvements as meaningful as those found in the West Bank.

Data and Information

The lack of data remains one of the biggest problems facing the Palestinian Water Authority. That is why the data and information provisions in Article 40 were of great importance to the newly established Palestinian Water Authority (PWA) at the time of the signing of the agreement. Since the signing of the agreement, official data and information transfer can be described as minimal and fragmented despite the efforts of the other involved parties in the peace process. Little serious effort was made to expedite data transfer and sharing of information from the official Israeli side. This has been especially true for data characterizing the Northeastern and Western aquifers and the Jordan River.

At the same time a much better data- and information-sharing process has emerged at the unofficial level through bilateral and multilateral research activities. Reports, plans, studies, research, and project documents flowed in both directions between Israeli and Palestinian researchers. A variety of joint efforts took place to collect data for research purposes. These efforts were supported by the donor community, such as USAID, EU, and many individual European countries.

In conclusion, data and information sharing, especially on the official level, have not met Palestinian expectations. At the same time, joint data sharing and joint research on the nonofficial level have been good and can offer a good model for other sectors of common interest.

The Joint Water Committee (JWC)

The JWC was established after the signing of the Oslo Agreement. The function of the JWC is to serve as the main coordinating player for the two sides in the sphere of water and sewerage. The JWC's role ranges from coordination, management, and exchange of information to overseeing and monitoring. This role was directly affected by the ongoing political conditions that have prevailed since the signing of the agreement. This can be seen from the number of meetings of the joint technical subcommittee.

The technical subcommittee has convened a total of fifty-two meetings during the past 10 years. For the first 4 years, the committee met at almost a constant rate of five meetings every year. In the years 2000 to 2001, the committee was doing much better with about ten meetings per year. From the Palestinian perspective, this momentum is due to the fact that the Labor party was in power in Israel during that period of time. After the year 2001, the subcommittee met only twice a year, which appears to be a function of the political conditions on the ground and the orientation of the Likud-led and, subsequently, the Kadima-led governments.

From the above, one can see that the JWC was not able to fulfill its role according to Article 40. On the other hand, the JWC is doing far better than many of the other joint committees established under the Oslo Agreement.

Cooperation

Cooperation in the sectors of water and sewerage has not been uniform across the many sectors that were to work together pursuant to the Oslo Peace Accords. The level of cooperation dramatically varies between official bodies and nongovernmental entities. On the official level, communication continues to exist between the Israelis and Palestinians officials, but it cannot be described as meaningful cooperation.

An example of the need for improved cooperation is the Jenin Project. Internal networks, reservoirs, and a pumping station were constructed for eleven villages in the Jenin district that have a total population of 45,000. According to Article 40, Jenin's water was to come from a well to be drilled in 1996 in the Jenin area. The Israeli representative rejected the requests for drilling of this well, however, and proposed selling water to these villages from Israel through the Israeli water company Mekorot instead. The Palestinians were very reluctant to accept this offer, but in the end they accepted it. The Israelis then changed their mind again so that the well was not drilled until 1999.

At the same time, fruitful cooperation has existed between different Israeli and Palestinian nongovernmental bodies, especially in the area of research. Different research projects were implemented, both on the bilateral level and on the multilateral level. The problem with these cooperative efforts is their tendency to be fragmented and uncoordinated.

To conclude, there is a need to improve cooperation, especially between the official water bodies on both sides. Areas of priority include issues concerning regional development programs, promotion and development of water- and sewage-related joint projects, water-related technology transfer, research and development, training, and setting of standards.

Obstacles

Political instability is considered to be the major obstacle in implementing the provisions of Article 40. In addition to political instability, full implementation of Article 40 faces many other obstacles and practices. There are delays in discussing the projects for approvals within the technical subcommittees; delays in convening JWC meetings; delays in issuance of approvals from JWC and signing of the protocols of the meetings; delays in issuance of permits, especially in area C of the West Bank; donor funding commitments which are ultimately dependent on issuing approval and permits; a limited number of qualified drilling companies (mainly for drilling of wells); a long duration of implementation from start to finish, especially for certain types of projects, such as drilling of wells; delays in land acquisition procedures; and unavailability of funds to implement approved projects.

Some of the above-mentioned constraints and obstacles could be easily lifted with goodwill. Others are more difficult to be lifted, such as funding, which requires third-party involvement, in particular, from the donor community.

Lessons Learned

Based on the above dynamics, the following are the major lessons learned from the Palestinian experience in implementing Article 40, in general, and in participating in the JWC, in particular. First, goodwill and a genuine spirit of equality should prevail in implementation. Neither side should veto the water projects of the other side without just cause and risk to critical national interests. Second, cooperation between the two parties remains essential. Cooperation should include water resources, supply, and infrastructure. When it existed, it enabled coordinated management and provision of effective services in the water sector. Third, implementation needs to be timely enough to meet the basic water needs of the Palestinians, and unilateral implementation of projects should be avoided. Implementation needs to cover all areas, including area C, where there is the greatest need for water. Fourth, lengthy procedures should be avoided and data should be exchanged regarding all relevant elements, especially water abstractions.

REFERENCES

CDM/Morganti. 1997. *Comprehensive planning framework for Palestinian water resources development*. Ramallah: Palestinian Water Authority.

Hydrological Service of Israel. 1999. *Development of utilization and status of water resources in Israel until fall 1998*. Water Commission, Ministry of National Infrastructure (in Hebrew).

Ministry of Planning and International Cooperation—Environmental Planning Directorate. 1996. *Gaza water resources—policy directions in groundwater protection and pollution control*. Gaza: Palestinian National Authority.

Palestine Consultancy Group. 1995. *An updated study of water supply and demand in Palestine*. Cambridge, MA: Harvard Middle East Water Project.

Palestinian Water Authority. 1998. *List of projects of top priority for PWA*. Ramallah, Palestine: Palestinian Water Authority.

Water and Environmental Studies Center. 1995. *Middle-East regional study on water supply and demand development*. Revised Draft Report Phase I. Nablus: WESC.

Article 40

AN ISRAELI RETROSPECTIVE

DORIT KERRET

In 1995, an interim agreement between Israel and the Palestinians was signed in Washington. As implied by its title, it was supposed to be an interim agreement that would pave the path toward the Permanent Status Settlement. The Permanent Status Settlement, in fact, was to have been signed by 2000. Sadly, 15 years later, there is no sign of a permanent agreement. An unfortunate chain of events and harsh political climate diverted the implementation of this agreement from its original goals. However, regardless of its background, the agreement still stands.

This chapter will present Israeli perceptions regarding the implementation of one of the important chapters of the interim agreement: "Article 40: Water and Sewage." The first section will briefly present the most significant principles of Article 40 according to Israeli perceptions, along with initial expectations regarding their implementation. The second section will present the status of implementation of these principles. First, the main problems associated with the implementation will be presented, followed by important achievements. The last section will present lessons and recommendations based on the experience of implementing the interim agreement. This essay is based on interviews with Israeli key actors in the design and implementation of the interim agreement.

The Israeli Perception of the Main Principles of Article 40

Interviewees indicated a number of principles as the most important elements in Article 40. In this section the importance of these principles and the expectations regarding their implementation will be briefly presented from the Israeli point of view. The principles are categorized according to the main themes they refer to and not according to the specific clauses of the agreement.

Development of Additional Water Resources

Israeli interviewees unanimously indicated the obligation of both sides to develop additional water sources (Principle 2) as one of the most important principles of the agreement. Both Israelis and the Palestinians are aware that natural water resources will not be able to provide all water necessities of both sides regardless of their distribution, in light of the water scarcity in the region. Therefore, there is no escape from developing new water sources. In this regard Israelis expected that the

Palestinians would support the development of additional water sources, especially desalination solutions as well as restoration of brackish water.

Balanced Management of Quantity and Quality of Water Resources

Facing chronic water shortages in the Mediterranean, preserving the integrity of existing water sources should be a paramount priority. This principle is anchored in some of the clauses that are all considered as fundamental and important principles of the agreement. Generally, Israelis expected the Palestinians to cooperate in preserving both the quality and the quantity of existing water sources.

Water Pollution Prevention

Untreated sewage is considered by Israeli water resources experts to be one of the most serious threats to the natural water resources in the area that are mainly groundwater aquifers. Sewage treatment is considered a challenge even in the most developed countries; recently, complaints regarding the sewage treatment in the United States were filed in the U.S. Congress. The Israeli sewage system is far from perfect, although it has significantly improved during the previous years. At the time the agreement was signed, Israeli experts sensed that awareness about the severity of the sewage situation and the need for upgrading treatment in Israel was in its infancy, while in the Palestinian areas it was practically nonexistent. Irreversible damage to the groundwater aquifer has already started due to sewage contamination. Both sides acknowledged the need to prevent water pollution in sections twenty-one and twenty-three. Therefore, one of the main expectations of the Israelis was to establish Palestinian sewage treatment infrastructure and even expedite the use of treated effluents as an additional water source for irrigation.

Protecting Water Systems

Both sides recognize that water systems and water supplies are necessary for the survival of the civilian community. Therefore, both sides are obligated not to harm water systems even in armed actions.

Water Allocation to the Palestinians

In Israelis' views, one of the most important elements of the agreement was to clearly allocate water to the Palestinian population to avoid water shortage and thirst. Section 6 of the agreement specifies the immediate needs of the Palestinians, which are 28.6 mcm/yr. Section 7 specifies their future needs as 70 to 80 mcm/yr. The specific allocation requirements are important for achieving order and clarity.

Cooperation Mechanism

Coordinated Management of Water and Sewage

The basic principles of water management in the agreement involve "coordinated" management of water and sewage. Coordinated management (as opposed to joint management) means that each party is in charge of water supplies and treatment for its population. Each water source is assigned a manager who is in charge of water allocation to the other party. The Northern and Western Aquifers are managed by Israelis and the Eastern Aquifer is managed by Palestinians. The basic understanding is that the management of water resources should follow an overall view that would take into account the natural qualities of the resource. The understanding that any harm caused by either of the sides affects all parties calls for cooperative actions under some conditions. Some frameworks for cooperation were set within the agreement to establish the de facto required cooperation.

Joint Water Committee (JWC)

The JWC is the main mechanism for cooperation. In this committee all the joint water and sewage issues are discussed. In practice, under the JWC, additional specific committees for cooperation were established as well. The Joint Technical Committee was established for dealing with technical aspects of problems and for providing the professional and technical background to the discussions of the JWC. The technical committee was comprised of subcommittees that were responsible for groundwater supply, sewage treatment, drilling (where, in terms of the aquifer, there should be drilling), and pricing (for establishing water prices). In addition, ad-hoc committees were established in light of a specific need. The JWC was perceived as a flexible mechanism that would provide solutions to the changing needs and realities.

Joint Supervision and Enforcement Teams (JSETs)

The JSETs, a series of teams whose Palestinian and Israeli members were to work jointly on enforcement, were considered by Israelis to be one of the most important mechanisms in the agreement. The JSETs were supposed to monitor the implementation of the agreement and, especially, to eliminate unauthorized water uses and drilling. The JSETs are important both in eliminating illegal activities and in establishing cooperation between the parties. The required level of cooperation within the JSETs' units is particularly high as they have to operate in full cooperation.

In sum, Israelis expressed high expectations from the agreement. In particular, it was hoped that the agreement would produce cooperation in the field of developing additional water resources, preserving the existing resources, allocating water to the Palestinians, and establishing institutional cooperation in both technical areas and enforcement.

Implementation Status

The following sections evaluate the implementation of the main principles of Article 40 as viewed by Israeli representatives. Many areas are deemed as problematic, with inadequate implementation of the main principles indicated above casting a shadow over the entire implementation of Article 40. And yet, the agreement has not been entirely a failure. On the contrary, this section concludes with the primary achievements in water and sewage management due to the implementation of Article 40.

Developing Additional Water Resources

One of the main disappointments in the implementation of the agreement from the Israeli side involved the lack of developing additional water resources. Two main reasons were raised by the Israeli interviewees to explain the reluctance of Palestinians to develop additional water resources. The first reason is connected to the differences in the interests and expectations of the sides regarding water issues and the establishment of grounds for the Permanent Status Agreement. The Palestinians approached the negotiations toward the interim agreement with a strong interest that their water rights be acknowledged by Israel. The Israelis, on the other hand, adopted the pragmatic approach that seeks solutions on the basis of needs. Israelis also did not want to harm their existing water uses.

In the interim agreement, in fact, a compromise was reached: in the first principle of Article 40, "Israel recognizes the Palestinian water rights in the West Bank." However, the specific rights are to be negotiated in the permanent status negotiations and settled in the Permanent Status Agreement. Therefore, the differences in the interests and approaches of both sides still exist. In the implementation of the agreement, regardless of principle 2, which recognizes the necessity to develop additional water, Palestinians still hold their position that Israel should provide them with all the natural water resources at the first stage (including water from the Jordan River and Kinneret Lake) and only then will they be willing to consider developing additional water resources.

The interviewees indicated that another claim that stands in the way of cooperation in the development of additional water resources involves the different economic conditions of the two sides. The Palestinians claim that the Israelis are rich enough to solve their own needs with desalination, so they can provide the Palestinians with the natural water and use desalination to solve whatever water shortages they may have.

Israelis believe that reluctance by Palestinians to develop additional water resources is also connected to their perceptions about the connection between land and water. They perceive the water rights as a part of their proof of sovereignty over the land.

Nonetheless, despite the general reluctance of Palestinians to develop additional water resources, at certain stages they seemed more open to the idea and there is heterogeneity in the opinions of different individual Palestinians. For instance, the Palestinian Negotiation Support Unit (NSU) adopted an interim approach according to which Israel should transfer some of its water rights to the Palestinians and, in parallel, additional water resources would be adopted.

The following list briefly presents the current status of projects for developing additional water resources:

- Water allocation to the Gaza Strip. The interim agreement states that Israel is to supply Gaza with water that may come from desalination. The Mekorot Company, in fact, did build the required pipelines that should transfer $5\,m^3$ of water from Ashkelon to Gaza in accordance with the interim agreement. The Americans started building the continuation of pipelines but have not finished the construction due to the rise of the Hamas government. The Norwegians decided to finish the setting of pipelines and to pay the desalination price of one year. Currently, American consent is still pending.

- Buying desalinated water from Ashkelon. Past Israeli water commissioner Shimon Tal offered Nabil Sharif, the Palestinian water commissioner at the time, to sign a contract with the Ashkelon desalination plant to provide Gaza with desalinated water with American funding. The Palestinian politicians would not hear of it. One of their main reasons for their declining this initiative was their desire to establish water rights over allocations from the Jordan River and Kinneret Lake.
- Desalination facility in Hadera. The Israelis offered to build a desalination facility in Hadera for the Palestinians, funded by the donor countries. Israel and the donor countries planned the route of the pipeline. The capacity of this facility should have been 50 m³ for the use of the northern West Bank. However, despite the approval of the professional staff of the Palestinian Authority, the Palestinian politicians refused to approve the project, and currently, implementation is nowhere in sight.
- Brackish water. The Palestinians acknowledge that using brackish water for irrigation is a necessary part of any future plan. However, they are afraid that the water may be too expensive due to the associated sewage treatment system and the necessary winter impounding. Israelis recognize that Palestinians irrigate in the area of Jerusalem with brackish water but perceive the quantities utilized as negligible.
- Red-Dead Canal. The Palestinians are designated to be a beneficiary in the planned project of transferring water from the Red Sea into the Dead Sea. Israelis agree that if implemented, the Palestinians should also enjoy one of the outcomes of this project—that is, desalinated water. Accordingly, recent Palestinian agreement to receive desalinated water from the project is seen as revealing a softening in their resistance to relying on desalinated water.

Balanced Management of Quantity and Quality of Water Resources

Under the principle of balanced management of water resources, Israeli interviewees generally expressed their satisfaction about the protection of water resources, as will be elaborated in the following sections. Nevertheless, they articulated significant disappointment about Palestinian efforts to preserve the quality of water through upgrading insufficient sewage treatment as well as their efforts to preserve water quantity by preventing water losses (water consumption that is unaccounted for that may mainly be caused by leakage from pipelines and water thefts). These two phenomena will be described later.

Water Pollution Prevention (Sewage Treatment)

One of the main claims of the Israeli side toward the Palestinians involves the insufficient sewage treatment by the Palestinians. All interviewees indicated the sewage problem as one of the gravest disappointments in the implementation of Article 40.

The following assumptions were raised as possible explanations for the lack of progress in sewage treatment during the first years of implementing Article 40:

- The Israelis are blamed for not treating the sewage in the Palestinian territories during the occupation. While these allegations may have some justification, the Israelis had hoped that Article 40 would open a new era.
- Palestinians hoped that the donations would eventually be transferred to other issues that they consider as more pressing.
- The observable harm was mostly in the Israeli territories as sewage flows downstream in the wadi.

Since the inception of Article 40, 250 million dollars (U.S.) have been allocated to sewage treatment in the Palestinian Authority. And yet, sewage still flows into Israeli wadis. Lately, however, there are signs of modest improvement due to some actions that were taken.

- Bureaucracy in the procedure of authorizing sewage treatment plans was inefficient and sluggish. Until 2002, the procedures were mostly the following: Palestinians submitted partial and unsatisfactory (in Israelis views) sewage treatment plans. Israelis recommended modifications and the discussions would invariably be delayed for another half a year each time. In 2003 both sides signed a Memorandum of Understanding (MOU) for promotion of sewage treatment plans. The MOU indicated that each side was in charge of treating its own sewage and that the treatment facilities would be established in two stages. The first stage was to provide a "20/30" level of treatment for chemical oxygen demand (COD) and total suspended solids (TTS), respectively. During the second stage, treatment levels were to be upgraded to reach the discharge levels recommended by the Inbar Committee, which set future sewage treatment standards for wastewater reuse.
- Both sides realized that they should develop a united front if they wanted to generate international financial aid. As soon as they approached the donors with a joint agenda, they started receiving financial aid for sewage treatment projects.
- Donors reformed their donation system so that it would be targeted to support specific infrastructure projects. Money allocated to support sewage treatment facilities could not be used for other purposes any longer.
- The Palestinian population did not accept the "solution" of discharging raw sewage into the sea.
- The Israeli government reimbursed itself with ninety million shekels due to damages that were caused by lack of sewage treatment by the Palestinians.

The aforementioned changes are perceived by the Israelis as having led to some improvements, but there are still some major obstacles to proper sewage treatment:

- Political problems. There is a "disconnect" between the professional staff of the Water and Sewage Authority in the Palestinian Authority and municipal officials. The professional staff that is in charge of water and sewage within the Palestinian Authority understands the importance of sewage treatment. However, decision makers and politicians in the municipalities do not appear to care or to understand these issues. The professional staff is unable to provide any solutions without the support from the political level.

- Palestinian priorities. The Palestinian authority places water supply as a top priority, whereas sewage treatment is a much lower priority. In accordance with this prioritization, the Water Authority is in charge of sewage treatment, and not the environmental authority.
- Capacity problems. Maintenance and operation are major challenges of sewage treatment even in highly developed countries. Therefore, construction of sewage treatment facilities does not solve the problem of sewage treatment in and of itself when the relevant authority does not have maintenance capacity. Most sewage treatment facilities that are currently built by donors are funded for an additional 3 years of maintenance and operation, above and beyond the construction of physical plants. For the long-term, maintenance of sewage treatment facilities bears costs. In Israel, residents are required to pay for their water consumption. These costs are supposed to include costs of sewage treatment. In the Palestinian Authority, Israelis sense that residents do not pay for the full costs of water consumption (presumably because they do not have the income to pay for it).
- General external problems. In addition to the three aforementioned specific problems, sewage treatment is stalled due to the general external problems that will be discussed.

Current Status of Sewage Treatment Facilities

Israeli experts take a dim view of the present conditions prevailing in Palestinian sewage infrastructure. The only facility that is properly functioning is the Ramallah treatment facility. The following facilities are in different stages of construction or their construction ceased from some reason:

- Hebron. The construction of the sewage treatment facility that was funded by the United States was stopped due to the overall policy regarding financial assistance to a Hamas-led government.
- Northern Gaza Strip. A forty-million-dollar facility is under construction, funded by the World Bank.
- Center of the Gaza Strip. An eighty-million-dollar sewage treatment facility project is ready for a tender.
- Tul Karem-Nablus, Jenin, and Ramallah. This year large projects are planned to start.

Water Losses

Water loss due to unauthorized drilling and water theft by Palestinian farmers is perceived as one of the three main problems associated with implementing

Article 40, as identified by Israelis. The most common method of water theft is simply drilling a hole in a water pipe. The impression of some of the interviewees was that although it seems that this activity is privately initiated by Palestinian farmers, Palestinian authorities are either incapable or reluctant to put an end to this phenomenon.

The most significant incidents of water thefts identified by Israelis have been the following:

- When Israel evacuated the Gaza Strip, wells, pipes, and equipment were left for the use of the Palestinians; but ,instead of using them, pipes and equipment were stolen and two thousand unauthorized wells were drilled that practically ruined the aquifer.
- In the West Bank the problem of unauthorized drilling is less severe as deep drills are required in order to reach the water and they are less accessible. Only deep drills may severely harm the aquifer. Deep drilling requires special machinery that can easily be located by the JSETs. In addition, the Palestinians have learned from the experience with the Gaza Strip and have taken measures to stop the theft. But still water theft is a widespread phenomenon as Palestinians hook into pipe lines, stealing from Palestinians and Israeli settlements alike.

Water depression resulting from losses within the pipeline system reaches an extreme percentage in the Palestinian Authority. According to the Palestinian Water Authority reports, it reaches 36% of all water losses. The Israeli government offered to assist the Palestinian Authority in implementing the Israeli system of prevention of water losses and reduction in domestic water consumption, but Palestinians refused to take advantage of this system.

Problems in Cooperation

Information Transfer

Israeli authorities hold that the Israel Water and Sewage Authority for some time has provided Palestinians with information regarding drills, quantities, and water levels. However, information transfer is deemed as potentially problematic when the information might be used against the Israeli water interests, esjwETspecially in a Permanent Status Settlement. Much of the transferred information is passed through unofficial channels or in the different joint committees.

Water Management

Israelis would have liked to witness a stronger, more organized and economic Palestinian water system management with citizens paying for their water consumption and their part in sewage treatment. Israelis would like to see the water and sewage system treated as a holistic system where effluents are treated and at least some of them utilized. The Israelis offered the Palestinians the benefit of their experience. For instance, the Palestinians were invited to learn water management practices from the Mekorot Water Company. Although several individual Palestinians took some classes and tours, they have not yet implemented their knowledge, perhaps due to internal difficulties. Another initiative that has not been realized is a joint center for desalination that was to train technicians and workers in desalination facilities. Despite a mutual agreement, international support, and German assistance, this project has never been implemented.

External Problems Affecting the Implementation

The Lack of a Permanent Agreement

Now 15 years have passed since the initiation of the interim agreement, even though its life expectancy was only supposed to be 5 years, at which time a permanent agreement would have been signed. The anticipation of the ultimate Permanent Status Agreement stymies development in several areas, such as development of water resources. Until the Permanent Status Agreement is signed, both sides try to avoid actions that may weaken their position regarding negotiations over a permanent agreement. One of the questions still open involves the determination of the final jurisdictional borders. As water rights are immediately connected to land ownership, disputes acknowledging the Palestinians' rights to certain aquifers may be viewed as acknowledging their land ownership in these areas. Similarly, the Palestinians' sewage treatment responsibility is also related to the sovereignty over these areas. Joint infrastructure projects, while possibly efficient in the short run, may be perceived by Palestinians as implicitly granting sovereignty and are avoided due to political considerations. For instance, joint sewage programs with Israeli settlements were declined by the Palestinians as it may be considered as acknowledging the legitimacy of Israeli settlements.

Security

Israelis also see a link between lack of progress and the security situation. The current unstable security situation in the area—with bombing and assassinations still occurring on a regular basis—serves to drive away donor nations that prefer to invest money in more stable and promising initiatives. In addition, when money is available, contractors are often prevented from reaching the relevant areas, equipment is stalled, and projects end up with excessive cost.

Budget

Sewage systems and water supply systems cost money. Israelis believe that at present Palestinians do not have the required amount for solving all the existing problems. However, some of the interviewees think that solutions were available that might have overcome budgetary problem. For instance, approaching donors with a commonly agreed upon agenda tends to generate interest and investment. A holistic approach to water and sewage (such as using brackish water for irrigation) could also save money and improve water allocation and might also be popular with donors.

Political Problems

Two main political problems have made a difficult situation even worse. The first is the rise of the Hamas government, followed by the boycott of the Palestinian Authority by the Israeli and U.S. governments. As a result, much of the activities that are defined in the interim agreement have been suspended, many donations to the Palestinians were denied, and projects have been stalled.

Another internal political problem that Israelis see as existing since the initiation of the interim agreement is the friction among the water professionals and the central government officials and the local governments. After the rise of the Hamas, the problem became aggravated as local authorities are often from the Fatach and the government is from the Hamas. The two levels do not communicate, and budget allocations are not transferred.

Significant Achievements

General Evaluation

All interviewees agreed that despite the mutual complaints, the agreement and its implementation have been relatively good and the agreement has fulfilled its intended purpose. It is telling that no Israeli expert interviewed wants to breach the agreement or cancel it. All sides want to preserve its main principles (a stable agreement is the best indication of a successful agreement). In addition, ensuring the water supply during the summer was mentioned as an indication of the successful work of the Joint Water Committee. Despite the potential gravity of water problems during the summer season and exacerbated scarcity, there has not been a single summer when the Palestinian Authority faced a humanitarian water crisis.

The most encouraging outcome of the agreement, from the Israeli perspective, therefore, is the enhanced cooperation between the sides. Before the agreement there was no cooperation whatsoever. Naturally, the Joint Water Committee did not exist. The agreement facilitates cooperation and sets the groundwork for its implementation.

Cooperation

JWC

Intervieweens agreed that the JWC was an important and good mechanism. Via the JWC, sides reached many understandings and projects were approved. This was the only committee that was spawned by the interim agreement that continued to operate, despite the Intifada, continuous political problems, and the Hamas victory in the Palestinian Authority elections. When political or security problems prevented physical meetings, creative solutions were adopted, such as telephone discussions and meetings in neutral places to sign the necessary protocols.

The main achievement of the JWC has been its ability to work together, raising problems and finding solutions. For instance, before every summer, a joint meeting is held where the Palestinians raise problems. Israel assisted the Palestinians in the maintenance of drillings, found creative solutions, brought water in tankers, etc. Prior to the last official meeting of the JWC all the issues that were raised by the committee were taken care of. A new list has been created, but the Hamas government was elected, and things ground to a halt.

One possible explanation for the successful operation of the committee is mutual need. The Palestinians could not drill any additional wells without the authorization of the JWC, and the Israelis were duty bound to coordinate regarding their settlements. Therefore, both sides needed one another in order to conduct any kind of activity in the West Bank. In addition, the JWC was largely composed of professional staff and not politicians. The decision by the Israeli government to allow the committee to keep working was unique to the water field. In practice, the JWC has been a vehicle for updating and keeping the agreement alive after it should have been replaced by the permanent agreement.

JWETS

Officially, five teams worked jointly till 2000. After an unfortunate incident in which a Palestinian officer shot an Israeli officer in the joint policing force, the teams were disbanded. For the next 2 years no control unit operated. In 2002 new enforcement teams of the Israeli Water Commission started operating. There is some cooperation with the Palestinians, who have teams of their own. At present, the teams no longer operate together, according to the instructions in the interim agreement. But they do cooperate in the area of information transfer. Israelis believe that the Palestinian teams feel threatened by Palestinian civilians and that this compromises their actions.

However, claims have been made that even while operating quite rapidly, the cooperation between the teams has been less than successful. The Palestinians were not motivated to cooperate in the joint teams since all the enforcement resources were targeted at the Palestinians. At the same time the Palestinian JSETs' members were considered to be "rats" by their own people if they reported offences. Israelis were under the impression that their complaints were not addressed.

Preserving Water Systems

Generally, the overall objective of the interim agreement—to preserve the water systems from physical harm—is considered to have been quite successful. From the Israeli side, the military is deemed as having done its best not to harm water systems, though occasionally during violent episodes, water systems were harmed. The Palestinian side also tried not to deliberately harm water systems, nor did it poison wells or bomb them. Even terrorist activities have not targeted water systems.

Based on the interim agreement, subsequent agreements were signed by the Israeli water commissioner and the director of the Palestine Water Authority for preventing harm to water resources. Also, the water commissioners issued joint statements to the Arabic press with a call for the Palestinian population not to harm the water systems as both sides rely on the same natural systems.

Water Allocation

One of the prominent achievements of the interim agreement was the significant rise in water supply to Palestinians homes. In 1967, at the start of the Israeli occupation of the West Bank, only 10% of the Palestinian households were connected to the water supply system. Today 90% of the Palestinian households are connected to the water system.

While signing the agreement the Palestinians were supplied with 120 mcm of additional water yearly. In fact, following the interim agreement water supply exceeded even the quantities Israel undertook to provide. Currently, the quantity provided by Israel is almost double the quantity that was promised in the agreement. Israel provides 50 m³ extra, beyond its obligations under the agreement, a matter that is confirmed by Palestinian records. Two main reasons caused the decision to increase the water supply beyond the amount stipulated in the agreement. The first was the fact that the interim agreement was in force longer than anticipated so that the hydrological situation had to reflect demographic and other changes. The second explanation involves miscalculation from the Israeli side, in part because no one was in charge of joining the provided quantities.

Lessons and Recommendations

The implementation of Article 40 and the cooperation that was achieved through the JWC surmounted many political and other obstacles. The experience under the interim agreement involving water governance proves that when goodwill exists, true cooperation is possible. Although water-related issues are unique in many ways, general lessons are possible as well. Arguably, one of the most important tools of Article 40 was the JWC. The updating mechanism that was implemented by the JWC left the agreement alive long after it was supposed to have perished.

However, the true cooperation was also the result of the unique relationships that were built between human beings who spent a significant amount of time with each other in the negotiations toward the agreement and during its implementation. It is enough to hear the Israeli appreciation about the professional staff in the Palestinian Authority to understand that personal relationships play a significant role in the realization of different goals. This observation may constitute a double-edged sword, as personal staff may change, affecting the conciliatory nature of the cooperation.

In addition, in cases where both sides were mutually dependent to act, the agreement worked smoothly. In several instances the cooperation proved worthwhile as both sides achieved more donations when their requests were uniform and coordinated. However, when both sides face great deficiencies (such as the case of sewage treatment facilities) significant problems arose.

REFERENCES

Kantor, Shmuel, advisor to the Water Authority. 2007. Interview by author. Tel-Aviv, March 1.

Keidar, Jackob, acting deputy director general for the Middle East, Ministry of Foreign Affairs. 2007. Interview by author. Jerusalem, February 27.

Nagar, Baruch, West Bank director, Water Authority. 2007. Interview by author. Tel-Aviv, March 25.

Raisner, Daniel, former head of International Affair, Israeli Defense Forces. 2007. Interview by author. June 3.

Shamir, Uri, advisor to the Water Authority. 2007. Interview by author. Tel-Aviv, April 30.

Tal, Shimon, water commissioner, 2001–2006. 2007. Interview by author. Hertzelia, February 16.

Editors' Summary

Objectively, there are areas of clear progress that can be identified with the execution of Article 40 of the interim peace accord with its provisions for cooperation in water management. And yet there are also clearly disappointments on both sides. Palestinians have a difficult time translating "objective" indicators of progress associated with implementation with a general reality of day-to-day deterioration with which they are familiar. For example, while Palestinians today objectively have access to greater quantities of water than they did prior to the agreement, the effect on the pervasive scarcity is hardly recognizable. The 60 l/day allocation to average Palestinian families is only half that of Jordan's, where water scarcity is considered a major problem. With a population that is still growing exponentially, along with a water delivery infrastructure that still suffers from chronic leakages, substantial numbers of Palestinians rely on cisterns and rain collection to meet their basic needs. Article 40 did little to change that.

Israeli disappointment involves the broader breakdown of the peace process. From its perspective far more money went into Palestinian military hardware than into water infrastructure. Moreover, while copious quantities of international support were available following the interim agreement, Palestinians did not prioritize water resource development and sewage infrastructure.

The most obvious inadequacy of Article 40 of the interim agreement is that while the provisions were intended to be an ephemeral stop on a much broader route that was to redefine the hydrological reality of the region, after almost 15 years the agreement functions as a permanent accord, for which it is poorly equipped. Hence, a clear definition of Palestinian water rights remains unresolved. Palestinians had little reason to anticipate Israeli goodwill in this area when there was constant enmity between the parties. Water is clearly one of the areas that Israel will want to use as a bargaining chip in the overall jockeying toward a final peace treaty. Therefore, Israel has not shown alacrity about making "concessions" up front.

One of the failures of Article 40 involves the lack of meaningful progress in the establishment of upgraded Palestinian sewage systems. Despite considerable investment by donor nations in the Palestinian economy, only some 6%–7% of sewage is fully treated. Political instability offers much of the explanation for the lack of progress. Yet, all the same, the agreement has not served to help garner the necessary resources to transform the sewage profile and establish the hygienic infrastructure necessary for a modern, healthy land. Palestinians are miffed that Israel has unilaterally deducted funds from development funds for the Palestinians in order to cover the expenses of sewage treatment plants and to remunerate their expenses associated with transboundary discharge of pollution.

While the stamina of the Joint Water Committee, with its ability to maintain operations during the most tumultuous of times, is often held up as one of the greatest achievements of Article 40, the institution itself is the target of considerable criticism. Outside commentators have pointed to an inherent flaw of the JWC involving the absence of symmetry between the sides. The interim agreement requires Palestinians to run all water-related projects through the JWC. But no parallel expectations are made of Israel in its ventures in the water management field. This lack of symmetry is considered unfair, giving the JWC a reputation as an exploitive body that perpetuates Israeli domination.

The JWC is also an excellent example of the gap in perceptions between the two sides. Because of the requirement for consensus in making its decisions, Palestinians for the most part see the committee as a continuation of Israeli domination, which serves to stymie independent hydrological initiatives and perpetuate Israeli control over their water resources. They argue that important sewage projects were delayed because one Israeli representative had reservations. Israelis typically point to the committee for proof that cooperation, while far from perfect, can persevere and produce positive results.

Clearly, Article 40 has produced important progress. Palestinian water rights were recognized and the quantities that they received expanded dramatically. The sides showed a willingness to create a joint enforcement program which although not yet fully operational, could easily be activated as the framework has already been agreed upon. Notwithstanding Palestinian frustration with the JWC, it has proven to be a forum where problems can be addressed and on occasion solved together. But it is important that efforts begin to move forward toward a final agreement, which can offer a more equitable and sustainable arrangement.

PART 3

THE WATER CULTURE OF ISRAELIS AND PALESTINIANS

This part offers insights into the culture of water for Israelis and Palestinians. For a final agreement to be sustainable, it is important that it enjoy broad popular support. Hence, it is important to explore how Israelis and Palestinians think about water and its relationship to the larger issues of Israeli-Palestinian relations. The two essays also offer an opportunity to consider how a shared water culture might emerge from the present conflict, rather than two separate cultures aspiring to attain sustainable management of common water resources.

Water Culture in Palestine

ZIAD ABDEEN

There are several objective differences between the water resources in the Palestinian sector and those in Israel. The most obvious one involves absolute quantities of available water. Israel currently has the upper hand in control of both surface and ground waters of the Jordan River watershed, including those areas in occupied West Bank. At the same time, water delivery infrastructure in Palestine is not as developed as it is in Israel. This means that water quality is not as high a concern in Israel as it is in Palestine. The discrepancy in both water quantity and quality is an important factor in the water culture of Palestine. The water consumption pattern by Palestinians is thus due in large part to political constraints.

The most basic disparity between Israeli and Palestinian attitudes toward water can be traced to how much they receive, or per capita allocation rates. The average Israeli consumes roughly 350 m³/yr while a Palestinian uses roughly 100 m³/yr.

In absolute terms, agriculture is a far smaller consumer of water in Palestine than in Israel. The Palestinian domestic/industrial and agricultural usage is roughly 89 mcm for agriculture and 57 mcm for the domestic sector. Ironically, this makes Palestinian agricultural a relatively greater consumer of water than the Israeli agricultural sector. Of course, the water management profile of agriculture in the West Bank is completely different than in the Israeli sector (see part 6). For example, irrigation techniques in the West Bank do not rely on capital-intensive drip systems, although this depends on the region and crop. Traditional Palestinian reliance on rainfall and streams, along with a lack of an irrigation-based agricultural sector, is considered by leading Palestinian experts to have ecological advantages (Assaf et al. 1998).

Another difference is the relative contribution of surface water to overall resources. For example, there are some 527 known springs in the West Bank, providing roughly half of domestic consumption. As these springs historically were not regulated by the Israeli authorities, historic rights remained in force. Some 67% of these streams are utilized—roughly two-thirds by agriculture in the West Bank with the other third used for domestic purposes.

The enormous magnitude of lost water to delivery systems has been documented in a number of contexts, with as much as 30% loss of local waters attributed to leaky pipes. While, theoretically, this problem falls in the technological rather than the social realm, expanding water efficiency in the municipal sector through investment in infrastructure is driven by social/political considerations.

For example, the hesitancy of Palestinians to rely on Israeli technology can be linked to the general hesitation to allow for ongoing control and influence of Israeli sovereignty of water resources over Palestinian territories and resources.

In general, the relative scarcity of water (both in terms of quantity and quality) in Palestine drives local perceptions and attitudes toward this resource. An additional factor driving attitudes is the traditional use of water in some villages in the West Bank. Where local control of water still remains intact, water allocations for agriculture are socially determined. Unfortunately, these systems are under threat as centralized authorities such as the Palestinian Water Authority begin to assume control. Further, the dominant role of political instability and the recent Intifadah within the day-to-day reality of Palestinians have enormous manifestations for the social dynamics of this society regarding water. In fact, it is a key element in the water culture of Palestine due to the perceived hegemonic position of Israel.

While Israelis are vaguely aware of the geopolitical conflict in the area as a source of tension regarding water allocations, these issues are extremely high in the perceptions of Palestinian communities. The Oslo Accords brought with them a spate of public works projects, largely American funded, with the goal of strengthening the water infrastructure of the West Bank. Yet, due to a variety of factors, most of these did not change the conditions on the ground, and water scarcity only grew worse. This has surely not been lost on the Palestinian public.

The impact of the military activities of the Israel Defense Forces (IDF) on water infrastructure is frequently cited as exacerbating a situation that was already extremely deficient. The freezing of critical water infrastructure projects (e.g., the sewage treatment plant in Hebron or Sulfit) as a result of the present hostilities suggests that to a large extent there is justification for linking water policies with the broader context of Israeli-Palestinian relations. In a word, for the West Bank, the present round of hostilities affects everything, with water management and perceptions of water issues being no exception.

This point becomes acutely salient during periods of curfew. At these times, water delivery becomes a critical issue for all Palestinian citizens, regardless of socioeconomic class. Basic access to drinking water becomes the primary focus of households. Showers and personal hygiene are delayed so as not to waste valuable water. As bottled water is too expensive for much of the population, tap water (or water delivered in tankers for the 200 villages that remain without running water) is the critical resource, and during summer months, supply is sometimes interrupted.

As such, Palestinians tend to blame Israel for water scarcity problems. A pervasive sense of injustice in the allocation of water resources is a common feature of almost all Palestinians' personal ideology, regardless of the individual's political or theological inclinations.

Cisterns and storage of rainwater constitute basic elements in many Palestinian homes. This direct involvement by citizens, while, on the one hand, a form of empowerment, also offers a constant reminder of perennial shortages. In other words, the citizens' experience in generating their own water makes them appreciate the resource, and they are acutely conscious of its value. This contrasts with urban residents of Israel who are largely buffered from personally experiencing scarcity due to an efficient water distribution infrastructure.

With scarcity dominating local perceptions, other uses of water are often perceived as frivolous or irrelevant. For example, should a conflict between nature and human needs arise, the acute shortage among Palestinians makes concern for ecological values or for increased supply to the Dead Sea seem like a luxury. With the expansion of supply for basic human needs, increasing quantities is considered to be the pre-eminent priority in discussions. A peace treaty that includes a redistribution of water for the region and allocations for nature (as well as generating expanded supply) may be able to change this perception, but only if it also leverages a parallel increase in water allocations to consumers in Palestine.

Water prices are set at an artificially low level in Palestine in order to ensure universal access, regardless of economic capabilities. Bottled water, although widely available in stores, is only utilized by a small (but growing) percentage of the local population due to the high (relative to income) associated costs. Tap water is sufficiently expensive and in many cases unavailable to justify a variety of "collection" activities by local populations in Palestine, where individuals drive to springs or private treatment centers and fill up containers.

Farmers typically do not pay for water at all in Palestine. Stream supplied irrigation is received free of charge due to the persistence of historical rights. This suggests that any direct expenses assigned to them for water usage will have an immediate affect on agronomic decisions and will be unpopular. Unlike in Israel, where there exists a certain level of animosity toward the agricultural sector for "wasting" limited water resources, Palestinian farmers do not appear to be the subject of resentment by their urban countrymen. The general public is aware of the poor quality of effluents, which are occasionally used by the agricultural sector, and tends to have an inflated view of its contribution to irrigation supply. As such, most city-dwellers have little desire to compete for these sources of water.

Moreover, there is no perceived agricultural lobby driving public policy in water in these sectors as there is in Israel. The poorly organized subsistence farmers (*fellahin*) are less likely to wield direct influence in the corridors of power, but at the local level they can be a powerful force. In either case, the political process in Palestine does not lend itself to making water a hot political issue in the domestic context, if for no other reason than because of the issue's public persona as one of many areas of conflict involving Israel.

Water conservation constitutes a highly developed ethos in Palestinian society. Regulation of agricultural utilization is often done via social pressures, with the wasting of water considered to be an inappropriate behavior which brings with it social repercussions.

There are great gaps in the availability and quality of water in Palestinian societies. Palestinian communities without access to running water are typically more indigent and rural. More importantly, they are more vulnerable to contamination of springs, which provide a sole source of water for the at least 200,000 people in these villages. There are a growing number of reports of utilization of polluted streams by Palestinians, notwithstanding their classification as a resource unfit for consumption.

REFERENCES

Abu-Zeid, M. A. 1998. Water and sustainable development: The vision for world water, life and the environment. *Water Policy* 1:9–19.

Assaf, K. K., M. Ben-Zvi, J. S. Clarke, H. El-Naser, S. Kesselman, M. N. Landers, M. F. Nuseibeh, and C. J. Wipperfurth. 1998. *Overview of Middle East water resources: Water resources of Palestinian, Jordanian and Israeli interest.* U.S. Geological Service, EXACT Middle East Water Data Banks Project.

Burmil, S., T. C. Daniel, and J. D. Hetherington. 1999. Human values and perceptions of water in arid landscapes. *Landscape and Urban Planning* 44:99–109.

Feitelson, E. 2000. The ebb and flow of Arab-Israeli water conflicts: Are past conflicts likely to resurface. *Water Policy* 2:343–363.

Hillel, D. 1994. *Rivers of Eden: The struggle for water and the quest for peace in the Middle East.* New York: Oxford University Press.

Hoekstra, A. Y. 1988. Appreciation of water: Four perspectives. *Water Policy* 1:605–622.

Hutson, S. S., L. N. Barber, F. J. Kenny, S. K. Linsey, S. D. Lumia, and A. M Maupin. 2004. *Estimated use of water in the United States in 2000.* U.S. Geological Survey.

Isaac, J., N. Hrimat, K. Rishmawi, S. Saad, M. Abu Kubea, J. Hilal, M. Owawi, G. Sababa, M. Awad, F. Ishaq, and I. Zboun. 2000. *An atlas of Palestine: The West Bank and Gaza.* Bethlehem, Palestine: Applied Research Institute Jerusalem.

Pandey, J. 1990. The environment, culture and behavior. *Applied Cross-Cultural Psychology* 14:254–277.

Trottier, J. 1999. *Hydropolitics in the West Bank and Gaza Strip, Passia, Jerusalem.*

Water Culture in Israel

CLIVE LIPCHIN

With at least 60% of water going to agriculture in Israel, its unique role in local Israeli culture and heritage must be understood and the practical manifestations integrated into an assessment of water culture in Israel. Agriculture has historically enjoyed a privileged place among Israeli decision-makers. Explanations for this were somewhat self-evident during the 1950s and 1960s, when agriculture provided some 30% of the country's GNP and most of the top political leadership had either immediate or historical connections with agricultural communities.

Zionism, the nationalistic ideology of the Jewish people, always elevated agricultural pursuits, encouraging "pioneer" immigrants to establish new settlements. A variety of philosophers, most notably A. D. Gordon, espoused a Tolstoyic perception that only through work connected to the land and soil could personal redemption be achieved. Among agriculture's additional merits that were traditionally cited are its contribution to "food security" as a means of self-sufficiency, its role in stymieing land claims by Arabs, its establishment of territorial claims in the periphery of the country and in the past, its socialization of new immigrants, and its reduction of unemployment.

This ideological and cultural bias provides some explanation for present water policies, which today are frequently inconsistent with economic and environmental considerations. To begin with, the economic contribution of agriculture to Israel's economic profile has fallen to 3% of GNP and 2% of overall employment. Crop subsidies nevertheless remain high for certain crops. Large-scale water diversions for agriculture have also left a hydrological legacy of dry streams and depleted aquifers. Chief among these is the National Water Carrier that diverts water from the Sea of Galilee in the northern part of the Jordan River watershed to the south of the country for irrigation. The project changed the way Israelis perceived their water resources and made almost the entire country dependent on a single water-supply system. This large-scale diversion scheme plays an important role in reducing the flow of water in the lower Jordan and hence the amount of water that can reach the Dead Sea. The building of the canal was also a source of friction with Syria in the build up to the war of 1967.

Part of the reason for Israel's societal commitment to water infrastructure can be attributed to the political elites who continue to dominate governmental decision-makers. Senior politicians and government officials are disproportionately affiliated with the agricultural sector, affecting their decisions about water allocation, pricing, and distribution. The political patronage of Israel's top leader-ship to agricultural interests continues, and they remain protected in recent years regardless of party affiliation. For example, past Prime Minister Ehud Barak, a "left-ist" politician, was raised on an agricultural kibbutz, while recent Prime Minister Ariel Sharon, head of a right-wing party, makes his home on a ranch in the Negev. Recently, a plan by the Israel Treasury to raise water prices by 70% for the agricul-tural sector was tabled after intervention from the minister of agriculture.

While the general public is increasingly urban in its domicile (over 90% of the population in Israel live in moderate to large cities), Zionist's veneration of ruralist living remains a critical factor in the water culture of the national psyche. This is true from an ideological perspective, with farming still considered among the more admirable (albeit barely profitable) professions. Youth movements, a critical social-ization factor for large segments of upper-middle-class Israeli youth, still spend considerable time in summer work camps in agricultural communities.

Agriculture also holds a place in the national aesthetic psyche. A study by Fleisher and Tsur (2000) from the Hebrew University based on a "willingness to pay" survey suggests that the value for passive use (among tourists) for agricultural production in Israel's Jezreel valley and Israel's Huleh valley exceeds the actual pro-duction amounts. This is not inconsistent with similar preferences in England, which has protected its bucolic countryside with legislation to subsidize rural landscapes. Quite simply, Israelis like farms, and farmers have convinced decision-makers (and to a certain extent the public at large) that the resulting prodigious water consumption is justified.

Hence, it can be argued that there are dominating "ideological and cultural" factors that explain the country's ongoing commitment to agriculture and that by association, water is just too valuable to flow freely in the country's rivers and streams. By this logic, the price now being paid by the Dead Sea's alarming decline is due to the veneration of water for agriculture among all other needs. Within this context, however, the agricultural sector has increasingly come to understand that freshwater is a scarce resource that will be largely replaced by treated wastewater and desalination. At the same time, the growing of certain crops may become pro-hibitively expensive or impossible due to the salinity levels in effluents and avail-able brackish waters. The transition to drip irrigation for many crops from the 1970s onward has allowed many Israelis farmers to maintain productivity even as actual allocations were cut periodically.

Reductions in allocations of water to agriculture were primarily enacted in the face of droughts but also reflected a growing domestic demand for water. The adaptability of Israel's agricultural sectors and the relatively consistent fluctuations in allocations over the past decade confirm that while agriculture's general support is fairly unquestioned, the actual quantity of water consumed is open to change and influence of additional factors. In fact, recent data show that water consumption in agriculture is declining (table 3.1).

Not only the actual magnitude, but also the form of the agricultural commu-nity's water portfolio can be considered a dynamic factor. Past experience suggests

Table 3.1 Potable water consumption by purpose (percentages)

	1983	1993	2003
Agriculture	71	64	56
Domestic	23	29	38
Industry	6	7	6
Total	100	100	100

Source: Israel Central Bureau of Statistics, 2004.

Table 3.2 Water production in agriculture by type (percentages)

	1993	2003
Potable	71	56
Effluent	12	24
Brackish	6	11
Surface	11	9
Total	100	100

Source: Israel Central Bureau of Statistics, 2004.

that it is a nimble sector that has frequently changed its crop profiles in order to exploit market opportunities or to respond to the agronomic constraints posed by different water qualities. This same flexibility can be seen in its utilization of wastewater, which, as already mentioned, provides it with a growing percentage of its hydrologic needs (table 3.2). Cultural resistance to wastewater, which has been an obstacle to its utilization in certain Arab societies, constitutes less of a barrier among Israeli communities. The use of wastewater for domestic purposes, however, has been shown to be unpopular. The amount of freshwater (potable) being consumed by agriculture is declining somewhat, although the savings of freshwater in agriculture are being rapidly consumed by the growing domestic sector.

From an empirical perspective, the primary factors that can be associated with any reduction in agricultural productivity, and hence water, involve land conversion. For many years, the powerful stature of agriculture in Israeli political culture was bolstered by the Planning and Building Law (1965) that gave agricultural zoning preference as a "default" to any land that was not designated otherwise. During the 1990s, a series of decisions changed that and led to a softening of zoning lines, which had previously locked farmers into agricultural usage. At the same time, economic conditions and high inflationary loans pushed many farmers to take advantage of the new speculative opportunities and sell out. This transformation can be seen in such regions as Sharon and Galilee. It also changed the perception of farmers among environmentalists, who increasingly valued agriculture as a hedge against urban sprawl.

Israel's national water management system since its inception has been designed to subsidize agricultural production. Water prices constitute one of the clearest economic manifestations of the aforementioned ideological commitment to agriculture. Under Israel's Water Law (1959) farmers pay a low-base price for the first 50% of their water allotment. The price increases for the next 30% and 20%, respectively. Water prices for water with high concentrations of salinity or effluents can be as much as 100% cheaper. This provides a disincentive to water conservation, as low-grade saline water is cheap to use. Urban uses can be charged as much as eight times more. In recent budgets, the cost of water subsidies has been roughly $73 million (U.S.).

In the past, drops in domestic water use came through moral suasion. When the Israeli public was convinced that the water shortage was acute and genuine, it responded by reducing its consumption. Lawns were dried up and even cemented over, shower times shortened, and water-saving devices installed in bathrooms, etc. The agricultural sector was also politically more willing to accept water allocation reductions. For example, when Israel's Supreme Court disqualified Spartan water quotas issued by Water Commissioner Dan Zaslavsky in the early 1990s, he was left with little alternative. Zaslavsky made a direct appeal to the public. Given the 3 successive years of drought that had depleted and overdrawn Israel's freshwater resources considerably, he asked Israelis to cut back. The public responded positively. Subsequent to Zaslavsky's request, some 10% drop in overall use was recorded. Albeit, this drop was temporary, as the following above-average rainfall years resulted in cutbacks being withdrawn. During the summer of 2009, public participation was even more dramatic with an 18% drop in domestic utilization responding to an aggressive public relations campaign and a "drought tax."

In other areas, Israelis have shown an impressive willingness to pay for public natural resources when they felt they were threatened, their crushingly high tax burden not withstanding. For example, in the wake of arson in the Carmel forests, citizens made substantial donations to telethon campaigns designed to cover the replanting expenses (Shechter 1998). Entrance fees to nature reserves and parks have not excessively deterred visitation rates. As the availability of desalinated water increases, Israelis will, for the first time, be able to manifest their "willingness to pay for water" with a potentially unlimited supply. But there will be a price. Here, societal support for alternative users of water (nature, agriculture) can be expected.

Ironically, higher rainfall may have an important role in influencing this particular factor. That is to say, when there is drought, the predictable efforts to galvanize the public to reduce water consumption have varying degrees of success, depending on the integrity of the appeal and the message. During wet periods, however, while basic infrastructure improvements continue (for example, dissemination of two-tank toilets, etc.) there is less of an actual appeal for restraint and conservation and the issue of demand management remains tucked far away from public consciousness. In other words, a crisis management response dominates the public's behaviour. The challenge is to convert this response to a sustainable one that pre-empts crisis rather than responding to it.

In sum, the water culture in Israel is driven by the hegemony of agriculture that is rooted in Zionist ideology. Demand management and conservation tend to be retroactive and are short-term responses to crises and not proactive and long term. Supply-side management dominates with special attention being focused on technological panaceas to the water crisis, such as the building of desalination plants on the Mediterranean coast and the proposed Red-Dead Conveyance project.

REFERENCES

Abu-Zeid, M. A. 1998. Water and sustainable development: The vision for world water, life and the environment. *Water Policy* 1:9- 19.

Assaf, K. K., M. Ben-Zvi, J. S. Clarke, H. El-Naser, S. Kesselman, M. N. Landers, M. F. Nuseibeh, and C. J. Wipperfurth. 1998. *Overview of Middle East water resources: Water resources of Palestinian, Jordanian and Israeli interest.* U.S. Geological Service, EXACT Middle East Water Data Banks Project.

Burmil, S., T. C. Daniel, and J. D. Hetherington. 1999. Human values and perceptions of water in arid landscapes. *Landscape and Urban Planning* 44:99–109.

Feitelson, E. 2000. The ebb and flow of Arab-Israeli water conflicts: Are past conflicts likely to resurface. *Water Policy* 2:343–363.

Fleischer, A., and Y. Tsur. 2000. Measuring the recreational value of agricultural landscape. *European Review of Agricultural Economics* 27(3): 385–398.

Hillel, D. 1994. *Rivers of Eden: The struggle for water and the quest for peace in the Middle East.* New York: Oxford University Press.

Hoekstra, A. Y. 1988. Appreciation of water: Four perspectives. *Water Policy* 1:605–622.

Hutson, S. S., L. N. Barber, F. J. Kenny, S. K. Linsey, S. D. Lumia, and A. M Maupin. 2004. *Estimated use of water in the United States in 2000.* U.S. Geological Survey.

Isaac, J., N. Hrimat, K. Rishmawi, S. Saad, M. Abu Kubea, J. Hilal, J. Owawi, G. Sababa, M. Awad, F. Ishaq, and I. Zboun. 2000. *An atlas of Palestine: The West Bank and Gaza.* Bethlehem, Palestine: Applied Research Institute Jerusalem.

Kislev, Y. 2002. *Urban water in Israel.* Discussion paper no. 6.02. Jerusalem, Israel: Hebrew University of Jerusalem.

Lipchin, C. 2000. Water use in the southern Arava Valley of Israel and Jordan: A study of local perceptions. *Journal of the International Institute* 11:112–114.

Pandey, J. 1990. The environment, culture and behavior. *Applied Cross-Cultural Psychology* 14:254–277.

Shechter, M., B. Reiser, and N. Zaitsev. 1998. Measuring passive use value: Pledges, donations and CV responses in connection with an important natural resource. *Environmental and Resource Economics* 12(4): 457–478.

The cultural contexts of Israelis and Palestinians in the realm of water have noted similarities and differences. But they inform and will influence the future discourse about water resource management.

The role of agriculture in each society is markedly different, but the implications for water policy may not be. In Israel, the commitment to the farming sector constitutes a hold over from Zionist ideology that gives the agricultural sector a preferrential status. Despite any economic and social indicators that say otherwise, farming as an honorable profession still resonates strongly with the Israeli public. While agriculture's "stock" has dropped in recent years, there remains a pride in Israel's agrarian heritage and a willingness to pay for maintaining a verdant countryside.

Palestinians also enjoy a rich agricultural heritage, albeit the role of irrigation and high-tech, export-driven farming has never been as salient. There also is less historic tension between different water-using segments as to the legitimacy of the dominant agricultural allocation there. (There are signs, though, that as urban population needs grow, there may be less tolerance for profligate utilization of water by Palestinian farmers.)

During the Intifidah periods, when the Palestinian economy imploded, agriculture provided many households with subsistence support. This left many Palestinians with the sense that, at the very least, providing water for agriculture can be critical in tough times for economic and human survival. It can therefore be assumed that any peace agreement will have to maintain reasonable allocations to agriculture. Calls for abandoning cultivation and opting for the "virtual water" that imported produce can provide will probably not be politically palatable in Israel or Palestine. Yet, the continued transition from freshwater to wastewater as a source of irrigation water for farmers will surely find greater support with time.

There is a growing concern among both the Israeli and Palestinian public about the quality of drinking water. This is reflected in the expanded utilization of bottled water. Israel's economic circumstances allow for greater consumption by a larger segment of the population (according to some surveys, over 70%). But sales in the West Bank and Gaza suggest that water is increasingly becoming a consumer product for Palestinian households as well. At present, the issue of water quality from bottled water is not well regulated in the Palestinian sector (see part 5). Given the strong links between the two society's retail economies, this might be an important area of cooperation in the future.

There are also fundamental differences between the two societies' views about water resources. For Palestinians, the ongoing conflict, the occupation, and the inequity in supply are important factors that shape their thinking on the subject. Even were there to be plentiful water (and the promise of desalination may make this possible), Palestinians will most likely still deem it critical to receive Israeli recognition of Palestinian water rights. Israelis are reminded periodically by politicians about the role of water in the Arab-Israeli conflict, but most do not perceive it as a critical issue in the negotiations and the resolution of the geopolitical enmity.

Another factor where major cultural divisions exist is in the area of technology and the economy. Israel has enjoyed enormous agricultural benefits from computerized drip-irrigation systems. Recently, its desalination plants have been called the most efficient in the world. Israelis see a sophisticated and efficient water supply network such that any discussion of water scarcity and the idea of "running out of water" is a theoretical abstraction to most people. In short, Israel is about as technologically optimistic about water supply as any Western nation on the planet, and for good reason. Water supply and, for the most part, water quality have improved due to the country's faith in technology. With water technology now identified as a strategic priority for national economic development, this position will only gain strength.

In contrast, Palestine water shortages are an everyday part of life that is exacerbated by the occupation. There is a sense that many of Israel's high-tech solutions for wastewater treatment and water desalination may be inappropriate at present for Palestinian society as it lacks the economic resources and, in some cases, the human capacity to maintain such a high-input infrastructure. Israel's assumption that desalination can solve any water quantity discrepancy will have to address this perception. In addition, some Palestinians express the view that water production facilities are temporary, with limited life spans. Tapping ground and surface water resources is perceived as far more sustainable and desirable as a source of supply.

The two parties' water quantity and quality realities are very far apart. Israel possesses a sophisticated infrastructure for supplying water to all economic sectors consistently with few interruptions in supply or degradation in quality. By contrast, in Palestine there is minimal infrastructure, there are frequent disruptions in water supply, and often the water quality provided is poor, contributing to public health insults. The reasons behind this asymmetry are well known and well documented and so, too, is the political nature of the water dispute between Israel and Palestine. Beyond the complexities of the local hydrology, the dispute also involves water rights, nationalism, aspirations for statehood, and religious tradition. In short, just as the hydrological picture in the two societies is very different, so are water's modern cultural ramifications.

PART 4

WATER LEGISLATION

The legal framework for Palestinian and Israeli cooperation on water issues must address issues of both quantitative allocation of shared water resources and protection of water quality. Protection of water quality is related to protection of water quantity in several ways.

These two essays first set out the existing Palestinian and Israeli legal regimes for water quantity allocation and for protecting water quality. They then consider what legal adjustments would be needed to allow the two regimes to work together.

The Palestinian Legal Regime
for Water Quality Protection

HIBA I. HUSSEINI

The legal heritage in Palestine dates far back to various historical eras including the Ottoman rule, British Mandate, Jordanian/Egyptian rule, and the Israeli military orders issued during the Israeli rule. Then there are Palestinian laws and regulations. In respect of water, the various legal traditions have had significant impact on shaping water issues. The Sharia deems water a source belonging to all, i.e., public property held in common. The Ottomans, between the sixteenth century and beginning of the twentieth (1917), maintained Sharia principles but established rules for use. During the British Mandate (1917–1948), the same rules remained in operation, but for the first time, concepts involving management were introduced. During the Jordanian rule (1948–1967 in the West Bank) and Egyptian rule (1948–1967 in Gaza), the laws of Jordan reinforced the principle of management of water resources. In Gaza, the British Mandate principles continued unchanged. Effectively, management principles emerged early and became operative in British Mandate Palestine. The Israeli Military Orders (1967–1994) considerably altered the principles of water use and management of water resources.

After the 1967 war Israel declared all water resources in the region as state property (Military Order 2 of 1967). Military Order (MO) 92, on August 15, 1967, transferred the authority over Palestinian territories' water resources to the area military commander; and MO 158, on November 19, 1967, forbade the unlicensed construction of new water infrastructures. With increased settlement construction in the Palestinian territories, Israel imposed stringent restrictions on the Palestinians concerning the development of the water resources. These regulations were intended to meet the growing consumption, which often exceeded supply.

Pursuant to the interim agreement signed between the Palestinians and Israelis on September 28, 1995, Article 40 (1), the Palestinian and Israeli sides agreed on transitional measures regarding water issues while they agreed to cooperate on developing programs that address water management, water rights, and equitable utilization of joint water resources. Under this article, Palestinians will purchase water from Israel. A Joint Water Committee (JWC) was established to coordinate the management of water and sewage resources and systems. The Palestinian Authority commenced its activities through Presidential Decree No. 90 of 1995. This decree called for the establishment of the Palestinian Water Authority (PWA) with a head and deputy head. Law No. 2 of 1996, the Establishment of the

Palestinian Water Authority, set the parameters for the PWA and established the National Water Council.

In 2002, the Palestinian Authority adopted the Water Law. This law was adopted by the legislative council following extensive deliberations. The draft law had been initiated in the late 1990s by the Palestinian Water Authority in order to develop a modern and harmonized legal framework for water legislation applicable in the Palestinian Authority.[1] In effect, since 2002, one water law applies in both areas and regulates water-related issues.

Present water administration and regulations in the Palestinian territories, which are stipulated in the Water Law, are derived from Islamic water law principles together with concepts and interpretations which have been imposed on pre-existing regulations, local uses, and customs. The Water Law encompasses the whole water sector. It aims to develop and manage the water resources, to increase capacity, to improve quality, to preserve, and to protect against pollution and depletion. The law provides an expanded legal basis for the Water Authority and grants it a legal personality.

The philosophy of this new Palestinian legislation is that the water resources of Palestine are common public property; they are controlled and managed by the government for the benefit of the people and for the development of Palestine (proposed Article 2). The same article entrusts the government with the protection of water resources from depletion and pollution. The main highlights of the law concern private ownership, beneficial uses, and licensing.

The private ownership concept of water resources is altogether eliminated (proposed Article 3); there is only a private right of use. The right to water allocation is linked to a specific use. There is no right to sell or transfer the right even for another private use. Accordingly, and even prior to final enactment, a special transitional/gradual program is under way in Palestine. It is aimed at fundamentally changing the legal concepts that have prevailed for centuries, i.e., land ownership included the right to use the water flowing through the land, beneath it, or drawn from wells situated on the land.[2] Under the new legislation, a regime of licensing production and use will replace ownership. The licensing extends to use for a landowner's own private consumption. The proposed law allows private water production, pumping, and supply. There is, equally, no public ownership of water; there is only management.

Within the legislation, water is allocated to specific beneficial uses including domestic, agricultural, industrial, commercial, and tourism uses. These uses must be licensed pursuant to the law (proposed Article 5[2]). Licensing for special activities is regulated by proposed Article 4. These licenses include terms for use, production, recharge, drilling, excavation, extraction, operation, collection, wastewater treatment, and desalination.

The Institutional Framework for Water Management in the Palestinian Authority (1995–Present)

When the Palestinian Authority took over the water sector, administration and regulations in the area were severely underdeveloped. However, this water sector was immediately recognized as an important strategic sector. The Palestinian Authority found that the roles and responsibilities in the water sector were scattered, fragmented, and unclear during the occupation period, which lent itself to inefficient management and uncoordinated investments. In 1995 the Palestinian Water Authority was established by Presidential Decree No. 5. It found that there was an urgent need to restructure the water sector in order to regulate, monitor, and control the managerial, technical, and financial performance at the national, regional, and local levels.

Having capable institutions is central to creating a comprehensive water management system. The acuteness of the water crisis in the Palestinian territories requires setting long-term strategies and allocation policies. Like the legal framework, the institutional framework is characterized by numerous agencies that often perform competing duties.

The Palestinian Water Authority (PWA) and the Ministries of Energy and Natural Resources, Agriculture, and Health set the environmental standards related to the quality of water for various uses and minimum public health standards. Responsibilities are divided statutorily to the PWA, the Cabinet of Ministers, and the National Water Council. The PWA is an independent entity that aims to efficiently administer the management of water resources and develop them to implement the water policies adopted by the National Water Council, to undertake water projects and supervise their implementation, and to achieve full coordination among the municipal agencies and other distribution bodies. The council sets the policies and strategies for the management of water resources; the PWA is the administrator and manager. The National Water Council (NWC) is responsible for overarching water policy and strategic matters. The council consists of the president of the NWC as chairman and members from the ministries, municipal, and private sector as representatives involved in water issues, with the PWA as secretariat. The main objectives of the NWC are to approve the national water policy and to support the work of the Palestinian Water Authority.

Article 7 of the Water Law grants full responsibility for managing the water resources and wastewater in the Palestinian territories to the PWA. In the area of water quality protection, the PWA is tasked with the following:

- Create reserve areas for protection from the danger of pollution, exercise oversight and supervision over such areas, and approve transfer of water between the different geographic areas.
- Study water and wastewater projects and projects that integrate them; set design standards, quality assurance, and technical specifications; and work to control their implementation.
- Regulate and supervise research and studies relating to water and wastewater and follow up with the concerned and specialized parties.
- Participate in setting approved standards for the water quality for the different usages in cooperation with the relevant parties and ensuring promulgation.

The Cabinet of Ministers, based upon the recommendation of the council, may issue any regulations that it finds suitable to implement the provisions of this law.

The Cabinet includes several ministries and directorates, which are briefly described here.

The Ministry of Health is responsible for public health aspects, water quality standards, and the alleviation of water-related health risks. In the Gaza Strip this ministry conducts all the water quality testing. The Ministry of Local Government is responsible for local (urban) planning, organization of the operation of the systems via the municipalities, and participation in hearings regarding licensing. The Ministry of Planning and International Cooperation (MOPIC) holds a mandate for the coordination of international cooperation and national planning issues. Its Directorate for Urban and Rural Planning (DURP) is responsible for overseeing the general policies, plans, and programs for spatial planning at the national and regional level.[3]

The Environmental Quality Authority is responsible for environmental policies, strategies, and criteria to ensure ecologically and environmentally sound development of the surface water and groundwater resources. The Palestinian Legislative Council (PLC) has a mandate to recommend the enactment of different regulations and bylaws. The Ministry of Justice (MoJ) has a mandate with regards to justice and legal enforcement.

Legal Rules on Water Quality

The Water Law of Palestine, like that of Israel, sets out general standards for protecting water quality. The various agencies and ministries are tasked with setting more specific standards. The PWA is the primary agency for implementing water quality standards. Currently, the PWA acts upon the principles of the Water Law; it has developed a master water plan; it coordinates with various Palestine Authority agencies and ministries on the various uses of water and the applicable rules, especially with the Ministry of Agriculture and the Environmental Protection Authority; it has embarked on preparing the water regulations which include licensing for use, abstraction, and well drilling, among others.

There are still, however, a number of impediments that keep the PWA from going beyond the preliminary stages of developing specific regulations. Among the greatest of these obstacles is the magnitude of coordination with the Israeli side that is still required. Other factors include the nature of acquired rights, inherited over decades and passed on from one generation to the next. Altering and restricting use has been a daunting task for the PWA. Another factor is enforcement. The PWA lacks the tools and means to enforce the laws and its regulations against violators, and this permits breaches to go unsanctioned. Other impediments included limited financial and human resources that are available to the PWA to enforce the law. The PWA lacks the technical means to monitor use and hold anyone accountable. The water infrastructure is underdeveloped in the Palestine Authority, which precludes effective and efficient monitoring.

Even with these impediments, the PWA is responsible for ensuring the protection of water resources and prevention of pollution. The PWA is empowered by the Water Law to regulate the use of agricultural and industrial materials that may cause pollution to the water resources or their supply systems. The PWA coordinates with the Ministries of Agriculture, Health, Local Government, and National Economy and the Environmental Protection Authority to regulate and prevent pollution and issue standards for quality of drinking water and wastewater standards.[4] The PWA uses this authority to test and verify and enforce the standards. The PWA relies on monitoring and posts notices in events of violation. It works closely with local government units (municipal and village councils) to enforce the standards and educate.

The PWA must prepare special guidelines for the environmental impact assessment for any activity relating to water resources or their supply systems. The PWA in cooperation with twelve ministries and agencies—like the EQA, Health, Agriculture, and Local Government—adopted in 2000 the National Environmental Impact Assessment (NEIA) Policy. The policy addresses national and local environmental impact issues regarding all types of activities and projects. A national committee comprised of the relevant ministries and agencies sanctions these assessments.

The Water Authority also participates in preparing special mechanisms for crisis management when there is drought, flooding, or a plague that is spread via water, or in response to major pollution events. The PWA participates and plays an active role with the EQA and the Ministries of Health and Local Government in preparing the mechanisms for crises. They work at the national level and the local government level, laboring in remote areas to provide water in the event of drought or take active measures in case of flood, or there might be bacteriological contamination found in areas where raw wastewater is used for irrigation.

The PWA is particularly concerned with pollutants. The PWA has prepared a list of water-related pollutants whose discharge requires licensing and compensation for damages resulting therefrom.[5] The notion of licensing pollution exists in the Environmental Law, but the notion of "polluter pays" is not yet prevalent. The Water Authority may halt the production or supply of water if it appears that its source or supply system is polluted, and it may close the source or system if pollution continues.[6] The PWA is also responsible for supervising well drilling and qualifying contractors in the field of constructing water facilities in accordance with procedures that are set by the law.[7]

Other Statutes and Regulations

Beyond the 2002 Water Law, several scattered statutes affect the way in which the PWA must regulate water and are worthy of brief mention. Public Health Law No. 20 of 2004 authorizes the Ministry of Health to supervise public sewage networks and wastewater treatment facilities. Chapters 3 and 4 of Environmental Law No. 7 of 1999 empower the EQA to safeguard water and marine environmental quality. The rules prohibit the disposal of materials and substances in sewage systems or seawater.

City Planning Law No. 28 of 1936 (applicable in the Gaza Strip) requires a building permit and the approval by municipal/local government units of the construction of buildings, roads, and public and private sewage systems. Any construction or sewage system, etc., must be in compliance with the national and local plans which proscribe causing any harm to the environment.[8] The PWA, EQA, and local governments all must give prior approval to such projects.

Building and Planning Law No. 79 of 1966 (applicable in the West Bank) is far more sophisticated than its counterpart law applicable in the Gaza Strip due to the timing of its enactment. Therefore, it has express and clear language prohibiting water pollution and safeguards for sewage controls. All construction at all levels (national, regional, and local), including the construction of water and sewage connections, cesspools, and septic tanks, requires a license.

Municipal Sewerage Law No. 1 of 1936 requires the construction of sewerage networks with all buildings and homes connected to the networks. The law further requires and authorizes local governments to set up and operate sewage collection and treatment systems. It further calls for the prevention of pollution of water resources.

Local governments also have authority under various national laws to enact local bylaws on issues of water quality. Many local governments have enacted such bylaws, particularly in the area of pretreatment requirements for industry. In addition to the laws mentioned above, several other statutes address water quality issues. One such example is the Drainage and Flood Control Ordinance of 1941. Other sources of legal authority include regulations that have been issued pursuant to the various laws listed here or the standards adopted.

National, Regional, Local, and Detailed Plans

The aforementioned National Water Plan of 2000 constitutes a strategic blueprint for the water sector. It sets the general direction and objectives until the year 2025 and proposes actions to be taken to achieve these goals. The document describes the role of service providers. It holds that regional water utilities will be responsible for the following services: preliminary investigations and design, construction and/or rehabilitation, research, repairs, operations, and maintenance. Moreover, it states that services would cover the fields of municipal and industrial water supply; wastewater collection treatment and reuse; storm-water collection, treatment, and reuse; and water and treated wastewater supplies for irrigation. Until all the regional water utilities are established, the PWA is to maintain responsibilities in these areas. To date, only the Coastal Water Utility is established and in operation.

The PWA has overall responsibility for wastewater treatment, licenses treatment facilities, and undertakes supervision and regulation. The PWA has prioritized the establishment of infrastructure for the treatment of wastewater, but not all wastewater is treated at present. The PWA has a number of plans, ranging from annual plans to 3- or 5-year ones that emanate from the National Water Plan and address issues like wastewater treatment, among other topics, as mentioned above. There are no penalties for lack of treatment at present because not all areas are serviced and have wastewater treatment facilities.

Methods of Implementation

Business Licenses and Building Permits

The PWA is responsible for licensing the exploitation of water resources, including the construction of public and private wells and their regulation, water exploration and drilling, testing and production of wells, and any other matters or activities relating to water or wastewater, in cooperation and coordination with the relevant parties.[9] As mentioned above, the PWA licenses wastewater treatment facilities, but it is the Ministry of Health and the EQA that are responsible for industries that discharge polluted effluents. All industrial facilities receive a license to operate from the Ministry of Health. The national committee overseeing the EIA policy requires the relevant ministries and agencies to issue the required licenses and ensure that the emission of effluents is monitored and inspected. Further, the EQA inspects licensed facilities and has adopted schemes and issued instructions for related standards.

Penalties for Noncompliance

Article 32 requires anyone who causes pollution in any water resource or its supply system to remove the pollution to that source or system at his/her own expense. In the event that he/she refuses or fails to do so, the Water Authority must remove the pollution and carry out the cleaning operations. This is done at the expense of party causing the pollution after notifying him/her of this, regardless of the costs, which shall be levied upon him/her in accordance with the Law for Collecting Public Monies.

The Water Law imposes criminal penalties on violations of specific provisions, including fines and imprisonment. These include polluting any water resource or supply system, or causing such action and failing to redress it within the period set by the Water Authority; drilling groundwater wells without a license or contradicting the terms of the license; violating any water resource or sewage system, causing it damage or leading to its destruction; or supplying water to oneself or to others without a license to do so.

The penalties for the above violations range from 1 month to 1 year in prison and fines of up to five thousand dinars.[10] The penalties are doubled for repeat offenses.[11] Article 37 of the Water Law provides the judiciary with discretion for adding additional penalties, including payment of the cost of the repair and cleanup. Issues related to water pollution enforcement have not yet reached the court system; as such there is no precedent or direction from the courts on water pollution.

Enforcement by the State

The Water Authority has the right to inspect water resources and systems of supply and any place where pollution is suspected. The associated legal authorities have the right of entry into any private or public property or building to accomplish this purpose in accordance with proper procedures.[12] The Water Law and Environmental Law both set out criminal provisions for violators, who many be subject to both fines and imprisonment. Specially, the Water Law lists six incidents of violations, including causing pollution to water resources, where penalties and/or imprisonment may be imposed. The law requires the violator to pay and remove the pollution. The Environmental Law stipulates similar provisions. Enforcement is limited.

Enforcement by Local Governments

The PWA and water utilities are charged with ensuring continued service to their local populations. The lack of specific regulations and a weak infrastructure, however, make enforcement at the local level very difficult. The minister of local government and a representative for the regional utilities are included in the National Water Council and provide a voice for local concerns.

Enforcement by Private Parties and by NGOs

Multiple environmental organizations have come into being and act as watchdogs and a voice for the public. The National Water Council also provides a seat for representatives of the Water Unions and public societies as well as Palestinian universities. Organizations working in the water and environmental sector are numerous, conducting considerable research and contributing to public awareness. Typically, they collaborate with the PWA and other related government bodies in preparing the standards, working during periods of crises, providing support and awareness to schools and the public, and participating in administrative forums. However, NGOs and civil society play no role in taking public or private polluters to court.

Protection of Groundwater and the Seas

The Water Law expressly sets out provisions for declaring an area containing groundwater a protected area if the quality or quantity of water is in danger of pollution, or if carrying out the water policy requires such action, on condition that it provides alternate water resources. In this respect, the Palestinian Water Law is in line with present Israeli law. Although many scientists agree that water reuse policies are helpful in protecting water quality, the Palestinian Authority has not yet developed water reuse policies.

The Water Law and Environmental Law are expressly clear that water and marine environments shall be safeguarded from discharges into the sea, whether directly or indirectly.[13]

General Comments

Palestine has developed the national, regional, and local plans for controlling water pollution. It has adopted a system for licensing use of water sources and placed stringent restrictions on water pollution. Three national government ministries/agencies are involved: the PWA, the EQA, and the Ministry of Health. At the local government level, the Ministry of Local Government has oversight through municipalities, village councils, and other local government units. Through the National Water Plan and its subsidiary plans, as well as the National Environmental Impact Assessment Policy, governmental bodies monitor and supervise water quality and seek to enforce against pollution of water and water resources. Enforcement of the legal requirements is emerging but requires considerable strengthening. Enforcement through the courts is not practiced yet. A number of local and international environmental NGOs work in water and environmental fields, especially in the area of public awareness. For the most part, they do not serve as watchdogs against polluters, nor do they have the authority to take violators to court.

NOTES

1. The West Bank and Gaza laws reflect two sets of laws and different legal systems. Thus, the Palestinian Authority in 2004 set out to harmonize laws prevailing in these areas to achieve unity and at the same time update legislation.

2. The Israeli Military Orders laid the groundwork for the elimination of private ownership.

3. The MOPIC is now separated into two different ministries, the Ministry of Planning and the Ministry of Foreign Affairs.

4. Industrial licenses are issued by the Department of Industry at the Ministry of National Economy; Palestine Institute of Standards rules, PSI 41 and PSI 742.

5. Water Law of 2002, Art. 29.

6. Water Law of 2002, Art. 30.

7. Water Law of 2002, Art. 7, Sec. 9.

8. The reference to environment issues in the law is in passing. It is a date law, where such issues were not examined when the law was adopted. See, by contrast, the equivalent law in the West Bank, which is more detailed and refers to prohibitions against pollution. In practice today, the National Environmental Impact Policy bridges the gaps in the law, and the same is true of the Environmental Law, which applies in both the West Bank and the Gaza Strip.

9. Water Law of 2002, Art. 7, Sec. 5.

10. Water Law of 2002, Art. 35.

11. Water Law of 2002, Art. 37.

12. Water Law of 2002, Art. 34.

13. At present, the Dead Sea is not accessible to Palestinians.

REFERENCES

Diabes, F. 2003. Water related politics and their legal aspects: A progressive approach for solving the water conflict. In *Water in Palestine, Problems—Politics—Prospects*, ed. F. Diabes, 5–56. Jerusalem: PASSIA Publications.

Daibes-Murad, F. 2005. *A new legal framework for managing the world's shared groundwaters: A case study from the Middle East*. London: International Water Association.

Husseini, H. 2007. Palestinian Water Authority: Developments and challenges—legal framework and capacity, water resources in the Middle East. In *Israel-Palestinian water issues—from conflict to cooperation*, ed. H. Shuval and H. Dweik, 301–309. Berlin: Springer.

Nassereddin, T. 1998. Legal and administrative responsibility of domestic water supply to the Palestinians. In *Joint management of shared aquifers*, ed E. Feitelson and M. Haddad, 117–126. Jerusalem: Truman Institute/Palestine Consultancy Group.

Stephan, R. M. 2007. Legal framework of groundwater management in the Middle East (Israel, Jordan, Lebanon, Syria and the Palestinian Territories). In *Israel-Palestinian water issues—from conflict to cooperation*, ed. H. Shuval and H. Dweik, 293–299. Berlin: Springer.

Van Edig, A. 1999. *Aspects of Palestinian water rights*. Ramallah: Ramallah Center for Human Rights Studies.

Legal Framework for Allocation of Water and for Protection of Water Quality in Israel

MARCIA GELPE

Water Ownership and Quantity Allocation

The ownership of water is based on a system of public, rather than private, ownership. All water sources in Israel are designated by statute to be public property, subject to control of the state. The state is to exercise its control in a way that serves the needs of the residents of the state and development of the country. No individual has rights in water except as provided in the Water Law of 1959; ownership of riparian or other real property carries with it no water rights.

Laws

Water allocation policies are partly controlled by the Water Law. In addition, both the government and the Water Council have a role in setting water policy, subject to the provisions in the statute. The Water Law of 1959 is the main statute on allocation of water quantity. Several other laws supplement the authorities provided in the Water Law. These include the Water and Sewage Corporations Law, 2001; the Supervision of Water Drilling Law, 1955; and the Water Measurement Law, 1955.

Institutions, Policy, and Planning

Government Water and Sewage Authority (Water Authority) administers the statutorily established system of rights to use freshwater. It is headed by the director, who is appointed by the government upon the recommendation of the minister of national infrastructures. The eight-member Water Council operates within the Water Authority. It supervises Water Authority policies and their implantation in such areas as water pricing, extraction, and licensing. Five members of the council represent governmental ministries, and two, appointed by the government, represent the public. The director of the Water Authority is the chairperson. An administrative court has authority over issues arising under the Water Law. Water allocations policies are partly controlled by the Water Law. In addition, both the government and the Water Council have a role is setting water policy, subject to the provisions in the statute.

Legal Requirements, Implementation, and Enforcement

The Water Law of 1959 sets out a complex scheme for allocating rights to use water. Anyone seeking to use water must obtain the "right to use" under that scheme. The allocations are implemented through a system of permits. Those who use water without complying with the law are subject to administrative and criminal enforcement.

Water Quality Protection

While the legal regime for water quantity allocation is found mainly in one statute, the legal scheme for water quality protection is scattered among several different statutes. There are probably a number of reasons for this less-than-unified approach to water quality. Because of the arid nature of the region, the need to deal with water quantity allocation quickly became clear with the growth of population after the establishment of the state in 1948. Israel could support its growing population, agriculture, and industries only with careful use of its limited water supplies. The need to deal with water quality issues was recognized more slowly and brought about by two factors: the growing awareness of the importance of water quality protection throughout the developed world and the increasing pressure the growing population put on the quality of Israel's water resources.

Main Regulatory Laws

A large number of laws deal with water quality. They invoke different approaches to sometimes similar problems and scatter authority among a variety of administrative agencies. The main law dealing with regulation is the Water Law of 1959. In 1972, provisions on preventing pollution were added to this law. These were later amended several times to reflect increasingly stringent policies.

The Public Health Ordinance authorizes protection of water quality where water quality deterioration has an adverse impact on public health. Most water pollution has an adverse impact on public health, so the reach of this statute is broad.

The Business Licensing Law of 1968 requires a business that is likely to have an adverse effect on water quality to have a business license. Water quality protection provisions are included in the license. The Building and Planning Law of 1965 requires that any building must have a building permit before construction and must be constructed in compliance with National, Regional, Local, and Detailed plans. New projects such as roads must also comply with these plans. The law requires consideration of environmental matters in approving plans, sometimes through preparation of an environmental impact statement and sometimes through other less formal means. As a result, new buildings and projects should receive approval only after their effect on water quality has been considered.

The Law on Prevention of Sea Pollution from Land-Based Sources was passed in 1988. This statute addresses discharges directly into the Mediterranean, the Dead Sea, or the Red Sea (via the arm called the Gulf of Eilat by Israel and called the Gulf of Aqaba by other states in the region) and also discharges to freshwater streams that flow into these bodies of water. The law sets up a system of specific permits separate from those issued under the Business Licensing Law.

In addition, local governments have authority under various national laws to enact local bylaws on issues of water quality. Many local governments have enacted such bylaws, particularly in the area of pretreatment requirements for industry. For example, the Local Authorities (Sewerage) Law of 1962 authorizes local governments to set up and operate sewage collection and treatment systems.

In addition to the statutes listed above, several other laws address water quality issues in more specific contexts. These included the Lake Kinneret Ordinance of 1947 and the Drainage and Flood Control Law of 1957. Other key sources of legal authority are the many regulations that have been promulgated under the statutes listed here.

Institutions

The allocation of authority among different agencies is based partly on rational allocations of authority and partly on the basis of political struggles for control over bureaucratic power. In some cases, the authority to deal with certain types of environmental problems resides in agencies that do not see their primary mission as environmental protection. Treatment of many environmental problems is complicated by the need for concerted action by many different agencies.

The minister of environmental protection has regulatory authority over water quality protection under the Water Law, the Business Licensing Law, and the Public Health Ordinance, subject to those areas that are carved out as being under the authority of the minister of health or the Water Authority. The Government Water and Sewage Authority (Water Authority) has primary responsibility for administrative enforcement of the Water Law's water quality provisions. The authority to issue regulations on water quality remains primarily in the hands of the minister of environmental protection, although coordination with the Water Authority is required.

The minister of health has authority over the quality of drinking water, including control of water resources designated for use as drinking water. Because so much of the water is used for drinking, this is an extensive authority. In addition, the minister oversees the quality of sewage discharges, both before and after their treatment in wastewater treatment facilities. Wastewater reuse standards for agriculture are also set by the Ministry of Health. Israel reuses 77% of its treated sewage, so the authority over those waters is also important.

Local governments derive their power from the state and are subject to state control. This control is exercised largely through the minister of interior, who oversees a large portion of local government budgets and approves local bylaws and local government actions under a variety of laws, including those governing water pollution control. As a result, the minister of interior is involved in many important local government actions involving water pollution prevention and control, such as construction and operation of water treatment facilities. In addition, the minister of interior has extensive responsibilities under the Building and Planning Law.

The Committee for Granting Permits operates under the Law for Prevention of Sea Pollution from Land-Based Sources. The committee comprises representatives of seven ministries and one representative of the recognized Israeli environmental nongovernmental organizations (NGOs). The minister of environmental protection is the chairperson of the committee. Authority for plan development and approval is in the hands of the Local and Regional Planning Commissions, the National Planning Council, and their subsidiary bodies.

Municipal and regional councils are both forms of local government in Israel. Local governments hold four types of authorities that are crucial to protection of water quality. They administer the business licensing scheme under the Business Licensing Law; they comprise the local planning commissions under the Building and Planning Law; they operate many of the country's sewage treatment systems; and they enact and enforce their own bylaws on water pollution control.

Policy and Planning

The National Planning Council has enacted thirty national plans, some of which still require further additions or revisions. Several plans have direct impacts on water quality; these include the National Plan for Impoundment, Infiltration, and Utilization of Surface Water, the National Plan for Waste Disposal, and the National Plan for the Water System (Waste). Other national plans, such as the National Integrated Plan for Building, Development, and Conservation, have more indirect, but still important, impacts. Regional plans must be consistent with all national plans, providing a greater level of detail for zoning in the country's six planning regions. Local plans must be consistent with all the applicable regional plans and add yet a greater degree of specificity. Detailed plans, for specific projects, must be consistent with the applicable local and regional plans and have the highest degree of detail. Regional, local, and detailed plans have significant influence over planned projects on water quality.

Under the planning rules, if a plan is likely to have a substantial adverse effect on water quality, an environmental impact statement must be prepared along with a proposed plan or amendment to a plan. The statement must be considered in deciding whether to accept, modify, or reject the provisions in the proposal. The regulatory requirements are quite detailed, with provision for less formal methods for considering environmental impacts when impacts are less significant. Courts have been fairly strict in requiring planning institutions to observe these environmental consideration provisions. In addition, significant elements of water pollution control policy are set out by the Ministry of Environment and the Ministry of Health.

Legal Requirements

The Water Law, on its face, prohibits any change in the quality of any surface or underground water, whether that water is natural or is an artificially created body of water and whether it is clean or already polluted. Of course, in practice this broad and absolute prohibition is subject to many exceptions. In general, only water pollution that violates a rule, license, permit, or order, or is otherwise unreasonable, is prohibited.

Public Health regulations set water quality standards for drinking water and proscribe the use for drinking water of water sources not meeting those standards. The regulations do not require cleanup of substandard bodies of water, but only prevent their use as drinking water.

The discharges of various industries and of sewage treatment facilities must meet regulations that limit concentrations of biological oxygen demand and of suspended solids. For large facilities, the regulations set out the discharge limitations. For smaller facilities, the director general of the Ministry of Health sets out the limitations on a case-by-case basis. As is described in part 8, sewage treatment standards are being upgraded to require tertiary treatment of wastewater. In addition, a variety of regulations provide more specific requirements for particularly troubling types of industries and practices. These include requirements to engage in certain practices designed to prevent pollution or to avoid certain polluting practices as well as requirements to use certain types of pollution control equipment. The number of such rules is too great to enumerate in the present context. A listing of just some of them provides of sense of the breadth of their coverage. Rules of this type apply to use of chemical spraying equipment, fertilizers, and detergents; operation of cesspools, septic tanks, and gas stations; and the electroplating industry.

Sources discharging into the Mediterranean, the Dead Sea, or the Gulf of the Red Sea must meet additional regulatory requirements. These regulations require that all such dischargers must have a special permit and that no permit shall be granted if there is an economically viable alternative of on-land disposal. Permits that are granted have detailed requirements on the amount of pollutants allowed in discharges and on the location of the discharge. In theory, these requirements apply to any discharge that would eventually reach the specified bodies of water, even through indirect means. In practice, indirect discharges are not always subjected to the requirements.

Implementation

Most sources of water pollution must obtain a building permit, a business license, or a marine discharge permit. These permits require the source to comply with all statutes and rules and may set out additional water quality requirements. Building permits are issued by local planning authorities, with input from the Ministry of Environmental Protection through environmental impact statements for projects likely to have a significant impact on water quality. Business licenses are issued by local governmental authorities, with permission from the minister of environmental protection for businesses that may have an adverse impact on water quality. Marine discharge permits are issued by the inter-ministerial Committee for Granting Permits.

Enforcement

All of Israel's environmental laws can be enforced in a variety of ways. They are subject to enforcement by the State of Israel and its national administrative agencies, by the local governments, and by private individuals. Enforcement may be through criminal sanctions imposed by courts, through administrative remedies imposed by the national or local governmental authorities, or through civil orders issued by courts.

Until recently, the state rarely took action against water polluters, while in those cases that were prosecuted, the courts imposed insubstantial fines and hesitated to incarcerate offenders of environmental laws. The number of cases prosecuted has now increased substantially, although it is still debatable whether the number of enforcement actions is adequate. Larger fines have become more common in the last few years. The largest fine for a water pollution that had been imposed against an individual source at the time of this writing was about $195,000. Most water pollution fines have been considerably lower, raising questions about the implementation of the "polluter pays" principle in practice.

If a corporation or local governmental unit violates the law, corporate officers, public officials, and facility managers are also subject to fines and imprisonment. In fact, individuals are rarely penalized for violations, although the threat of individual liability may lead the corporation or local government to agree to pay a penalty in return for dismissing claims against individuals. In a criminal action, courts may also order the polluter to clean up the pollution and to undertake other specified actions.

Administrative enforcement under the Water Law is problematic. Although the minister of environment has general authority for the water pollution control, authority to issue administrative orders is in the hands of the director of the Water Authority, who has no formal connection to the minister of environment.

The administrative authority under the Business Licensing Law is very important. It allows issuance of an administrative order to close a business that is violating its business license or operating without a business license. This can provide immediate relief from water pollution.

Israeli law is unusual in that it allows private criminal enforcement of environmental laws. Standing to bring private criminal enforcement actions under the Water Law is granted to anyone adversely affected by violation of the laws, as well as to established environmental NGOs. Few such cases have actually been brought. Management of a criminal case is complicated. Furthermore, the successful plaintiff does not necessarily get a personal remedy for any injury suffered, so the financial incentive for a private person to bring such an action is weak.

A person who has been injured or might be injured by water pollution can seek a court order to stop the pollution under a special civil statute on environmental enforcement. Under the same law, such actions can sometimes be brought as class actions. Neither provision has been used extensively for any type of environmental problem; individuals who are bothered by pollution usually want financial compensation, which is not available under this law. Civil nuisance claims and other tort claims are also available, and there are more such cases, although the problem of proving that a specific polluter caused a specified harm can be daunting.

Israeli law allows individuals to bring civil actions against governmental authorities for failure to observe any legally imposed requirements. In the water pollution control field this is important because it allows private actions against local governments that cause water pollution by their failure to operate adequate wastewater treatment facilities. Environmental NGOs have brought such actions.

Groundwater Protection

Israel has no separate legal scheme for preventing groundwater pollution, nor does it have specific statutes on soil pollution, although proposed laws on these topics are now under consideration. The general legal scheme on water pollution described above applies to pollution of groundwater as well as surface water, although proof of causation of groundwater pollution is more difficult than proof of causation of surface water pollution. In addition, several laws apply to solid waste or toxic waste disposal. These laws are designed in part to prevent seepage of waste material from a disposal site through the soil into underground water and resultant contamination of the underground water. Such laws include the Law on Preservation of Cleanliness, 1984, which prohibits unauthorized disposal of waste on public and private property, and the Business Licensing Regulations (Disposal of Waste from Hazardous Substances), which require that most hazardous wastes be disposed of in a special facility, Ramat Hovav, in the southern part of Israel. Both laws are administered by the Ministry of Environment. In addition, under the Building and Licensing Law, conditions designed to prevent groundwater pollution are imposed on new solid-waste disposal facilities. These conditions include installation of liners below the disposal cells and wastewater collection and treatment systems.

Water Reuse

Much of Israel's sewage is treated for reuse in agricultural irrigation. In a water-poor country, this reuse is essential. There are several water quality implications for this system. On the one hand, reuse of sewage brings with it the danger of increasing pollutants such as salinity, nitrates, and pathogens. If polluted water is used to irrigate plants, the pollution can enter surface water and groundwater. On the other hand, by reducing use of Israel's existing water resources, reuse helps save water for other uses. Rules enacted under the Public Health Ordinance provide that untreated effluents cannot be used for irrigation and that treated effluents can be used for irrigation only if the treatment meets the requirements set out by the director general of the Ministry of Health (see part 7).

The Dead Sea

All laws described above apply to water flowing into the Dead Sea. Most importantly, the Law on Prevention of Sea Pollution from Land-Based Sources, 1988, and rules enacted under that statute apply to all discharges into the Dead Sea, whether they reach that body of water directly or indirectly.

General Comments

Israel has an extensive and complex system for controlling water pollution. This system covers most significant sources of water pollution and involves a number of different types of licensing and permitting schemes. Authority for operating the system is spread through a substantial number of governmental agencies. Enforcement of the legal requirements, while not as strong as some would wish, is well established. In addition, a number of Israeli environmental NGOs operate as watchdogs over the system, working through the administrative agencies and through the courts to see that legal requirements are implemented and enforcement is taken against the most prominent violators. These organizations are working to establish a broad expectation that the law will be observed. The last few years have seen increasing efforts by the state and its agencies to enforce water laws and increasing willingness of the courts to impose meaningful penalties on violators.

REFERENCES

Adam, R. 2000. Government failure and public indifference: A portrait of water pollution in Israel. *Colorado Journal of International Environmental Law and Policy* 11:257.

Civil Wrongs Ordinance. 2008. Israeli Legislation based on British Mandate Ordinance. Available at Israel Ministry of Environment, Legislation (in Hebrew).

Cr. C. 714/04 *State of Israel v. Chatam Araaf*, Krayot Municipal Court, March 11, 2008.

Cr. C. 4831/01 *State of Israel v. Carmel Chemicals*, Haifa Municipal Court, June 12, 2006.

Cr. C. 9467/04 *State of Israel v. Dan Association of Cities for Sewage*, Tel Aviv Municipal Court, June 25, 2007.

The Israel Union for Environmental Defense v. Minister of Interior. 1994. 2004 H.C.J. 1131\93, Takdin Elyon 94(1) 324, January, 19.

The Law on Prevention of Environmental Nuisances (Civil Complaints). 1992.

Merom-Albeck, O., and A. Tal. 2000. Upgrading citizen suits as a tool for environmental enforcement in Israel: A comparative evaluation. *Israel Law Review* 34:373, 423.

Planning and Building Rules (Environmental Impact Statements). 2003.

Rotenberg, R. 1998. Enforcement strategies of the Israel Ministry of Environment. Paper presented at the Fourth Annual International Conference on Environmental Compliance and Enforcement, http://www.inece.org/4thvol2/rotenber.pdf (accessed November 8, 2009).

Talitman, D., A. Tal, and S. Brenner. 2003. The devil is in the details: Increasing international law's influence on domestic environmental performance—the case of Israel and the Mediterranean Sea. *New York University Environmental Law Journal* 11:414.

Editors' Summary

Water Quantity Allocation

It is assumed that water quantity allocation will be addressed in an agreement between Palestinians and Israelis and that such an agreement may require changes in the existing domestic legal rules of both parties. For the most part, both entities have legal regimes in place for water quantity allocation, and these could be used to divide up the amount of water the entity receives under any agreement. The two legal regimes differ in that there are private water-use rights under the Palestinian regime but not under the Israeli regime. These use rights can be controlled and even extinguished by the central authority. It is likely that with the shortage of water, both regimes will have to alter current allocations of rights to use water, and doing so may create either a legal or political need for compensation.

Water Quality Protection

Water quality will probably continue to be driven by domestic legislation. Because Palestinians and Israelis share many of the water resources, and the failure of either to protect water quality severely affects both parties, it will be essential to find a way to make the two systems for water quality protection compatible. This will be especially important in cases where the actions of one side affect the water quality of the other side, such as in the following cases:

- wastewater disposed of in one area can reach the other, either via the surface or through shared groundwater;
- land disposal of solid waste or building construction in one area can pollute shared groundwater sources;
- joint planning for water pollution prevention projects.

Coordination of water quality standards will be essential. Israel traditionally has taken a position which expects the Palestinians to meet Israeli requirements, even as compliance with them in Israel and in Israeli West Bank settlements is frequently deficient. Environmental expectations must be adjusted to meet available capacity. To some extent, the answer to this quagmire involves phasing in more stringent performance standards through realistic timetables. Just as East German industries were allotted several years to meet the higher West German environmental expectations after unification, Israelis and Palestinians will need to agree that Palestinians need a grace period to allow for the improvement of both the physical infrastructure and human capital. Here the role of donor nations in providing resources directed specifically to this goal will be critical.

Another possible model is that provided by U.S. and Mexican cooperation in restoring their shared water resources. Given compelling American interests in environmental improvement, the United States demanded higher levels of performance but was willing to participate in the associated investment within Mexico.

While it will be hard for Israeli environmentalists to swallow, it may also be prudent to accept somewhat less stringent standards in the interest of ensuring high compliance levels. The alternative could be creating a pattern of "lip service" and alienation from shared environmental standards for years to come. The primary legal challenge at present involves implementation and compliance monitoring. The pervasive use of raw sewage by some Palestinian farmers and the excessively polluted discharges of industrial and municipal facilities in Israel are examples of the gap that exists between theory and practice.

One difference between the Palestinian and Israeli systems for protecting water quality lies in the licensing arrangements. In theory, any business or operation in Israel that is likely to cause water pollution needs a license of some sort that will include pollution prevention provisions; therefore, the regulatory authorities have prior knowledge of any such operations and the specific conditions that apply to a business are set out specifically. Under the Palestinian system, the law sets out general prohibitions on water pollution but no licenses are required. This can make it more difficult to identify and account for all potential sources of pollution and can leave unclear the precise way the general legal requirements apply to specific sources. Both of these characteristics are problematic in the search for greater transparency between the sides. In practice, the Israeli regime does not work as well as it should, and many businesses operate without business licenses or in violation of them. It is recommended that both sides put in place and operate a comprehensive scheme for licensing sources that may pollute the water, that both vigorously enforce the licenses, and that both licensing provisions and enforcement efforts be transparent to everyone on both sides.

At present, only Israel makes substantial use of treated wastewater and has water quality standards for the treated wastewater. If wastewater treatment is undertaken by the Palestinians, it too will need treatment standards. Coordination of the standards for treated wastewater will be necessary where the treated wastewater can flow as runoff from one area to the other, or where it reaches a shared groundwater resource. In other cases, each entity can set its own wastewater treatment standards.

Enforcement

The law is only effective when it is observed, and neither compliance nor enforcement is sufficient on either side. No legal system has the funds to catch all violators. The goal of the environmental regulatory system on both sides therefore must ultimately be the creation of incentives for polluters not to violate environmental laws. This is the heart of a deterrence system.

At present, the Palestinians find that the political situation and pervasive poverty inhibit strong enforcement. It is not now clear whether a change in the political situation would be sufficient to bring about strong and consistent enforcement of the water laws. The Israelis also have a serious enforcement problem, based on a lack of a tradition of fines large and consistent enough to deter violation of the environmental laws, although recent steps are ameliorating, but not eliminating, this problem. Both sides must greatly improve their enforcement of legal requirements, whatever the obstacles. Otherwise, the existing water resources will be overused and polluted and mutual blame will continue in a way that displaces the accountability that cooperation will necessitate.

Transparency

Israel has in place a wide-reaching Freedom of Information Law, although agency responses to requests for information are not always timely and complete. The Palestinian Authority is working on a Freedom of Information Law. Such laws on both sides are essential to allow the building of trust needed to deal with the shared water resource. Both the Palestinians and the Israelis have active environmental NGOs. These groups should be encouraged to use their respective Freedom of Information Laws to monitor official action and to share their information with each other.

PART 5

GROUNDWATER MANAGEMENT

Much of the literature involving "water conflict" and the need for joint management between Palestinians and Israelis has focused on the Mountain Aquifer, which is shared by the two parties. This series of three aquifers contains the highest quality water of the natural reservoirs in the region and constitutes the only meaningful source of water for Palestinians in the West Bank. These two essays offer a review of this critical resource by two hydrologists/hydrochemists who for many years have been involved in research about water quality and the hydrological properties of the aquifer.

Shared Groundwater Resources

ENVIRONMENTAL HAZARDS AND
TECHNICAL SOLUTIONS IN PALESTINE

KAREN ASSAF

Transboundary or shared water resources imply hydrological interdependence, connecting different riparian countries within the one shared system by the use of these waters for their various needs. The borders of groundwater and surface catchments and national boundaries are obviously not congruent, and international law and practices are to be followed to define the right of all riparian states to their water needs in any international water basin.

The water sources in Palestine (e.g., the inland region of the West Bank and the coastal region of the Gaza Strip) are primarily from groundwater wells, the only surface water being from springs and the seasonal flow in wadis during the rainy season. All the water from the Jordan River that runs along Palestine's eastern border is unavailable to Palestinians as it is totally militarily controlled by the Israelis. Thus, the main source of water supply in Palestine for all uses—domestic, agricultural, and industrial—originates as groundwater.

The gap between water demand and water consumption in Palestine has widened since 1948. The population has increased, but the quantity of available freshwater has remained essentially the same. The access to water resources has been constrained and restricted due to the political situation. Throughout the Middle East, there is a gap between water supply and water demand. In Palestine, this gap is growing with time because water supply is artificially constrained by the stagnation of the Peace Process. This gap is having severe adverse effects on both current and future Palestinian socioeconomic development. This essay considers specific measures that need to be implemented to change the present trends.

Palestinian Groundwater Resources

The existing water resources of Palestine are derived from four aquifer basins (the Western, Eastern, Northeastern, and Coastal) as well as a series of springs that emanate from the groundwater. The Eastern Aquifer basin is not considered a shared aquifer.

The Western Groundwater Basin is considered as one unit called the Nahr El-Auja-Tamaseeh (Yarkoun-Taninim in Hebrew) Basin. Water is discharged into the coastal plain. A small portion of the rainwater that seeps through the exposed parts of the Cenomaniam and Turonian aquifers in the Western Aquifer Basin flows in springs draining the sloping aquifers—but most of the water reaches the shared aquifer and is tapped by wells—especially along the West Bank's 1948 Armistice Line with Israel, with the greater usage being now on the Israeli side. The natural drainage outlets of the Western Aquifer are two separate spring systems, the Nahr El-Auja (Yarkoun) Springs and the Temaseeh (Taninim) Springs near Carmel. Most of the aquifer is cut off from contact with the waters of the Mediterranean Sea by aquicludes that penetrate to a great depth.

The Northeastern Groundwater Basin is subdivided into two overlying aquifers—both discharging in the valleys of Beisan and Zerein (now called Yizra'el by the Israelis). The two aquifers are the Cenomanian/Turonian Aquifer, and the Eocene Aquifer. The natural drainage outlets of West Bank's Cenomanian/Turonian Aquifer are for the most part all in Israel, mainly the springs in the Beisan Valley (four major springs and twenty small springs). The water level in this aquifer is constantly declining, which deteriorates and depletes the West Bank underground water supply. In fact, the Jenin area's many springs have dried out completely—a city that historically was known for its lush landscape due to numerous natural springs.

The Eastern Groundwater Basin drains into the Jordan Valley and includes six almost separate groundwater basins. These aquifer basins are not considered to be shared resources. Israel currently, however, employs several wells, pumping an unknown amount from these strata.

Groundwater is also the only freshwater resource in the coastal region of Palestine, i.e., the Gaza Strip. The aquifer in the Gaza Strip is composed of a number of subaquifers made up mainly of sand, sandstone, and gravels of the Quaternary Age that are at times separated by impervious and semi-pervious clayey layers. The over-pumping of the coastal aquifer of the Gaza Strip and the resulting increase in salinity in most of the well water of the area is the subject of part 12.

Natural recharge (replenishment) of all the aquifers in the central hilly chain of the West Bank between the Mediterranean Sea and the Jordan River occurs predominantly in the West Bank.

There are two surface catchment areas in Palestine: the Western catchment area that drains to the Mediterranean Sea and the Eastern catchment area that drains in to the Jordan River and the Dead Sea basins. The only permanent source of surface water within the present boundaries of Palestine is the Jordan River (figure 5.3). The situation there will be presented in part 11. (It should be noted that, topographically, Egypt is riparian to the Jordan River Basin; however, Egyptian territory does not contribute water to the basin, except for the possibility of intermittent, seasonal wadis.)

The source of water supply in Palestine is from rainwater. The level of rainfall varies according to the topography and location. The prevailing rain-bearing winds are westerlies on which the rising ground acts to force the moist air upwards, causing precipitation in the hills of the West Bank inland region. The rainwater which

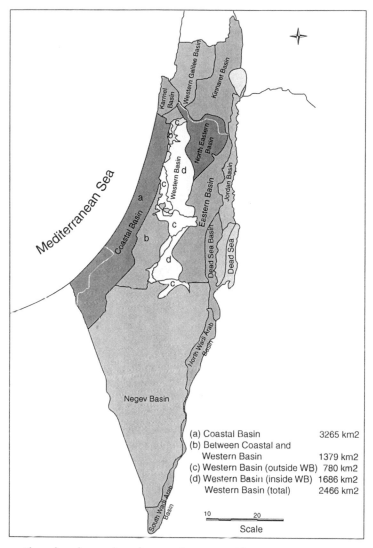

Figure 5.1 Shared and non-shared groundwater aquifers (Kinneret Basin = Tiberias Basin).
From the Palestinian Hydrology Group (PHG) 2004.

falls in the West Bank flows to the east and west following the natural slopes of the central mountain range. As the western slopes are gentler than the eastern slopes and receive more rainfall, the western groundwater aquifers have a higher natural recharge rate. Rainfall on the eastern slopes, however, feeds the springs along the eastern slopes as well as the deep aquifers that dip toward the Jordan Valley that are tapped by Israeli settlers. In the Gaza Strip coastal area, the rainfall that remains after evapotranspiration infiltrates the sandy soil and recharges the groundwater aquifers.

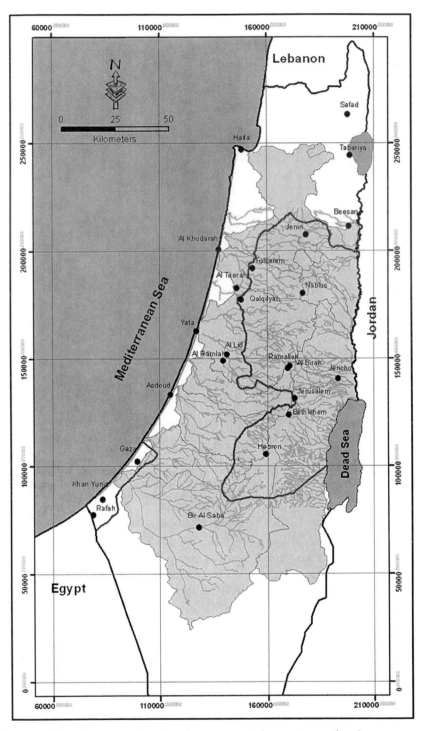

Figure 5.2 Shared and non-shared surface water catchments (map also shows network of wadi runoffs).
From Aliewi and Assaf 2006.

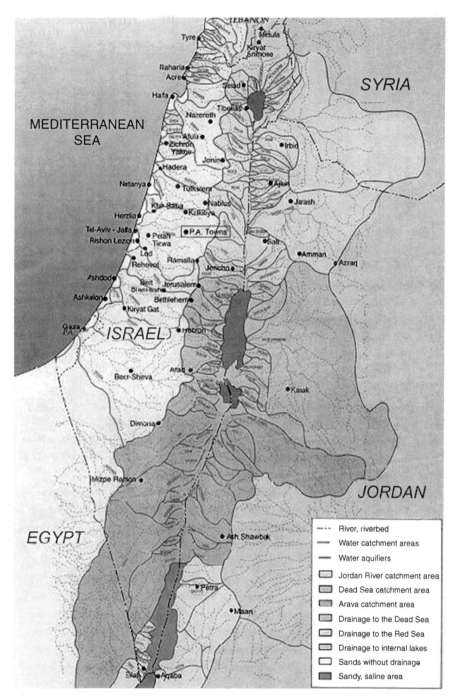

Figure 5.3 The Jordan River, Dead Sea, and Wadi Arava catchment area. The Palestinians are co-riparians in the Jordan River Basin and the Dead Sea Basin. From Aliewi and Assaf 2006.

Table 5.1 Natural water recharge of the aquifer basins

Basin	Range of Recharge (mcm/yr) INSIDE THE WEST BANK	Recharge (mcm/yr) OUTSIDE THE WEST BANK
Eastern	125–197	0
Northeastern	132–177	35
Western	317–366	37
Total	574–740	72

As can be seen from the above, another transboundary issue is natural water recharge of the aquifer basins, as estimated in table 5.1. For example, the recharge area of the unconfined part of the productive Western Aquifer inside the West Bank is 68% of the total unconfined aquifer area. The area outside the Green Line is 32% of the unconfined aquifer area, which is mainly a discharge or abstraction area, except in Jerusalem. The area of the confined part of the Western Aquifer (light gray in figure 5.1) is entirely outside the West Bank and it also is mainly a discharge or abstraction zone (Palestinian Hydrology Group 2004).

Toward Sustainable Water Management

The dual threats of water insufficiency for basic needs and development and inequality in the right to use—and the control over—both water resources and water supply constitute a most urgent environmental and human rights crisis for Palestinians. Increasing availability of basic water supply and sanitation also constitutes a cost-effective measure for promoting public health.

Intensive use of water, fertilizers, and other agricultural inputs for crop production at present are the major cause of problems in soil and groundwater salinization, nutrient imbalances, and environmental degradation. Add to this the pollutant potential of untreated wastewater and runoff and leakage from solid waste dumps.

The approach to water resource management in this region should evolve together with the social and economic development of the area as the growing demands of water for sectorial use and waste products disposal increase the stress on the available supplies of adequate water quality. Every cubic meter of water deemed unusable due to poor quality or improper utilization is, in reality, a direct loss in the water supply of the region. Deteriorating water quality can reduce available water supplies just as surely as drought. The fact is that the amount of water available for any purpose in any location is a function of the quality of available water supplies.

Groundwater Management

The major management options for the sustainable development and environmental protection of shared water resources are developing groundwater supply, harvesting storm water, improving water and wastewater infrastructure, importing water, and increasing desalination. Groundwater supply development consists of drilling new production wells while monitoring and rehabilitating existing wells. Harvested storm water can be used for irrigation or for artificial recharge of groundwater for storage.

In order to improve water and wastewater infrastructure, there must be rehabilitation of water networks, spring conveyance systems, and leak detection. The installation of new water networks, reservoirs, and main transmission lines should be encouraged. More wastewater collection systems, treatment plants, and reuse systems for agriculture are needed.

The combination of political strife, resource overuse, and continued contamination of water sources means that freshwater scarcity will reach critical levels. The problem, as mentioned, is not only quantity, but also quality. Critical resource threats include pollution of freshwater by industrial activities and untreated human wastes and contamination of wadis and aquifers due to runoff from fertilizers, pesticides, and wastewater. The immediate task facing Palestinian water managers is to solve actual problems that have occurred, or will occur, in specific areas. This will require coordination with their Israeli counterparts.

The ever-dwindling supply of freshwater (both in quantity and in quality) and the irrevocability of inappropriate policy measures by some require regionally unified and internationally supported, definitive, and ecologically sound changes to current policies and practices to ensure an adequate future water supply for all peoples in the region.

Frameworks for Cooperative Groundwater Management

Water resource management encompasses assessment of all available water resources and water resource utilization in all its forms as well as water protection and conservation methods. Water management, especially in this semi-arid area, essentially means the formulation and implementation of a sustainable socioeconomic development policy with corresponding regulations and guidelines. These management areas can be conceptualized or divided into three components—water supply, water utilization, and water discharge. Palestinian and Israeli joint water management decisions should address the concept of water resources in all three phases in what can be called the "water usage cycle," which should be visualized from the very beginning of any planning phase as non-separable elements of a process.

The pollution from nonpoint sources may be the most significant cause of water contamination. It must be remembered that groundwater is susceptible to contamination not only from current discharges, but also from those that occurred even many decades ago. Fertilizer residues, toxic chemicals, and other materials discharged onto the soil can pose a serious hazard to groundwater for many years.

The Palestinians have a finite supply of drinking water—under pressure from population growth, but also by the demands placed on it by so-called progress. Many of the products of modern civilization that are dumped in the groundwater

Table 5.2 Water usage cycle

Water supply component: Allocation of water resources	Water extraction, regulation, distribution, and maintenance techniques that aim toward an efficient and integrated management of water sources
Water utilization component: Demand management of domestic, industrial, and agricultural uses	Sectorial uses of water, seeking more efficient production processes that minimize water requirements and emphasizing the efficient use of water by all end-users and the need to minimize water use per unit of end product
Water discharge component: Pollution control of water resources	A controlled management of waste disposal in order to avoid pollution and to combat environmental and health hazards due to deteriorating water quality before and after use

supplies are proving to be surprisingly persistent. The compounds ending up in the water supply (and wastewater effluent) are playing an increasingly important role in the life cycle of all creatures. Chemicals being poured into the water supplies are likely to interact, exposing humans and animals to unpredictable additive and synergistic effects.

Water supply in the Mountain Aquifer is by definition finite. The mechanisms to manage water scarcity (whether due to climate change or to outside constraints) must include conservation and demand management, along with education programs and strategies for addressing water quality. Economic utilization, protection, and conservation of water should constitute the fundamental goals of every measure or action undertaken in pursuit of a rational management of water resources. Issues must be addressed that relate to water utilization techniques in the framework of minimizing the negative secondary effects during all phases of water supply—distribution, utilization, and disposal, i.e., the water usage cycle. These water management goals should include a set of techniques, structural measures, and related policies required to achieve an efficient allocation, distribution, operation, and utilization of water resources as well as adequate environmental, agricultural, health, and pollution controls.

Objectives for the basis for the rational protection and development of Palestinian water resources should include assessments of the availability of water resources, comparisons of possible uses of water resources, development of managerial activities dealing with both administrative and non-structural measures, initiation of water protection and conservation techniques, and a review of agricultural practices and policies.

A Comprehensive Strategy for Sustainable Development and Environmental Protection of Shared Water Resources

Fluctuations in annual precipitation patterns and the unpredictability of aquifer recharge are likely to grow worse for the foreseeable future due to climate change.

A strategy of adaptation to periodic or increasing drought conditions in the region as a whole must be assembled and implemented. One of the technical solutions that will be important to this strategy is the reuse of regional water. Conservation of valuable water resources can be benefited by the reuse of treated wastewater, the reuse of collected and treated storm water and urban runoff, and small- to large-scale rainwater harvesting and artificial recharge schemes.

Adaptive agricultural practices such as changing cropping patterns are likely to help protect water resources as well. Pilot programs for the development of economic industrial crops in the agricultural sector (such as jojoba, aloe vera, and biofuels) should be implemented, along with pilot projects for trees and ground covers to combat desertification. Farmers should be encouraged to plant rain-fed and drought-resistant crops. They can also help conserve water by lining irrigation canals, reusing drainage water, and improving the efficiency of their irrigation practices.

In order to protect these valuable resources, both public and private participation must be utilized in water, sanitation, and environmental projects involving the entire community. Average citizens can help save water by using water-saving and efficient household fittings and dual piping. These new technologies can be promoted to the public through demonstrations and pilot projects. Citizens should also be encouraged to plant trees to expand the greenery of the region.

Wadis are extremely important for the maintenance and development of water resources. The utilization of intermittent wadi flows, the development and preservation of small springs, land use studies, and extensive land terracing for rainfall conservation are all steps necessary to retain the resources in wadis.

The storage and distribution of scarce waters can be facilitated through leak detection surveys and maintenance programs, household water-tank surveys and water quality testing, and artificial recharge of groundwater and aquifer storage.[1] In addition, studies should be done examining different types of small- to large-scale reservoirs and pools, to determine the best methods for water storage.

Infrastructure and Expanded Recharge

More specifically, the future management strategy for shared groundwater resources needs to ensure development of infrastructure schemes in order to utilize the runoff flow in the wadis of the Eastern Aquifer, which is the Palestinian side of the Jordan River Valley, on the basis of a comprehensive technical and socioeconomical analysis of the major wadis. This should include construction of storage dams or water retention structures on main wadis of the western bank of the Lower Jordan River Valley, Palestine. There is also a need for geological studies and rehabilitation and development of major springs, including civil works and storage reservoirs, based on seismic and geophysical surveys.

Feasibility and technical studies should be made with an eye to artificial recharge of aquifers from seasonal wadi runoff, urban runoff, or treated wastewater for either seasonal storage or as a barrier for saltwater intrusion. These should involve implementation of the use of winter runoff waters collected in floodplain areas, such as Marj Sanour of the Jenin District.

There is also a need to supplement natural rates of recharge through artificial recharge. Artificial recharge can be accomplished either indirectly, by percolating water through the soil profile of percolation basins, or by injecting water directly into the aquifer. The possibilities for artificial groundwater recharge also open the prospect of groundwater storage or groundwater banking. This should begin with the implementation of pilot projects for artificial recharge and aquifer storage along with recovery and utilization of excess surface flows or treated wastewater. This requires hydrological and meteorological monitoring networks, including gauging, monitoring, and sampling systems with all necessary equipment and vehicles (for water and soil monitoring). Pilot projects for the use of renewable energy (solar and wind) for water extraction and/or distribution should be considered.

Research and Pilot Studies for the Use of Brackish Water

A comprehensive strategy needs to include measures that can manage water demand. In-depth studies of existing cropping patterns with a recommendation for a change in policy toward economic rain-fed cropping (or with supplemental irrigation) in the entire Jordan River Basin area should be undertaken.[2] For example, almonds, olives (with quality grading specifications), herbs and spices, barley, vetch and maize/sorghum (not corn), and jojoba are all promising. And the feasibility of brackish water use should be better characterized on crops such as industrial tomatoes and melons (cantaloupes), for example.

Permit systems need to be enforced for point-source industrial discharges, including the requirement to use the best available technology to treat wastewater prior to discharge into a sewerage system. Firms need to be encouraged to recycle and reuse both processing and cooling waters. Quotas and/or pumping taxes are the usual tools recommended for the regulation of groundwater extraction.

Wastewater reuse provides a drought-proof resource for a community that automatically increases as population growth increases. Technologies for wastewater collection include gray-water separation as an alternative management scheme for individual households, transportation of wastewater to decentralized treatment plants, and alternatives to conventional gravity sewerage which are applicable to small communities.

A water resources protection and development program for the sustainable development and environmental protection of shared water resources should also include sectors for public awareness (dissemination of information) and capacity-building programs.

Recommendations

Meeting the sustainability challenge for water resource development will require an advanced level of regional management. The regional water resource management structure (institutions and organizations) must manage two systems: the natural water resources system (existing water, floods, and droughts) and the human activity system (water demands and pollution).

Regional management must be multipurpose, addressing domestic water supply, irrigation, industry, and the needs of nature. It must have multiple objectives, ensuring economic productivity, environmental quality, social equity, and human health. These objectives can be maintained through the use of physical structures, regulations, dissemination of information, and economic incentives.

What is needed is to move away from the technical-fix-dominated and largely supply-oriented management structure of water resource management. The focus has to be extended from "blue water" to incorporate also "green water" issues, and from water quantity to incorporate water quality as well. An integrated approach is necessary for environmental management and water management. Planning should incorporate a multi-sectoral framework. All sorts of interdependency linkages and implementation barriers need to be addressed in an overarching and integrated manner. The conventional setup of sectoral water management institutions is not able to cope with the present water problems facing the area. The solutions to these problems require an integrated approach to water, land use, and ecosystems, addressing the role of water within the context of social and economic development and environmental sustainability.

Problems that are facing water resource management in the area can be summarized as an increase in demand and waste production due to population growth and socioeconomic development, a decrease in the availability of water per capita, high losses of urban water, and the increasing depletion and pollution of groundwater.

Water is the driving force of sustainable development. Thus, rational water management in this region should be founded upon a thorough understanding of all the types of water available and their movement. A major objective should be to view hydrological processes in relationship with the environment as well as human activities, emphasizing the multipurpose utilization and conservation of water resources to meet the needs of economic and social development throughout the area.

Proper management of Palestinian water resources requires consideration of both supply and demand. Naturally occurring water resources in Palestine and the demand for their usage are currently critical political, economic, and technical issues. Palestinian water usage, management, protection, and conservation constitute a top-priority strategic package that must be freely developed. With ever-declining safe and sufficient water sources, it is imperative that Palestinians manage their most valuable natural resource—water—if a continued reliable and sustainable water supply is to be expected in the future. The fact is that water problems in Palestine are caused not so much by a shortage of freshwater as by its uneven distribution due to practices during the occupation. Applying more science and technology, rather than bureaucracy, can help mitigate some of the effects of people's indifference to and abuse of the limited water resources in the area.

Water availability is essential to Palestinian socioeconomic development and food security. The agricultural component of the Palestinian economy is the largest user of water and takes the "lion's share" of total water utilized in Palestine, in both the West Bank and Gaza Strip. This fact is also true for Israel and Jordan.

The ongoing rapid growth of the Palestinian population, together with the desired extension of irrigated agriculture and industrial development, is sure to stress the quantity and quality aspects of the natural system of water resources in Palestine because of the limited water resources and the increasing problems associated with the expected imposed limitations.

Emphasis should be on proper water utilization and water conservation—stressing water demand management, rainwater harvesting, dry-farming of rain-fed crops, methods and techniques of using refined sewage waters, irrigation with brackish water, desalinization, etc. It should be recognized that there exist varying cultural traditions (e.g., urban versus rural), social structures, and degrees of economic development or scientific and physical infrastructure; and these differences—even within the small area of Palestine—can affect the choice, use, and sustainability of different water resource options.

The development of Palestinian water resources has as its aim—in common with Palestinian development generally—the enhancement of the conditions of human life and must be recognized as an integral part of the social and economic programs. It must always be remembered that development goals are not realizable in the absence of water adequate in quantity and quality.

To date, supply-oriented and resource-oriented water management dominates the scene in Palestine, with emphasis on structural measures to cope with supply of water and water-related services. Since the establishment of the Palestinian Water Authority, intensive and extensive institutional development programs have been initiated, aimed at developing the management tools necessary for a sound, sustainable, integrated water management policy.

In summary, both the supply and demand management stages of water resource development will have to run concurrently in order that the concept of water supply will not exclude the processes of collection, cleansing, and discharge of wastewater, which must be directed and seen as being under the same planning umbrella as water resource development (the water usage cycle).

Intensifying water scarcity (whether due to climate change or due to outside constraints) will remain a dominating feature in the Palestinian-Israeli water scene for the foreseeable future. Water scarcity will be managed by a variety of techniques including augmentation of supplies, pricing, education, water-saving technologies, and water recycling. Limited water supplies need to be stretched and protected in order to serve the growing demands for additional water from almost every water-using sector.

What is spoken of as a water problem in the area is not solely a hydrological problem, but a societal problem. The main task is to master the political forces, to build up the balancing forces, and to develop competent management systems. Water is the source of life and a natural resource that sustains the environment and supports livelihoods—but it is also a source of risk and vulnerability. From the beginning to the end, it is poverty, power, and inequality that are the roots of the water scarcity problem in the region.

NOTES

1. The effects of climate variability are exacerbated by the underdevelopment of water resources infrastructure. Without aggressive strategic programs that include storage infrastructure development, vulnerability cannot be overcome.

2. The number of irrigable donums in the Lower Jordan River Valley—Palestinian Side—is 200,000 (20,000 hectares). Currently, 71,898 donums (7,189 hectares) are irrigated (when possible).

REFERENCES

Aliewi, A., and K. Assaf. 2004. Planning for water resources development in the lower Jordan River valley. *Proceedings of the international conference on regional hydro-political challenges of sustainable management of transbondary river basin*. Beirut, Lebanon: Ministry of Water and Irrigation.

———. 2006. Shared management of Palestinian and Israeli groundwater resources: A critical analysis. In *Water resources in the Middle East, Israel-Palestinian water issues—from conflict to cooperation*. Vol. 2 of *Hexagon Series on Human and Environmental Security and Peace*, ed. H. Shuval and H. Dweik, 17–32. Berlin/Heidelberg: Springer-Verlag.

———. 2007. Beyond scarcity: Power, poverty, and the global water crisis: Water rights in the Palestinian Territories. *United Nations Development Programme: Human development report 2006*, 217.

Assaf, K. 1985. *Food security in the West Bank and Gaza Strip*. Water resources, 23–77. UN ESCWA/FAO Joint division and AOAD of the Arab League. Rome: FAO.

———. 1994. *The hydrogeological conditions in the Palestinian Territory and the need for information management systems and training in the water sector*. Paris: UNESCO.

———. 1994. Replenishment of Palestinian waters by artificial groundwater recharge as a non-controversial option in water resource management in the West Bank and Gaza Strip. *Water and Peace in the Middle East, Studies in Environmental Science* 58:301–314.

———. 2000. The need for joint management and monitoring of the water "usage" cycle in management of shared groundwater resources. In *Management of shared groundwater resources: The Israeli-Palestinian case with an international perspective*, ed. E. Feitelson, and M. Haddad, 75–82. Ontario: International Development Research Centre.

———. 2000. The Palestinian situation: The need to legally define "Palestinian Water Rights." Expert group meeting on legal aspects of the management of shared water resources, Sharm El-Sheikh, June 8–11. Economic and Social Commission for Western Asia (ESCWA) and Center for Environment and Development for the Arab Region and Europe (CEDARE).

———. 2004. Joint projects and programs promoting Middle East cooperation and knowledge in the water sector. *Proceedings of the 2nd Israeli-Palestinian International Conference Water for Life in the Middle East, Antalya, Turkey, October 10–14*, Israeli Palestinian Center for Research and Information, Vol. 1, 236–249. Jerusalem: IPCRI.

———. 2007. The Palestinian situation: Riparian rights in the Jordan River and Dead Sea basins, transboundary natural resources governance in regions of extreme conditions. Paper presented at the NATO advanced research workshop, Ein Gedi, Israel.

Assaf, K., A. K. As'ad, M. Haddad, T. Nassereddin, R. Koning, and P. Roark. 1994. *Water conservation in Palestine*. World Bank Report. Ramallah: Center for Engineering and Planning.

Assaf, K., and Said Assaf. 1986. The water situation in the West Bank and Gaza Strip. In *Water resources and utilization in the Arab world*, 93—136. Kuwait: Arab Fund for Social and Economic Development (in Arabic).

Assaf, K., and Shireen Assaf. 2005. Basic needs in development focus on Palestine. *Proceedings of the international conference on water values and rights, Ramallah, Palestine, 2–4 May*, 589–603. Palestine: Palestine Academy Press.

Assaf, K., B. Attia, A. Darwish, B. Wardam and S. Klawitter. 2004. Water as a human right: The understanding of water in the Arab countries of the Middle East—A four country analysis. *Global Issue Papers* 11:168. Berlin: Heinrich Boll Foundation.

Assaf, S. 2004. The need for implementation of water for peace strategy for the Jordan River Basin countries through a shift in cropping patterns. *Proceedings of the 2nd Israel Palestine Conference Water for Life in the Middle East, Antalya, Turkey, October 10–14*, Israeli Palestinian Center for Research and Information. Vol. 2, 851–864. Jerusalem: IPCRI.

Attilli, S. 2001, Palestinian water, conflict and issues for negotiations, in Arabic at Al-Jazeera Web site, http://www.aljazeera.net/in-depth/water/2001/2/2-6-1.htm.

Committee on Sustainable Underground Storage of Recoverable Water. 2008. *Prospects for managed underground storage of recoverable water.* National Research Council of the National Academies. Washington: National Academies Press.

Gleick, P. 1999. The human right to water. *Water Policy Journal* 1 (5): 487–503.

Palestinian Hydrology Group. 2004. *Water for life—Israeli assault on Palestinian water, sanitation and hygiene during the Intifada.* Water, Sanitation and Hygiene Monitoring Program (MaSH MP), funded by UNICEF.

———. 2006. *Water for life—the dilemma of development under occupation: The obstacles to achieving the millennium development goals and water rights in the occupied Palestinian territory.* Water, Sanitation and Hygiene Monitoring Program (MaSH MP), funded by UNICEF.

Sustainable Management of the West Bank and Gaza Aquifers. 2001. *Technical background on water issues for the final status negotiations—technical report.* Working report no. SUSMAQ-NEG #08 V1.0. Palestine: Palestinian Water Authority.

United Nations Development Program. 2006. *Human development report beyond scarcity: Power, poverty, and the global water crisis.* New York: UNDP.

United Nations—Economic and Social Council. 1999. *Protocol on water and health to the 1992 convention on the Protection and Use of Transboundary Watercourses and International Lakes.* London. http://www.unece.org/env/water/text/text_protocol.htm (accessed July 20, 2009)

———. 2002. *General comment No. 15, the right to water (Articles 11 and 12 of the International Covenant on Economic, Social and Cultural Rights).* www.unhchr.ch/html/menu2/6/gc15.doc (accessed July 20, 2009)

Ziad, M., and A. Aliewi. 2005. Sustainable development of the Palestinian water sector within IWRM. *Proceedings of Groundwater Protection workshop organized by UNESCO*, September 15–18, Damascus, Syria.

The Mountain Aquifer

SHARED GROUNDWATER RESOURCES,
ENVIRONMENTAL HAZARDS, AND
TECHNICAL SOLUTIONS

DROR AVISAR

Background

The dispute between Israelis and Palestinians over the shared water resources of
the Mountain Aquifer is one potential obstacle in the path of peace in the Middle
East. One of the largest freshwater sources in Israel and Palestine is the Mountain
Aquifer, a particularly vulnerable resource. This aquifer is the only source of water
for Palestinians in the West Bank and provides about 50% of Israel's drinking water.
Due to the chronic groundwater deterioration occurring within the Coastal
Aquifer, the significance of this water source appears to be increasing.

The majority of the Mountain Aquifer's natural recharge area lies within the
West Bank territories, with two of its three basins flowing naturally toward Israel.
In 1967, Israel occupied the West Bank and imposed strict control policies over the
utilization of the Mountain Aquifer water. This policy aimed at preventing irre-
sponsible drilling and groundwater exploitation by citizens, which could lead to
saltwater intrusion and pollution. Due to hydrological characteristics, it is vulnerable to additional sources of groundwater pollution.

The geology of this mainly carbonate aquifer is complex—water flows in several
directions and quite rapidly for an aquifer. But in the main section of the aquifer, the
flow is from east to west, which means that in many cases the actual recharge takes
place in Palestinian areas and the outlets are located in Israel. While 90% of the catchment lies under the West Bank, 60% to 70% of the storage potential lies under Israel's
pre-1967 borders. This asymmetry is the basis for the continuous disagreement over
water rights and constitutes a challenge for future management strategies.

Along the mountainous backbone of Judea and Samaria mountains, the subsurface water divide is determined by structure, stratigraphy, and karst developments,
creating two groundwater basins. The western one is known as the Yarkon–
Taninim Basin (figure 5.4), in which groundwater flows in the mountain aquifer, of
Cretaceous age. This aquifer is a major resource of freshwater for both Israelis and
Palestinians. The groundwater of the eastern basin, which flows to the Dead Sea
and Jordan Valley, is fully exploited by pumping wells, which supply freshwater to
both Palestinian and Israeli settlements.

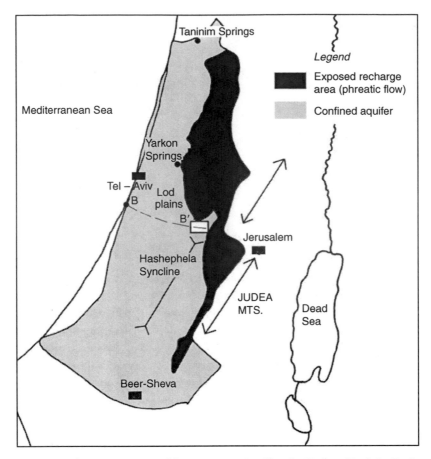

Figure 5.4 The western part of the Mountain Aquifer, the Yarkon-Taninim Basin.

The Mountain Aquifer succession is composed of a thick (600–800 m) sequence of hard, karstic (cracked), and permeable limestone and dolomite interbedded with argillaceous beds of lower permeabilities. Such low-permeability rocks separate the upper and lower parts of the Judea Group sequence, thereby creating two aquifers (Avisar et al. 2001): the lower subaquifer, composed mainly of massive dolomite and limestone layers, which contains groundwater of low salinities (up to 100 mg/l chlorides) and the upper aquifer, which also contains dolomite and limestone.

The recharge area of these aquifers is mainly exposed in the western parts of the Judea and Samaria mountains, covering an area of about 1,800 km². Generally, groundwater flows west and northwest to the Yarkon and Taninim springs, which are traditionally considered as the natural outlets of the two aquifers. For the most part, the water wells that tap the aquifer are located on the margins and in the foothills of the high (600–1,000 m) Judea–Samaria anticlinorium (figure 5.4). In the western foothills of the mountains and further westward, beneath the coastal plain, the Mountain Aquifer beds are uncomfortably overlain and confined by the Mount Scopus Group, composed of massive chalk and bituminous chalk of Senonian Age and by Early Tertiary (Paleocene) chalk, marl, and shales, attaining a thickness of 300 m to 2000 m.

Because of the prevailing chalky-shaly composition of the lithological ensemble, the Mount Scopus Group was always regarded as a regional aquiclude overlying the Mountain Aquifer beds (Blake and Goldschmidt 1947). The thick sequence of shales of the overlying (mostly Neogene) Saqiye Group and the laterally aligned chalky marl of the Albian Talme Yafe Group act as semi-impervious barriers along the western boundary of the Yarkon-Taninim Aquifer (Avisar et al. 2003).

Environmental Hazards

The State of Israel and the Palestinian Authority are located in a region with an acute water shortage; the issue of water use and allocation constitutes one of this region's most pressing problems. In order to meet growing demand required by both Israel's and Palestinian Authority's urban, agricultural, and industrial sectors, Israel is currently fully exploiting its water resources; and in only a few years the underground resources available will be depleted even under conditions of maximum efficiency.

Dependence on precipitation and the seasonal fluctuations of the Sea of Galilee (Lake Kinneret), in combination with the dire conditions of the Coastal Aquifer—conditions created by pollution from industrial sources, urban sewage, pesticides, effluents from waste disposal sites, and others—have put serious limitations on the amount of available quality drinking water. The importance of the Mountain Aquifer has thus grown as Israeli's main supply of potable water. Moreover, the weakening conditions of other water sources will force Israel in the not-too-distant future to lean even more heavily on this resource (Avisar 1996).

The Yarkon-Taninim Basin runs the length of the central mountain range in Israel. The aquifer is structurally complex, with a diverse lithology, many faults, and a dissected anticlinorium. The rock formations in the recharge zone, the region in which precipitations penetrates vertically below ground, are hydrologically varied and have different levels of fragility. This differentiation is the key to understanding the level of impact of the pollutants on the groundwater. In addition, this differentiation makes it possible to divide this region into several sub-regions on the basis of their susceptibility to pollution and, thereby, to recommend a sustainable plan for this region. Portions of this region are karstic, a characteristic that increases the hydraulic conductivity of those areas and that accounts for a danger of the aquifer's water being polluted heavily and rapidly by sources of human pollution, such as urban, agricultural, and industrial wastewater and leakage from gas stations.

The potential sources of pollution to the Mountain Aquifer can be found in both Palestinian and Israeli development. Palestinian urban centers have grown in the past several decades in the West Bank, and consumption of drinking water has increased, while a sufficient sewage and waste disposal infrastructure remains absent. The steady discharge of municipal wastewater from Palestinian towns and cities constitutes a significant pollution source that needs to be addressed.

The most significant regional change, however, may have taken place during the 1970s and 1980s, when, as a result of political and ideological policy, a large Jewish population began settling above the Mountain Aquifer. Motivated by political considerations, these new rural and urban settlements were established without sufficient environmental planning or regard for the protection of water resources. These demographic changes did not bring with them technical solutions for the pollution that the new settlements would generate above this aquifer. The resulting discharges have begun to disturb the groundwater's chemical balance.

In general, the major demographic and, consequently, environmental changes that threaten the Mountain Aquifer include a high birth rate, increasing urbanization and settlement, lack of planning and inspection, creation of industrial areas containing a wide variety of factories, lack of modern wastewater treatment plants (WWTP), unsupervised solid-waste dumps located at the edge of settlements and villages, and deficiencies in sewage infrastructure resulting in raw sewage discharge into river/stream basins. These factors have also contributed to the contamination of the local groundwater and the destruction of natural ecosystems (Avisar 1996).

Large quantities of untreated sewage run on the surface of the Mountain Aquifer, percolate into the ground, and threaten the continued utilization of vital water resources. It is undisputed that the pollution sources are both Palestinian and Israeli in origin and that they constitute a significant threat to future water supply. Evidence shows that groundwater in some locations has already been polluted. The lower deep limestone aquifer is especially prone to contamination due to its karstic nature and the quick transport of pollutants through it. Overexploitation may lead to a rapid rate of saline water infiltration from surrounding saline water sources.

Technical Solutions

Israelis living inside the nation's 1967 boundaries consume about three times as much water per person for household use as do Palestinians. The real issue over water is not whether the Palestinians will get more water, due to Israeli concessions on water quantity. Implicitly, Israel has already agreed to allow for additional transfers of water beyond the interim agreement, and new desalination plants will make this possible. Rather, the main question is whether both Israel and the Palestinian Authority will share management of the water, particularly the Mountain Aquifer, and act to protect this critical resource.

Under decades of Israeli control over the mountainous recharge region, no meaningful steps were taken to develop adequate resources for the preservation of the Mountain Aquifer. Development in the region was hurried and advanced without sufficient consideration regarding sustainable water management. The planning and building process, driven by short-term political considerations, did not take into account the hydrological fragility of the aquifer.

In particular, the governments never took responsibility for the future of this critical water resource. This neglect is perfectly demonstrated by the chronic lack of solution for the wastewater of Arab villages and Jewish settlements. No government (on either side) allocated effective inspection and enforcement of pollution sources above the most important water resources in the region.

With the recent renewal of the peace process in the Middle East, Israelis and Palestinians have struggled to define the content and nature of an agreement concerning the allocation of the water of the Mountain Aquifer. It is clear to all that the coming years will be characterized by geopolitical changes. It is important that they strengthen the capacities of the parties involved to maintain this essential source of water.

Taking into account both the physical characteristics of the region and the expected growth in its population, Israelis and Palestinians at this stage must seek to better understand the environmental impacts of the rapid demographic changes and the development anticipated to support it. The link between the fates of these two nations and that of the Mountain Aquifer demands a radical improvement in understanding the relationship between human activities and this critical natural resources—the Mountain Aquifer.

The Israeli-Palestinian peace process may have been stalled for several years, but scientists from both sides have continued to work and have made substantial progress in resolving one of the key hydrological questions. At present, Palestinians and Israelis are moving toward a political resolution of their more than half-a-century-old conflict. The overall mission of a peace agreement regarding the Mountain Aquifer, therefore, should be to reduce or to eliminate groundwater pollution arising from Israeli and Palestinian municipalities, settlements, industries, and gas stations. Future collaboration will need to eliminate the myriad sources of groundwater pollution that arise from anthropogenic activity; establish guidelines for monitoring, managing, and reducing sources of groundwater pollution in Israeli and Palestinian municipalities, settlements, and villages; strengthen technical know-how and build a network of Israeli and Palestinian water practitioners at the municipal level; and create commitment within Israeli and Palestinian municipalities to improve environmental performance in their jurisdictions.

REFERENCES

Avisar, D. 1996. *The impact of pollutants from anthropogenic sources within a hydrologically sensitive area—Wadi Raba Watershed—upon groundwater quality.* Tel Aviv, Israel: Israel Union for Environmental Defence.

Avisar, D., J. Kronfeld, J. Kolton, E. Rosenthal, and G. Weinberger. 2001. The sources of the Yarkon springs. *RadioCarbon* 43:793–799.

Avisar, D., E. Rosenthal, A. Flexera, H. Shulmana, Z. Ben-Avrahama, and J. Guttman. 2003. Salinity sources of Kefar Uriya wells in the Judea Group aquifer of Israel. *Journal of Hydrology* 270:27–38.

Blake, G. S., and M. Goldschmidt. 1947. *Geology and water resources of Palestine.* Jerusalem: Government Printer.

El-Fadel, M., R. Quba, N. El-Hougeiri, Z. Hashisho, and D. Jamali. 2001. The Israeli Palestinian Mountain Aquifer: A case study in ground water conflict resolution. *Journal of Natural Resources and Life Sciences Education* 30:50, 61.

Weinberger, G., E. Rosenthal, A. Ben-Zvi, and D. G. Zeitoun. 1994. The Yarkon-Taninim groundwater basin, Israel: Hydrogeology; case study and critical review. *Journal of Hydrology* 161:227–255.

Editors' Summary

The crux of the historic disagreement between Palestinian and Israeli negotiators in the water realm has involved rights to the Mountain Aquifer. Both sides have conveniently adopted theoretical positions which support their hydrological interests. Hence, Israel argues that it enjoys historic rights to the aquifer, pointing to the storage capacity and established wells inside Israel's 1967 borders. Palestinians maintain their rights as riparians, relying on the location of the aquifer recharge area, where the rainfall actually originates. Resolving this "zero-sum-game" dynamic through other formulations, such as "equitable use" or the "needs" of the parties, has only been moderately successful. Ultimately, as was the case in the Israeli-Jordanian peace accord, a political compromise must be made, which should be far easier today given the availability of alternative desalinated sources for both sides. Yet, taking concrete measures to protect the aquifer cannot wait for such diplomatic resolution.

There is a sense that while politicians have naturally focused on the "allocation" debate, which is easy to grasp, the more complex dynamics of joint management and the associated technical challenges for sustainable management of the Mountain Aquifer have not received adequate attention. As a result, the sources of contamination have not abated. In particular, municipal sewage and nonpoint source pollution involving runoff from agricultural and urban sources have not been addressed. The importance of the many projects and practices for protecting the Mountain Aquifer that have been detailed in this part is not disputed by technical experts on either side.

Regardless of ultimate water allocation, there needs to be a coordinated system of management and regulation between the two parties that is overseen by technical experts. These experts need to be freed to the greatest extent possible from political constraints and need to take the necessary measures to ensure future sustainable, high-quality yields of groundwater. Continued neglect of pollution-prevention technologies and infrastructures and oversight could lead to a shared resource which is of little value. The grave situation of the Coastal Aquifer, underlying the Gaza Strip, is a sobering reminder that hydrological systems will not wait for political harmony, but are easily compromised given the relentless flow of contaminants and uncontrolled tendencies toward extraction beyond sustainable levels.

Upgrading sewage systems in the recharge area remains the single greatest imperative for protecting the Mountain Aquifer. Over the past years a litany of sanitary projects has been discontinued in the West Bank and Gaza due to the political instability. Ironically, funds were available from international aid agencies for treating most of the sewage from Palestinian cities. Already, fecal contamination can be measured in many of the West Bank streams, portending water quality problems in the underlying aquifer. An "emergency" initiative to collect and treat all untreated sewage in the Palestinian sector and shift the existing cesspool systems to connect to these centralized facilities must be initiated immediately.

Even after allocations find a political resolution, water quantity will continue to be an open problem that must be addressed dispassionately and creatively. The effects of the anticipated climate change on aquifer recharge have been sufficiently considered. If projections of the models endorsed by the United Nations International Panel on Climate Change (IPCC) are correct, recharge will be diminished. Indeed, it has been argued that the allocation schemes that emerged from the interim Oslo agreement in the mid-1990s relied on the rainfall levels of the preceding years, a relatively wet period. Hence, many wells have essentially been mining groundwater resources. The present drawdown on the aquifer due to continuous pumping will probably grow worse due to effects of global warming, and the hydrological damage could be irreversible.

In the past, agriculture served in Israel as a buffer for drought periods. But, with the shift to wastewater, the impact of cuts to agriculture will be far more painful—with orchards and mature trees being sacrificed rather than a single year's annual yields, for which compensation can be provided. Preparing for such droughts should be done in a coordinated fashion. Desalination offers protection against these fluctuations.

PART 6

STREAM RESTORATION

While the term "river" is a misnomer in water-scarce areas, the many natural streams of the area are in chronically poor condition. Beyond sewage treatment, industrial wastes, nonpoint source discharges, and a host of other pollution sources need to be treated. These two essays—written by a Palestinian sanitary-wastes expert and environmental expert and Israeli ecologists—suggest that there is room for cooperation in the area of stream restoration and that a final agreement can play a key role in facilitating this.

The Condition of Streams and Prospects for Restoration in Palestine

NADER EL-KHATEEB

Stream Contamination: A Transboundary Problem

While a rich variety of streams flow through the Palestinian Authority, most of them are highly polluted, mainly from untreated wastewater and other polluting activities. The pollutants not only flow in the surface water, but often infiltrate the groundwater which both parties use for drinking and for other purposes. The present condition of the streams is exacerbated by the geopolitical context. Many streams in the Palestinian Authority are transboundary and do not recognize political borders. The end result is that contaminated waters flow across the border in both directions, causing pollution and degradation of water quality. As a result, both sides suffer. Because so much of the problem is transboundary in nature, it is impossible to repair these problems without Israelis and Palestinians cooperating. Without working together, stream restoration turns into a "lose-lose" situation.

Israelis frequently focus on streams that flow west—from the West Bank toward the Mediterranean Sea, with Palestinian pollution reaching Israel. But there are numerous examples of streams that flow east, from Israel to Palestine. These include the Kidron Stream, whose flow begins in the neighborhoods of West Jerusalem, continues through East Jerusalem, and moves on to the Bethlehem area and out into the Dead Sea. At present this sewage in the streambed is raw, without any systematic treatment, although there is some natural decomposition of contaminants that takes place during the flow. Little if anything has been done thus far by Israel to prevent the raw sewage from flowing. The same situation can be seen in the Jordan River, which is polluted by wastewater from the Beit She'an region below the Degania dam. Untreated wastewater also flows into the Jordan from the Wadi Qelt catchment area around Jericho when there are heavy storms and floods.

Examples of streams that flow west from Palestine to Israel include the Zomar-Alexander catchment that flows from Nablus through Tulkarem and into Emek Hefer and down the Mediterranean. The Besor, the largest watershed in the region, flows through three political entities from Hebron to Beersheva and then into the Gaza Strip and eventually to the Mediterranean. In short, rather than pointing fingers about who bears a greater responsibility for past contamination, it is time to begin to work together to address these significant environmental challenges.

The Importance of Clean Streams in Palestinian Culture

In Islam, water is life and everything was created from water. In fact, this is no different from the way water is perceived in many cultures around the world. Palestinians know how vital water is to life. Despite the difficulties we face, citizens and the government must make a substantial effort to prevent pollution from wastewater.

Local streams have particular religious significance for Christian Palestinians as they do for Christians around the world, especially the baptism site on the river Jordan. It is the dream of many Christians to visit this site and to be baptized in the Jordan. Unfortunately, the water at the baptism site is not in sufficiently good condition to serve this traditional function. Despite the pollution, in many places you will still find people trying to enjoy the water and the beauty of nature.

Palestinians are an agricultural people. The presence of freshwater streams has resulted in a variety of agricultural practices that make optimal use of the flow. However, since so many of the streams have become heavily polluted with sewage, for many years farmers have been basically using sewage water to grow crops, including salad vegetables. Given the groundwater depth in the West Bank, there is limited access to groundwater for irrigating crops. For many Palestinians to remain farmers, they had no choice but to use the polluted surface water.

With produce moved from north to south and, of course, east to west across the borders to Jordan and into Israel, consumers are often unaware that the fruits and vegetables they are purchasing frequently are grown with sewage water. It can be assumed that they would have been highly reluctant to purchase the vegetables if they knew. The Palestinian Authority has begun to address this problem, and irrigation with raw sewage has largely been phased out. However, in Area C, the region controlled by Israeli authorities, such dangerous practices can still be found.

Ground versus Surface Water

There has been joint research and policy analysis conducted between Palestinians and Israelis about the Mountain Aquifer for many years. Considerable monitoring, evaluation, and discussions ensued about how this resource could be jointly managed, with allocations of quantities for each party recommended and scenarios about responding to problems considered. There has been far less joint research and discussion about surface water. Limited attention has been focused on questions such as how to improve the flow of the springs and streams, how to protect the streams in summer, and how to promote wastewater systems and decentralized sewage treatment plants for small communities.

Accordingly, Palestinian experts have traditionally focused their hydrological research and expertise in the area of groundwater, rather than surface water. Yet, the effects caused by polluted surface water are surely as serious: local people suffer from raw sewage flowing beside their home, which can leave severe health impacts, as well as from the acute nuisances associated with the constant smell and the mosquitoes. However, at the official level, priority has been given to ensuring the supply of drinking water from the Mountain Aquifer. After the interim Oslo Peace Accords, international donors also prioritized freshwater drinking supply, without giving parallel support to wastewater infrastructure development. These issues are, however, clearly linked. If raw sewage is flowing on the surface, it is easy for it to percolate into the Mountain Aquifer and cause pollution. The karst/ limestone aquifers allow wastewater to penetrate very easily, and the end result could be catastrophic for drinking-water supply. As such, it is essential to consider the two issues in parallel.

Pollution Sources

Sewage wastewater is undoubtedly the major source of pollutants in Palestinian surface water resources. Most urban areas in the West Bank have little or no sewage treatment, discharging the effluents in a raw form. The associated organic loadings and bacterial contamination leave their mark on the streams, their ecosystems, and the underlying groundwater. The odor and mosquito nuisance created can become unbearable.

There are, in fact, a variety of other contaminants that must be addressed as part of a stream restoration strategy. For example, there is also considerable leachate which derives from inappropriate management of solid waste. In practice, safe disposal of solid waste can only be found in the northern sections of the West Bank, where the first modern landfill sites were built. In the center and the south of the West Bank, rubbish is simply dumped and leachate easily flows, with rainwater reaching nearby creeks and streams during the rainy season. The leachate can, of course, infiltrate the groundwater as well.

Industrial wastes also constitute a source of pollution, although a less significant one in Palestine than in Israel, due to the absence of heavy industry. For example, wastewater from the dye industry and from slaughterhouses is typically discharged into rivers and streams without treatment. As mentioned, there is also a steady flow of industrial waste from the Israeli settlements into Palestinian streams without treatment, sometimes it is even hazardous waste. A good example is the Barkan Industrial Region, located near the city of Ariel in the north of the West Bank. Israeli regulations on wastewater treatment are not strictly enforced there. Since the 1970s many industries have relocated there, presumably to take advantage of the lenient environmental enforcement and tax incentives for settling in the Wet Bank. In some cases, such as the leather-tanning industry—a substantial portion of a heavily polluting industry appears to have coordinated their geographical migration.

As a result, Palestine's streams receive effluents from a myriad of industrial sources: from small-scale electroplating industries to car repair garages. Regardless of the location, the contaminants eventually find their way into the streams. The potential health risk is not well characterized but surely is ever present. The problem is one of not only technology and enforcement, but also economics. Pollution prevention requires a good economy so that businesses can start paying for these services rather than dumping their waste because they cannot afford to pay for treatment.

Wastewater from olive mills is also a major pollutant in Palestinian streams. Palestine is famous for its olive production. Despite the short picking season, the consequences of the wastewater from olive oil residuals flowing into streams are very severe. Olive water has a high load of organic pollutants and increases the salinity of a stream. In a recent research initiative, it was found that during the olive production season, Israelis actually stopped using the water that flows into their part of the catchment because of high salinity. The consequences of the olive oil production on the ecosystem of streams on the Israeli side during the olive season can also clearly be seen. The impact was especially prevalent in those areas where the stream had been restored, with massive damage to aquatic life and significant fish kills due to organic loadings and oxygen depletion. The unfortunate impacts highlight the imperative of cooperation, without which there will be ecological suffering.

These environmental hazards can be addressed. Recently, as part of a Palestinian-Israeli research initiative assessing the conditions in the Zomar-Alexander Stream, the full impact of the olive oil discharges were quantified. As a result, for the first time last year, with support from an outside company, the Palestine Water and Environmental Development Organization helped arrange for the wastes to be collected from the Palestinian olive mills and transported to special treatment plants in Israel so that they would not be dumped in the stream.

Ephemeral versus Permanent Flow Dilemma

The fact that wastewater now flows more or less continuously in their streams presents Palestinians with a dilemma. It is clear that capturing and treating the wastewater that flows in the wadis is important, since the present pollution damages the ecosystem and threatens ground and surface water integrity. However, if wastewater is not flowing, the volume of water in the wadis will drop precipitously, especially during the summer time. This could also leave the ecosystems which have emerged there much poorer.

It is important to find a way to ensure that good quality water flows in the rivers and that people can enjoy the value of restored areas. Small segments of the Alexander River have already been restored in Israel and serve as a wonderful recreational resource for the general public. Here too, the flow during the dry season is almost entirely based on treated effluents. Palestinians can use examples like this to demonstrate to the public how we can improve a section of river and make it much more attractive, providing recreational benefits for everyone, especially the public, who otherwise would not have access to water resources.

Toward Restoration

The first step in cleaning up Palestine's streams requires the prevention of further pollution from point sources. This will require significant investment in regional wastewater collection and treatment systems. Once the contamination ceases, it will be possible to consider repairing and restoring these streams.

If we are to collect, treat, and reuse wastewater, Palestinians can learn from Israel with regards to how they might effectively treat it for reuse. Israel has a great deal of experience and is a worldwide leader in the field. Israel could, and should, provide training about the technical aspects of treating the water as well as guidance with regards to the implementation of the associated agricultural and irrigation practices. The Palestinians can benefit from the Israeli experience and use it to show Palestinian farmers the benefits of reusing treated wastewater. Should treated wastewater become a valuable commodity, it will be possible to demonstrate to Palestinian industry the benefits of paying for wastewater treatment.

The costs of fully treating and reusing wastewater may well reach hundreds of millions of dollars on the national scale. It is important that policy makers recognize that the move toward tertiary treatment is not a luxury. From the perspective of water management, there is no other alternative. The only directly available source of potable water available in the West Bank is the groundwater. If wastewater is not collected and treated, the aquifer will be destroyed. While gathering the necessary financial resources is a charge, the longer we wait, the greater the degradation and suffering will be.

Bilateral Cooperation in Research

Recently, a 3-year research initiative between the Arava Institute for Environmental Studies and the Palestine Water and Environmental Development Organization was completed. It was funded by U.S. AID's Middle East Research and Cooperation program. This was the first comprehensive study that focused on transboundary surface water rather than groundwater in Palestine. It highlighted the level of ecological destruction that is happening in many of the catchment areas and what will need to be achieved in both Israel and Palestine to restore the catchment areas. Despite the critical data that the project generated, it did not succeed in generating additional funds so that it might continue or expand to other transboundary watersheds.

One of the major outcomes of the study was capacity-building for Palestinians. Students were sent to the United States to receive training about preparation and implementation of hydrological models for water management and stream restoration. Palestinian experts gained important experience in working with these models, and equipment for the first time became available for monitoring surface water flow and quality. These can be utilized in other surface water projects with the now-experienced graduates and engineers who are better able to contribute in these fields. No less important is the practical experience gained. The Palestinian team had to learn to work in severe weather conditions—floods and snow—to make sure that the equipment was operating so that data could be collected.

Another valuable benefit of the project was the provision of technical support, for the first time, between Israelis and Palestinians. The research offered an excellent opportunity for Palestinians to learn from Israeli experience as the Israelis have done much more advanced research in the field of stream monitoring and have well-equipped laboratories to this end. They have also developed a relatively broad infrastructure and network for regular monitoring.

Many misunderstandings between the two sides were clarified as a result of the project. It also offered a rare opportunity to present the outcomes and associated recommendations to official decision-makers on both Israeli and Palestinian sides. The project suffered, however, due to its inability to access streams in the Gaza region. As one of the watersheds examined was the Hebron-Besor Basin, which eventually flows to the Mediterranean via the Gaza Strip, it was unfortunate that this section of the watershed could not be monitored.

Despite initial discussions, the Palestinian Water Authority (PWA) did not participate officially in the research project. This was largely due to the political dynamics of that period. While it was certainly interested, especially given the clear institutional interests in developing its laboratories, the political situation at that time meant that the PWA could not be a partner. In retrospect, this was valuable for the Palestinian research team, which developed in-house expertise. Results of the project were disseminated to all relevant parties, governmental and non-governmental. Yet, in the future, the monitoring of streams and rivers needs to be done by national authorities on a larger scale.

The Good Water Neighbors Project and Other Cooperative Stream Initiatives

Beyond research, public interest, action, and educational-oriented programs have emerged that address the problem of stream water quality. Friends of the Earth Middle East, a regional environmental NGO with Jordanian, Palestinian, and Israeli offices, has for several years been engaged in a public awareness and protection initiative called the Good Water Neighbors Project. The project focuses on cross-border co-operation on environment and water issues between neighboring communities. Due to its activities, Palestinians and Israelis have been able to consider water conservation techniques, such as recycling gray-water, and build small-scale treatment plants such as wetlands. The project also works in schools on initiatives such as reusing water to flush toilets and for irrigation as well as learning how to conserve water and harvest rainwater. Friends of the Earth Middle East works with the community to look at the impacts of community water usage and organization on the local stream flow and quality as well as the aquifer recharge. The project also actively promotes organic agriculture.

One of the perceived obstacles to Palestinian efforts to reduce contamination of streams involves capacity and technology. Small, dispersed communities with little funds and no highly trained personnel are not considered capable of stopping wastewater flow. The Good Water Neighbors Project shows that small communities can easily handle their wastewater with small-scale, low-cost technologies. The biggest problem faced by the GWN Project involves a chronic lack of financial resources. This means that only pilot initiatives, workshops, and demonstrations can be pursued and that more meaningful interventions involving nationwide, fully operational projects are not possible. In short, the GWN Project can and should be much bigger. Other communities are asking to join. On the Palestinian side, it enjoys the full support of the Palestinian Authority and seeks to include as many communities as possible. Working with small communities has helped to highlight their problems among decision-makers and donors, using methods such as petitions. These methods have helped keep some donors committed.

A good case about the potential of cooperation on surface water is the discussion that emerged about how to coordinate joint sewage treatment plants between continuous communities. For example, between Emek Hefer and Tulkarem (in the Zomar-Alexander catchment area) such facilities have been established as well as between Baqa Shartiya and Baqa el-Garbiya. The project showed that all communities involved are willing to work jointly, and the national authorities are also willing to provide encouragement to such grassroots efforts. Due to the catalyst of civil society, mayors on both sides met to discuss in more detail how to proceed to ensure that water reaching streams is of higher quality. Such cooperation often catches the attention and support of donors.

Indeed, transboundary projects that attempt to improve stream quality tend to be win-win projects—in which all sides benefits as do water resources. At the end of the day, the reality of transboundary water dynamics is either a win-win or a loose-loose proposition. Residents of all communities want to get rid of the raw sewage flowing by their homes and stop the associated smells and the mosquitoes that the sewage brings. Everyone wants a healthy environment and cleaner streams.

Palestinians were often surprised to find that the Israeli authorities are also very supportive. Projects that lead to concrete activities to improve the biological integrity of streams and abate pollutants provide real support not only for the peace process but also for the future sustainability of these communities. They can bridge the gap between the two peoples. Both sides soon learn that it is in their interest to work together so the projects don't collapse and to protect their shared water resources.

A Research Agenda for the Future

The U.S. government–funded Middle East Research and Cooperation (MERC) research initiative showed the potential of Palestinian and Israeli experts to work together in a joint scientific framework. But the results also pointed to numerous areas where further investigation is necessary.

To begin with, more research on organic loads in transboundary catchments is required, as well as additional chemical and biological analysis. Among the essential questions is the link between surface water and groundwater issues and the implications for future drinking-water quality. More information needs to be collected about surrounding land-use patterns and public health-related issues. It would help to establish permanent stations in the wadis for testing, especially weather stations, because there was not enough weather data generated in the Palestinian sector.

The project also revealed the extent to which progress in surface water monitoring and modeling has taken place during the past ten years. In particular, building an HSPF (Hydrologic Simulation Program–Fortran) model that can offer water managers for both sides the ability to make informed decisions about optimizing control efforts is an important task. Ultimately, the political situation has improved, allowing for the involvement of more international partners and greater involvement by research agencies. Moreover, Gaza needs to be integrated in future hydrological monitoring research. Beyond surface water and groundwater, such efforts could provide important information about the future prospects for Mediterranean marine water quality.

Future Stream Function and Designation

In the future, Palestinians should seek to treat the wastewater so that it does not pollute streams and restore them for ecological and recreational use. Each Palestinian region should be the site of a high-level wastewater treatment facility, allowing for economies of scale and reuse by agriculture. At present, Palestinians lack the financial resources to construct this critical infrastructure.

Agriculture will, of course, continue, but irrigation will be based on recycled effluents treated to a high standard rather than on freshwater. This is because the supply of available freshwater is becoming more and more depleted, while at the same time the supply of recycled wastewater will grow. A program will need to be established that works with consumers and farmers. Farmers will need to learn which crops can be safely grown in the treated wastewater and how to protect the soil from being salinized. At the same time, consumers must be willing to accept that crops grown using high-quality, recycled wastewater are perfectly healthy to eat. The quality of the water must be constantly monitored in order to reassure the consumer that it is safe. The final water utilization will ultimately be driven by the types of crops grown, with Palestinian agriculture certain to retain some plants that will require freshwater. This strategy should leave reasonable amounts of water available for streams in the Palestinian state.

Palestinian awareness, like its infrastructure, remains inadequate to address the wastewater treatment and stream restoration challenge. Much of the problem involves economic capacity, because Palestine is not a first-world country like Israel. It would be well for Israel to consider funding even a single project inside Palestine aimed at improving the wastewater quality and the biological integrity of transboundary streams. Such an investment would clearly be of benefit to both sides and would certainly benefit Israel, as it is the major user of the groundwater which continues to flow from Palestine into its borders. Given its present economic capabilities, there is no reason why Israel should not begin to act like one of the donor countries from Europe.

REFERENCES

Abramson, A., A. Tal, N. El-Khateeb, A. Assi, N. Becker, L. Asaf, and E. Adar. 2009. Stream restoration as a basis for Israeli-Palestinian cooperation—a comparative analysis of two transboundary rivers. *Journal of River Basin Management*, forthcoming.

Assaf, K., N. El-Khateeb, E. Kally, and H. Shuval. 1993. *A proposal for the development of a regional water master plan*. Jerusalem: IPCRI.

Assaf, L., N. Negaoker, A. Tal, J. Laronne, and N. El-Khateeb. 2007. Transboundary stream restoration in Israel and the Palestinian Authority. In *Integrated water resources management and security in the Middle East*, ed. C. Lipchin and E. Pallant, 285–295. Dordrecht: Springer.

Haddad, M. 2007. Politics and water management: A Palestinian perspective, water resources in the Middle East. In *Israel-Palestinian water issues—from conflict to cooperation*, ed. H. Shuval and H. Dweik, 41–52. Berlin: Springer.

Tagar, Z., T. Keinan, and G. Bromberg. 2004. *Sleeping time bomb: Pollution of the Mountain Aquifer by sewage*. Tel Aviv: Friends of the Earth Middle East. Tamimi, A. H. 2006. Wastewater characterization and the reuse of recycled effluent in irrigation of agricultural crops. In *Water for Life in the Middle East, Conference Proceedings*, 768–778. Jerusalem: IPCRI.

United Nations Environment Programme. 2003. *Desk study on the environment in the occupied Palestinian Territories*. Nairobi: UNEP.

Stream Restoration under Conditions of Water Scarcity

INSIGHT FROM THE ISRAELI EXPERIENCE

AVITAL GASITH

YARON HERSHKOVITZ

Prior to the establishment of the State of Israel in 1948, many of the coastal streams had significant perennially flowing water habitats. Today, two-thirds of the population, a majority of the industry, and a considerable share of intensive agriculture activities are located in the coastal plain. Population increase and the ensuing agricultural and urban development resulted in augmented demand for water. For many years water has been diverted for human use (mostly agriculture) directly from the streams or indirectly from the aquifers. Stream channels lost dilution capacity and some dried out. The demographic growth was also followed by increasing production of wastewater that ended up in the streams. Presently, many of Israel's streams only flow because of the discharge of effluents.

Since the early 1990s, stream rehabilitation measures and recovery of streams' environmental and social functions have taken an increasingly important place on the public agenda in Israel. The nature of the attempts to restore streams in Israel where water resources are fully exploited is fundamentally different from efforts conducted in relatively water-rich countries due to the severe competition by different sectors for the limited resource. Presently, reclaimed wastewater is the only alternative water source for replenishing water abstracted from the streams. Moreover, most of the watersheds are shared with neighboring countries, with which, for geopolitical reasons, there is virtually no cooperation of watershed management. This worsens the environmental effects and compounds the problems that need to be solved. The situation is further aggravated by relatively low priority given to solving environmental problems in Israel and its neighboring countries. Also, administrative complexity in Israel emanating from the fact that at least five governmental ministries (Interior, Health, Agriculture, Notional Infrastructure, Environmental Protection) have jurisdiction over applicable aspects of the water law negates effective enforcement. And, not the least, severe financial constraint of relevant governmental ministries holds back implantation of rehabilitation projects. Consequently, in the beginning of the second millennium most of the streams in Israel and its neighboring countries are still severely impacted anthropogenically.

In this essay we selectively discuss issues of the attributes and current state of streams in Israel, elucidate on recently studied transboundary-polluted streams, and present principles for stream rehabilitation under conditions of fully exploited water resources.

Climate Setting, Geomorphology, and Geographic Variation

Fluvial systems (streams and rivers) are shaped by climate, geomorphology, and human activities. Israel is situated at the eastern part of the Mediterranean Sea ($29°-33°$N, $34°-35°$E) and is governed by a Mediterranean climate, distinguished by relatively hot and dry summers (June–September) followed by mild and wet winters (December–April). The precipitation regime is characterized by high seasonal predictability combined with high inter-annual variability (low constancy). Annual rainfall in Mediterranean regions can be similar to that in temperate areas, but the seasonal pattern of rainfall distribution is strikingly different. For example, in Frankfurt, Germany, on the average, rain falls every month of the year over a total of 173 days, averaging 638 mm. In contrast, in Tel-Aviv, Israel, where average yearly rainfall amount is only slightly lower (546 mm), rain falls during a period of about 5 months, for only 56 days.

Precipitation in Israel declines on a north-to-south gradient, from wet Mediterranean regions in the north (>700 mm/yr), through Mediterranean regions at the center (600–400 mm/yr), semi-arid in the south and eastern valley (400–200 mm/yr per year), and arid regions in the extreme south (less than 100 mm/yr) (Goldreich 1998). Large perennial streams are scarce and historically were situated where large karstic aquifers maintain spring flow (e.g., upper tributaries of the Jordan River at the north and the Yarqon and Taninim rivers in the central coastal region).

From the perspective of watershed formation, the most important local topographical formation is the Jordan Rift Valley (a part of the Great Rift Valley), stretching approximately 400 km from the upper Galilee Mountains in the north, along the Judean and Samaria hills in the center, down to the Arabah Valley in the south. This geographical configuration divides the landscape into the western (coastal) catchment, draining into the Mediterranean Sea, and the eastern catchment, draining into the Jordan Valley. Streams in the Golan Heights and upper Galilee drain into Lake Kinneret (Sea of Galilee), located in the northern part of the Jordan Valley. The coastal streams are relatively short (most are less than 50 km), perennial or intermittent, and typically lowland. Standing water and slow-flowing habitats are predominant (Gasith 1992). The eastern streams are mostly intermittent and ephemeral (wadis) and are relatively short, steep, and fast-flowing during storm events. Selected geophysical characteristics of Israel are shown in table 6.1.

Mediterranean-Climate Streams

Streams and rivers in Mediterranean-climate regions (five such regions exist globally) are physically, chemically, and biologically shaped by sequential, seasonally predictable events of flooding (late fall and winter) and drying (summer and fall)

Table 6.1 Selected geophysical characteristics of Israel

Area	(km²)
Total area	20,700
Surface area	20,271
Lakes area	429
Sea of Galilee (Lake Kinneret)	164
Dead Sea	265
Coastline	*(km)*
Total	205
Mediterranean Sea	194
Red Sea	11
Lake Kinneret	54
Dead Sea	121
Altitude	*m above/below SL[a]*
Lowest point in the world, the Dead Sea	−421
Lake Kinneret	−213
Length of selected streams	*(km)*
Jordan River (Jordan Valley)	172
Soreq Stream (Coastal plain)	92
Qishon Stream (Coastal plain)	49
Yarqon Stream (Coastal plain)	25

Source: Israel Central Bureau of Statistics, 2006.

[a] Sea level, August 2008.

(Gasith and Resh 1999). Winter floods act as the stream's "reset mechanism"; they scour accumulated sediment and debris, wash away in-stream and encroaching riparian vegetation, redistribute streambed substrate, and contribute to the mortality of organisms (Lake 1995, 2000; Gasith and Resh 1999). Drying involves a gradient of events from reduction in flow, through formation of isolated pools, to complete channel drying (Boulton 2003).

Abundance of water, coinciding with mild environmental conditions during the intermediate period between flooding and drying (spring and early summer), presents an ecological "window of opportunity" for the biota. Biological interactions and reproduction during this period are at their peak. The organisms found in such streams are evolutionarily attuned to these seasonal sequential changes in stream conditions (Bonada et al. 2007). One example is the reproductive strategy of a small cyprinid fish (the Yarqon bleak, *Acanthobrama telavivensis*), endemic to the coastal streams of Israel. It breeds in late winter and early spring, between flash floods and habitat desiccation. Breeding at this time of the year in Mediterranean-climate streams puts early stages somewhat at risk of being washed away by late floods but also provides them a longer period of growth under favorable in-stream conditions (Elron et al. 2006).

Multiple Stressed-Stream Ecosystems

Mediterranean-climate regions are naturally water stressed because of the relatively short rainy season and the high annual water losses due to evapotranspiration during the long hot summer (Gasith and Resh 1999). Moreover, the mild winters, abundance of sunshine, and fertile soil for millennia have made the Mediterranean region attractive for human settlements and development of intensive agriculture. This, in turn, led to competition for the limited resource—freshwater—and to the diversion of water from streams and rivers for human use, especially during the dry season.

Israel's water resources (about 1,100 to 1,500 mcm, under consecutive drought and rainy years, respectively) are fully exploited. The competition for water intensified dramatically during the second half of the twentieth century, following the re-establishment of the State of Israel (in 1948). Rapid population growth since the 1950s (from about 8% per year during the 1950s to 2% at the present) (Central Bureau of Statistics 2006) and the ensuing agricultural and urban development augmented demand for water, creating severe competition by different sectors. For instance, Israel witnessed an increase in consumption of water for domestic purposes from 25% to 37% and a decrease in use for agriculture from 68% to 56% in 1986 and 2003, respectively (Central Bureau of Statistics 2006). This resulted in diminished freshwater available for natural ecosystems (Gasith 1992).

The aforementioned demographic growth, along with low environmental awareness, resulted in severe pollution of streams and rivers (Gasith 1992; Bar-Or 2000). Except for the upper Jordan River and its tributaries that feed into Lake Kinneret (a major national drinking water reservoir), most other streams in Israel are polluted. Human activity imposes multiple pressures on the Israeli stream ecosystems. These include diversion of water directly from the stream channel or indirectly by pumping the groundwater, discharge of domestic and industrial effluents (point-source pollution), drainage of fertilizers and pesticides from agricultural runoff (nonpoint pollution), as well as stream-bank modification and channelization as flood prevention measures. One frequently overlooked additional source of ecological stress is the salinization of water in stream ecosystems, an increasingly common environmental insult, particularly in dry-land regions. We describe this environmental pressure as "silent pollution" as it is colorless and odorless and often goes unnoticed. There is, however, a negative relationship between biodiversity and salt content in perturbed freshwater ecosystems (Ben-David 2005).

Table 6.2 Maximum and average values of readily degradable organic matter in selected streams in Israel (mg/l biochemical oxygen demand)

Year Stream	2000		2001		2002		2003		2004	
	MAX	AVERAGE	MAX	AVERAGE	MAX	AVERAGE	MAX	AVERAGE	MAX	AVERAGE
Na'aman	135	20	42	18	110	26	28	9	153	17
Qishon	96	39	38	13	34	10	16	12	31	10
Daliyya	15	7	26	13	26	14	11	5	19	7
Taninim	5	3	12	6	8	4	7	3	10	4
Hadera	153	42	45	18	452	82	62	28	297	63
Alexander	84	28	440	66	165	61	433	19	24	8
Yarqon	34	12	114	13	55	16	28	12	84	17
Soreq	353	79	120	36	292	42	42	15	253	40
Lakhish	27	12	136	30	120	32	433	77	380	47
Harod	165	29	370	51	252	42	42	15	39	20
Lower Jordan	13	4	14	6	31	10	180	52	16	8

Source: Israel Central Bureau of Statistics, 2006.

Note: This includes coastal streams from north to south and two northeastern streams, 2000–2004.

Notwithstanding, the predominant pollution stressors in Israeli streams remain organic matter and nutrients discharged into streams with municipal effluent.

Israel has emerged as the world's leader in recycling wastewater. It is estimated that from a total of about 500 mcm of sewage produced each year, about 96% is collected by central sewage systems, and about 72% of that (350 mcm) is reclaimed (Inbar 2007; Tal 2008). Following recent consecutive drought years, the proportion of reclaimed wastewater is expected to increase. The untreated and un-reclaimed wastewaters are being discharged directly into stream channels. In the year 2000, the Ministerial Economics Committee decided to appoint an Inter-Ministerial Committee (the Inbar Committee) for the purpose of reviewing existing regulations (since 1992) and recommending new regulations for effluent use for irrigation or for disposal to streams and receiving waters (see part 8).

Yet, it is not clear that these standards are sufficiently stringent to allow for stream restoration in naturally low-flowing and ephemeral streams. Consider, for example, two common pollution measures, the readily degradable organic matter (biochemical oxygen demand, BOD) and total suspended solids (TSS). The presently recommended maximal and average concentration in discharged effluents for both these variables is 10 mg/l (Inbar 2007). The level of BOD exceeding 10 mg/l is at least twofold higher than the maximum level recorded in natural, unpolluted

Table 6.3 Maximum and average values of total suspended solids in selected streams in Israel (mg/l TSS)

Year Stream	2000 MAX	2000 AVERAGE	2001 MAX	2001 AVERAGE	2002 MAX	2002 AVERAGE	2003 MAX	2003 AVERAGE	2004 MAX	2004 AVERAGE
Na'aman	173	92	172	102	844	125	101	61	103	44
Qishon	95	57	454	142	352	81	508	135	177	76
Daliyya	117	41	296	99	1,346	211	95	37	78	35
Taninim	32	16	150	59	130	35	80	36	82	31
Hadera	490	89	86	46	120	64	122	48	429	102
Alexander	111	50	1,500	176	210	62	319	58	120	46
Yarqon	63	24	95	34	112	29	114	29	104	37
Soreq	168	51	160	38	1,013	156	87	27	238	47
Lakhish	1,360	360	68	23	80	39	183	60	310	73
Harod	802	253	272	149	662	206	272	97	186	90
Lower Jordan	269	67	203	51	316	90	276	100	296	71

Source: Israel Central Bureau of Statistics, 2006.

Note: This includes coastal streams from north to south and two northeastern streams, 2000–2004.

streams. The high level of degradable organic matter existing in the streams is usually associated with depletion of dissolved oxygen and increased mortality of aquatic organisms, diminishing natural biodiversity (discussed below under "stream health assessment").

Recent measurements of water quality in eleven selected streams in Israel indicate that in most of the streams the level of BOD and TSS far exceeds the recommended concentration (see tables 6.2 and 6.3).

The high level of pollution reflects the low quality of the discharged effluent, a result of relatively poor wastewater treatment in plants that still comply with the old 1992 standard of secondary effluent (20 mg/l for BOD and 30 mg/l for TSS). A compounding factor is the low or completely absent dilution capacity of the streams, generally as a consequence of water diversion for human use. In some cases, if not for the effluent discharged into the stream, the channel would dry out during the dry season (e.g., the central segment of the Yarqon Stream, the central coastal plain, and the lower Jordan River).

Stream Health Assessment

The authors studied the ecological impact of secondary effluent discharged into streams under conditions of water scarcity and reduced flow by assessing macroinvertebrate community integrity. This methodology is based on the notion that healthy, undisturbed streams are characterized by a rich and diverse macroinvertebrate community (high biodiversity).

Human impact significantly reduces biodiversity and enhances dominance of pollution-tolerant species. These responses can be detected and followed (i.e., bio-monitored) by sampling the community and by manipulation of the data (number of species combined with species abundance) in a way that weighs the results by scaled scores. These scores are interpreted on a scale of percentage of biological integrity, which is associated with health categories (Hershkovitz 2002). This approach was used to assess the ecological state of coastal streams in Israel.

These results indicated that although recommended effluent quality for stream discharge (Inbar Committee) can improve the ecological state of streams in Israel, it is yet inadequate. For example, under the recommended concentration of 10 mg/l BOD, the integrity of the macroinvertebrate community in the Yarqon Stream was less then 50%. This is equivalent to a state lower than "fair" on the scale of stream health.

Transboundary Pollution

Israel shares many of its stream catchments with its neighbors, Lebanon (Iyyon Stream), Syria (Yarmouk River), Jordan (Jordan River), and the Palestinian Authority. Fifteen streams flow from the Palestinian Authority westward into Israel. The upper tributaries within the Palestinian Authority are naturally intermittent but presently carry sewage or treated effluent downstream. Likewise, there are polluted tributaries that originate in Israel (three major ones are Harod, the upper reaches of the lower Jordan, and Og Stream) and flow easterly to the lower Jordan River and cross into the Palestinian Authority. A special case is that of the Hebron/Besor Stream that originates in the Palestinian Authority territory (West Bank), flows westward, crossing into Israel, and ultimately crosses again into the Palestinian Authority territory in Gaza Strip on the Mediterranean coast.

It is estimated that of about 74 mcm of sewage produced in the West Bank (Palestinian and Israeli settlements) annually, only 20% is being treated before being disposed of in cesspits or discharged untreated into streams (Cohen et al. 2008).

The magnitude of cross-boundary pollution was demonstrated in joint Israeli-Palestinian research in which the authors participated, assessing conditions in two major streams and their upper Palestinian tributaries: Hebron (El-Halil)-Besor and Shekhem (Nablus)-Alexander (Tal et al. 2008). The predominant source of pollution is raw domestic sewage or effluent as well as industrial wastes from Hebron's leather and tanning industry and limestone-cutting factories. It is estimated that about 5.5 mcm/yr of sewage flows over 120 km downstream until reaching Israel's Besor Reserve. This steady base flow of discharged effluents fundamentally alters the character of the stream, transforming it from an ephemeral desert stream where high-quality runoff water flows for only a few days a year to a perennial stream with a constant flow of sewage. A recent study (Hassan and Egozi 2001) showed that in ephemeral transboundary streams in the Negev and the Judean deserts, perennial flow of wastewater enhanced the development of riparian vegetation, which reduced water velocity and increased deposition of sediment along bar edges. This process resulted in lengthening and widening of the stream bars, relative to that recorded in unpolluted situations. In addition, the channel bed of streams receiving discharges from limestone-cutting factories (Hebron Stream) was significantly modified.

Analysis of water quality revealed extremely high pollution as reflected, for example, by the levels of BOD and TSS (an average range of 130–500 mg/l and 700–3,800 mg/l, respectively) (Tal et al. 2008). Estimates suggest that from 40% to 90% of the wastewater discharged along the stream (8,000–11,000 m³) infiltrates into the groundwater along the stream's first 60 km, before crossing into Israel.

The poor water quality of the stream was also reflected in the low diversity of aquatic organisms per site (e.g., three to eleven macro-invertebrate species, such as molluscs, crustaceans, and insects); all were pollution-tolerant species. Health assessment of the above two transboundary streams (Zomar/Alexander and Hebron/Besor) indicated a "poor" to "very poor" state. The grave pollution state of the Zomar/Alexander and Hebron/Besor streams is representative of the situation in most of the other cross-boundary streams.

Stream Restoration under Conditions of Water Scarcity

Ecological restoration is an attempt to repair damage to ecosystems by eliminating or minimizing man-made effects. The term "restoration" is sometimes interpreted differently by ecologists and engineers; to overcome this obstacle we advocate using a terminology that distinguishes between different levels of ecosystem repair. Accordingly, the term "restoration" is restricted here to situations in which the ecosystem is fully restored to its original state. "Reclamation" is used in connection with limited repair, mostly aesthetic, and "rehabilitation" is used when the purpose is to restore ecosystem structure and function and its ability for long-term self-regulation under constraints that prevent restoring it to its original state. Together they may be termed "the triple R ecological repair." In this connection we wish to introduce a new term of ecosystem transformation that is often confused with rehabilitation. The former lacks ecosystem repair, but rather the ecosystem is transformed from one state to another. A relevant example is "greening the desert" by modifying an ephemeral stream into a perennial one, usually by discharging sewage or effluent (e.g., the Besor Stream).

For the past 15 years effort has been made to restore streams in Israel. Such effort is yet to be implemented in the Palestinian Authority territory. Since the early 1990s, stream rehabilitation measures and recovery of a stream's environmental and social functions have taken an increasingly important place on the public agenda. As a result, rehabilitation master plans have been developed and partly implemented by the Israel River Rehabilitation Administration (established 1993) in cooperation with different stakeholders such as local stream authorities (e.g., Yarqon and Qishon), local municipalities, drainage authorities, the Nature and Parks Authority, the Jewish National Fund, and Israeli academia (Kaplan 2004). So far the effort made in Israel to repair stream ecosystems has only led to reclamation at best.

River rehabilitation plans are conducted on different scales, from a stream section to the whole catchment basin. The rehabilitation must consider the natural hydrology of the rehabilitated stream (perennial, intermittent, or ephemeral), its surrounding landscape features (e.g., natural, agricultural, and urban), the potential ecosystem services (e.g., maintenance of nature's values, provision of drinking water, recreation, and pollutant retention), and the social and economical benefits. This calls for cooperative team effort by ecologists, hydrologists, engineers, economists, and sociologists.

Rehabilitation of streams in Mediterranean-climate regions is fundamentally based on restoring the unique hydrological pattern and maintaining the multi-annual flow variability. Under the situation of water scarcity, allocation of water for the streams may be achieved by applying the following five management principles.

- "Drink the water and have it too": Maximizing reclamation and reuse of the reclaimed wastewater, primarily for use in agriculture and in industry, leaves more freshwater for nature.
- "Have the water and drink it too": Stream disturbance can be minimized by letting most of the water flow in the channels and diverting it for human use further "downstream." Maintaining natural flows along a large stream section maximizes public gains of "ecosystem services" (e.g., recreation together with irrigation). One of the mechanisms for achieving this goal is by differential pricing for upstream and downstream pumping (adopted in Israel since 2006).
- "Preferential flows for spring and summer": Maximum restoration of historic hydrograph patterns is done by discharging allocated water differentially on a seasonal basis. Rather than releasing constant amounts of water year round, more water should be discharged during spring and early summer, a period of peak biological activity ("window of opportunity" for the biota) in Mediterranean-climate streams.
- "Maximize water saving": Water stress of natural ecosystems can be reduced by maximizing saving of water. The latter can be achieved by government regulative intervention (e.g., differential pricing and use of local arid-land-adapted vegetation in public parks and private gardens).
- "Enlarge the cake" by desalination: In 2008 desalination in Israel added to the yearly renewable volume about 130 mcm (10%). Beyond 2010 the volume of desalinated water is expected to increase by an additional 20%. However, the alarming trend of declining average annual precipitation by about 12% during the past 16 years (possibly an effect of global warming) may require even greater investment in desalination. In addition to enlarging the renewable volume of water, desalination will relieve the pressure of groundwater withdrawal, which reduces natural spring flow and threatens groundwater quality. Moreover, the added desalinated water is expected to reduce salinity of the wastewater, increasing the quality of the reclaimed wastewater.

Water Management as if Nature Matters

In 2004 a regulation recognizing nature's right for water was introduced in Israel, leading to the allocation of 50 mcm of freshwater yearly for stream flow (excluding the Jordan River). Consecutive drought years and increasing water deficit in the aquifers (about 40% of the renewable volume in 2008) holds back implementation of this critical regulation. For the time being, rehabilitation of streams using reclaimed wastewater seems to be the only practical alternative. Attempts, thus far, to ecologically rehabilitate the streams using wastewater effluent, however, have consistently failed. To succeed using this approach will require use of high-quality effluent. Use of tertiary-treated effluent was recently proposed (e.g., Bar-Or 2000). However, production of high-quality effluent is expensive and inherently handicapped because of the competition for this water by many sectors. The costs will surely be prohibitive for the Palestinian sector.

In order for effluent quality to be sufficient to contribute to ecological restoration, we propose using a low-tech, relatively inexpensive, constructed wetland technology to upgrade existing sewage treatment. In such systems the effluent flows above and through a porous medium (e.g., gravel) planted with hydrophytes. In this technology contaminants are removed by physical (e.g., filtration and sedimentation), chemical (e.g., oxidation-reduction), and biological (e.g., microbial degradation) processes. This methodology is presently planned to be applied in Israel for the Alexander and Yarqon streams and is already examined on a small scale (e.g., Dan Region wastewater treatment plant, Shafdan site; Yad Hana waste water impoundment site).

Restoration of Transboundary Streams

Streams and rivers are strongly influenced by watershed processes. Therefore, cross-boundary cooperation is mandatory for achieving effective rehabilitation of transboundary streams. In the present reality in the Middle East, this is easier said than done, but surely not unattainable. Lack of adequate wastewater treatment capability, particularly at the stream source (upper tributaries), combined with the erroneous concept that one of the services of the fluvial ecosystem is to transport polluted water, leads to the present grave situation of many of the streams. This conclusion comes as no surprise to anyone dealing with stream restoration. Under the poor ecological state characterizing most of the streams in the region, the first and most immediate effort must be to stop the pollution discharged on both sides of the border. Reclamation of the wastewater and reuse in agriculture and industry may be a strong incentive for diverting the polluted water out of the streams. This, however, may result in desiccation of many streams' sections, especially during the summer time. Yet, this may be an unavoidable transitional state until the potential of water in the region is enlarged by desalination.

In this troubled region the countries involved are currently unable to overcome political and economic obstacles on their own, and the assistance of the international community for achieving these goals is needed. The absurd situation of the Israeli-Palestinian reality can be demonstrated by the fact that a master plan prepared for the Alexander transboundary stream (Brandeis 2003) won the prestigious Thiess Riverprize (from Brisbane, Australia). Nevertheless, 5 years later the target stream is still gravely polluted. Although efforts are being made with some success to involve the international community, it is time that the sides find the political will and use the help of the international community to overcome geopolitical and financial constraints that impede the implementation of this outstanding rehabilitation plan. The success of such a project may lead the way for further cooperation in rehabilitation of streams in our region.

ACKNOWLEDGMENT

We are indebted to the many students and technicians at the laboratory of freshwater research, Faculty of Life Sciences, Tel-Aviv University, who were involved in the study of Mediterranean streams.

REFERENCES

Bar-Or, Y. 2000. Restoration of the rivers in Israel's Coastal Plain. *Water, Air and Soil Pollution* 123:311–321.

Ben-David, E. 2005. Streams rehabilitation: Sensitivity of macroinvertebrates to salinization. Master's thesis, Tel-Aviv University (in Hebrew).

Bonada, N., M. Rieradevall, and N. Prat. 2007. Macroinvertebrate community structure and biological traits related to flow permanence in a Mediterranean river network. *Hydrobiologia* 589:91–106.

Boulton, A. J. 2003. Parallels and contrasts in the effects of drought on stream macroinvertebrates assemblages. *Freshwater Biology* 48:1173–1185.

Brandeis, A., Itzkovitz N., and Almon N. 2003. The Alexander River restoration project. Report.

Central Bureau of Statistics. 2006. *Environment Data Compendium 2006*, No. 2, 148. Jerusalem, Israel.

Cohen, A., Sever Y., Tzipori A., and Fiman D. 2008. West Bank streams Monitoring: stream pollution evaluation based on sampling during the year 2007. Environmental Unit, Israel Nature and National Parks Protection Authority (in Hebrew)

Elron, E., A. Gasith, and M. Goren. 2006. Reproductive strategy of a small endemic cyprinid, the Yarqon bleak (*Acanthobrama telavivensis*), in a Mediterranean-type stream. *Environmental Biology of Fishes* 77:141–155.

Gasith, A. 1992. Conservation and management of the coastal stream of Israel: An assessment of stream status and prospects for rehabilitation. In *River conservation and management*, ed. P. J. Boon, P. Calow, and G. E. Petts, 51–64. New York: Wiley.

Gasith, A., and V. H. Resh. 1999. Streams in Mediterranean climate regions: Abiotic influences and biotic responses to predictable seasonal events. *Annual Review of Ecology and Systematics* 30:51–81.

Goldreich, Y. 1998. *The climate of Israel: Observations research and applications.* Ramat-Gan: Bar-Ilan University Publishers and Magnes Publications (in Hebrew).

Hassan, M. A., and Egozi R. 2001. Impact of wastewater discharge on the channel morphology of ephemeral streams. *Earth Surface Processes and Landforms* 26:1285–1302

Hershkovitz, Y. 2002. The use of macroinvertebrate community for biomonitoring streams in Israel: The Yarqon stream as model. MS thesis, Tel-Aviv University (in Hebrew).

Inbar, Y. 2007. New standards for treated wastewater reuse in Israel. In *Wastewater reuse: Risk assessment, decision-making and environmental security*, ed. M. K. Zaidi, 291–296. Proceedings of the NATO Advanced Research Workshop on Wastewater Reuse—Risk assessment, decision-making, and environmental security. Dordrecht: Springer.

Kaplan, M. 1999. Rehabilitation and development policy for Israel's rivers. Position paper presented to the editors of the national outline scheme for development and building (NOS 35). River Rehabilitation Administration, Division of Water and Rivers, Ministry of the Environment, Jerusalem, Israel.

———. 2004. *The rivers of Israel: Policy and planning principles*. Jerusalem: Ministry of Environmental Protection, State of Israel (in Hebrew).

Lake, P. S. 1995. Of floods and droughts: River and stream ecosystems of Australia. In *Ecosystems of the world 22*: River and stream ecosystems, ed. C. E. Cushing, K. W. Cummins, and G. W. Minshall, 659–688. Amsterdam: Elsevier.

———. 2000. Disturbance, patchiness, and diversity in stream. *Journal of the North American Benthological Society* 19(4):573–592.

Tal, A., N. Al Khateeb, L. Asaf, A. Nassar, M. Abu Sadah, A. Gasith, J, Laronne, Z. Ronen, Y. Hershkovitz, D. Halawani, N. Nagouker, R. Angel, H. Ackerman, and M. Diabat. 2005. *Watershed modeling: Biomonitoring and economic analysis to determine optimal restoration strategies for transboundary streams*. Annual Report, MERC project M23-019. Submitted to the U.S. Agency for International Development: Bureau for Economic Growth Agriculture and Trade (Middle Eastern Regional Cooperation).

Tal, A., et al. 2009. Chemical and biological monitoring in ephemeral transboundary Palestinian-Israeli streams. Article submitted for consideration to the *Journal of River Basin Management*

Editors' Summary

Stream restoration is still in nascent stages of evolution in the region. While there have been modest and isolated improvements in several Israeli streams, the general situation is still extremely polluted and water quality is far from the natural conditions. Aquatic ecological systems have not been restored and the present conditions are generally poor.

Among the clear challenges to future restoration efforts is ensuring that both parties perceive stream rehabilitation as a "win-win" dynamic. Palestinians argue that many sewage treatment plants have been built with Palestinian funds but that the treated water goes to Israel. (Furthermore, Israel, it is claimed, charges for upgrading the treatment and the utilization of water that it essentially receives for free.) In other cases, money from donors was available, but sewage treatment plants were not approved by the Joint Water Committee. Given Israel's location as a downstream riparian in which the majority of the recreational and ecological benefits appear to accrue, it is important that future management strategies create conspicuous benefits for the quality of life of Palestinians. If such benefits are provided, the popularity of stream restoration projects will increase and the Palestinian public will have greater motivation to invest in restoration efforts. At a theoretical level, a strong Palestinian commitment to stream restoration exists and has been confirmed in "willingness-to-pay" studies. Yet, to date, it is not clear that restoration projects have been appropriately packaged to engage the local population and inform them of the potential environmental benefits.

One of the challenges in designing a cooperative transboundary restoration strategy is identifying "common uses." This is due to the fundamental asymmetry in several watersheds. Historically, there was little serious flow in the upper parts of most of the shared watersheds. Swimming and boating were not an important part of the culture in the West Bank region even as some of the coastal streams served as "swimming holes" for the downstream, rural communities.

Palestinian public perceptions justifiably see effluent-driven streams as too small and narrow to allow for meaningful swimming in the future. A final agreement should encourage the establishment of parks, scenic walks, sporting facilities, lawns, picnic areas, etc. along streams to draw people outdoors—rather than facilities that focus on boating and swimming. It is unlikely that future flow will be able to support such activities. Pools could, however, be established in the adjacent parks. If flow is sufficient, then the streams could be stocked and recreational fishing could be encouraged. But much remains dependent on improving access of Palestinian populations to the streams.

One possible new approach to increasing Palestinian support for investment in transboundary stream restoration is riparian parks, which should be recommended within the context of international economic assistance. To date the Palestinian public has minimal access to its streams. There are several reasons for this. There are constraints on movement associated with Israeli occupation and security concerns; lands are often controlled by private landowners or farmers who are disinclined to turn their property into public parks without adequate compensation; and there is a lack of access roads to the streams.

In Israel, the situation is different with several new parks emerging along the lower portions of transboundary streams, not withstanding their poor water quality. As a result, a growing number of Israelis see the streams as tourist and picnic destinations, where in the past they were largely perceived as environmental hazards. Bike paths have been developed, observation points built to view unique natural assets (e.g., the soft-back turtles), and picnic areas established that draw large crowds on a regular basis.

Palestinian villages have few open spaces, and public parks per capita are low due to past planning priorities. With the growing population density in the Palestinian sector, establishing natural "sanctuaries" for the Palestinian public would contribute greatly to general quality of life. Accordingly, among the list of possible projects for funding, along with sewage infrastructure, should be a variety of urban parks and recreational infrastructures along the streams. If monies are granted for stream restoration, then funds should be available to purchase or lease the lands adjacent to the streams so that land might be set aside for public use and access roads to parking facilities. Local NGOs could be utilized to take a lead in planning and establishing the parks. Already, Friends of the Earth Middle East has launched "Neighbor's Paths," an initial step toward a future Peace Park. The separation fence, of course, truncates the stream flow in many cases, hindering the founding of Palestinian and Israeli "transboundary parks." Ideally, in a future peace agreement, physical barriers that limit stream utilization could be removed.

With 60% of the Palestinian population defined as "rural," agriculture continues to provide a livelihood to a considerable percentage of the Palestinian population. At present, Palestinian farmers do not benefit from the treatment undertaken by Israeli facilities to improve stream water quality. If a final agreement regarding stream restoration is perceived as coming at the expense of the agricultural sector, it will not enjoy popular support. Rather, environmental agreements must be considered a win-win proposition for all sectors. While agricultural produce today contributes a far more modest percentage of the Israeli economy, given the strength of the Israeli farm lobby and historic and cultural affinities for agriculture, this dynamic remains true for Israel as well.

While there is some benefit in terms of stream restoration for treating sewage prior to pumping it into the stream, there are, of course, clear hydrological reasons for treating wastewater as close to the source as possible. The high percolation levels of sewage measured in several watersheds suggest that, from the perspective of groundwater protection, Palestinian treatment of its waste is a top priority.

It is likely that money can be raised to improve wastewater treatment and even to establish parks around the banks. Yet, the question of the long-term financial viability of these ventures is a critical one. If the tax base is not sufficient to support maintenance of environmental infrastructures, their performance will quickly drop. The creation of shared watershed management units is an important institutional measure, but their funding must be secured, either through governmental or international support, in order for stream restoration and management to be successful. In addition, the creation of a variety of commercial enterprises that utilize the newly restored natural resources must be considered seriously. Park concessions—from parking lots and boat rentals to restaurants and bathrooms—can bring in funds to ensure that the parks are well managed and clean. But the economic assessment needs to be larger in its scope.

PART 7

DRINKING-WATER STANDARDS

Historically, there have been clear links between drinking water and health, with epidemics occurring in both the Israeli and Palestinian sectors as a result of cholera, polio, dysentery, and a host of other water-borne diseases. While for the most part water quality has improved, there is no shortage of problems which require ongoing monitoring and measures to reduce exposure to contamination. These essays consider the source of drinking water for each entity, threats to its integrity, and existing regulatory frameworks for its protection.

Drinking-Water Quality and Standards

THE PALESTINIAN PERSPECTIVE

ALFRED ABED RABBO

Drinking-Water Resources and Supply

The Southern West Bank

The principal source of drinking water in the southern West Bank is that part of the eastern basin of the Mountain Aquifer which drains to the Dead Sea. This is a deep area within the Mountain Aquifer, with a depth ranging between 800 m and 850 m in strata of Albian to Turonian age, and is made up of two principal subaquifers. The upper, unconfined subaquifer, in Cenomanian-Turonian strata, is between 50 m and 80 m higher than the lower, confined subaquifer, of Albian-Cenomanian age. According to borehole data, an impermeable stratum of bluish green clays and marls and some chalks in the Lower Cenomanian form a separation between these two subaquifers.

Exploitation of this part of the aquifer is concentrated in the Herodian Beit Fajjar field and to a lesser extent further south in the Riheyeh-Samou well field, including the Fawwar wells. A more recent development is located in the Bani Naim well field. The Herodian Beit Fajjar well field is located to the east of the line between Bethlehem and Hebron. The northeasterly plunging syncline controls the flow direction in the unconfined aquifer toward the major discharge of the Feshkha springs along the Dead Sea shore. In general terms, rainwater entering the recharge area of the phreatic aquifer in the Hebron Mountains will take about 40 years before it is discharged at Feshkha.

The Northern West Bank

There are two main aquifer systems in the northern West Bank. The Eocene aquifer is contained within a shallow synclinal structure of the flanking and underlying Upper Cretaceous strata. Groundwater flows in a northeasterly direction in the Eocene basin. As well as deep production wells for domestic uses, there are many hundreds of relatively shallow private wells utilized primarily for agricultural purposes. The relatively constant discharge rates indicate an abundant reservoir source of water.

Gaza

In the Gaza Strip, the groundwater exists in the Coastal Aquifer (a shallow aquifer), which consists mainly of sandstone, sand, and gravel. The groundwater system is, in fact, the extension of Israel's Coastal Aquifer. The aquifer is highly permeable with a transmissivity of about 1,000 m²/day and an average porosity of 25%. The depth to water ranges between 70 m in the highly elevated area in the east and 5 m in the lowland area. The total annual recharge of the aquifer is estimated at 46 mcm. A deficit of 50 mcm/yr is observed in the water balance due to overpumping. Therefore, the aquifer is subject to infiltration from the brackish or seawater, which results in a quality deterioration.

Drinking-Water Availability and Allocation

Palestine is a land that suffers from severe water stress. The full extent of the severity emerges from a comparison with international standards for per capita water availability. The World Health Organization (WHO) (1993) sets the figure for minimum water requirements at 100 m³/yr per capita for domestic, urban, and industrial use, plus a minimum of 25 m³/yr per capita for fresh food for local consumption. In contrast, the annual supply of water for the almost three million Palestinians in the West Bank and Gaza for their domestic, industrial, and agricultural needs is a mere 246 mcm/yr. According to Israel's annual allocation, Palestinians have 93 mcm/yr for industrial use and 153 mcm/yr for agricultural use. Average per capita Palestinian supply is 82 m³/yr, of which only 26 m³ is provided for domestic consumption.

While there has been considerable improvement, access to tap water is by no means universal in the Palestinian National Authority. For instance, the hill villagers, who frequently eke out a subsistence agricultural existence, lack an adequate supply of domestic water, with little available locally for irrigation. In the Bethlehem region, 89.8% of households enjoy running water in their homes, while just to the north in the Hebron Governorate, the figure remains as low as 66.3%. Supply is hardly regular; roughly a quarter experience periodic cutoffs in water supply.

Palestinian water consumption is low for a variety of reasons. Chief among them are physical restrictions as well as an Israeli policy that for many years essentially froze Palestinian allocations. This created considerable resentment when new wells were drilled to provide water to Israeli settlements. Eventually, Palestinians came to focus their efforts on changing unequal distribution of water between the Israelis and Palestinians, with improvement of local efficiency or conservation taking a secondary role. At present, roughly 80% of the water from aquifers under the West Bank and Gaza is exploited by Israel, largely inside its pre-1967 borders.

Shortages of drinking water can also be attributed to domestic allocation priorities. The Palestinian agricultural sector consumes 70% of available water, even though irrigated agriculture represents only 5% of the total land available for farming. Less than 1% of the land available for agriculture is irrigated in the southern West Bank. Palestinian agriculture in the West Bank consumes 84 mcm/yr of water.

One of the most unfortunate infrastructure problems involves widespread leakage in the Palestinian piping system. The Palestinian Water Authority estimates that the overall loss of water in the system ranges between 25% in Ramallah to 65% in Jericho with an average of 44% of total supply trickling out of the system due to faulty infrastructure. In the Gaza Strip, the overall loss rate is estimated at 45%, of which 35% is due to inadvertent leakage while another 10% is tapped away by unregistered connections.

The low per capita water consumption and water shortage in the West Bank can to a great extent be associated with the historic Israeli occupation and the artificial barriers placed on water resource development in the Mountain Aquifer among the Palestinian population. The occupation of the West Bank by the Israeli army in 1967 brought together two distinct and asymmetrical entities; the Palestinian society remained an agrarian, capital-poor, low-income economy. In contrast, the State of Israel boasted an industrial, capital-rich, high-income economy. In retrospect, the dependency of the Palestinian water system on the Israeli institutions should not be surprising.

One of the distinguishing characteristics behind the organization of the water sector on the West Bank has been the integration of services from the Israeli water supply network. The Israeli network supplied domestic water to some of the larger communities in the area from the early 1970s. Israel's Mekorot Corporation's involvement in water supply to the Palestinian sector undoubtedly improved the quality of life for dozens of communities that finally became connected to a freshwater grid.

From the Palestinians' perspective, however, providing a resource as essential as water was frequently perceived as giving the occupying power another form of domination. Israel can correctly respond that water supply was never used as a "weapon" to pressure Palestinians during the periodic times of violence and military conflict. Yet Mekorot's activities undoubtedly limited Palestinian sovereignty even after the establishment of a Palestinian Water Authority (PWA) that assumed responsibility for the provision of drinking water to the Palestinian people. Palestinians quickly came to feel that Israeli authorities routinely rejected sites selected by the PWA and refused permits for drilling new wells in the West Bank.

In the long run, drinking-water supply for Palestinians is riddled with serious problems. Engineers working for the PWA on new wells estimate a further 100 m drop in the water table over the next quarter of a century. Other estimates expect conditions to be far worse, far sooner, on the assumption that the eighteen new wells in the southern part of the eastern basin of the Mountain Aquifer will be pumping at the projected rate of 250 m³/hr while the seven older wells will continue to pump at their present rates. European and American donors have been blamed for bankrolling the unsustainable exploitation of the aquifer. Clearly the PWA, now in a position to supply the Palestinian population, deprived for so long, with an abundance of water, did not have conservation or even sustainability as a major priority.

Water Quality and Pollution

Water quality in the West Bank is generally considered acceptable. For the most part, there are no serious indications of pollution in the deep aquifer. There is, however, no shortage of instances involving contamination of water in the more shallow aquifers and springs in the West Bank. Both the Nablus and the Jericho areas, for example, have shown nitrates levels in excess of the recommended 45 mg/l.

In contrast, drinking-water quality in the Gaza Strip is substantially worse, with only 4.0 mcm out of 44.1 mcm supplied by municipal wells reaching homes at an acceptable standard (PWA 1999). The main quality problem is the increase of salinity due to saltwater intrusion from overpumping. Salinity can reach as high as 1,500 mg/l in the western areas of Khan Yunis and the southeastern part of Rafah governorates, a concentration that makes growing many crops practically impossible. Equally severe is the problem of pollution from nitrates, due to the usual agricultural and sewage sources. Nitrate concentrations also have emerged as an acute public health problem, reaching up to 400 mg/l.

The Water and Soil Environmental Research Unit (WSERU) at Bethlehem University noted bacterial contamination of water from three of the Mekorot wells (Abed Rabbo et al. 1998). During pump testing of four of the new PWA wells, bacterial contamination was also detected (CDM/Morganti 1997; personal communication 2000; WSERU laboratory 2001). Karstic aquifer drainage allows rapid flow from the surface to below the water table, permitting colonial growth of coliform bacteria at depths around 250–280 m. Most of the wells penetrate the clay-marl seal separating the unconfined subaquifer from the confined subaquifer and reach depths of between 700 m and 800 m. Consideration of sectional profiles through the aquifer reveals that emptying the upper phreatic subaquifer seems very likely. Politicians and aid agencies deny that this is the case (PWA and USAID, personal communications 2000). Exploitation of the confined subaquifer will be considerably more expensive than that of the phreatic subaquifer. Conservation and sustainability, despite protests to the contrary, are not treated as a priority by those political and engineering agencies engaged in exploiting the aquifer.

The area to the south of Jerusalem has two distinct regions separated by the northeast to southwest axis of the anticlinal structure forming the Hebron Mountains that contain the southern part of the Mountain Aquifer. To the east the land descends from elevations exceeding 1,000 m to the Dead Sea, more than 400 m below sea level. Prevailing moist westerly airstreams deposit most of their load on the windward side of the Hebron Mountains. To the east a rain-shadow desert results from the descending air mass. To the west, springs have been the main source of water until recent times. For the Palestinian population, the eastern basins of the Mountain Aquifer are now the principal source of high-quality drinking water.

The results of past chemical analyses conducted offer a reasonable assessment of the suitability of the water for its designated purposes. Monitoring was based on internationally accepted chemical and biological standards for drinking water and other uses as published in WHO (1993). These results may be found in Abed Rabbo and Scarpa (2000, 2001).

The relative importance of the spring water for different groups depends on alternative sources of supply. Some communities are supplied with water derived from the deep aquifer and provided either by Israeli or Palestinian water authorities. Those lacking access to such sources utilize local spring discharge or, if they can afford it, buy water from privately owned or PWA water tankers.

A few villages have neither network provision nor direct access to any spring and cannot afford the expensive tanker water. Many households rely primarily on rainfall collection. But collection of rainwater in household cisterns depends on an uncertain precipitation during the winter season. Rainfall in the 2001–2002 seasons seemed to return to the 1961–1990 averages (Scarpa et al. 2002). Since that time, the very low rainfall of the subsequent rainy seasons brought considerable hardship to these villages.

Of the major springs sampled in each of the three seasons (end of the dry, middle of the wet, and end of the wet seasons), many were detected as having high nitrate concentrations and are contaminated by coliform bacteria, with more than 1,000 colonies/100 ml. Rainfall kept in home cisterns often serves to dilute the concentration of the nitrate and the bacteria.

In another study, a detailed chemical analysis of samples collected by WSERU from the shallow wells of two unconfined aquifer systems in the northern West Bank that are utilized for drinking water revealed substantial levels of pollution. With the low level of monitoring and regulation, there is a constant risk of potential health hazards. It is important that the Palestinian Water Authority effectively apply well-protection policies and monitor drinking-water quality.

The major sources of groundwater pollution in the northern part of the West Bank are ill-considered agricultural activities and careless wastewater disposal. Pollution due to agricultural activities is caused by an excessive use of fertilizer, coupled with over irrigation, facilitating passage though the unsaturated zone to the groundwater aquifer. Farmers in the West Bank use chemical fertilizers to improve their crops. The most commonly used fertilizers are ammonium sulfate, urea, potassium nitrate, and super phosphate. Therefore, the most important ions added to the recharge areas of the shallow aquifer are nitrate, ammonium, potassium, sulfate, and phosphate.

The pollution due to these agricultural activities is manifested in increasing levels of salinity (as measured by electrical conductivity) and nitrates. In some cases, high concentrations of potassium and sulfate are recorded. The concentration of potassium in the groundwater is normally low. This is because most of the potassium is absorbed by plants or adsorbed by mineral particles, particularly clay minerals, in the soil. Clear directives must be given to farmers concerning the safe application of fertilizers.

Uncontrolled wastewater disposal sometimes contaminates other waters, causing an increase particularly in electric conductivity (EC, an indicator of salinity) values and high concentrations of chloride, sodium, nitrate, and sulfate. In those areas not served by sewage systems, wastewater from septic tanks can pollute the shallow aquifer systems. Communities that are served with sewage systems frequently have leakages from the sewage network or from poorly sealed wastewater collection pools. This absence of an adequate infrastructure leaves raw sewage flowing from cesspits into wadis. In some cases, because of the karstic nature of the aquifers, there can be percolation into the groundwater systems. Facilities for solid waste disposal, another potential source of pollution of the aquifers, are also often inadequate.

Biological contamination is common among the shallow wells in the northern West Bank. A few of the wells were found to be chemically unsatisfactory for drinking-water purposes. It is important that these shallow wells be protected and rehabilitated, where possible, and that proper storage facilities be provided. This would facilitate upgrading the water to good potable standards by disinfection and other appropriate methods of treatment. Legislation preventing sewage disposal into wadis would provide some protection for the aquifer from this form of pollution. Cesspits are common, particularly in the rural villages, and present a pollution danger to the aquifer and spring discharge. Strict regulations requiring proper seals to cesspits or their replacement, where possible, with proper sewage networks could remove this danger. As mentioned, unregulated use of fertilizers has led to water quality degradation. This, together with excessive irrigation, a combination observed in some agricultural areas in the northern West Bank, is a source of contamination that could be avoided with proper legislation and implementation.

The quality of drinking water available from all sources, springs, rain-fed cisterns, and municipal delivery networks, is reduced even further during the dry periods, in many cases reaching levels of contamination that represent a danger to health. Reduced flow of water in springs also reduces the quality of the drinking water in those villages dependent on spring water for the drinking supply. This presents a serious health hazard, especially for the children. Significant incidences of amoebic dysentery among both children and adults were reported in most of the villages of this study (Scarpa 2000). The water supply from the springs and shallow wells could not accommodate even the basic domestic needs of the population.

Drinking Water in Gaza

The Gaza Strip has an area of 365 km² with a population of about 2 million Palestinians. The water quality of its aquifer has for many years been so poor as to constitute a hazard when it is pumped and delivered as drinking water. This phenomenon is not getting better. There continues to be a decline in water quality from the shallow coastal aquifers that are located in an interfingering complex of sands and sandstones separated by impermeable clay seals.

Direct rainwater infiltration is about 40 mcm/yr, while underground flow from the Mountain Aquifer can be 10–20 mcm/yr. However, a series of Israeli wells to the east of the Gaza border extracts a considerable amount of this westward-flowing groundwater. Excessive exploitation of the delicate Coastal Aquifer is unsustainable. But with domestic water availability being extremely low (about 60 l/day per capita) residents often seek to extract as much water as possible from the aquifers, legally or illegally.

Pollution to the aquifer there comes from the surface, from sewage flows, cesspits, agricultural wastes, pesticides, and fertilizers, and from seawater intrusion as a result of unregulated drilling and consequent pressure releases and from saline waters located under the coastal aquifers, again, rising as a result of pressure release. Agricultural use of water is inappropriate but continues because of livelihood pressures, cash cropping, and food security. Citrus is an extremely water-intensive crop but remains an important cash commodity for local and foreign markets as do other water-demanding crops. Wastewater treatment provides an increasing amount of irrigation water but is not treated sufficiently.

Since the PWA has taken responsibility in Gaza, losses through leakage from pipes have declined considerably. It seems unlikely that the Gaza Coastal Aquifer can be saved, even if the necessary but very difficult political decisions concerning water prioritization and allocation can be put into effect. Some form of desalination would seem to be essential for providing good-quality drinking water.

Conclusions

For the foreseeable future, Palestinians will continue to live under conditions of significant water stress. According to World Bank estimates, the present shortfall between demand and supply is 32%, but this will reach 55% in 2020. Given existing resources, it would seem that freshwater in the region should be reserved for domestic use, with treated wastewater supplying agriculture and industry. Half a century of mismanagement, including draining of wetlands and overpumping of aquifers, has reduced the quantity and quality of available water resources in the area.

The official position of the Palestinian Authority is that, in the long term, provided that Palestinians receive their full water rights, there will be a surplus for the West Bank population. This provision assumes that the present Israeli settlements in the West Bank will be evacuated, leaving only Palestinians with access to the West Bank aquifers. It is to be hoped that the final status agreements reached in the bilateral peace talks between Israeli and Palestinian negotiators might lead to a more responsible shared management of these scarce water resources.

REFERENCES

Abed Rabbo, A., D. J. Scarpa. 2000. *A comprehensive study of the water resources of the southern Mediterranean drainage from the Mountain Aquifer*. Final implementation report to Ireland Aid. Bethlehem: WSERU, Bethlehem University.

Abed Rabbo, A., and D. J. Scarpa. Forthcoming. *Public dissemination program to raise awareness of water quality in the southern West Bank*. Implementation report to Ireland Aid, 2000–2001. Bethlehem: WSERU, Bethlehem University.

Abed Rabbo, A., D. J. Scarpa, and Z. Qannam. 1998. A study of the water quality and hydrochemistry of the Herodion-Beit Fajjar wells. *Bethlehem University Journal* 17:10–28.

Abu Ju'ub, G. 1998. *Regional plan for the West Bank governorates: Water and wastewater—existing situation*. Ramallah: Ministry of Planning and International Cooperation.

Aliewi, A., and A. Jarra. 2000. *Technical assessment of the potentiality of the Herodian wellfield against additional well development programmes*. Ramallah: Palestinian Water Authority.

Allan, J. A. 1997. "Virtual water": A long-term solution for water short Middle Eastern economies? Paper presented at the 1997 British Association Festival of Science, Water, and Development Session. University of Leeds.

———. 2001. *The Middle East water question: Hydropolitics and the global economy*. London: I. B. Tauris.

CDM/Morganti. 1997. Two-stage well development study for additional supplies in the West Bank, State 2: Well development study. Task 19, USAID for PWA.

CH2MHILL. 2003. Personal communication. West Bank Production and Monitoring Wells, November 1, 2003.

De Bruijne, G., J. Moorehead, and W. Odeh. 2000. *Water for Palestine: A critical assessment of the European Investment Bank's lending strategy in the rehabilitation of water resources in the southern West Bank*. Jerusalem: Palestinian Hydrology Group.

Farinelli, X. H. 1997. *Fresh water conflicts in the Jordan River Basin*. Geneva, Switzerland: Green Cross International.

Feitelson, E., and M. Haddad. 2001. *Management of shared groundwater resources: The Israeli-Palestinian case with an international perspective*. Dordrecht: Kluwer Academic Publishers.

Gass, G., A. MacKenzie, Y. Nasser, and D. Grey. Forthcoming. Groundwater resources degradation in the West Bank: Socio-economic impact and their mitigations (1st draft). Wallingford: British Geological Survey.

Guttman, J. 2000. Hydrogeology of the eastern aquifer in the Judea Hills and Jordan Valley. Multi-lateral project 02WT9719 within the framework of the German-Israeli-Jordanian-Palestinian Joint Research Program for the Sustainable Utilization of Aquifer Systems, Sub Project B, Final Report No.468, Tel Aviv.

Isaac, J., and M. Saade. 1999. *Strategic options for sustainable natural resource management in Palestine*. Bethlehem: ARIJ.

Israel-Palestinian Bilateral Negotiating Team. 1995. Water supply and sewage disposal. *Interim Accords, Article 40*, Washington.

Ministry of Environmental Affairs. 2000. *Palestinian environmental strategy: Main report*. 2nd ed. Al-Bireh: Palestinian National Authority.

———. 2001. *Water resource programme phase III*. Hebron Wastewater Master Plan. Jerusalem: Palestinian National Authority.

Ministry of Planning and International Cooperation. 1998a. *Sensitive water resources recharge areas in the West Bank governorates: Emergency natural resources protection plan*. 2nd ed. Ramallah: Directorate for Urban and Rural Planning.

———. 1998b. *Map 7 valuable agricultural land in the West Bank governorates: Emergency natural resources protection plan*. 2nd ed. Ramallah: Directorate for Urban and Rural Planning.

———. 1998c. *National policies for physical development: The West Bank and Gaza governorates*. Jerusalem: Directorate for Urban and Rural Planning.

Palestinian Central Bureau of Statistics. 1997. *The demographic survey in the West Bank and Gaza Strip: Final report*. Report. Ramallah.

Palestinian Economical Council for Development and Reconstruction. 2001. *People under siege*. Report. Ramallah.

Palestinian Water Authority (PWA). 1999. *Water sector strategic planning study*. Vol. 3: *Specialist Studies, Part B: Focal Areas*. Report. Ramallah.

PASSIA. 2000, 2001, 2003, 2004. Palestinian Academic Society for the Study of International Affairs. Report. Jerusalem.

Scarpa, D. J. 1994. Eastward groundwater flow from the Mountain Aquifer. In *Water for Peace in the Middle East*, ed. J. Isaac and H. Shuval, 193–203. Amsterdam: Elsevier Science Publications.

———. 2000. The sustainability of Palestinian hill villages to the west of the hydrologic divide in the southern West Bank. *Water Science and Technology* 42:1–2, 331–336.

———. 2004. *Water resources and the sustainability of towns and villages in the Bethlehem and Hebron governorates, Palestine*. PhD diss., London University.

Scarpa, D. J., M. Abed Rabbo, R. Zeitoun, and A. Abed Rabbo. 2002. Rainfall in Bethlehem (1992–2002). *Bethlehem University Journal* 21:39–45.

World Health Organization. 1993. *Guidelines for drinking-water quality*. 2nd ed., vol. 1. Recommendations. Geneva.

WSERU Laboratory. 2001. Data base, Bethlehem University, Palestine.

Israeli Drinking-Water Resources and Supply

RAMY HALPERIN

Sources of Natural Waters in Israel

Fresh drinking-water supply in Israel is based on three principal sources: two groundwater aquifers, the Coastal Aquifer and the Mountain Aquifer (the latter is also known as the Yarqon-Taninim Aquifer), and one surface water source, the Lake Kinneret basin. In addition, there are a number of other minor water sources. The Coastal Aquifer extends along the Mediterranean Sea shore, from Haifa in the north to the Gaza Strip in the south. The primary quality of the water in this aquifer was once excellent, with low salinity and no pollution, but over the years this aquifer has become the most severely polluted of the three main sources. Causes for the pollution include the following:

1. The greater part of Israel's population is concentrated in the areas overlying the Coastal Aquifer, and large industrial plants are still located over this area. Urban and industrial activities in the overlying area have resulted in the penetration of pollutants into the aquifer. The main pollutants include fuel products, heavy metals, toxic organic materials, and many micro-pollutants. The heavy metals, organic materials, and micro-pollutants can cause many illnesses, including cancer and other fatal illnesses.
2. The Coastal Aquifer has undergone a process of salinization as a result of pumping in excess of its natural replenishment, irrigation with water from the Kinneret Basin (which has relatively high salinity levels), as well as irrigation with reclaimed wastewater. The chloride content of the water detracts from its suitability for agricultural irrigation, whereas its effect on potable water quality is secondary.
3. Irrigation with effluents and the general fertilization of agricultural crops give rise to an increased concentration of nitrate in the water. The nitrogen oxides (nitrates) in the drinking water may cause illness to day-old babies, such as blue-baby syndrome (cyanosis).

Water quality in the Mountain Aquifer is generally excellent. Yet, the water is exposed to a variety of pollutants that arises from the wastewater and other pollutants from settlements that are located over this area. Israel is making many efforts to prevent the penetration of sewage or chemical contamination to the Kinneret water and keep this water safe for drinking. Yet, the water has a high level of natural salinity, which flows into the lake from the encircling aquifers.

Illness Associated with Drinking Water in Israel

Israel experienced a large number of waterborne disease outbreaks between 1975 and 1985, followed by a steep decline in such episodes between 1986 and 1992. Large-scale community waterborne disease outbreaks occurred primarily in 1970 and 1985. A massive public health insult caused by drinking-water contamination occurred in the Krayot—the suburban region north of Haifa—in 1985. The event was attributed to a break in a sewage pipeline that was laid near a drinking-water well. Water supplied to residents of the Krayot caused intestinal diseases for more than ten thousand people. Water-associated morbidity declined from about five per year between 1976 and 1985 to less than one case per year between 1986 and 1992 and ceased entirely after that. It is believed that the mandatory chlorination of all community water supplies and more stringent microbiological standards, which came into effect in 1988, were the main reasons for the dramatic progress.

The Evolution of Drinking-Water Treatment and Standards

Drinking-water quality standards are intended to assure the health of the water consumers and to provide palatable water because it is important that one drinks enough water, especially in the generally warm prevailing climate. This means that the color, taste, and the smell of the water must be adequate. Drinking-water standards all over the world are changing in recent years, to a great extent due to the enhanced capacity to detect pollutants in minute concentrations as well as new health research findings.

Israeli standards conform to general regulatory patterns found in international drinking-water criteria, such as guidelines promulgated by the World Health Organization, directives of the European Communities, and U.S. EPA regulations. In Israel, a guidance document was in effect until 1974. At that time the Ministry of Health issued the Drinking-Water Quality Regulations. These regulations have been updated about every 10 years and recently were reviewed by a special expert's committee known as the Adin Committee (after the chairman's last name). The regulations include microbial, chemical, physical, and radiological standards as well as monitoring-frequency requirements for each of these groups of standards. In general, the committee recommended that Israeli drinking-water standards be set at more stringent levels.

Since Israeli regulations are based on the leading international bodies regulating drinking-water quality, including the U.S. EPA., the WHO, and the EU, standards adopted in the Israeli regulations are generally consistent with international norms. Israeli drinking-water standards are divided between recommended levels and required levels. In some cases, such as with nitrates, there are modest differences between the concentrations that are actually allowed and the more stringent recommended standards.

Microbial Standards

Detection of pathogenic bacteria is very difficult. All microbial standards are therefore based on the detection of indicator bacteria. These standards are very strict,
since small quantities of pathogenic bacteria can cause immediate illness to the
water consumer. Israeli standards strive to ensure that water contains no fecal coliform bacteria. In the past, international rules allowed up to ten coliform bacteria
per 100 ml of water. This number was later reduced to three and later to zero in
more than 95% of the water sampled. The Israeli standards presently allow up to
three coliform bacteria per 100 ml water, but the Adin Committee has already
decided to reduce it to zero, commensurate with other international standards.

In order to assure this standard and prevent the entry of parasites into drinking
water, the committee suggests that all surface water be filtered (by deep sand filtration) before entering the drinking-water network. The existing regulations also
require that all the drinking water in Israel contain active chlorine, in order to prevent contamination within the water network.

Chemical Standards

Chemical standards are intended to ensure public health over a consumer's lifetime. Accordingly, stringent values are set, based on empirical data suggesting that
chronic exposure to these concentrations poses no risk of illness. The Israeli chemical standards are generally similar to those of the U.S. EPA standards or the WHO
recommendations and also were reviewed by the expert's committee.

Chemical contamination of the aquifer waters makes it necessary to treat some
of the water in order to reduce the level of contamination. One of the methods to
reduce contamination of the water is by dilution of the contaminant with water
that contains a low level of a particular substance. The Ministry of Health now
allows the dilution method only for organoleptic pollutants (chlorides) or other
semi-natural contaminants, like nitrates. The Adin Committee recommended that
the dilution of all natural contaminations be allowed as an effective strategy to
reduce the use of chemicals in the process of the treatment.

Water Parasites and Viruses

Parasites (giardia and cryptosporidium) and viruses in drinking water have already
caused serious outbreaks of illness in numerous countries. The detection and elimination of such parasites and viruses are very difficult since the chlorination has a
very low effect on them. Thus, the U.S. EPA requires adequate filtration of all surface water to ensure a reduction of water parasite and virus presence by two to four
orders of magnitude. The Adin Committee has demanded such treatment for all
upper waters in Israel, so the turbidity of the filtered water will be not more than
0.1–0.2 NTU. (The units of turbidity from a calibrated nephelometer are called
nephelometric turbidity units (NTU).

Physical Characteristics of Drinking Water

The physical characteristics of drinking water include parameters such as the turbidity, pH, taste, odor, and color of the water that influence the palatability of the

water. Turbidity also has important health effects because it can prevent effective disinfection of the water. Therefore, over the past few decades, the maximum allowable turbidity in water was reduced from 25 NTU thru 5 NTU to 1 NTU under existing regulations. The reduction of the maximum allowed turbidity to 1 NTU has led to the filtering of most of the surface water that is utilized for drinking, including water of the national carrier that derived from the Sea of Galilee (Lake Kinneret).

The Adin Committee is now discussing a suggestion to reduce it to 0.5 NTU within the water network and to 0.1 NTU after the filtration of surface water. Such strict turbidity standards and the requisite filtration are intended to prevent the passage of parasites from surface water to the treated water.

Disinfection and Disinfection By-products

Israeli regulations mandate the disinfection of all drinking water and demand that all of the water supply contain between 0.1 to 0.5 ppm of chlorine (or other disinfectants) in order to disinfect any contamination that can penetrate into the water network. This is essential for protection of the microbial quality of the water. On the other hand, it is well known that each disinfection process causes the formation of harmful disinfection by-products, and it is necessary that they be reduced. The main problem arises in the disinfection of surface water (such as Kinneret water) with chlorine because of the formation of trihalomethanes (which are suspected to cause cancer). The ozonation of the Kinneret water is also problematic since it contains a high concentration of bromine, and the ozonation can cause the formation of bromide, which is also harmful to health.

The water of the Israeli National Water Career (that supplies the Kinneret water) is disinfected using chlorine dioxide (ClO_2) as a strong sterilizer, followed by chloramines as a disinfectant that remains in the water system for prolonged periods (table 7.1).

Monitoring of Drinking-Water Quality

Israeli regulations require that the supplier of the water control and supervise the quality of water supplies at a frequency specified by the regulation. There is a basic difference in monitoring frequency between microbial and the chemical water tests. Bacterial contamination of the water may cause illness after drinking the water only once. Therefore the regulations require the frequent testing of the bacterial quality of the water, with monthly testing in small settlements and daily testing in large cities (population over 200,000).

The standards for chemical parameters are set at a level which permits the drinking of the water for a lifetime without excess morbidity, and therefore the frequency of the chemical testing is low. The intervals between the testing of water sources fluctuate between 1 to 6 years, according to the level of contamination that was found earlier in the water.

According to the regulations, testing of the water quality must be done by the water supplier, including the local municipality that supplies the water to its

Table 7.1 Summary of the existing Israeli drinking-water standards

Organic substances

1. Volatile organic compounds (V.O.C.)

Element or compound	Maximum level (mg/l) [A]	[B]
Benzene	0.01	0.005
Benzo(a)pyrene	0.0007	0.0005
Dichlorobenzene (1,2)	1	0.6
Dichlorobenzene (1,4)	0.3	0.075
Dichloroethane (1,2)	0.005	0.004
Dichloroethylene (1,1)	0.03	0.01
Dichloroethylene (1,2)	0.1	0.05
Trichloroethane (1,1,1)	0.2	
Trichloroethylene	0.05	0.03
Tetrachloroethylene	0.04	0.01
Chloroform	0.1	0.08
Carbon tetrachloride	0.005	
Monochlorobenzene	0.3	0.1
Formaldehyde	0.9	
Toluene	0.7	
Xylene	1	0.5

2. Pesticides & herbicides

Element or compound	Maximum level (mg/l) [A]	[B]
Ethylene dibromide	0.00005	
Lindane	0.002	0.001
Alachlor	0.02	0.004
Heptachlor	0.0004	
Chlordane	0.002	0.001
Methoxychlor	0.02	
Endrine	0.002	
Atrazine	0.002	
DBCP (1,2 Dibromo-3-chloropropane)	0.001	0.0003
Aldicarb	0.01	
Trifluralin	0.02	
2,4,5 TP (Silvex)	0.01	
Simazine	0.002	
Permethrin	0.02	
DDT	0.002	0.001

Parameter	[A]	[B]
Styrene	0.05	
Organoleptic effect parameters		
Zinc	5	
Iron	1	
Total solids	1,500	
Chloride	600	400
Anionic detergents	1	0.5
Copper	1.4	
Magnesium	150	
Manganese	0.5	0.2
Phenols	0.002	
Oil and grease	0.3	
Turbidity	1 NTU	
pH	6.5–9.5	
Taste and odor	Acceptable	
Color "platinum cobalt"	15	
Fluoride	1.7	
Radioactive radiation		
Effective radioactivity/person	0.1 mSV/yr	

Parameter	[A]	[B]
2.4-D (Dichlorphenoxy acetic acid)	0.03	
Vinyl chloride	0.002	
Trihalomethanes (total)	0.1	
Monochloroamines	3	
Di(-ethyl-hexyl-phthalate)	0.008	
(di-octil-phthalate)		
Inorganic substances		
Arsenic	0.05	0.01
Barium	1	
Mercury	0.001	
Chromium	0.05	
Nickel	0.05	0.02
Selenium	0.01	
Lead	0.01	
Cyanide	0.05	
Cadmium	0.005	
Silver	0.01	
Nitrates	70	

Note: [A] equals the existing values; [B] equals the recommendations of the Adin Committee. Sulphates are 437.5 ppm, minus 1.25 times the concentration of magnesium.

residents. Supervision and enforcement of the regulations is conducted by the Ministry of Health.

Trends in Drinking-Water Quality

Israel has suffered over the years from a shortage of freshwater; moreover, existing sources of natural water (especially the Coastal Aquifer) continue to suffer contamination and are thus excluded from supplying drinking water. As a result, Israel has begun desalinizing seawater to increase its water resources. It is anticipated that the contamination of the water resources will continue and Israel will be forced to increase the production of desalinized water.

The decline in the quality of the water resources raises the question of how the quality of the drinking-water supply is improving. The explanation is that each contaminated source of water is excluded from supplying drinking water (usually it is transferred to supply agricultural irrigation), and so the drinking-water system receives only high-quality water.

Bottled Water

In Israel many people drink bottled water. One of the plausible explanations for the phenomenon is the actual taste of the water itself. The taste of the chlorinated Kinneret water, which supplies most cities of Israel via the National Water Carrier, is often deemed offensive and may increase the desire to drink bottled water. A new large filtration plant that treats all the National Water Carrier water has begun operation and has improved its taste to some degree. Other reasons for consumer preference for bottled water may be the reports in newspapers, electronic media, and even the reports of the state comptroller, which do not distinguish between the contamination of the water in the aquifers and the better quality of the drinking water in the water supply network.

Conclusion

Israel's drinking-water quality has improved dramatically over its history. Standards have been steadily more stringent, consistent with international trends and expectations. Even as the quality of water resources themselves have deteriorated, water management interventions have for the most part prevented contamination at the faucet. Yet the public in Israel seems to be losing confidence in the quality of its drinking water and shows a preference for bottled water, its high price not withstanding.

REFERENCES

Council Directive 98/83/EC of 3 November 1998 on the quality of water intended for human consumption. http://europa.eu/legislation_summaries/environment/water_protection_management/l28079_en.htm (accessed July 20, 2009).

Halperin, R., and A. Adin. 2002. Treatment of polluted groundwater in Israel: Problems, costs and benefits (in Hebrew). http://geography.huji.ac.il/emppp/courses/Adin's%20lecture.doc (accessed July 20, 2009).

Ministry of Health, State of Israel. 2000. *Israeli sanitary quality of drinking water, 1974.* Consolidated version (English translation of the Hebrew original). Jerusalem: Ministry of Health.

Shelef, G., R. Halperin, and N. Icekson-Tal. 2007. Fifty years of wastewater reuse in Israel. In *Wastewater reclamation and reuse for sustainability,* ed. I. S. Kim, J. Cho, and S. Kim. Selected papers from the 5th International Conference on Wastewater Reclamation and Reuse for Sustainability (WRRS2005), held in Jeju Island, Korea, November 8–11, 2005. IWA Publishers.

Tulchinsky, T. H., et al. 1993. Water quality, water borne disease and enteric disease in Israel, 1976–92. *Israel Journal of Medical Sciences* 29(12):783–790.

U.S. EPA. 2004. 2004 edition of the drinking-water standards and health advisories, EPA 822-R-04–005. http://www.epa.gov/waterscience/drinking/standards/dwstandards.pdf (accessed November 8, 2009).

World Health Organization (WHO). (2004). Guidelines for drinking-water quality. 3rd ed. http://www.who.int/water_sanitation_health/dwq/gdwq3/en/ (accessed November 8, 2009).

There is a significant gap in the quality of drinking water available to Palestinian and Israeli households. While Israel's drinking-water quality has largely improved, there are many examples of chronic contamination in Palestinian West Bank communities. Drinking much of the water supplied in the Gaza Strip has for some time been defined as unhealthy.

For the foreseeable future, Palestinian and Israeli drinking-water systems will remain intertwined. Today some 40.3 mcm of drinking water is supplied by Israel's Mekorot water utility to houses in the West Bank—well over 60% of present municipal use. An additional 3.2 mcm of water is still delivered by Mekorot to the Gaza Strip. This is among the highest-quality water presently available. To change the associated infrastructure and piping that supply this water will take many years and may not make hydrological or economic sense. This means that drinking-water standards between the two parties must at least be harmonized and in the long run should probably be identical.

While economic differences exist, the reality is that if Palestinian municipalities provide drinking water that is of poor quality, the population will simply choose to purchase bottled water. This constitutes a disproportionate economic burden on the poorest populations. Bottled water currently sells at rates of 36¢/l in the West Bank. While this is orders of magnitude higher than tap water, large segments of the population are paying for it.

Adopting tougher drinking-water standards through harmonization in and of itself will not be enough to improve the Palestinian situation. There are fundamental infrastructure measures which will be required for the present contamination to be reduced. For example, septic tanks will need to be cemented so that wastewater does not escape and percolate directly into the ground and reach drinking-water sources. Cisterns, which in many Palestinian villages are so critical for capturing rainwater, are subject to considerable biologically contamination from bacterial outbreak, bird excrement, and waterborne diseases. Because taps have filters, the population is frequently unaware of the actual water quality and illness is common. Education along with drinking-water protection measures and disinfection kits are needed. Establishing and upgrading sewage treatment is, of course, a critical effort in virtually every Palestinian community. Here, it may make more sense to have differential standards, dependent on the ultimate use of the effluent and its potential to contaminate water resources. In either case, efforts to upgrade Palestinian water infrastructure will be extremely costly for a society whose resources are quite limited.

Accordingly, a steady process of ratcheting down drinking-water contaminant levels is envisioned by Palestinian experts. They compare their situation to Israel's experience. Initial Israeli drinking-water standards were low and gradually became more demanding as the country's economic conditions improved. For instance, Israel understood that a standard of 90 mg/l was desirable for nitrates but couldn't afford it. Today it can make this commitment. The same is true of the BOD standard for sewage treatment. Today plants are expected to drop to 10 mg/l, whereas initial standards could only require that sewage sit for 5 days in an oxidation pond.

Palestinians also envision a steady phase-in of higher-quality drinking-water standards. It can be argued that the present contamination is so severe with pollutants that cause acute health effects (e.g., bacterial pollutants) that the correct approach should be impatience and intolerance for low standards. But for many drinking-water standards, a gradual ratcheting-down strategy, based on clear timetables and quantitative targets, is one which should be considered favorably by Israeli negotiators, if common drinking-water standards become a negotiating topic.

Because Palestinians receive considerable water from springs, there must be better monitoring to ensure their integrity. But again, while identifying polluted water sources is important for public health, it will not change the need to address the actual pollution sources. The Palestinian Water Authority envisions a decentralization process by which local municipalities will play a larger role in monitoring drinking-water quality. This will require consider upgrading in human capacity, laboratory and field kits, etc. This is an important area for international assistance which will both improve public health and strengthen human and scientific capacity in a new Palestinian state.

A broader, strategic question that needs to be considered in negotiations is the effect of "privatization" of water resources. While Palestinians are used to the present system, which accommodates private rights, there may be less tolerance for the traditional system as scarcity becomes more severe due to population growth and expanded contamination. Yet, nationalization of drinking-water supply systems may not be an optimal solution either. Creating a regional water market has been widely advocated as an important step not only for depoliticizing water issues, but also for improving water quality. As bottled water consumption becomes a more prevalent solution, there is a slow shift in perceptions regarding drinking water. Where once people expected to be able to receive their drinking water free or at trivial prices from the tap or the well, many households now budget water as an essential commodity. Creating regional water utilities will allow households, presumably on both sides of the border, to purchase high-quality drinking water at a fraction of the price which is now spent on bottled water.

PART 8

SEWAGE TREATMENT

From a practical standpoint, upgrading sewage treatment constitutes the single most important priority for improving water quality. The rapid population growth in both Israel and Palestine has increased the quantities of wastewater produced, while there has not been a concomitant expansion of associated infrastructure. Given Israel's dependence on wastewater recycling as a source for irrigation, the quality of effluents has special importance. This part considers the issue of sewage treatment from the perspectives of the two sides.

Sewage Treatment in Gaza and the Quest to Upgrade Infrastructure

KHALIL TUBAIL

The Gaza Strip is one of the most densely populated areas in the world with a population of 1,472,000 in 2005 and an area of only 365 km^2. The Gaza Strip is located in a semi-arid area where water resources are scarce. Due to increasing groundwater pumping for human use as well as for irrigation purposes, the extraction of groundwater currently exceeds the recharge of the groundwater aquifers. As a result, the groundwater level is falling and the salinity is increasing, making the water unsuitable either for human consumption or for irrigation purposes. The environmental situation in the Gaza Strip is critical: depletion of water resources, deterioration of water quality, shoreline and marine pollution, and land degradation. This needs regional and international efforts to enhance and protect it.

Reclaimed wastewater reuse for agriculture has been recognized as an essential component in the management strategy for water shortage in the neighboring countries. In arid and semi-arid countries, reuse of treated wastewater in agriculture is gaining more attention in planning and developing strategies for Palestinian water resources as it represents an additional renewable and reliable water source, which would reduce the water deficit and the decline in groundwater quantity and quality.

There are several benefits in using treated wastewater. Using treated wastewater for irrigation will reduce the demand on the groundwater for irrigation, will preserve high-quality and expensive freshwater for potable use, and will reduce the degradation of the groundwater quality. Collecting and treating wastewater protects existing sources of valuable freshwater, the environment, and public health. If managed properly, treated wastewater can sometimes be a superior source for agriculture. It is a constant water source, and nitrogen and phosphorous in the wastewater may result in higher agricultural yields than with freshwater irrigation, negating the need for additional fertilizer application.

Current Situation of Wastewater in the Gaza Strip

Currently, there are three wastewater treatment plants (WWTPs) in operation in the Gaza Strip, receiving about 24 mcm of raw sewage per year. These are the Beit Lahia, Gaza, and Rafah WWTPs (table 8.1). In the middle zone there is no WWTP; instead, wastewater is collected through sewage network and pumps directly into Wadi Gaza without any treatment. Such a sewage network was recently established

Table 8.1 Wastewater treatment plants existing in Gaza governorates

Governorate	Name of WWTP	Year of establishment	% population connected	Processes	Inflow mcm/yr	Outflow
Northern	Beit Lahia	1978	78	2 anaerobic ponds, 2 aerated lagoons, and 3 stabilized ponds	2.8[a] 5.5[b]	Surrounding sand dunes (artificial lake)
Gaza	Gaza	1977	85	2 anaerobic ponds, 1 aerated lagoon, and 2 trickling filters	11.7[a] 19.8[b]	Mediterranean Sea and Wadi Gaza
Mid Zone	—	1997	70	No treatment	0.0[a] 3.5[b]	Wadi Gaza
Khan Younis	—	2004	25	Not operated	—	—
Rafah	Rafah	1982	60	1 aerated pond and 1 lagoon	0.7[a] 2.7[b]	Mediterranean Sea

Source: Palestinian Water Authority, 2005.

[a] Designed flow.

[b] Actual flow.

in Khan Younis Governorate to serve only 25% of the population; however, this network is not operating now and the people are still widely using cesspools.

The existing WWTPs currently produce primary and secondary effluents based on the pond system of treatment. As a result of rapid population growth, the actual flow of the three WWTPs far exceeds the design flow, leading to overloading and flooding of wastewater. Such floods in the Beit Lahia WWTP created an artificial lake of about 35 hectares (ha) in the surrounding sand dunes. Most of the effluent produced in the Gaza WWTP is discharged to Wadi Gaza, and from there it flows to the Mediterranean Sea, representing a significant loss of water resources and a violation of the international ban on land-based source discharges into the sea. The biological and chemical properties of effluent of the Gaza WWTP for 2005 are shown in table 8.2.

Effluent from the existing Gaza WWTP is currently being used by farmers through pilot projects funded by the Spanish and French governments, principally

Table 8.2 Current effluent quality (chemical and biological)
of the Gaza wastewater treatment plant

Parameter	Value	Unit
BOD	37.3 (74[a])	mg/l
COD	111.2 (230[a])	mg/l
TSS	59.1 (175[a])	mg/l
Ph	7.79	
EC	3.13	mmhos/cm
Ammonium-N	72.6	mg/l NH_4^+
Nitrate	35.9	mg/l as NO_3^-
Chloride	576.4	mg/l as Cl^-
Sulfate	128.9	mg/l as SO_4^{-2}
Potassium	31.3	mg/l as K^+
Sodium	377.5	mg/l as Na^+
Alkalinity	520	mg/l as $CaCO_3$
Copper	0.6	mg/l as Cu^+
Boron	1.2	mg/l as B
Fecal coliform	2.6E+06	CFU/100 cm

Source: Palestinian Water Authority, 2005.

[a] Average values of months January, February, and March 2007

for irrigation of citrus and olive trees in the Gaza area (around 10 ha) and forage crops in the northern area (4 ha).

It is proposed to construct three new WWTPs in the north, middle, and south zones of the Gaza Strip that will replace the existing ones, with an effluent capacity reaching 116.8 mcm by 2020. Effective and economical management of the effluent reuse system is essential for the long-term success. With the planned construction of three regional WWTPs, it is widely recognized that the treated effluent will provide an opportunity to reduce the current reliance of farmers on groundwater for irrigation both by direct supplies to farm land and indirectly by recharge to the aquifer.

Effluent Standards

Palestinian standards for effluent quality and limit values for its reuse are broadly consistent with those of neighboring countries. Standards for effluent reuse have recently been adopted (PWA 2003). Four classes of effluent quality are recognized (table 8.3), classified by BOD, TSS, and fecal coliform concentrations. The heavy

Table 8.3 Classification of effluent quality (PS 742/2003)

Class	Quality	BOD (mg/l)	TSS (mg/l)	Fecal coliform (MPN/100 ml)
A	High	20	30	200
B	Good	20	30	1,000
C	Medium	40	50	1,000
D	Low	60	90	1,000

Table 8.4 Comparison of expected effluent quality from Central Gaza WWTP with local quality standards

Parameter	Expected effluent quality new WWTP	Palestinian standard (PS 742/2003)	
		IRRIGATION	RECHARGE
BOD (mg/l)	20	20–60	20
TSS (mg/l)	30	30–90	30
TDS (mg/l)	1,800	1,500	1,500
EC (μS/cm)	2,700	—	—
T-N (mg/l)	25	45[a]	100[a]
Na (mg/l)	430	200	230
Cl (mg/l)	550	500	600
SAR	8	9	—
B (mg/l)	0.6	0.7	1
F. coliforms (MPN/100 ml)	10^6	200–1,000	200–1,000

[a] Sum of nitrate, ammonia, and organic N limit values.

metal limit concentrations given in the Palestinian standards fall broadly in line with values commonly adopted internationally. The following hygiene standards, consistent with WHO guidelines, are recommended for effluent reuse in irrigation. Fecal coliform (FC) is used as an indicator of potential pathogen content in the effluent at the point of irrigation:

- <1,000 MPN (most probable number) FC/100 ml for restricted reuse, including crops normally eaten cooked and fruit from trees, etc.
- <200 MPN FC/100 ml for unrestricted reuse, including crops normally consumed uncooked and green areas with public access.
- <1 nematode ovum/l for all reuse by irrigation

Effluent Management Concept

It is by now well established that treated effluent must play a key role in re-establishing a water balance in the Coastal Aquifer to aid sustainable development in the Gaza Strip. This will require farmers to substitute effluents for groundwater as the principal irrigation source, wherever feasible, and require effluent that is surplus to agricultural demand to be recharged to the aquifer.

Such a strategy is recognized as optimal and could be implemented in an integrated and flexible manner, according to strategic water management decisions and demands for water. Irrigation of agricultural crops is the only feasible option for the direct reuse of treated effluent and will also reduce the reliance of farmers on wells. Existing irrigated crops that are currently suffering yield reductions due to the high salinity of the groundwater, particularly citrus in the area, should recover some of their yield potential and return to more economic levels. In addition, aquifer recharge by strategically located infiltration ponds is clearly identified as a crucial component of effluent reuse strategies in Gaza. The major advantages with regard to the local water resources are the recovery of declining groundwater levels and reduction of salinization of the aquifer from seawater intrusion and upconing of saline water. For recharge purposes, the hydrogeological conditions in Gaza Strip will provide effective filtering of any pathogens within the surface layer. Nonetheless, additional treatment of effluent at the WWTP would be advisable to minimize the loading of solids on the filtration surface.

It is also clear that discharge of treated effluent to Wadi Gaza has the potential to improve the environmental conditions and recreational potential of the area. But for this and other initiatives to be implemented, there needs to be an expressed willingness to use and pay for reclaimed water. One of the main concerns is willingness of farmers to use treated wastewater for agriculture. A number of surveys have been conducted in the context of studies on the reuse of reclaimed water which dispel concerns about cultural barriers to wastewater recycling. In the northern area, 86.1% of all interviewed farmers accepted the use of reclaimed water for irrigation (Tubail et al. 2004).

The general acceptance level for using reclaimed water for irrigation in Gaza and the middle area is also very high (89.9% of all farmers). The most important reason for wanting to use reclaimed water as an alternative to groundwater is related to anticipated higher incomes, either due to irrigation cost reductions or improved yields. On average, farmers would be willing to pay 0.36 shekels/m³. Farmers expressed a number of concerns about reclaimed water regardless of their acceptance or refusal to use it for irrigation. Their principal concern is that customers might refuse to buy their products if they become aware about the source of irrigation water.

Strategic Assumptions and Implications

Future Palestinian sewage policy relies on several assumptions: that farmers are willing to use and pay for effluent; that the quality of the effluent is suitable for the intended outlets and in compliance with appropriate standards; that the cropping

Table 8.5 Criteria recommended by PWA for effluent standards in
the Gaza Strip

Criteria	Recharge by infiltration	Restricted irrigation	Unrestricted irrigation
BOD (mg/l)	10–20	10–20	10–20
SS (mg/l)	15–25	15–20	15–20
T-N (mg/l)	10–15	10–15	10–15
Helminths (no./l)	—	<1	<1
Fecal coliform (no./100 ml)	—	<1,000	<200

practices of farmers can be controlled to ensure that specific crops (mainly vegetables) are not grown where restricted reuse is necessary; and that the Coastal Aquifer can accept large quantities of effluent by artificial recharge at appropriate locations that will benefit groundwater levels and reduce saline intrusion.

Potential Impacts

The main implications of the current Palestinian effluent reuse standards are that some parameters are significantly more stringent than the well-established WHO and FAO guidelines. For example, the limit values set for salinity and chloride concentrations according to the Palestinian standards would prevent any reuse of effluent in agriculture or aquifer recharge. The standards would also set a limit for effluent recharge of 25 mg N/l and an equivalent concentration of 110 mg NO_3/l. At this level, the effect would be to increase, or at least maintain, the currently high concentrations of nitrates in groundwater. Exclusion of all vegetable crops from effluent irrigation, however, is considered unnecessarily restrictive since the hygienic standards for effluent are appropriate for unrestricted reuse and meet the WHO guidelines.

The area in Gaza in which vegetables are grown has increased from 26% of the agricultural land to 44% during the last years. A fecal coliform limit of less than 200 MPN/100 ml should be adopted for unrestricted reuse on all crops. For irrigation and aquifer recharge, PWA has already recommended criteria for effluent quality standards in Gaza as shown in table 8.5.

Additional Effluent Treatment

The new Palestinian WWTPs must be designed to achieve an effluent quality suitable for discharge into Wadi Gaza. However, for reuse, additional effluent treatment is considered necessary to achieve disinfection of fecal microbes. Sewage treatment should reach a level that will permit unrestricted reuse for irrigation. The minimum level of pathogen and parasite removal should achieve WHO guidelines (fecal coliforms <1,000 MPN/100 ml and nematodes <1 ovum/l).

The technical means to achieve this have been reviewed; and from a practicable, environmental, and economic perspective, rapid sand filtration and UV disinfection are reliable methods to achieve this.

Excess nitrogen also needs remediation. The design of the WWTP is expected to achieve a maximum total nitrogen concentration in effluent of 25 mg N/l. Further reduction of nitrogen is considered necessary for the recharge of effluent to protect the groundwater from additional loading of nitrate and to allow gradual rehabilitation of groundwater quality. A standard of 10 mg N/l is broadly equivalent to the WHO standard for nitrates in drinking water and is considered appropriate. In order to reach these concentrations, oxygen must be provided during wastewater treatment by aeration. The second step of nitrogen removal, denitrification, is the reduction of the nitrate to elemental nitrogen (N_2).

Both irrigation and aquifer recharge of effluents require a low content of total suspended solids (TSS). Effluents with low suspended solids are also necessary to reduce the risk of clogging drip irrigation emitters and the infiltration surface of recharge ponds.

The WWTP will need to be designed to achieve about 30 mg TSS/l, which is acceptable for irrigation and recharge; but for efficient disinfection the suspended solids should be reduced to 10 mg/l or less. Rapid sand filters are recommended as the most cost-effective option.

Conclusion

It has been well established by previous strategic studies that treated effluent must play a key role in re-establishing a water balance in the Coastal Aquifer to aid sustainable development in the Gaza Strip. This requires farmers to substitute effluent for groundwater as the principal irrigation source, wherever feasible, and for effluent that is surplus to agricultural demand to be recharged to the aquifer. The existing three WWTPs in the Gaza Strip are overloaded and poorly operated. As a result, the three planned WWTPs should be engineered in order to produce substantial quantities of treated effluent; this is a valuable agricultural resource. But successful treatment and reuse requires careful planning and management to ensure that appropriate quality standards are achieved and the maximum sustainable benefits are realized economically.

For unrestricted reuse of effluent to be acceptable, additional effluent treatment is necessary, for which rapid sand filtration and disinfection by UV are recommended as the most suitable options. Nitrogen removal from effluent that is recharged is required to protect and improve groundwater quality.

REFERENCES

Nashashibi, M., and L. A. Van Duijl. 1995. Wastewater characteristics in Palestine. *Water Science & Technology* 32 (11):65–75.

Ouda, O. K., and M. R. Al-Agha. 2000. Treated wastewater use in Gaza District: The question of public acceptance. Paper presented at the Fifth International Water Technology Conference, Alexandria, Egypt.

Palestinian Central Bureau of Statistics. 2000. *Population, housing and establishment census 1997.* Palestinian National Authority.

Palestinian Water Authority (PWA). 2000. *Water sector strategic planning study.* Final report, vol. 3: Specialist studies, Part B: Focal areas. Ramallah: Palestinian Water Authority.

———. 2001. *Coastal Aquifer Management Program (CAMP).* Integrated Aquifer Management Plan, Task 25, Gaza Strip, Palestine. Ramallah: Palestinian Water Authority.

———. 2003. *Effluent reuse standards (PS 742 / 2003).* Palestinian Standard Institute, Gaza Strip, Palestine. Ramallah: Palestinian Water Authority.

———. 2005. *Evaluation of water quality in Gaza Strip.* Annual Report, Gaza Strip, Palestine. Ramallah: Palestinian Water Authority.

Pescod, M. B. 1992. Wastewater treatment and use in agriculture. *FAO irrigation and drainage paper 47.* Rome.

Tubail, K., J. Al-Dadah, and M. Yassin. 2004. Present situation of wastewater and its possible prospect for reuse in the Gaza Strip. *KA-Abwasser, Abfall* 51 (8):866–872. Germany.

World Bank. 2000. *Wastewater treatment and reuse in the Middle East and North Africa region.* Cairo, Egypt.

World Health Organization (WHO). 1989. Health guidelines for the use of wastewater in agriculture and aquaculture. Technical Report Series 778, Geneva.

Wastewater Treatment and Reuse in Israel

YOSSI INBAR

The total area of arable land in Israel has increased from 1,600 km² in 1948 to approximately 4,200 km² in 2001. Irrigated land has increased from 300 km² in 1948 to 1,866 km² in 2001. Water scarcity has traditionally been the primary limiting factor in Israeli agriculture. Agriculture is the number one factor in the protection of open space and prevention of desertification. It also serves as a sink for waste produced in the urban sector, including effluents, sewage sludge, or compost.

The combination of severe water shortage, densely populated urban areas, and highly intensive irrigated agriculture makes it essential that Israel put wastewater treatment and reuse high on its list of national priorities. In fact, national policy calls for the gradual replacement of freshwater allocation to agriculture by reclaimed effluents. In the past, sewage has constituted a major source of water pollution. Yet, a steady process of sewage infrastructure expansion has improved the situation dramatically, with only isolated cases remaining of untreated sewage. Currently about 72% (>300 mcm) of the wastewater produced in Israel is reclaimed for agricultural reuse.

A new standard for unlimited use of effluents was recently adopted by the government. The standard encompasses thirty-six parameters, taking into account public health, soil, hydrological, and flora considerations. This new standard will enable the re-allocation of nearly 50% of all freshwater (about 500 mcm) from agriculture to the municipal and industrial sectors. The operational objective is to treat 100% of the country's wastewater to a level enabling unrestricted irrigation by the year 2010.

Wastewater

Out of a total of 500 mcm of sewage produced in Israel, about 96% is collected in central sewage systems and 72% of the effluent is reclaimed (300 mcm). By law, local authorities are obligated to treat municipal sewage. In recent years, new or upgraded intensive treatment plants were set up in municipalities throughout the country. The ultimate objective is to ensure that all of Israel's wastewater is sufficiently clean to allow for unrestricted irrigation in accordance with soil sensitivity and without risk to soil and water sources.

The following facts provide a synopsis of the condition of Israel's municipal sewage profile:

- Some 500 mcm of wastewater are produced in Israel every year, of which 450 mcm/yr are treated.
- Some 330 mcm/yr of the effluent is reclaimed (about 72%).
- About 4% of the wastewater is discharged to cesspools (20 mcm/yr).
- The rest, about 96%, is collected in central sewage systems.
- About 33% of the wastewater/effluents is discharged into the environment (approx. 160 mcm/yr).

Wastewater Treatment

There are upwards of five hundred sewage treatment facilities in Israel today, of which some thirty-five are advanced wastewater treatment plants (purifying over 360 mcm/yr) with minimum annual capacity of more than 0.5 mcm each. Recently, Israel has begun to divert Palestinian sewage that flows over the green line in waste treatment plants to prevent contamination of streams and groundwater.

Regulations promulgated by the Ministry of Health in 1992 require secondary treatment to a minimum baseline level of 20 mg/l biochemical oxygen demand (BOD) and 30 mg/l total suspended solids (TSS) in urban and rural centers with populations exceeding ten thousand people. Local authorities are responsible for the construction and operation of wastewater treatment plants.

Israel's wastewater treatment plants use intensive (mechanical/biological) and extensive treatment processes. Intensive treatment plants use activated sludge methods while extensive processes are based on anaerobic stabilization ponds, which are integrated with shallow aerobic ponds and/or deep facultative polishing reservoirs. Treatment facilities may include nitrogen and phosphorous removal. After treatment, the effluent is placed in seasonal reservoirs, which also serve to regulate the constant flow of treated wastewater and the seasonal demand for irrigation.

Because of the combination of severe water shortage, contamination of water resources, densely populated urban areas, and intensive irrigation in agriculture, wastewater treatment and reuse are high on Israel's list of national priorities. There appears to be a steady improvement in the quality of sewage effluents produced. In 2001, some 46% of the effluents produced in the country (200 mcm) complied with the standards set in regulations (20/30 BOD/TSS). This reached 60% (256 mcm) in 2002 and 72% (300 mcm) in 2005.

The organic load in Israel's municipal wastewater is much higher than in the Western world. Furthermore, due to the high rate of effluent reuse for irrigation purposes, environmental sensitivity to the salt content of sewage is especially great.

The adverse environmental impacts of domestic sewage may be reduced through the following activities:

- reduction of salt emissions to the sewage system through discharge of industrial brines to sea as well as reduction in the use of salt in dishwasher and laundry detergents;

- changes in the chemical composition (especially reduction of boron) of detergents to environment-friendly materials;
- legislation to limit the use of domestic garbage disposals because in Israel each person generates some 0.5 kg of organic waste per day, such that use of garbage disposals and disposers would increase the organic load in wastewater treatment plants tenfold;
- steps to assure that industrial sewage discharged to municipal treatment systems will undergo pretreatment to remove toxic or harmful materials.

Effluent Disposal and Reuse

Sewage treatment of effluent is the most readily available water source and provides a partial solution to the water scarcity problem. National policy calls for the gradual replacement of freshwater allocations to agriculture by reclaimed effluent. In 1999, treated wastewater constituted only about 22% of the consumption by the agricultural sector. It is estimated that effluent will constitute 50% of the water supplied to agriculture in 2010 and as much as 70% in 2020.

The Ministry of Health maintains a permit system designed to ensure that irrigation with effluent is limited to non-edible crops such as cotton, fodder, etc. Only highly treated effluent, after disinfection, is used for irrigation of orchards, such as citrus and avocado groves. Effluent is not used for irrigating crops in which there is direct contact between the water and the edible part of the plant (e.g., lettuce).

Upgraded Effluent Quality Standards

Because of the decision to increase the use of effluent to a total of 500 mcm, the Ministers Committee for Economics (Decision 46, July 2000) decided to nominate an Inter-Ministerial Committee (Inbar Committee) in order to review existing regulations and recommend new ones for the use of effluents for irrigation or for disposal to streams and receiving waters.

The recommended values, designed to minimize potential damage to water sources, flora, and soil, call for much higher treatment levels in existing and future wastewater treatment plants. An agreement in principle has been reached on the new effluent quality standards, and a techno-economic review of the standard has been conducted. The objective is to treat 100% of the country's wastewater to a level enabling unrestricted irrigation in accordance with soil sensitivity and without risk to soil and water sources.

The proposed regulation included thirty-six biological and chemical parameters classified in three groups (table 8.6):

- Organics, nutrients, and pathogens: BOD, TSS, COD, fecal coliforms, dissolved oxygen, residual chlorine, mineral oil, pH, total nitrogen, ammonia, and total phosphorus;
- Salts: electrical conductivity (TDS), SAR, chloride, sodium, boron, and fluoride;
- Heavy metals: arsenic, barium, mercury, chromium, nickel, selenium, lead, cadmium, zinc, iron, copper, manganese, aluminum, molybdenum, vanadium, beryllium, cobalt, lithium, and cyanide.

Table 8.6 Proposed New Israeli standards for effluent (average levels)

Parameter	Units	Unrestricted irrigation	Rivers
Electric conductivity	dS/m	1.4	n/a
BOD	mg/l	10	10
TSS	mg/l	10	10
COD	mg/l	100	70
$N-NH_4$	mg/l	20	1.5
Total nitrogen	mg/l	25	10
Total phosphorus	mg/l	5	1.0
Chloride	mg/l	250	400
Fluoride	mg/l	2	n/a
Sodium	mg/l	150	200
Fecal coliforms	Unit/100 ml	10	200
Dissolved oxygen	mg/l	>0.5	>3
pH	mg/l	6.5–8.5	7.0–8.5
Residual chlorine	mg/l	1	0.05
Anionic detergent	mg/l	2	0.5
Mineral oil	mg/l	n/a	1
SAR	$(mmol/l)^{0.5}$	5	n/a
Boron	mg/l	0.4	n/a
Arsenic	mg/l	0.1	0.1
Mercury	mg/l	0.002	0.0005
Chromium	mg/l	0.1	0.05
Nickel	mg/l	0.2	0.05
Selenium	mg/l	0.02	n/a
Lead	mg/l	0.1	0.008
Cadmium	mg/l	0.01	0.005
Zinc	mg/l	2	0.2
Iron	mg/l	2	n/a
Copper	mg/l	0.2	0.02
Manganese	mg/l	0.2	n/a
Aluminum	mg/l	5	n/a

(continued)

Table 8.6 Proposed New Israeli standards for effluent (average levels) *(continued)*

Parameter	Units	Unrestricted irrigation	Rivers
Molybdenum	mg/l	0.01	n/a
Vanadium	mg/l	0.1	n/a
Beryllium	mg/l	0.1	n/a
Cobalt	mg/l	0.05	n/a
Lithium	mg/l	2.5	n/a
Cyanide	mg/l	0.1	0.005

Note: From soil, flora, hydrological, and public health considerations.

To achieve the threshold values recommended for the parameters in the regulation, the quality of the effluent must be upgraded. The way to reach this objective will be different for any group of parameters. The group of organics, nutrients, and pathogens can be treated at the wastewater treatment plants under present conditions or with some technical upgrading. Salts and heavy metals, at the present level of wastewater treatment, have to be treated at the source. Therefore, recent years have seen a flurry of new regulations (by the Ministry of the Environment in collaboration with other ministries) designed to improve wastewater quality. In some instances, regulations are based on European standards (e.g., regulations limiting the discharge of heavy metals); in others, they are specifically developed to address conditions that are unique to Israel (e.g., regulations prohibiting the discharge of brines into municipal sewage systems and detergent standards setting limits on concentrations of chlorides, boron, and sodium). Special attention is currently being given to problems relating to the high salinity of municipal sewage. This is an issue of particular importance in Israel, where wastewater recovery for agricultural purposes is imperative.

Conclusions

Israel's experience with wastewater reuse suggests that it can be an invaluable component in water management strategy for dry lands. However, there are strong public health and environmental implications that must be considered prior to adopting a final policy. A water management system that is not based on extremely high treatment levels will not be sustainable or beneficial in the long run. Inadequate sewage treatment limits the range of crops that can be safely grown with wastewater irrigation. Consequently, the government of Israel decided to upgrade its treatment of effluents to the above-proposed advanced standards, enabling unrestricted irrigation in accordance with soil sensitivity and without risk to human health, flora, soil, and water sources. Despite the apparent progress domestically, the lack of adequate treatment of Palestinian sewage is not a problem that Israel can ignore as it pursues its water quality goals.

REFERENCES

Aharoni, A., and H. Cikurel. 2006. Mekorot's research activity in technological improvements for the production of unrestricted irrigation quality effluents. *Desalination* 187:347–360.

Gabbay, S. 2002. *The environment in Israel.* Jerusalem: Israel Ministry of Environmental Protection.

Israel Ministry of Environmental Protection. N.d. Water. www.sviva.gov.il/bin/e_sviva.jsp?z =water_top (accessed July 21, 2009).

Life and Environment. 2005. *Paths to sustainability.* Tel Aviv: Life and Environment.

Research News. 2002. *Besa Bulletin* 14:1–4.

Tal, A. 2006. Seeking sustainability: Israel's evolving water management strategy. *Science* 313:1081–1084.

Editors' Summary

There is probably no area in water management where the gap between Palestinian and Israeli environmental performance is greater than in sewage treatment. While Israel's present level of treatment is often lacking, the present infrastructure and treatment levels are world's apart from those that existed 15 years ago. At the same time, despite the general sense of progress, some of the assumptions about future wastewater utilization in Israel may require reconsideration. For instance, as urbanization expands in some regions, the agricultural demand for wastewater will continue to drop. Ultimately, transferring effluents great distances to where demand exists may make less economic sense. As the ecological integrity of streams improves, there will be a need to continually upgrade wastewater treatment, and better freshwater sources will be expected. Many environmentalists also argue that the country has not made an adequate commitment to sewage infrastructure and that many municipal governments have found other areas in which to spend local taxes. But if present trends are any indication, it is fair to assume that Israel will continue to expand its usage of sewage treatment and that the quality of effluents will continue to improve.

While Israel has made slow but steady progress first in connecting homes to sewage systems and then upgrading its level of treatment, sewage treatment remains anomalous for the vast majority of Palestinian communities. Existing treatment facilities suffer from lack of maintenance and are increasingly over whelmed by the growing organic loadings that have come with the population increase. Palestinians have not made sewage treatment a high enough priority. The long-term impact on soil and water resources is still not well characterized but should be a source of apprehension. The effect of mosquitoes, poor odors, and periodic outbreaks of related diseases is more apparent and of immediate concern to the general public. In the context of future negotiations, sewage treatment constitutes environmental priority number one. Any negotiated solution and international assistance should reflect this commitment.

There is also probably no other area of water management (with the possible exception of overpumping) where there is a greater need for coordination between Israelis and Palestinians. The integrity of ground water or the aquatic systems in local streams will never be ensured unless dramatic improvement takes place. Common standards for sewage treatment are important because of the impact that sewage discharges have on shared water resources. It is clear from Israel's experience that recharging aquifers with poorly treated sewage will ultimately degrade groundwater quality. Massive irrigation with poorly treated effluents has also led to groundwater contamination, with industrial solvents appearing in wells throughout Israel's coastline when they were not removed in wastewater treatment plants. Salinization of soils and wells is often attributed to Israel's alacrity to utilize wastewater. But there is a limit to the demands that can be made in an international agreement when the issue of sewage treatment standards arises.

There is a link between environmental infrastructure and economic conditions. Several Palestinian sewage treatment plants have been established that ceased to function effectively due to lack of funding. Donors should ensure that financial mechanisms are in place to prevent these dynamics from occurring in the future. More importantly, the limitations of present capacity have clear implications for the establishment of common treatment standards. Essentially, "perfection" is indeed the enemy of the "good." Better to install reasonable secondary treatment across the board then to have expensive tertiary treatment facilities that are not functioning.

A critical question that needs to be addressed in negotiations involves a coordinated response to the present transboundary dynamics of sewage treatment. In recent years, Israel unilaterally has begun to establish treatment facilities to capture and treat Palestinian sewage as it crosses the border. This was initially described as a pragmatic response, taken to protect Israeli water resources given the lack of progress in Palestinian wastewater treatment. But it is not clear whether what was once an exigency has now turned into a strategy. It is now clear from hydrological research that much of the sewage flowing from the Palestinian Authority percolates into the ground prior to reaching the Israeli treatment facility. A substantial percentage of this "lost" wastewater will make its way to the groundwater.

Accordingly, a final agreement about water should therefore internalize a fundamental axiom of environmental management: the proximity principle. The proximity principle holds that it is essential that water be treated as close to its source as possible. While future infrastructure and normative frameworks should consider waste treatment and utilization of effluents at a regional level, the focus on treatment must be local. Alternatively, and in the interim, untreated wastes can be transported to regional treatment centers via pipelines in order to prevent water loss/contamination and the risk of human exposure while it is in transit.

Until this principal is applied, there remains the thorny issue of costs. Israel has traditionally charged Palestinians for treating their waste in ad-hoc facilities in Yad Hana and Nahal Beer Sheva. It has not, however, been willing to pay out similar funds in areas like the Kidron Valley, where Israeli sewage is a source of pollution in the Palestinian Authority. Palestinians justifiably object to this asymmetry. Moreover, they perceive the interim agreement, which requires high levels of coordination with Israel, as one of the primary reasons why there has been so little progress in upgrading their sanitary infrastructure during the past decade.

Surely, it is in Israel's hydrological self-interest to facilitate the construction of Palestinian sewage treatment plants via monies either donated by international donors or generated by local taxes. Moreover, in the long run, siphoning off Palestinian "tax funds" for a sub-optimal sewage plant in Israel will make no sense hydrologically. Eventually, Palestinian plants and reuse of wastewater will render these facilities useless in any event. Israel should think about making strategic investments from its own funds in Palestinian infrastructure—over the border and close to pollution sources. A long term "sustainable" allocation of water in the region will require both Israelis and Palestinians to utilize treated effluents in agriculture and as part of their stream restoration program.

PART 9

AGRICULTURE AND WATER

Agriculture constitutes the greatest consumer of water in both the Israeli and the Palestinian economies. Besides its dominant role in water quantity issues, agriculture contributes a variety of pollutants. Given its central role in both Zionist and Palestinian culture and the fact that food is not an ordinary product, clearly, public policy toward agriculture will be different than for other industrial sectors. It is also clear that agriculture is no longer perceived as an "environmental adversary" but rather as a partner in a sustainable solution to water issues. This part considers the unique role of water for each side, written by two experts who are known for their expertise in sustainable agriculture.

Sustainable Water Supply for Agriculture in Palestine

SAID A. ASSAF

The geographic and historical area known as Palestine has been inhabited continuously by Palestinians whose forefathers thousands of years ago and even before Christ's time were the Canaanites and Polista tribes of Greece.[1] The Canaanites were the first to plow the earth and cultivate it. The farming of rain-fed olive trees and olive oil production has been the backbone of Palestinian agriculture from the old times of the Roman rule and the more recent Ottoman rule of historical Palestine, which was followed by the British Mandate on Palestine after World War I.[2] This mainly dry-farmed, rain-fed agricultural activity continued with more vigor on the hilly lands of the West Bank even after the Jordanian administration and the Israel occupation. Similarly, citrus cultivation in the Gaza Strip expanded under the Egyptian administration and the Israeli occupation. Jewish settlers, especially from Western Europe and the United States, expanded on the existing irrigated citrus orchards (growing the famous "Jaffa oranges") established by Palestinian farmers before 1948 in the fertile coast of Palestine along the Mediterranean Sea and the adjoining plains. Yet, they ventured little into olive cultivation, which takes a longer time to produce economically.

Following the aftermath of World War II and Israel's creation, the more fertile Palestinian coastal lands and water resources were controlled by Israel. This became especially true after the 1967 Israeli-Arab War. These disastrous events, from the Palestinian perspective, pushed and squeezed many of these farmers after the 1948 war to the southern part of Palestine to become refugees in the small coastal Gaza Strip. Israeli occupation of the West Bank in 1967 also resulted in the Palestinians being pushed into the center of the country, to the hilly area that is now known as the West Bank, truncated from the previous connection with Jordan in the east. Palestinian farmers in the coastal Gaza Strip concentrated on citrus and vegetable production, as they still do. On the other hand, in the West Bank's hills and valleys, Palestinians focused their agricultural activities on rain-fed agriculture as water resources for irrigation were limited and under Israeli military control and restrictions. Irrigated lands were mostly concentrated in the northwestern and northeastern parts of the West Bank, especially the semi-coastal northwest areas near Tulkarem and Qalqilyah.

Of even greater significance in terms of irrigated lands are those at the extreme eastern borders of the West Bank. These Palestinian lands are unique for being near the Jordan River. Their location is unique, being at the lowest elevation on earth, from 50 to 350 m below sea level, and the warmest area in Palestine. Especially during the winter season these lands serve as a large natural greenhouse.

After the Israeli occupation of Palestine's coastal irrigated lands, these Palestinian Jordan Valley lands became the major contributor to irrigated crops including citrus, bananas, and vegetables. Rain-fed agriculture has been and still remains the dominant production mode of the West Bank, mainly for olives, grapes, and some fruit trees such as almonds, plums, and other stone fruits which are dry-farmed without irrigation. In addition, Palestinians grow field crops and summer vegetables there.

Only about 5% of all the cultivated lands in the West Bank are currently under irrigation, and that is mostly, as was indicated, in the semi-coastal and northern areas of the West Bank as well as the Jordan Valley areas. Most of these are used for citrus and vegetables, with water provided from springs, especially in the Jordan Valley around Jericho. The Jordan Valley has become the main source for agricultural production in the winter season while the northern areas serve that role in spring and summer months.

Palestinian development of water resources to support agricultural activity has been stymied in the past by the political situation. Israeli military laws which were issued immediately following the occupation of the West Bank and Gaza Strip in 1967 effectively prevented the drilling of new underground water wells (or expansion of existing ones) in the West Bank, especially for agricultural use. These decrees controlled the pumping of wells inside the Gaza Strip as well, whose water resources were already poor, both in quantity and quality. The Israeli policy led to the water resources of the West Bank hilly Mountain Aquifer being utilized largely by Israel consumers, leaving Palestinians in the West Bank to mainly depend on rain-fed agriculture.

Nearly 80% of the Gaza Strip population is comprised of refugees and/or their offspring. Many left their fields along the coastal plane. The existing inadequate and low-quality water resources have been used to grow citrus and irrigate other crops. The farmers in the West Bank continue to depend in their plant agriculture production on rain-fed trees and crops and in their animal production on sheep and goat milk and meat production using rain-fed wild pasture areas and animal feed imported from Israel.

Even after the establishment of Israel, Palestinian farmers were successful in overcoming the restrictions on free movement and access to lands and water resources by avoiding the most stringent measures of a harsh military occupation on agricultural production. These so-called traditional Palestinian farmers—as they have been called—have been able to successfully cultivate olives and produce high-quality extra virgin olive oil in the West Bank as well as cash crops such as strawberries, cut flowers, and vegetables for export. When restrictions do not prevent it, as is currently the case for all agricultural exports from Gaza, Palestinian farmers export large quantities of agricultural produce to Israel and to high-end markets in Europe and other countries.

Palestinian farmers have proven to be dynamic and versatile in changing cropping patterns and shifting from one vegetable crop to another, depending on Israeli
restrictions and market influences, either existing or anticipated. The extent to
which exports are facilitated or restricted to Israel and Jordan is a distinct factor in
the cultivation decisions of Palestinian farmers.

Current Land Use and Agricultural Situation in the West Bank and Gaza

Land use patterns in the West Bank and Gaza Strip are constantly changing due to
a number of factors, but mainly due to occupation and land confiscation by Israel
and the isolation of the Separation Wall, which is projected to take away over 8.5%
of the Palestinian West Bank lands and a very significant part of the groundwater
resources, especially on the northwestern part of the West Bank. This occupation
is, of course, in addition to the expected changes of trends in Palestinian land investments with time, due in part to political changes.

An analysis of land use in the West Bank and Gaza Strip (table 9.1) shows 27%
of the land in the West Bank and Gaza is used for agricultural purposes. The Gaza
Strip has a higher percentage, 30%, showing relatively little room for future expansion of agricultural lands in a total area of only 365 km². The West Bank, on the

Table 9.1 Land use in the West Bank and Gaza Strip in 2005 (km²)

Land use	West Bank	Gaza	Total
Permanent crops and pastures irrigated	73.3	46.6	119.9
Permanent crops and pastures rain-fed	1,079.4	10.0	1,089.4
Seasonal crops irrigated	84.9	32.6	117.5
Seasonal crops rain-fed	260.5	19.9	280.4
Total agricultural land	1,498.1	109.1	1,607.2
Forests	88.6	3.2	91.8
Nature reserves	54.4	1.0	55.4
Palestinian built-up area	531.9	53.8	585.7
Jewish settlements	187	0	128.3
Other	3,353.7	197.9	3,551.6
Grand Total	5,655	365	6,020

Sources: Agricultural, forests, and natural reserve lands from Palestinian Central Bureau of
Statistics (PCBS) Area Statistics, 2005. Built-up areas of Jewish settlements from PCBS
Israeli Settlements in the Palestinian Territory, Annual Statistical Report, 2006. Palestinian
built-up area from PCBS Palestinian Land Survey, 1999–2000.

Note: 1 km² = 1,000 dunams = 100 hectares.

Table 9.2 Key crops in the West Bank and Gaza Strip in 2006 (crops with highest
ton production)

Area	Fruit trees		Vegetables		Field crops	
	CROP	% OF TOTAL	CROP	% OF TOTAL	CROP	% OF TOTAL
West Bank	Olive	53	Cucumber	27	Wheat	32
	Grape	19	Tomato	26	Dry onion	20
	Lemon	5	Eggplant	11	Potato	19
Gaza Strip	Orange	48	Tomato	41	Potato	56
	Lemon	11	Cucumber	17	Dry onion	18
	Guava	8	Cut flower	16	Sweet potato	11
Palestinian	Olive	45	Tomato	32	Potato	32
Territories	Grape	17	Cucumber	23	Dry onion	20
	Orange	12	Eggplant	9	Wheat	19

Source: Palestinian Central Bureau of Statistics Agricultural Statistics, 2006.

other hand, has only 26% utilized for agricultural purposes. It has a much larger
total area of land that can potentially be expanded into for agricultural purposes.

The proportion of this land that is irrigated shows a very different profile for
agricultural water use in the West Bank versus the Gaza Strip. While only 5%–11%
of West Bank agricultural land is irrigated, in the Gaza Strip that proportion is 73%.
While this is a vast difference in terms of percentage, due to the small area of the
Gaza Strip, in practice the total irrigated land in the Gaza Strip is just half of the
total irrigated land in the West Bank.

The crop mix that leads to this irrigation profile is illustrated in table 9.2. One
explanation for the low percentage of irrigation levels in the West Bank is that the
leading crop is olives, covering over 60% of the agricultural land of the West Bank;
and olive trees are cultivated almost exclusively as a rain-fed crop. In the Gaza Strip,
citrus trees, which require irrigation, dominate fruit tree cultivation; and even the
cultivation of various vegetables is done there at much higher irrigation levels than
in the West Bank.

Land Use Trends before and after Occupation

A compilation of research on agricultural land use in the West Bank and Gaza Strip
before and after the Israeli occupation (table 9.3) shows a decrease in the percentage
of cultivated area in both the West Bank and Gaza Strip. The change over the past
40 years is very dramatic and may in part be due to different data collection methods over time, but certainly also has factual causes. The expansion of the population, particularly in the Gaza Strip, is due not only to natural population growth but

Table 9.3 Cultivated land in the West Bank and Gaza Strip before and after the
Israeli occupation

Area	Description	1964	1982	2006
West Bank	Total cultivated area (in hectares)	216,870	160,057	149,810
West Bank	Percentage cultivated area to the total area of the West Bank (565,500 hectares)	38.35	28.30	26.49
Gaza Strip	Total cultivated area (in hectares)	26,700	16,460	10,910
Gaza Strip	Percentage of cultivated area to the total area of the Gaza Strip (36,500 hectares)	73.15	45.10	29.89

Sources: 1964 and 1982 data from Food Security Study (1985) by ASIR for FAO/ESCWA;
2006 data from Palestinian Central Bureau of Statistics Area Statistics, 2006.

to the continued effects of the absorption of the refugee population from the 1948
war, along with restrictions on access to land, roads, and water resources. Such
restrictions are due to settlement expansion and the Israeli military occupation,
and that would account for the drastic shift in cultivated land areas and type of
crops seen between 1964 and 1982. In the West Bank, there has been only a minor
decrease between 1982 and the present day, but in the Gaza Strip this decrease continues dramatically and can probably be explained by a combination of high population growth and destruction of citrus crops by Israeli military incursions and
neglect of orchards due to water shortages.

The crop mix in the West Bank and Gaza Strip has also changed over time.
In the West Bank, there is a clear tendency toward expansion in fruit trees, which
are primarily olives, at the expense of field crops and vegetables. In the Gaza
Strip, there is an opposite trend, with the area of trees, which in Gaza are primarily
citrus, falling against rising areas of vegetables and field crops. (Potatoes and
onions are statistically considered as field crops as reported by Palestinian Central
Bureau of Statistics). While the reasons for these trends lie somewhat in market
issues, such as prices, these patterns are also linked to the Israeli occupation measures (table 9.4).

Olive cultivated areas were and still are on the increase to protect the land from
Israeli confiscation (table 9.5), as treeless lands have been more susceptible to confiscation. It is easily observed that the Palestinian farmers have used less area for vegetables due to their vulnerability to extraneous marketing measures by the Israeli
occupation authorities and the decrease in the water available for irrigation. In addition to the general water extraction restrictions, the Israeli government closed the
area around the Jordan River (the Zohr) to irrigation by Palestinian farmers.

A closer look at very specific changes in field crops due to Israeli land restrictions is shown in table 9.6. It should be pointed out that the lands cultivated by

Table 9.4 Type of agricultural crops cultivated before and after occupation in the West Bank (in hectares)

Area	Type of agriculture	1964	1982	1995	2006
West Bank	Field crops	112,810	50,092	52,560	43,154
West Bank	Vegetables	27,113	13,904	13,650	13,643
West Bank	Trees (olive and other)	76,927	96,061	105,743	107,963
Gaza Strip	Field crops	—	—	3,755	6,447
Gaza Strip	Vegetables	—	—	6,125	5,697
Gaza Strip	Trees (orange and other)	—	—	8,617	5,706
Palestinian Territories	Field crops	—	—	56,315	49,601
Palestinian Territories	Vegetables	—	—	19,775	19,296
Palestinian Territories	Trees (olive, orange, and other)	—	—	114,360	113,669

Sources: 1964–1982 from Food Security Study (1985) by ASIR for FAO/ESCWA; 1999–2006 from Palestinian Central Bureau of Statistics Agricultural Statistics.

Note: PCBS statistics classify potatoes and onions as field crops, but the Food Security study of ASIR considers them vegetables.

Table 9.5 Olive and olive oil production in the West Bank (various years)

Year	Total live trees production area (in hectares)	Total olive fruits production (in tons)	Total olive oil production (in tons)
1966	53,700	24,000	4,800
1974	61,800	124,000	24,800
1982	69,200	127,000	25,400
1987	88,000	160,000	35,000
2006	90,000	170,000	34,000

Sources: Author's Palestinian reports to the International Olive Oil Council, Madrid, Spain; and author's data in the Food Security Study (1985) to FAO/ESCWA.

Table 9.6 Changes in the cultivated area of wheat, barley, and
sesame in the West Bank, 1964–2006 (in hectares)

Year	Wheat	Barley	Sesame
1964	65,200	25,000	2,500
1976	33,000	20,000	1,000
1982	20,300	17,100	750
2006	18,008	10,058	399

Source: 1964–1982 data from Food Security Study (1985), ASIR; and 2006
data from Palestinian Central Bureau of Statistics Agricultural Statistics.

wheat decreased to less than a third of pre-occupation levels. Considering the recent significant price increases in wheat flour, the continued drop in wheat production has a direct impact on Palestinian income, food security, and poverty levels.

Palestinians argue that allowing the planting of field crops, e.g., wheat and barley, in restricted-use lands would constitute an important humanitarian gesture. Barley is currently a critical crop due to the skyrocketing prices of animal feed, the majority of which is imported from Israel. The decrease in the production of badly needed barley is continuing and reached critical stages in 2008, making further investments in sheep production very risky nowadays.[3] The several-fold decrease in the land cultivated with sesame, due primarily to the labor intensiveness of harvesting it, is also an important matter for Palestinians as sesame, when it is of the large, hardy type like the Palestinian Baladi variety, is needed for many food products in Palestine, as with *za'ater* (thyme) and, particularly, with tahini (sesame paste), which is manufactured locally with mostly imported sesame seeds.[4]

It is of interest to note that farmers in the Gaza Strip depend mainly on irrigated crops such as citrus and other fruit trees and, more recently, strawberries, cut flowers, and vegetables. These crops tend to be sensitive to handling and delays and are highly export based, not like the olives and field crops in the West Bank, which are more dependent on rain. Thus, as happened in the early months of 2008, the closures of borders and water scarcity made the people in the Gaza Strip more vulnerable to agricultural losses and suffering due to their inability to export to Israel and other countries as well as to the West Bank. Due to water shortages, farmers in the Gaza Strip have begun some expansion of their small olive orchards with some supplemental irrigation. The West Bank produces rain-fed products such as olives and olive oil and now the valuable jojoba oil as well as cereals and legumes, which tend to have lower returns than vegetables or flowers but are more stable and can be stored during closures. The distribution of cultivated land in the West Bank by the type of agricultural use emphasizes consideration of the factor of occupation measures in selecting the crops to be cultivated. Of course, vegetables are more susceptible to damage from handling and storage and thus have decreased, and the types of vegetables planted have changed during the occupation.

Water for Agricultural Use in the West Bank and Gaza

It is a matter of fact that one of the major obstacles for good plentiful agriculture production is water. Crops produce several times more when planted under irrigation as compared to rain-fed regimes. Even a desert plant such as jojoba, which is cultivated in both the West Bank and Israel (but only as a rain-fed crop in the West Bank), produces much more with supplementary irrigation and fertilizers. Furthermore, it is not easy to increase the productivity of rain-fed crops through fertilization as the rains do not come at regular intervals, whereas the fertilization of irrigated crops (fertigation) can be managed in terms of amounts and timing.[5]

The irrigation situation in the West Bank and Gaza Strip has been extensively studied and documented. The sources of irrigation water are groundwater wells and, secondarily, springs (see table 9.7). As would be expected, the Gaza Strip relies exclusively on wells while the West Bank obtains more than half of its irrigation water from springs.

It should be emphasized that even though there is an abundance of springs and shallow wells in the Jordan Valley, the lands there have a somewhat high salt and sodium concentration and require a lot of water for leaching and washing, whenever water is not restricted for use by the Israeli occupation. Also, as was illustrated in a previous study of the fourteen wells of the Arab Development Society (El-Alami) in Jericho, many of the wells have high salinity and higher than acceptable levels of total dissolved solids (TDS), water suitable for irrigation of only certain field crops, such as alfalfa and barley.

The great inadequacy in the water available in the Gaza Strip forces many of the farmers there to break the law, installing shallow wells in their backyard. Even though the water available is brackish, it still provides water for immediate use, albeit at the expense of the aquifer. It is estimated that the Gaza Strip has over 2,700 unlicensed private shallow wells in addition to the 80 official wells. Controlling the resulting over-pumping requires not only laws and regulations, of which there are many on the books, but enforcement of those laws.

Table 9.7 Irrigation water sources and amounts used (mcm)

Area	Springs in Gaza Strip	Underground wells	Total irrigation water
Gaza Strip	0	80.0	80.0
West Bank semi-coastal areas	20.7	0.1	20.8
West Bank mountainous areas	1.7	0	1.7
West Bank wadis zone	11.7	2.7	14.4
West Bank Jordan Valley	35.5	14.3	49.8
Total	49.0	117.7	166.7

Source: Ministry of Agriculture Report, 1999.

Table 9.8 Area of protected cultivation in the West Bank (in hectares)

Year	Surface tunnels	French tunnels	Greenhouses	Total
1994	866.0	26.2	385.8	1,477.4
2006	477.7	67.6	1,378.0	2,123.9

Source: Palestinian Central Bureau of Statistics Agricultural Statistics, 1993/1994 and 2005/2006.

Some sea and brackish water desalination projects have begun with success, but that is not sufficient to solve the water problems in the Gaza Strip. A basic improvement and continued hydrologically appropriate management of the Coastal Aquifer is needed. The greatest problem that needs to be overcome for sustaining agriculture in the Gaza Strip is the use of treated sewage and wastewater for agricultural crops. This requires infrastructure, education, and a whole manageable system.

The use of protected agriculture, particularly greenhouses, for vegetables and other crops has greatly increased, and this dramatic change has served to increase productivity and efficiency of water use. To illustrate, table 9.8 reports the percentage of protected agriculture cultivation in the West Bank. Note the increase of 44% from 1994 to 2006.

An increase in water conservation, as well as in the efficiency of water extraction and utilization, may also be realized by improving the condition of the Palestinian wells used for irrigation in both the West Bank and Gaza Strip. In the West Bank, a Ministry of Agriculture (MOA) report indicated that 5% of the agricultural wells were drilled before 1950, around 40% between 1951 and 1959, and about 50% between 1960 and 1967. Very few have been drilled since 1967 due to Israeli restrictions, particularly wells for agricultural use.

Potential Irrigable Land in the West Bank and Gaza Strip

At present, as mentioned previously, the total land area under irrigation in the West Bank varies from 5% to 11% of cultivated land. There is no precise estimation of the land that could economically be brought under irrigation. Nevertheless, the prevailing view is that the total land area that could possibly be irrigated in the West Bank may be as high as 53,000 ha, which can be divided, not by district, but by topographic areas, as shown in table 9.9.

Reaching these potential levels of irrigated land would first require allowing Palestinian access to agricultural land and water resources in the West Bank, which are restricted by Israeli occupation and settlement expansion. In addition, the estimated irrigable area could be increased if planting practices emphasized those crops that have a lower water demand. Spring flow in the West Bank could, if properly utilized, be a major source of water for bringing more land under irrigation and for increasing agricultural production.

Table 9.9 Feasible irrigatable land areas and the amount of irrigation water
        required

Topographical area	Approximate number of irrigatable hectares	Amount of water needed to irrigate the land (in mcm)
Jordan Valley	10,000	100
Jenin and Tulkarem	11,000	110
Hilly uplands	25,000	108
Eastern slopes	7,000	37
Gaza Strip	20,000	130

Source: Ministry of Agriculture Report, 1999.

Many of the conveyance systems for irrigation in the West Bank still consist of dirt canals and/or cement canals that are either in poor condition or are uncovered. Existing canals need maintenance in order to repair cracks and seepage from the base, and dirt canals need to be replaced with cement canals in order to prohibit infiltration. Utilizing the existing and potential spring flow in a more thorough and efficient manner would benefit the national economy and would allow individual farmers to have a more productive and diversified agriculture and, at the same time, would provide stability to family income and food security.

Many NGOs—both international and national—have begun work on spring development and provided support for protected agriculture using greenhouses and plastic tunnels. The Palestinian Water Authority has also initiated several spring development programs. Items that need either continued or further attention are maintenance of existing spring structures; development of natural spring sites in order to maintain, increase, and/or preserve the spring flow for economic purposes; development of more efficient water storage and transfer infrastructure; development and dissemination of information on more efficient irrigation methods; and, when possible, the development of know-how in planting profitable crops that utilize either a minimum amount of water or water of a lesser quality.

A Water-Based Cropping Strategy

Of significance to this discussion is a published proposal to implement a "water-for-peace" strategy for the Jordan River Basin countries through a shift in cropping patterns. Parts of this proposal cover the ways and means for sustainable use of water in agriculture. It is pointed out that the countries in the Jordan River Basin (Jordan, Palestine, Israel, Syria, and Lebanon) need to plant productive trees, such as jojoba, and economic crops that use minimum amounts of water and/or withstand salinity. This is most critical for Palestine, whose water resources at present are controlled and restricted. Still, even if a peace agreement should improve the situation, water supply will be very limited.

Table 9.10 Trees grown in the Jordan River Basin and their water sources

Tree type	Total water needs in cubic meters per hectare	Water source
Bananas	200	Irrigation
Avocadoes	170	Irrigation
Mangos	160	Irrigation
Date palm	150	Irrigation
Citrus	120	Irrigation
Guava	100	Irrigation
Figs	48	Rain fed
Olives	40	Rain fed
Apricots	40	Rain fed
Plums	38	Rain fed
Soft-shell almonds	38	Rain fed
Hard-shell almonds	35	Rain fed
Jojoba	30	Rain fed and/or supplemental irrigation
Cactus	15	Rain fed

Note: A similar tabulation is made for some field crops and/or forage crops under rain-fed conditions, as shown in table 9.11.

Table 9.10 shows the different total water needs of some major trees that are grown in the Jordan River Basin countries. Table 9.11 shows the water requirements of field crops grown in the basin. It should also be taken into consideration that certain crops withstand and do well in somewhat saline conditions. The differences in such crops with respect to the saline water and/or soil used for their growth are shown in table 9.12.

In experiments by Professor Dov Pasternak (Ben Gurion University of the Negev) in Israel and Egypt, tomatoes and melons (cantaloupes) were found to produce excellent yields only when irrigated with water with a chloride concentration of 1,200 to 1,500 ppm. Moreover, the quality of the product irrigated with the saline water was enhanced. The tomatoes had more solids and became tastier, while the melons became sweeter when using drip irrigation of that saline water. Better water conservation of irrigation water is realized by growing vegetables under protective covers such as plastic greenhouses and plastic tunnels, rather than planting these crops in open fields. As mentioned, these dynamics have been internalized by Palestinian farmers, who have increased their protected

Table 9.11 Field crops grown in the Jordan River Basin and their
            water requirements

Field crops and/or forage crops	Rainfall requirements for economic production in total millimeters annually
Corn	600
Watermelon	550
Melons (cantaloupe)	450
Wheat, sorghum, alfalfa	400
Tobacco	400
Chickpeas (garbanzos)	385
Barley	350
Thyme	350
Vetch	325
Lentils	325
Kirsanneh vetch	325
Cumin, anise, blackseed	225

Table 9.12 Salt-tolerant crops and maximum salinity for cultivation

Salt-tolerant crops	Salinity in total dissolved solids (ppm)
Cactus (prickly pears)	2,500
Jojoba	2,000
Melons	1,500
Tomatoes	1,200
Alfalfa	1,100
Hard-shell almonds	800
Olives	800
Citrus	500
Bananas	150

agriculture areas, especially with plastic greenhouses. Those who are unable to
have the expensive greenhouses use instead the low-cost plastic tunnels. The water
requirements of several highly consumed crops under open field and greenhouse
cultivation are shown in table 9.13.

Table 9.13 Water requirements of some vegetable crops under greenhouse and
open-field cultivation in cubic meters

Type of vegetable	Vegetables inside greenhouses	Vegetables in open fields
Tomatoes	600	1,000
Cucumbers	850	1,200
Green beans	750	900
Peppers	600	800
Thyme	300	350

Table 9.14 Water needs and productivity of jojoba and almond trees

	Jojoba	Almonds
Water needs	Very minimal	Minimal for the hard-shell type
Salinity tolerance	Excellent	Fair
Economic returns	Very high from the jojoba oil	Good
Need for insecticides	None	Some
Need for fungicides	None	Some
Percentage oil in the nuts	50	15
Oil price	$20/liter	$11/kg of nuts
Yield per hectare		
Irrigated crop	10 kg/hectare = 5 kg oil/hectare	13 kg/hectare
Rain-fed crop	4 kg/hectare = 2 kg oil/hectare	5 kg/hectare

Almond and jojoba dry-farmed cultivation in Palestine as well as in the other Jordan River Basin countries is an example of a sustainable crop strategy for economic water use in agriculture for the long term. This is reflected in the limited water needs of these nut-producing trees. Jojoba is an evergreen, a long-lived, environmentally friendly tree whose high-value oil production compliments olives, which are alternative bearing.[6] Almonds have a good market locally and, like jojoba, also require little care. Both of these tree crops do not require large amounts of water to produce economically (table 9.14). Their production and care do not require special technology, and they can be maintained in the same way as olives.

The water-thrifty crops that are cited here are those that Palestinian farmers should be planting on an expanded scale to replace water-guzzling crops such as bananas and mangoes. Crops that withstand long storage and rough handling without being harmed (such as jojoba nuts [seeds] and oil) have special merits that need to be realized when considering selection or change of cropping patterns. Also crops such as these can help in the alleviation of desertification and unemployment while providing a sustainable income in arid regions such as Palestine.

As a final comment, of course, the future use of treated wastewater will contribute to the sustainable water supply for agriculture in Palestine as well as in all countries in the region. However, this aspect is not emphasized in this essay as it is addressed already in part 6. Furthermore, a long timeframe is required for implementation of the appropriate wastewater treatment plants and their associated infrastructure and management systems. To date, there has not been much progress in the Palestinian Authority in expanding wastewater treatment due to the political conditions and the involvement of the Joint Water Committee, which is required to reach decisions by consensus. Based on this, the Israelis enjoy de facto veto power. At times, donor funding was jeopardized due to the failure to obtain required Israeli approvals. Without improvement in the political situation, it could be many years before the benefits of treated wastewater irrigation are realized by farmers in the West Bank and Gaza.

NOTES

1. With the exception of this discussion on the historical perspective, this essay will be focusing on sustainable water for agriculture and related agricultural practices in what is referred to by the United Nations as the "Occupied Palestinian Territories," or the "West Bank and Gaza Strip," including East Jerusalem, defined by the areas occupied by Israel in 1967, i.e., the areas within the 1949 armistice line.

2. Over 62 years ago, the author's passion for agriculture was inspired by witnessing his father diligently planting wild olives in his 5-hectare hilly land plot near Arrabeh, Jenin, then 3 years later methodically grafting the young olive stems with the local Souri (Nabali Baladi) variety and growing them for 15 more years until their production of olive fruits became economically viable. Today, this rain-fed orchard produces over four tons of pure organic olive oil from 5 hectares of that hilly marginal land with no irrigation.

3. A half-fat-tail hybrid sheep (a breed named Assaf, which is a hybridization of Awassi and East Friesian breeds) was introduced in the West Bank in 1981 by Dr. Assaf of the Arab Scientific Institute for Research and Transfer of Technology (ASIR) and this breed has proven to be more efficient in the production of twins, milk, and meat than the local full-fat-tail Awassi breed of sheep. More significantly, it does well within confined sheds on feed concentrates, vetch, and wheat hay; and thus they are not in need of large wild pasture lands, which the Israelis control in the West Bank. This breed has proliferated to more than 20,000 now in the West Bank, and even a few herds are also in the Gaza Strip.

4. Another crop of special interest and relevance in Palestine where Israeli occupation had an opposite effect is that of thyme. In the early 1980s thyme was not cultivated but picked and harvested from the wild thyme bushes in the hills, which rejuvenated the plants and spurred new growth. The Israeli military occupation, citing environmental protection, introduced an odd ban on this practice. In response to this problem, the ASIR Institute developed and distributed thyme seedlings from its greenhouses in the Jenin district and taught interested farmers how to make thyme seedlings from vegetative terminals of vigorous thyme plants and seeds, as there is no law against planting thyme. Thyme seedlings became widely available, and thyme is now even used in the various foods in Israel as well as by Palestinians. There are now 104 ha of cultivated thyme in the Occupied Palestinian Territory (Palestinian Central Bureau of Statistics 2006).

5. The term "fertigation" refers to direct application of dissolved fertilizers in liquid form through drip irrigation.

6. Putting this approach into practice, the author has planted thus far over 12,000 jojoba trees in several rain-fed hilly areas in the West Bank and 6,000 trees in his land plot that is 6 km east of the Jordanian international airport under a limited irrigation of eight times per year.

REFERENCES

Assaf, K. 2004. Water as a human right: The understanding of water in Palestine. Paper presented at the Third Forum on Global Development Policy, Berlin, March 25–April 1. Berlin: Heinrich Boll Stiftung Foundation.

Assaf, K., and S. Assaf. 1982. *The chemical and hydrological status of the wells at the Arab development society project.* Birzeit, West Bank, Palestine: Birzeit University Research and Documentation Center.

———. 2005. Basic needs in development: Focus on the water sector in Palestine. In *Water values and rights*, 589–603. Ramallah, Palestine: Palestinian Academy of Science and Technology and the Palestinian Water Authority.

Assaf, K., B. Attia, A. Darwish, B. Wardam, and S. Klawitter. 2004. Water as a human right: The understanding of water in the Arab countries of the Middle East—a four-country analysis. *Global Issue Papers* 11:168. Berlin: Heinrich Boll Foundation.

Assaf, S. 1982. *A comparative evaluation of the Assaf hybrid sheep with that of the local Awassi sheep in the production of twins, milk and meat.* El-Bireh-Ramallah and Arrabeh/Jenin: ASIR Publications.

———. 1989. *Thyme as a medicinal field crop in Palestine.* Abstracts. Baghdad, Iraq: Union of Arab Biologists.

———. 1993a. Dry-Farming of Jojoba by Palestinians in the West Bank and Gaza Strip. *Jojoba Happenings* 21(2):4–8.

———. 1993b. *Jojoba as an industrial oil-tree crop complementary to olives for the support of a Palestinian economy.* El-Bireh, Palestine: Arab Scientific Institute for Research and Transfer of Technology.

———. 1997. The pollution of Gaza's underground resources by nitrates. Paper presented at the Conference on Water and Environment, the Technion, Haifa, Israel.

———. 1998. *Water reuse and education of the Gaza Strip Palestinian farmers in the implementation of the Coastal Aquifer Management Program.* A USAID report with Engineer Fred Zobrist.

———. 2001. Existing and the future planned desalination facilities in the Gaza Strip of Palestine and their socio-economic and environmental impact. *Desalination* 138:17–28.

———. 2004. The need for implementation of water for peace strategy for the Jordan River Basin countries through a shift in cropping patterns. Proceedings of the 2nd Israel Palestine Conference Water for Life in the Middle East, Antalya, Turkey, October 10–14. Vol. 2, 851–864. Jerusalem: Israeli Palestinian Center for Research and Information.

———. 2005. Water in Palestine: Acknowledging the past, comprehending the present, and facing the future. In *Values and Rights*, 883–904. Ramallah, Palestine: Palestinian Academy of Science and Technology and the Palestinian Water Authority.

———. 2007. *What is Jojoba oil and what are its benefits.* ASIR booklet. El-Bireh/Ramallah: Arab Scientific Institute for Research and Transfer of Technology.

Assaf, S., and K. Assaf. 1985. *Food security in the West Bank and Gaza Strip.* A comprehensive study published by the United Nations ESCWA/FAO Joint Division and AOAD, the Arab Organization for Agricultural Development, the Arab League. FAO publication for ASIR. Rome: ASIR Publications.

———. 1986. The water situation in the West Bank and Gaza Strip. In *Water resources and utilization in the Arab world*, 93—136. Kuwait: Arab Fund for Social and Economic Development (in Arabic).

Attilli, S. 2009. Head of Palestinian Water Authority, personal communication.

———. 2001. Palestinian water, conflict and issues for negotiations (in Arabic). Al-Jazeera Web site. http://www.aljazeera.net/in-depth/water/2001/2/2-6-1.htm.

Badran, A. 1995. *Water in the Islamic world—an imminent crisis*. Amman, Jordan: Islamic Academy of Sciences.

Commission on Sustainable Water Supplies for the Middle East. 1999. *Water for the future in the West Bank and Gaza Strip, Israel and Jordan*. Washington, DC: National Research Council, National Academic Press.

Dillman, J. D. 1989. Water rights in the occupied territories. *Journal of Palestine Studies* 19:46–71.

International Olive Oil Council (IOOC). 1999–2006. *The biannual olive oil production reports*. Palestinian reports by S. Assaf. Madrid, Spain: IOOC.

Ministry of Agriculture. 1999. *Strategy for Sustainable Agriculture in Palestine*. Ramallah: Palestinian National Authority.

———. 2002. Medium term agricultural development plan. Ramallah: Palestinian National Authority.

Mizrahi, Y., and D. Pasternak. 1985. Effect of salinity on quality of various agriculture crops, plant and soil. Vol. 89 (1-2): 301–307.

Nijim, B. K. 1990. Water resources in the history of the Palestinian conflict. *New Journal* 21:317–323.

Palestinian Central Bureau of Statistics (PCBS). 1994–2006. *Agricultural statistics*. Ramallah, Palestine: PCBS.

———. 1998–2007. Ramallah, West Bank, Palestine: PCBS.

Palestinian Economic Council for Development and Reconstruction (PECDAR). 1995. Agricultural institutional policy study. Ramallah, Palestine: PECDAR.

———. 2001. *Palestinian water strategic study with PWA*. Ramallah, Palestine: PECDAR.

Palestinian Times. 2006. Palestinians olive farmers seek new trade avenues. *Palestinian Times*, November 27, 8.

Sbeih, M. 2004. The role of supplementary irrigation for food production in a semi-arid country, Palestine. In *Water resources of arid areas*, ed. D. Stephenson, E. M. Shemeng, and T. R. Chaoka, 191–200. London: Taylor and Francis Group.

Sustainable Water Supply
for Agriculture in Israel

ALON BEN-GAL

Development and Structure of Modern Israeli Agriculture

Since the beginning of the Zionist resettlement in Palestine around the turn of the twentieth century, Jewish presence has possessed a strong agrarian emphasis. Early pioneers believed in farming as an ideology that was needed to transform the occupational and social structure the Jews had in Eastern Europe into a natural organic national structure rooted in the soil. The preference for agrarian living was also thought to assist in transforming the Jews into a nation "like all other nations" (Elon 1971). In addition to its ideology, the early Jewish agricultural society was defined by rejection of traditional Middle Eastern farming and, alternatively, adoption and application of modern European cultivation approaches. Traditional agriculture of the time was fairly unsuccessful, with low yields, little irrigation, and no sense of land or soil conservation. The Zionist farmers, on the other hand, introduced soil conservation techniques, irrigation, and mechanized cultivation.

Israel's agriculture remains organized on cooperative principles which evolved during these first decades of the twentieth century. Two unique forms of agricultural settlement, the kibbutz and moshav, continue to dominate the Israeli agricultural landscape. The kibbutzim (plural of kibbutz) are collective intentional communities while the moshavim (plural of moshav) are rural villages with a more modest cooperative base. Both reflect the early pioneers' vision of rural agricultural communities based on social equality, cooperation, and mutual aid. Today, kibbutzim and moshavim continue to provide most of the country's fresh produce as well as processed food products and almost all meat, poultry, and fish.

Upon the founding of the State of Israel, large numbers of immigrants arrived to join the early settlers. The new government actively settled immigrants in agriculture-based communities, many situated in the arid southern, sparsely populated part of the country as a vehicle to assume ownership of the land. In addition, both pre-and post-state agricultural communities functioned as strongholds against military threats. The agricultural communities became the core of the nation's ethos, and many of their people belonged to the cultural, political, and military elite of the country. "Making the desert bloom" has become a national goal and slogan, making agricultural importance rise above mere food production and security.

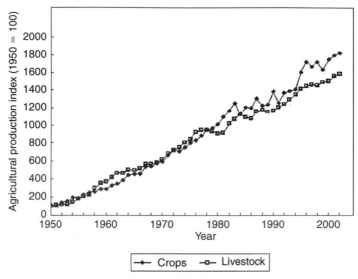

Figure 9.1 Quality index of agricultural production, crops, and livestock.
From Ayal Kimhi 2004.

The period of high immigration in post-state Israel was accompanied by tremendous expansion of agricultural production, much of which was due to increased irrigation. Early state agriculture was highly supported by the government; water was subsidized; price supports were offered for many basic crops; disaster relief was provided. A highly professional extension service brought state-of-the-art agricultural practices to the farmers; research was funded generously. The Ministry of Agriculture in Israel currently still invests some $70 million a year in agricultural research.

Up until a decade ago, the management of national water resources was the responsibility of the Ministry of Agriculture. Typically, the director-general of this office came from the agricultural sector and was very sensitive to its needs. Even today, after a steady weakening of the communal infrastructures, the agricultural sector accounts for about 2.5% of Israel's gross national product and approximately 3% of Israel's exports. Its lobby continues to be considered very powerful (figure 9.1).

The past few decades have seen a softening of state support for agriculture and a decline in the agronomic ideology of yore. Water prices have gradually increased and subsidies for agricultural water have decreased. The Jewish Agency, a Zionist development organization funded by Jewish donors from around the world, built and supported settlements for almost a century, only to discontinue its institutional support for agriculture and new agricultural settlements during the 1990s. Where previous governmental policies made it practically impossible to alter the status of agricultural lands, new flexible policies have allowed many farmers to change the zoning of their lands or to rent to commercial ventures, producing powerful incentives to cease farming.

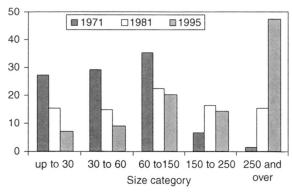

Figure 9.2 Size distribution of active farms among Israeli moshavim (in hectares). From Ayal Kimhi 2004.

Today, the general trend agriculturally is in the direction of economies of scale. To be competitive, farms have had to grow larger. Once, a 1.2 ha greenhouse was considered enormous, and now 4 ha is the standard. Figure 9.2 confirms the magnitude of the transition in Israel, with small family farms in the moshav villages giving way to larger agribusinesses.

Agriculture in Israel Today

After Israel's independence in 1948, cultivated area was 165,000 ha, managed by 400 agricultural communities. Today some 435,000 ha are cultivated by 900 communities. During the same time period Israel's population increased seven-fold, but agricultural production expanded sixteen-fold. Israel's varied climatic, topographical, and soil conditions (subtropical to arid, 400 m below to 1,000 m above sea level, sand dunes to heavy clay alluvial soils) allow a wide range of agricultural production. Table 9.15 provides a general breakdown of present production according to land use. As would be expected given the climatic conditions, the majority of agricultural lands are irrigated. Roughly a quarter of agricultural lands are dedicated to orchards, with citrus still comprising a major component of local fruits, even as the groves have migrated south to the northern Negev. Flowers and ornamental plants, intensely raised in greenhouses, have provided revenues far greater than their 1.6% of land space. In general, some 1,456 ha of land are utilized as protected screen, net, or plastic-covered hothouse or greenhouse facilities (figure 9.3).

Fruits account for some $280 million in annual exports, two-thirds of which are citrus. Other fruits cultivated include avocados, kiwis, mangos, bananas, dates, apples, pears, cherries, and vineyards for both table and wine grapes. Much of the fruit is harvested out of season for European markets. Approximately 1.7 million tons of fresh vegetables are produced annually, representing 17% of Israel's total agricultural production. Some 110,000 tons of these vegetables, valued at $100 million, are exported each year. Greenhouses today offer controlled conditions for lengthening seasons, increasing yields, and saving water, spawning prosperous tomato, melon, pepper, and other vegetable production. There are 220,000 ha

Table 9.15 Agricultural use of land in Israel

	Thousands of hectares	% of total lands
Total	382.2	100
Irrigated crops	192.3	50.3
Rain-supported crops	136.9	35.8
Orchards	84.8	22.2
Citrus	25.3	6.6
Vegetables, potatoes, melons	55.1	14.4
Flowers and ornamental plants	5.2	1.4
Field crops	183.0	47.9
Cotton	29.0	7.6
Wheat	86.0	22.5

Source: Ministry of Agriculture, 2001.

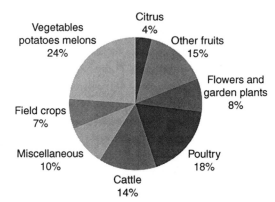

Figure 9.3 Breakdown of agricultural output by branch (% of value), 2004.
From the Central Bureau of Statistics.

of field crops grown, 160,000 ha of rain-fed winter crops (wheat, hay, legumes, safflower), and the remainder is summer crops such as cotton, chickpeas, beans, corn, and groundnuts. The irrigated crops (corn, cotton, groundnuts, potatoes) primarily consume recycled wastewater using drippers and traveling sprinklers. Dairy and beef products comprise some 17% of county's total agricultural production. Israel holds the world record for milk production with more than 10,000 kg of 3.3% butterfat milk per cow per year. Poultry for eggs and meat, beef cattle, and fish farming are all important in Israel. Over 100 flower varieties are cultivated, many of which are European "summer" varieties grown and exported in winter. Agricultural inputs produced in Israel are valued today at over $2 billion, of which 70% are exported.

Israel produces some 70% of its own food requirements. Grains, oilseeds, meat, fish, sugar, coffee, and cocoa are imported. Countering this are $800 million of

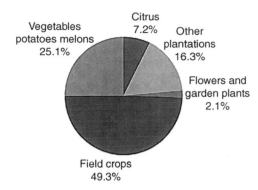

Figure 9.4 Breakdown of agricultural crop areas, 2003 (total = 2,820 thousands of hectares).
From the Central Bureau of Statistics.

annual agricultural produce and $600 million of processed foods which are exported (figure 9.4). The success of Israeli agriculture since the establishment of the state can be attributed to a number of factors (Tal 2007). In addition to a commitment to food security, innovative technological development, a steady increase in available work force, the unity of purpose in the agricultural settlement movements, the unconditional political/economic support, and the growing availability of export markets created a simply extraordinary record of water development and utilization.

Water in Israeli Agriculture

Water consumption from all sources and for all sectors in Israel has increased from 230 mcm in 1948 to 1997 mcm in 2002; only 82% of the present amount is annually renewable. The remaining water supplied must be derived by groundwater mining, through the use of reclaimed wastewater, or by desalination. Whereas per capita consumption in the domestic and industrial sectors has remained essentially the same over the years, today, per capita water available for agricultural uses is less than half its volume from the 1960s. Despite the reduction, agricultural production per capita today is more than 150% of that produced 40 years ago, reflecting a threefold increase in water productivity (Kislev 2001).

Freshwater use in agriculture has dropped from 950 mcm in 1998 to around 550 mcm today. Total water to agriculture has been maintained via the utilization of saline and recycled water. In this decade, agricultural production has continued to rise, and agricultural efficiency, whether measured as return per unit water or return per unit land, has steadily increased. Of particular significance in Israeli agriculture are the extent that marginal (brackish and recycled) water resources are utilized and the level of water use efficiency that is attained.

Brackish Water

Salts in irrigation water cause stress in crops and reduce yields. Salts introduced with irrigation water accumulate in soils and eventually are leached into groundwater. In spite of this, Israel's agriculture directly uses some 80 mcm of groundwater that is regarded brackish for irrigation. Salinity in water is commonly quantified by determining its electrical conductivity (EC). Measured in dS/m (desi Semins per meter), EC rises as dissolved salts in water increase. Much of Israel's water has low

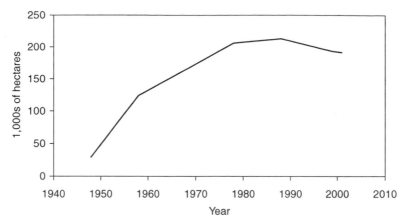

Figure 9.5 Extent of irrigated land since the establishment of the State of Israel.
From the Central Bureau of Statistics.

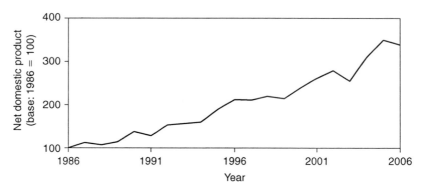

Figure 9.6 Agricultural production, 1986–2006.
From the Central Bureau of Statistics.

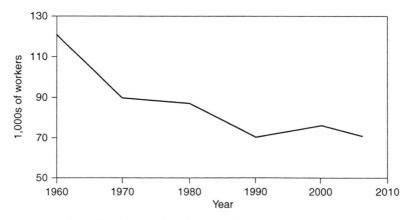

Figure 9.7 Number of people employed in agriculture, 1960–2010.
From the Central Bureau of Statistics.

to moderate salinity. The EC of the National Water Carrier's water is approximately 0.8 dS/m. Water from brackish wells in which EC reaches more than 2 dS/m is also commonly pumped and used for agriculture. The hottest and driest regions in Israel, including the Negev highlands and the Jordan and Arava valleys, use the most saline water. In parts of these regions, the best quality water for irrigation has EC values of 2.5–3 dS/m, and water of up to 5–5.5 dS/m is also used.

The combination of high concentrations of salts in water with particularly high crop water demand, resulting from the extreme climate in these regions, essentially creates a situation where salts are being added to the agricultural fields and crops at rates unknown in other parts of the world. Successful agriculture has been developed in the country's arid southlands in spite of this by choosing crops that are relatively salt tolerant and avoiding crops that are particularly sensitive. This is only sustainable through careful irrigation and soil management where salts are maintained lower in the active root zone of the crops and any accumulating salts are leached.

Recycled Wastewater

Israel has made wastewater recycling a central component of its water management strategy. A master plan presented in 1956 envisioned the ultimate recycling of 150 mcm of sewage, all of which would go to agriculture. Today three times that level is recycled, representing more than 60% of all domestic wastewater produced. Effluents (treated wastewater) today contribute roughly a fifth of Israel's total water supply and a far higher percentage of the irrigation supply for agriculture. The continued shift from fresh to marginal water use in agricultural production is expected to continue and is incorporated in national planning. Table 9.16 offers a Ministry of Agriculture projection of future crop area and water use.

The supply of water to agriculture continues to decline relative to total supply of water, as reflected in table 9.17. This makes farmers highly dependent upon a temporal water budget. During drought years, freshwater supply to agriculture is severely diminished, while the flow of wastewater is hardly affected. During the agricultural year 1999/2000 Israel faced an extreme drought. In that year, agricultural supply of freshwater was severely reduced, but farmers utilizing reclaimed wastewater continued to receive nearly full amounts of their water supply. In 2008 Israel is facing an additional serious drought situation in which allocations of freshwater are being cut by as much as 50%.

One of the criteria for successful utilization of recycled wastewater is that treatment level is high enough to ensure safe use of the effluent. In order for effluent to be the dominant water source for irrigation, water must be treated to a level allowing unlimited use on all crops and on all soils. The Shafdan plant, Israel's largest sanitation facility, is a large-scale project for processing sewage of the Tel-Aviv (Dan) region. Wastewater there undergoes biological treatment and then is recharged into aquifers before being pumped and transported to the Negev, where the effluent is used in agriculture. The aquifer serves both as a filter in which further purification occurs and as an underground reservoir in which the reclaimed

Table 9.16 Cultivated area, major crops, and irrigation water use, 1996 and
         predicted for 2020.

| Major crops | Cultivated area (thousands of hectares) | | Irrigation water use (mcm/yr) | | | | | |
| | | | FRESHWATER | | MARGINAL SOURCES | | TOTAL | |
	1996	2020	1996	2020	1996	2020	1996	2020
Tree plantations	84	82	490		70		560	
Field crops, vegetables, & flowers	233	240	185		205		380	
Flowers	43	55	175		25		190	
Fish ponds	3	3	30		70		100	
Fallow land	68	70						
Total	428	430	880	600	378	750	1265	1350
Irrigated land	183	200						
Dry & fallow land	245	230						

Source: Compiled from Central Planning Authority, Ministry of Agriculture, 1998.

Table 9.17 Supply of water to agriculture

| Calendar year | Total water supply MCM/YR | Agricultural supply MCM/YR | Reused wastewater | | |
			MCM/YR	% OF TOTAL SUPPLY	% OF SUPPLY TO AGRICULTURE
1965	1,329	1,075			
1970	1,564	1,249			
1980	1,700	1,235	80	4.7	6.5
1990	1,804	1,216	159	8.8	13.1
2000	1,924	1,138	269	14.0	23.6
2005	1,961	1,126	335	17.1	29.8

Source: Central Bureau of Statistics.

water can be stored seasonally with minimum losses for use in the summer months
when agricultural demand is high. About 110 mcm of Shafdan effluents are piped
annually to the western Negev for use in irrigation. As is discussed in part 7, additional sewage water purification plants are to be built based on this high standard of
purification, and older plants are to be brought up to this treatment level.

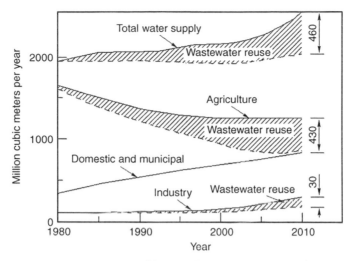

Figure 9.8 Wastewater reuse as part of the overall water balance (drought years excluded). From Shelef 2001.

Agricultural Water Use Efficiency

The average requirement of water per unit of land area in Israel has decreased from 8,700 m^3/ha in 1975 to 5,500 m^3/ha in 1995. At the same time agricultural output increased twelve-fold, while total water consumption by the sector remained almost constant. Such increased water use efficiency has been accomplished via a number of supporting factors, including precision irrigation technology, irrigation water control, and water policy covering water allocations, metering, and pricing.

Micro-irrigation and Fertigation

The wide-scale adoption of low-volume irrigation systems (e.g., drip, micro-sprinklers) and automation has increased the average efficiency (relative amount of water utilized by crops) to 90% as compared to 64% for furrow irrigation or 75% for sprinklers. Development of drip irrigation technology that allows low-flow application of water uniformly throughout agricultural fields, along with the application of this technology in agricultural water management, has been a cornerstone in Israel's advancements in water use efficiency. With drip irrigation, water is supplied when and where crops can utilize it. In addition, a significant advantage of drip-irrigation systems lies in their ability to supply nutrients as well as water.

Such fertilizing via the irrigation system (fertigation) allows precision nutrient management and results in increased efficiencies of both fertilizer and water as higher yields are achieved. Today, further irrigation efficiency is being attempted by regulating water application to each individual plant. Root volume water and nutrients can be further controlled by proper irrigation management where soil and crop types are matched with dripper spacing, flow rate, and irrigation frequency in order to ultimately achieve maximum plant water uptake and growth with minimum water.

Table 9.18 Agricultural water prices

Agricultural use	U.S.s/cubic meter
Freshwater	
Up to 50% of user's allotment	0.39
Next 30% of user's allotment	0.45
Rest of amount allocated	0.59
Average	0.45
Tertiary recycled wastewater (Shafdan)	0.24
Secondary effluent	0.18
Brackish water	
1.9–2.65 dS/m	0.25
2.65–3.4 dS/m	0.24
3.4–4.1 dS/m	0.21
4.1–4.8 dS/m	0.20
4.8–5.2 dS/m	0.19
.5.2 dS/m	0.17

Source: Israel Water Authority, 2008.
Note: US$1 = 3.5 NIS.

Irrigation Water Control

Drip irrigation systems are readily automated. Computers allow real-time response in the operation of the irrigation systems, providing precision, reliability, and savings in manpower as water application is controlled remotely. Sensors are also used to provide information on soil moisture and plant water status, allowing automatic operation of systems and providing tools that assist to avoid unnecessary excess or deficits in water applications.

Water Allocations, Metering, and Pricing

While traditionally subsidized, water prices for agriculture are graded according to water quality. Subsidies to agriculture that were approximately 50% in 1992 decreased to around 20% in 1996 and continue to be decreased. Water charges for various consumers are set by a parliamentary committee. Agricultural water is allocated by quota and purchased at prices that increase as use of the quota increases. The purpose of this price structure is to combine support for agriculture with economic efficiency and encouragement of conservation. Conservation is further encouraged by pricing brackish and recycled water (table 9.18) lower than the freshwater and according to level of quality (Kislev 2001, Nativ 2004).

A Critical Look at the Conflicting Roles of Agriculture in Israel's Water Economy

Israel's history suggests that agriculture plays multiple, sometimes conflicting, roles in Israel's water economy. First, irrigation technology and advancements in water use efficiency and agricultural productivity are banners of national pride. Israel is fast to promote its agricultural water-related achievements and even to attempt to export expertise and technology. At the same time, agriculture, as the largest single sector consuming water, is held responsible for water shortages in the country—both ongoing and those occurring periodically due to drought. Irrigation water is the first to be reduced when there is not enough water to go around. In spite of increasing replacement of freshwater with low-quality (not fit for drinking) water sources, the use of agriculture as a buffer for water supply management in the country is very hard on the sector that is forced in some years to forfeit up to 50% of normal freshwater allotments. The agricultural sector is also treated as a waste management solution. On the surface, application of wastewater in agricultural fields appears to be both a viable waste disposal solution and beneficial to agriculture, but it does not come without a pretty heavy price.

The salinity of the recycled water (and that of other marginal water sources) causes lower than optimal yields and demands irrigation with substantially greater volumes of water in order to maintain the best possible growing conditions (Ben-Gal et al. 2008; Dudley et al. 2008; Shani et al. 2007). Excess irrigation water for leaching salts not only raises water consumption rates but carries the salts and many other agricultural contaminants (fertilizers, pesticides, herbicides, etc.) into and beyond the soil of the fields. Eventually, management for optimized yields using salty water for irrigation causes pollution of soils and groundwater. The policy of waste dumping as an agricultural/environmental solution thus appears to be highly non-sustainable.

Desalination and Agriculture

Recently, desalination has begun to be considered economically viable for increasing water supply. In Israel, both incidental use and designed use of desalinated water for irrigation have begun to change the water supply portfolio for farmers. Water from the world's largest reverse-osmosis desalination plant in Ashkelon is being supplied to farmers in the northern Negev (Yermiyahu et al. 2007). A number of small- to medium-sized plants, designed to desalinate local saline groundwater and to serve irrigation needs, already exist in the south of Israel, and more, larger facilities are currently planned. Irrigation with desalinated water is beneficial as it allows for increased yields and decreased environmental degradation from leaching of salts. In spite of this, desalinated water lacks a number of minerals which are necessary for plant growth and which must be provided in intensively irrigated agriculture. These minerals, including calcium, magnesium, and sulfur, are present in all of Israel's water sources and therefore not commonly added as fertilizers, but they are removed during the reverse-osmosis desalination process.

The missing nutrients can be re-supplied either as fertilizer supplements to the water or soil or, alternatively, through blending of the desalinated water with saline water. Each of the options has advantages and disadvantages. Fertilization of the missing nutrients is costly, due the basic costs of the chemical additives themselves, and requires sophisticated equipment, especially since, due to problems of chemical mineralization and settlement, they cannot be simply added with the regular fertilizers. Blending, on the other hand, is less costly economically and increases the volume of irrigation water; but, due to the higher salinity of the blended water, increased leaching rates lead to higher overall water consumption and to elevated pollution of soils and groundwater with salts and other contaminants.

The Future

Israel's agricultural future will be faced with a number of essential issues. Many of the issues are water related, and all of these demand regional considerations which will require coordination with the Palestinian Authority and Jordan. Here are few examples:

- further development of water resources through desalination, rain augmentation, wastewater treatment, and utilization of brackish water;
- environmental responsibility through reduction (preferably, elimination) of ground and surface water contamination by salts and agricultural chemicals;
- greater economic efficiency through deregulation of the water economy; and
- international coordination in respect to the water rights of the Palestinian population.

REFERENCES

Ben-Gal, A., E. Ityel, L. Dudley, S. Cohen, U. Yermiyahu, E. Presnov, L. Zigmond, and U. Shani. 2008. Effect of irrigation water salinity on transpiration and on leaching requirements: A case study for bell peppers. *Agriculture Water Management* 95:587–597.

Ben-Gal, A., A. Tal, and N. Tel-Zur. 2006. The sustainability of arid agriculture: Trends and challenges. *Annals of Arid Zone* 45:227–258.

Dudley, L., A. Ben-Gal, and U. Shani. 2008. Influence of plant, soil and water properties on the Leaching Fraction. *Vadose Zone Journal* 7:420–425.

Elon, A. 1971. *The Israelis, founders and sons.* New York: Bantam Books.

Falkenmark, M., and G. Lindh. 1976. *Water for a starving world.* Boulder, CO: Westview Press.

Fedler, J. 2002. *Israel's agriculture in the 21st century.* Israel Ministry of Foreign Affairs. http://www.mfa.gov.il/MFA/Facts+About+Israel/Economy/Focus+on+Israel-+Israel-s+Agriculture+in+the+21st.htm (accessed November 2, 2009).

Feitelson, E. 2002. The ebb and flow of Arab-Israeli water conflicts—a past confrontation likely to resurface. *Water Policy* 2(4):343–363.

———. 2004. Implications of shifts in the Israeli water discourse for Israeli-Palestinian negotiations. *Political Geography* 2(3):293–318.

Haddadin, M. J., and U. Shamir. 2003. *The Jordan River Basin, Part I: Water conflict and negotiated resolution.* UNESCO report, supported by the Japanese government.

Hydrological Service of Israel. 2002. *The water resources of Israel 2001.* Jerusalem: HIS (in Hebrew).

International Federation of Organic Agriculture Movements (IFOAM). 2004. *Organic agriculture and biodiversity: Making the links.* http://www.ifoam.org/growing_organic/1_arguments_for _oa/environmental_benefits/pdfs/OA_Biodiversity_Links.pdf (accessed July 27, 2009).

Kimhi, A. 2004. *The rise and fall of Israeli agriculture: Technology, markets, and policy.* Rehovot, Israel: Department of Agriculture Economics and Management, Hebrew University of Jerusalem.

Kislev, Y. 2001. *The water economy of Israel.* Discussion paper no. 11.01. Rehovot, Israel: Department of Agricultural Economics and Management, Hebrew University of Jerusalem.

Lowi, M. 1993. *Water and power: The politics of a scarce resource in the Jordan River Basin.* New York: Cambridge University Press.

Nativ, R. 2004. Can the desert bloom? Lessons learned from the Israeli case. *Ground Water* 42:651–657.

Pasternick, D. 2002. Report on agricultural research at Ben Gurion University of the Negev. Beer Sheva, Israel.

Schwarz, J. 2007. *Water resources development and management in Israel.* Ramat Gan: Began–Sadat Center for Strategic Studies, Bar-Ilan University. http://www.biu.ac.il/Besa/waterarticle5 .html (accessed November 2, 2009).

Shani, U., A. Ben-Gal, E. Tripler, and L. M. Dudley. 2007. Plant response to the soil environment: An analytical model integrating yield, water, soil type and salinity. *Water Resources Research* 43.

Shelef, G. 2001. *Wastewater treatment, reclamation and reuse in Israel, efficient use of limited water resources.* Ramat Gan: BESA Center for Strategic Studies, Bar-Ilan University.

Sitton, D. 2000. *Development of limited water resources: Historical and technological aspects.* http:// www.mfa.gov.il/MFA/Facts+About+Israel/Land/FOCUS+on+Israel-+Development+ of+Limited+Water+Reso.htm?DisplayMode=print (accessed November 2, 2009).

Tal, A. 2007. To make a desert bloom—the Israeli agriculture adventure and the quest for sustainability. *Agricultural History* 81 (2): 228–258.

United Nations Development Programme. 2006. Human development report. *Beyond scarcity: Power, poverty and the global water crisis.* New York: Macmillan.

Yermiyahu, U., A. Tal, A. Ben-Gal, A. Bar-Tal, J. Tarchitzky, and O. Lahav. 2007. Rethinking desalinated water quality and agriculture. *Science* 318:920–921.

Zaslavsky, D. 1999. *Sustainable development of water resources and the fate of agriculture.* Technion Haifa, Israel: Faculty of Agricultural Engineering (in Hebrew).

Editors' Summary

Israeli and Palestinian agricultural practices and conditions are in many ways very different. Israel epitomizes an irrigation-driven, high-tech, high-input, high-production system, with an increasing utilization of wastewater and greenhouses. Palestinian agriculture remains primarily rain-fed, although the percentage of protected agricultural facilities and the general willingness to utilize treated effluents is increasing.

The internal discourse about agriculture in each of the parties, however, has certain similarities. The relative contribution of agriculture to both economies has generally declined over the years and, in the long run, will continue to do so. In both communities there are those who believe that the overall water scarcity mandates a steady down-sizing in agricultural production. The growing demand of the predominant urban sector is argued to be more important than maintaining production in a water-intensive agricultural sector, notwithstanding the cultural significance and heritage of farming. Expansion of "virtual water" through the increased importation of produce is considered to be inevitable.

Of course, agricultural advocates on both sides are more sanguine. They see an even stronger future for agriculture, based on scientific advancement. They also cite food security and aesthetic, historic, cultural, and economic justification for maintaining and even subsidizing the agricultural sector.

Neither internal Israeli nor internal Palestinian critics of present water allocations to agriculture would like to see an elimination of local farming. Most members of the general public believe that it is simply impossible to think about Palestinian or Israeli society without a robust farming sector. Yet critics argue that recycled wastewater must continue to become the predominant irrigation source. (Cattle and livestock, for example, will surely continue to require freshwater, although these quantities are trivial compared to the demands of field crops.) As in most countries in Europe and in the United States, subsidies for agriculture are widely considered legitimate, given concerns over social stability, food security, landscape, and heritage preservation. They should, however, find expression in areas other than water supply, such as general tax relief for agricultural production, subsidies on farm labor, etc.

Water pricing is another issue which separates the Israeli and the Palestinian agricultural sectors. Today, Palestinian farmers who wish to purchase water for irrigation face a rate of $1.20/m³—a rate far higher than their Israeli counterparts. This creates a clear competitive advantage in what may ultimately be a single market. A final agreement should address this discrepancy, with the advantages of the creation of a regional water market quite evident in the agricultural context.

The fact that many Palestinian farmers rely on private water rights for much of their own production means that reduction of water for the rural sector will not be as smooth as it might be in Israel. (Nationalization of water sources in Israel occurred 50 years ago and has long since become part of the culture of agricultural regulatory reality.) In the past, Palestinian communities have successfully negotiated the purchasing and transfer of rights for public use, and this is expected to continue naturally. The relative profitability of selling water as opposed to using it for rural Palestinians may offer a point of departure for the creation of a regional market for water supply. But whether through the pricing of water in an open market or through government allocation, there is a consensus that the amounts of freshwater that will be available from natural sources is not going to increase for the farming sector of either side in the foreseeable future. It most likely will decline.

Reductions in water, with the objective of downsizing agriculture, have greater social implications today than in the recent past for Palestinians. During the Intifada, when movement was restricted and half the population became unemployed, many people returned to subsistence farming. Agriculture offered an economic buffer, temporarily returning its economic significance for many members of the local Palestinian population.

Wastewater and desalinated water are considered to be the inevitable substitutes for future decreases in traditional freshwater supplied to farmers. Israeli farmers in particular have been criticized for exporting crops with high water demands at a time when there is a general shortage. As agricultural needs have become increasingly supplied by wastewater and (and in the future by market-priced desalinated waters), these charges appear less compelling. Desalinated water at its present marginal price level will be too prohibitively expensive for the foreseeable future to be used to irrigate many crops, although there may be some, such as flowers or avocadoes, which could afford the higher price for this high-quality irrigation source.

While recycled wastewater is discussed in greater detail in part 7, it can be summarized that without substantial upgrading of present treatment levels and oversight of wastewater recycling, dramatic expansion of present levels is inadvisable. The reuse of poorly treated wastewater may exacerbate present salinization of groundwater and lead to additional health problems. Setting common standards for agricultural recycling could be an important part of a future water agreement in order to enable a transboundary water market for recycled effluents to be used for farm operations.

There is a consensus that due to growing water scarcity Palestinian and Israeli farmers will need to be even more selective about crops and continue research that will ensure maximum crop water efficiency and salt tolerance. The anticipated precipitation drop associated with future climate change will only heighten the importance of such measures.

Donors can play a key role in supporting the Palestinian agricultural sector, just as Jewish philanthropies historically have boosted Israeli farmers by covering the costs of infrastructure, providing irrigation reservoirs, or preparing farmlands.

Such assistance (for instance, for restoring Palestinian well operation) should be done through the government or a public-interest agency, rather than given directly to private individuals whose interests may be too narrow to attain optimal economic and social results.

When considering the role of agriculture in a final water agreement, a few points are clear. To the extent that water supply will be allocated regionally, agricultural interests, as the largest consumers for both parties, must be consulted. The ultimate role of wastewater reuse that is mandated should ensure that high environmental standards are maintained to protect groundwater, ensure farmers' health, and allow for maximum flexibility in crop selection. Food security is an issue of common concern. Yet, as Israel is likely to become increasingly connected to the European market, and the future Palestinian state to the Jordanian and Egyptian markets, it is not clear whether the agreement should focus on cooperation in this realm.

PART 10

DESALINATION

Desalination has provided not only a new source of low-cost water, but also a source of optimism for a technological solution to water quantity controversies. The following chapters assess the present state of local desalination facilities along with the associated concerns of Palestinians and Israelis. The reviews offer a broader context for evaluating the ultimate role of desalinated seawater as a sustainable solution to present water scarcity.

The Coming Age of Desalination for Gaza

VISIONS, ILLUSIONS, AND REALITY

NAHED GHBN

The Gaza Strip is located along the coast of the eastern Mediterranean Sea, covering an area of 378 km² (United Nations Environment Program 2003), stretching over a distance of approximately 45 km from Beit Hanoun, a town in the north, to Rafah, a city in the south, with width of 7 to 12 km. The Gaza Strip is composed of five governorates, sixteen municipalities, and nine local councils. Each municipality has its own water source and a separate distribution system. Water consumption averages 80 to 100 l/c/d (liters per capita per day). Due to the deteriorating distribution network, water losses are very high, in the range of 35% to 50%. Growing population and deteriorating water quality have created a growing water "overdraft." The total deficit in domestic water supply for 2005 was more than 7 mcm for the Gaza Strip.

Gaza has no permanent surface freshwater resources. The Wadi Gaza is located at the middle of the Gaza Strip and, while the wadi has a large catchment in Israel, seasonal rainfall and dams on the eastern side of the border result in only intermittent flow, hence the primary water resource of the region for potable and agricultural uses is the Coastal Aquifer. The Coastal Aquifer in the Strip, however, has limited quantities. Its thickness fluctuates from few meters in the southeastern area to about 120 m in the western areas. Groundwater quality varies according to its depth from ground surface and also varies spatially from place to place. Groundwater levels have been in long-term decline, and water quality continues to degrade. Induced saltwater intrusion and infiltration from septic tanks have resulted in groundwater quality that fails World Health Organization drinking-water standards throughout the region. Agricultural production is also adversely affected by salinity, particularly citrus, for which the Gaza Strip is famous, resulting in orchards being abandoned in some areas.

Existing wastewater treatment plants are overloaded, causing pollution and releasing untreated wastewater to be discharged to the wadi from the central communities with unacceptable environmental impacts. Less than 10% of the supplied municipal water matches with international standards for domestic purposes. Some illnesses linked to unsafe drinking water are cancer, diarrhea, and methemoglobinimia. The incidence of enteric diseases is high, particularly in the refuge camps.

As a result, most Gaza residents use various techniques to improve their drinking water or they purchase bottled water. Operating home reverse-osmosis (RO) filters is an expensive method that is not affordable for most of the people, and the small desalination firms that have emerged are also inherently inefficient, selling relatively expensive drinking water in 20 l jerry cans.

There is an urgent need to develop new water resources in addition to upgrading and developing the storage and distribution facilities. The priority in Gaza is to reduce pressure on the aquifer by identifying other sources of freshwater and using non-conventional water resources, including seawater desalination. Large- and small-scale seawater desalination is widely perceived among Palestinians as providing a more sustainable water management strategy. Critically, it would decrease present dependency on the aquifer. The cost of seawater desalination has decreased in recent years as the technology and its efficiency levels have improved.

Ultimately, desalinated water from Gaza could relieve the water shortages in the West Bank. Yet, to date, no broader supply strategies have been designed beyond local production and supply of desalinated water for Gaza itself. This essay, therefore, will focus on present plans for desalination in the Gaza context, with the understanding that production could eventually be expanded to service all of the Palestinian territories.

Desalination Techniques

The need for pure water for drinking purposes is increasing in step with the technological progress. Many places in the Middle East have limited quantities of groundwater or none at all. This means that potable water has to be carried over long distances or must be produced by desalination of seawater.

There is no single best method of desalination that a Palestinian facility should automatically select. A wide variety of desalination technologies effectively remove salts from saline water or extract freshwater from salty water, producing the product stream—a water stream with a low concentration of salt and then the brine or concentrate stream with a high concentration of remaining salts. Most of these technologies rely on either distillation or membranes to separate salts from the product water.

Various processes are available for desalinating both brackish water and seawater. These processes are typically categorized as either thermal or membrane separation systems. The thermal process includes multiple effect distillation (MED), multiple stage flash (MSF), mechanical vapor compression (MVE), and some other variations of these three systems. The membrane separation systems include electrodialysis (EDR) and reverse osmosis (RO).

Seawater desalination by means of reverse osmosis (membrane technology) has been applied for more than 20 years and is emerging as the process of choice for large seawater facilities. The process is increasingly found in parts of the world where natural ground or surface water for drinking purposes is only present to a limited extent.

Membrane technology plays a large role in water treatment in general and in RO plants in particular. Advanced technology in manufacturing the membranes has made reverse osmosis the leading and most competitive process for desalinating water when compared to other desalination technologies. RO uses dynamic pressure to overcome the osmotic pressure of the salt solution, causing water-selective permeation from the saline side of a membrane to the freshwater side. Salts are then rejected from the membrane. The RO membranes used are semi-permeable thin polymeric layers, adhering to a thick support layer. Membranes are usually made of cellulose acetates, polyamides, polyimides, and polysulfones. They differ as symmetric, asymmetric, and thin film composite membranes. Membranes are sensitive to changes in pH, small concentrations of oxidized substances like chlorine and chlorine oxides, a wide range of organic materials, and the presence of algae and bacteria. Therefore, careful pretreatment is needed in order to prevent membrane contamination and fouling. Associated measures include pre-filtration to remove suspended solids from feed water and a dosage of acid (hydrochloric or sulfuric) to remove bicarbonate ions, followed by aeration to remove carbon dioxide and filtration by active carbon to remove dissolved organic materials and chlorine compounds. Different anti-scalants are used in order to prevent precipitation of dissolved salts due to increased concentration. Reverse osmosis is used for both small and large plants, amounting to about 22% of the world's larger plants' capacity of above 4,000 m^3/day. RO systems can easily be integrated within other thermal desalination technologies, namely, hybrid systems for efficient water production

Electrodialysis (ED), or the more modern reversible electrodialysis (EDR), is another promising alternative process. Ions are forced, by means of DC electrical power, to pass through semi-permeable membranes into concentrated streams. The water leaves behind dilute salt solutions. Its advantages involve the relative insensitivity of the membranes to fouling and the thermodynamic transfer properties. To date, the technique has not yet reached a significant market share relative to other processes. Currently, the technique is in use mainly for brackish water desalination and water purification.

The selection of a desalination process depends on site-specific conditions, including the salt content of the water, economics, and the quality of water needed by the end user, as well as local engineering experience and skills. The technology for desalinating water continues to improve, driven by advances in technology, the need to reduce costs, and commercial competition. The Gaza Strip is a special case, where selection of appropriate treatment processes deserves special attention.

Through the launched Water Master Plan and Integrated Aquifer Management Plan, many options and desalination techniques have been considered for use in the Gaza Strip as well as the most appropriate location for plant sites. It was concluded that establishing a large RO-membrane seawater desalination plant is technically feasible and a cost-effective water resource for bringing substantial quantities of new freshwater into the Gaza municipal system.

There were two basic reasons for this decision. Membrane technologies generally have lower capital costs and require less energy than other systems. Other processes for desalination of seawater are less attractive for Gaza. Because of economic reasons, pure distilled water quality is not required. Rather, drinking water with reasonably low turbidity levels (below 700 TDS) can be pumped into the distribution system. Ultimately, selection of the optimal technology was an economic process, allowing gradation in the product quality without requiring mixing to dilute the corrosive effects of distilled water.

The membranes should be properly selected according to the present water analysis and the quality requirements of the product water. A feasibility study conducted by Metcalf and Eddy concluded that the most economic combination of processes for seawater membrane desalination is to use RO systems with a seawater membrane in the first pass and nanofiltration membranes in the second pass in order to be most cost effective and meet product turbidity concentrations of 350 mg/l TDS (Camp Dresser and McKee International 1993).

The Desalination Status in Gaza

The increasing demand for freshwater to supply the Gaza Strip has driven decisions about establishing desalination facilities. The desalination market responded in two distinct directions. The first direction involved distribution of pure water for drinking purposes through small-scale private brackish desalination plants or slightly larger seawater desalination plants. The second direction involves implementation of large seawater desalination plants for domestic purposes that can distribute drinking water through the piping system to local customers.

Drinking-Water Desalination Plants

There are several brackish and seawater RO projects/plants in the Gaza Strip, varying in output productivity. Desalination of brackish water has already begun in several locations in the Gaza Strip with four major functioning RO desalination plants for brackish water presently operational. Yet, there is a limited quantity of brackish water available for expanding this kind of desalination, as shown in table 10.1 and figure 10.1.

The chronic scarcity also created a new, smaller market for desalinated water in Gaza through many small-scale, private brackish water desalination plants. The number of registered plants (or registrations under process) now reaches around forty plants, distributing water over all Gaza Strip. These private plants are simply RO membranes with a high-pressure pump fixed directly to the water well. No pretreatment is included and no reliable work mechanism is used by the private sector for the quality control monitoring or the marketing of the water.

In addition to the brackish desalination plants, it was decided to construct two small seawater desalination plants for drinking purposes in the Gaza Strip. These plants promise to provide the local Palestinian communities with good quality water for drinking purposes as an emergency solution to alleviate the unsafe supply of domestic water with its very high chloride and nitrate concentration. These plants will be expected to produce water that meets drinking-water quality standards. The sources of feed water will be beach wells located close to the seashore.

Table 10.1 Brackish and seawater desalination plants in the Gaza Strip

Name	Donors	Water source	Capacity m^3/hr	Productivity m^3/hr	Disposal
Industrial zone (the north)	USAID	Brackish well	95	75	Water to be disposed by tankers to the sea
Beit Lahia (the north) under construction	France	Sea well	60	50	Tankers to the sea
Deir El Balah desalination station	Before Palestinian Authority	Brackish well	78	45	The sea
Deir El Balah	Austria	Seawater	30	20	The sea
Khan Younis, El-Sharqi	Italy	Brackish well	60	50	The sewer system and the sea
Khan Younis, Al-Sa'ad	Italy	Brackish well	80	65	The sewer system and the sea

The treatment process consists of pretreatment (chlorination, coagulation, pH adjustment, sand filtration, safety cartridge filtration, dechlorination), RO process, post-treatment, and sterilization.

The northern plant is to be financed through a grant from the French government. The grant covers the first phase, with a capacity of 1,250 m^3/day, located north of Gaza Strip. The second one is to be financed through a grant from the Austrian government. The first phase involves a capacity of 600 m^3/day, with the facility located in the middle area of Gaza Strip.

In all the planned RO desalination plants, the salty water is discarded onto the adjacent grounds and/or into the sea through pipes or tankers delivering the brine water to the sea or to the sewerage network. Brine which is discharged into the seashore has a very high concentration of salts and could affect the surrounding environment. Table 10.1 summarizes the status of the brackish and seawater RO desalination plants in the Gaza Strip.

Projected Plans for Large-Scale Seawater Desalination Plants

To improve the domestic municipal water supply system in the Gaza Strip, an integrated water resources management plan has been developed through USAID funding. According to the plan, the projected water demand in the Gaza Strip will dramatically increase and reach about 260 mcm/yr by the year 2020, of which about 180 mcm will be needed for municipal purposes. The associated pressures on the aquifer will cause serious groundwater deterioration and produce a substantial water deficit in Gaza with water quality and quantity ramifications if significant

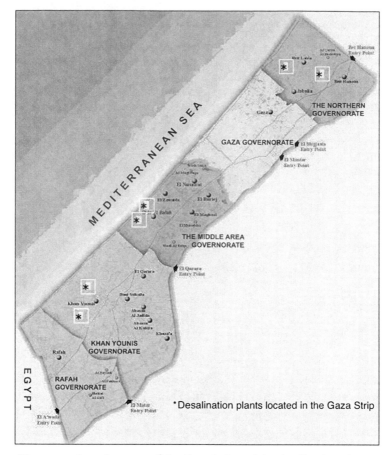

Figure 10.1 Location map of the Gaza Strip and the desalination plants.

measures are not immediately implemented. In order to alleviate this crisis and meet the domestic (municipal) water demand, RO seawater desalination was seen as the most realistic option for Gaza conditions.

In order to maintain a positive water balance and meaningfully improve the water situation in Gaza, the new large-scale seawater RO desalination plants will need to have a total capacity of 150,000 m³/day. Originally, USAID agreed to finance the design and construction of the first phase of a major RO seawater desalination plant as full donation with a capacity of 60,000 m³/day. The Gaza regional north-south water carrier would distribute this high-quality water throughout the Gaza Strip. In the second phase, the capacity would be expanded to 120,000 m³/day, and in the third phase it would grow to 140,000 m³/day. This planned desalination plant could be extended so that in the final phase it could reach a capacity of 150,000 m³/day in year 2020. The quality of the produced water would match WHO and Palestinian standards for drinking water. The desalination project includes sea intake, outfall, two pumping stations, storage, and a 2 km pipeline to the regional

Table 10.2 Environmental impact assessment of desalination plants

Category	Impact
Energy: Burning fossil fuels to generate power for desalination plants	Human health, climate change, agricultural crops, biodiversity, and noise level
Land use: Land-use impacts related to the loss of the open seashore for construction of desalination plants	Land degradation and soil contamination
Brine discharge: Rejected brine to the sea contains chemicals like anti-scalants and washing solutions	Brine discharge affects marine life

carrier. Some of this infrastructure would be built to meet an eventual capacity of 150,000 m³/day. However, implementation of these projects was suspended because of the political situation.

The Environmental Impacts of Anticipated Desalination Plants

Desalination, like any other major industrial process, has environmental impacts that need to be considered and mitigated. The impact includes the effects associated with the construction, operation, and effects of withdrawing large quantities of sea and brackish water from an aquifer or seawater and discharging large volumes of highly concentrated brine. Indirect impacts associated with the substantial use of energy must also be considered.

Rejected brine is a byproduct resulting from the desalination processes. The brine typically has at least twice the concentration of seawater. Brine water also contains chemicals like anti-scalants, used in pretreatment of the feed water, washing solutions, and rejected backwash from the feed water. In large-scale desalination processes, brine discharge detrimentally affects marine life. The high concentration of chemicals in brine water can have a substantial negative effect on marine life (table 10.2).

The constituents of brine water discharged from desalination plants ultimately depend on the desalination technology used; the quality of the intake water; the quality of water produced; and the pretreatment, cleaning, and RO membrane storage methods used. Distillation plants produce high-quality product water that ranges from 1 to 50 mg/l TDS, while RO plants produce product water that ranges from 10 to 500 mg/l TDS. Desalination plants produce liquid wastes that may contain high salt concentrations, chemicals used during de-fouling of plant equipment and pretreatment, and toxic metals. All desalination plants use chlorine or other biocides to clean pipes and other equipments and sometimes as pretreatment for the feed water. As mentioned, at high concentrations these can be hazardous to marine resources.

As part of the specifications for these large RO facilities, a variety of chemicals would have to be neutralized before they could be discharged into water bodies.

RO plants use a coagulant (usually ferric chloride) as a part of the pretreatment process to cause particles in feed water to form larger masses. Ferric chloride is not toxic but may cause a discoloration of the receiving water if discharged. In RO plants, cleaning and storage of the membranes can produce potentially hazardous wastes. The membranes must be cleaned every three to six months, depending on feed-water quality and plant operation. The membrane-cleaning formulations are usually diluted with alkaline or acid aqueous solutions. These chemicals are also considered toxic materials when discharged to the sea.

Conclusion

Seawater desalination as a source of potable water can relieve Gaza's acute water shortages. Indeed, at present, desalination is considered to be the only realistic and best technological hope for dealing with freshwater scarcity. Desalination would also improve the water quality supplied to the citizens and alleviate the looming water crisis and water deficit in the groundwater aquifer underlying the Gaza Strip. As Palestinians consider the use of non-conventional water resources, seawater desalination needs to be a major part of future strategies.

Expanded desalination in the Gaza Strip should in no way be considered as a concession of Palestinian water rights and should not affect final-stage negotiations in this area. Rather, it should be seen as an emergency solution to alleviate the present water crises and deterioration of groundwater quality. More of these plans should be closely evaluated, and any adverse environmental impact on the environment in the area should be prevented through proper mitigation measures to ensure protection of the marine life and the beach area.

The success of a plant's operation is very much dependent on good management. Progressive management encourages staff innovation, continued education, and detailed attention to technical and human resources aspects. Along with the physical implementation of desalination plans, comprehensive training and capacity-building programs should be introduced as well as free exchange of information between the management and operating bodies of the desalination plants in the region.

REFERENCES

Al-Mutaz, I. S. 1991. Environmental impact of seawater desalination plants. In *Environmental monitoring and assessment*. Netherlands: Springer.

Aqua Resources International, DAI & CDM. 2003. Feasibility study—Gaza sea water desalination plant. Copy available with author.

Argyrou, M. 2000. *Impact of desalination plant on marine macrobenthos in the coastal waters of Dehkelia Bay*. Internal report. Cyprus.

Camp Dresser and McKee International. 1993. *Strategic action for development of the environmental health sector in the Gaza Strip*. Gaza: Palestine Water Authority.

Ghbn, N. 2003a. Optimization of human resources development for water sector in the Palestinian Territories and the Middle East. In *Third World Water Forum*, ed. M. Abu-Zeid and A. Hamdy. Kyoto, Japan.

———. 2003b. The Palestinian Water Authority and Its Desalination Activities. *Watermark newsletter of the Middle East Desalination Research Center*. February 19.

Metcalf and Eddy. 2000. *Coastal Aquifer Management Program—integrated aquifer management plan.* PWA, CAMP.

———. 2001. *Coastal Aquifer Management Program—Gaza desalination master plan.* PWA, CAMP.

Palestinian Water Authority. 1999. *Strategy for water management in Palestine.* PWA, March.

———. 2000. *Standards of drinking water for Gaza Strip.* Gaza: PWA, July.

———. 2000. *Water National Plan.* PWA.

SOGREAH. 1999. *Technical assistance for the construction of desalination plant in Gaza.* Gaza: SOGREAH.

United Nations Environment Program (UNEP). 2003. *Desk Study on the Environment in the Occupied Palestinian Territories.* Nairobi, Kenya.

World Health Organization. 1989. *Health guidelines for the use of wastewater in agriculture and aquaculture.* Report 778 of a WHO Scientific Group, Geneva, Switzerland.

World Water Council. 2002. Water Vision for the Twenty-first Century in the Arab World. In *Third World Water Forum,* ed. Abu-Zeid and Hamdy. Kyoto, Japan.

Desalination in Israel

STATUS, PROSPECTS, AND CONTEXTS

YAAKOV GARB

Overview

Desalination is a marvelous technical feat, separating pure water out of the saltwater of seas, brackish aquifers, and wastewater. With membrane technologies improving and the costs of desalinated water dropping, this once exotic water source is fast becoming a mainstay of Israel's water system. The Ashkelon plant, for example, the first of five new facilities planned for Israel, is the largest reverse-osmosis plant in the world, producing 100 mcm/yr, or 15% of total domestic demand. This plant's successful operation has started to shift the perceptions and decisions of the water community in Israel, and some expect Israel to eventually derive half of its potable water from desalination (Dreizin et al. 2008).

Abroad as well, the pricing, technologies, and sophisticated fiscal and institutional structures of private-sector involvement in Israel's desalination projects have been regarded with keen interest by water professionals. The Ashkelon plant, for example, was voted "Desalination Plant of the Year" in the Global Water Awards of 2006 in Dubai, and the Ashdod plant was awarded the title of "Deal of the Year" for 2007 by Project Finance.

Desalination has been a technological holy grail for water-scarce regions, breaking the constraints of local hydrological circumstances with the prospect of a drought-proof, independent, and predictable supply of "new water." Some form of desalination has been developed in 130 countries, with over 10,000 plants (over a threshold of 100 m³/day) and an installed capacity growing at 7% a year (Cooley et al. 2006). But desalination must be located as one element within a range of approaches and technologies for managing water needs and provision, with ramified inputs and implications. In this broader context, the creation of new water through desalination in plants such as the Ashkelon plant is distinctive in the degree to which it is, at once, energy intensive, technology intensive, capital intensive, centralized, and privatized. Similarly, the costs of desalinated water should be contextualized to include the cost of land and negative externalities (the discharge of brine and chemicals, the energy use and air pollutants associated with this, thermal effects, and loss of coastal lands) as well as more subtle benefits, such as the value of water reliability and the benefits of relieving water stress, which may reduce political tensions or aquifer depletion.

This essay gives a brief history of desalination in Israel and an overview of the current scope and consequences of its adoption and frames these within some larger contextual questions regarding Israel's overall water system. While Israel's aggressive engagement with desalination is one of the more well considered internationally, and more justified than in some other contexts, questions remain about whether this should become the country's central escape path from water constraints, especially as the world stands at the threshold of an energy-limited and carbon-constrained era.

The Take-off of Desalination in Israel

Israeli decision makers and politicians have long had a soft spot for hard technical fixes, and from the state's early history there was a tradition of visionary thinking and bold execution related to water technologies. By the mid 1950s, Israel had extended irrigation pipes to the Negev Desert and was well on its way to a national-scale water carrier, and desalination had already been employed for drinking water in Eilat. In the late 1950s the Israeli government was presciently investing a relatively large amount of money on research and development on desalination, and Israel became an exporter of various desalination technologies, for example, vacuum freezing-vapor compression (the Zarchin process or VFVC) and a battery of other technologies commonly known only by their acronyms (SRFD, LT-MVC, LT-TVC, LT-MED, etc).

Despite this, Israel itself employed only a few small reverse osmosis plants in the southern Arava areas (which are not connected to the National Water Carrier), notably, a major facility in Eilat. Elsewhere, with prices typically upwards of $1/m^3$ of water, desalination was not considered as a feasible option on the supply side, with most of the country relying on the National Water Carrier and local aquifer utilization through wells. There was also room for demand-side improvements through increased agricultural water efficiencies and the use of treated wastewater for irrigation.

Given Israel's semi-arid and arid provenance, more sweeping visions of desalination's potential, which had been raised by Ben Gurion, were nurtured by water professionals. As early as 1965, TAHAL, the government (now private) company in charge of water resources planning and development in Israel, had formulated and obtained government adoption in principle for a grand (15 year, $100 million) desalination venture. The enthusiasm of engineers, however, repeatedly encountered the cold feet of decision makers (and, in particular, the Ministry of Finance) when it came to actually getting large desalination ideas funded. For a long time, the Ministry of Finance was convinced that other sources of water must be exploited, and agricultural use reduced (through pricing reform), before the "last resort" of seawater desalination could be considered. Additionally, the powerful agricultural lobby was hesitant about desalination, fearful that this would prompt such a reform, which would de-subsidize their water.

Desalination plans were quiescent for some decades, but by the 1990s several cycles of drought and instances of overpumping, accompanied by the steady growth of urban water consumption, made the crisis of Israel's water economy salient enough to prompt intensive desalination planning. The Israeli Water Commission embarked on the planning of mega-scale desalination solutions to meet the increasingly painful gaps between supply and demand and prevent further deterioration of groundwater. An intensive planning process was begun, and a desalination master plan was completed in 1997. This was the fruit of a comprehensive examination of various water sources and demand scenarios, of optimal sites for and capacities of desalination plants, and of desalination costs and benefits (both direct and indirect).

The commission's planners produced a flexible, staged "road map" for using these desalination plants to meet needs as they developed. The plan reserved, within the National Master Plan 34B, sites for eight desalination facilities plus an upgrading of the Eilat facility, which would come on line in an incremental manner, for a total capacity of 775 mcm/yr.

These plans crossed the threshold to execution at the end of the 1990s, with the combination of a sense of crisis, perceived exhaustion of demand-side and reallocation solutions, and an opened window of pricing feasibility. A prolonged drought and increasing urban water demand caused water levels in natural storage reservoirs to fall below their "red lines," notwithstanding meaningful reductions in per capita domestic, agricultural, and industrial uses of water. At the same time, technology advances brought down the price of seawater desalination dramatically. These circumstances led to the approval and budgeting in 1999 of a range of new water projects, including large-scale seawater desalination. On April 4, 2002, Government Decision 1682 formally adopted a schedule for establishment of four desalination facilities with a combined capacity of 400 mcm/yr. The Water Commission was instructed to prepare tenders for the immediate private-sector financing, construction, and operation of desalination facilities to provide 200 mcm/yr. In July 2007 the desalination master plan was updated so that the five coastal plants are projected to provide over 500 mcm/yr by 2013.

These five plants are now in various stages. A BOT (build, operate, and transfer) tender was issued for the most readily available of the Master Plan sites, at Israel's southern coastal town of Ashkelon, and a contract for the production of 50 mcm/yr was signed with the winning consortium. The contracted capacity was doubled to 100 mcm/yr a year later, and in 2003 financial closure was reached and a notice to proceed with construction was issued. The facility, which cost $250 million, began operation at 50% capacity in August 2005 and 100% capacity in December of the same year, with proven daily production of 348,000 m³/day.

In 2002 a 25-year BOO (Build, Own, Operate) concession agreement was signed by the special purpose company Via Maris Desalination, for the provision of 30 mcm/yr at a facility in Palmachim (north of the port city of Ashdod), though a request to double capacity was, reportedly, denied. (In a BOO scheme, as opposed to a BOT, the operator owns the site.) Financial closure on the Palmachim plant was reached, effective on January 1, 2005, and it began operation in September of 2007. In November 2006, Housing and Construction Holdings Ltd. and IDE Technologies Ltd. (through the special purpose company H_2ID) signed an agreement to build and operate a 100 mcm/yr desalination plant in Hadera for about $389 million, and it is expected to come on line at the end of 2009. A 45 mcm/yr plant at Ashdod is now being readied for tender, while the Shafdan 100 mcm/yr wastewater desalination plant is under longer-term planning. An additional 125 mcm/yr plant will be bid for by plant owners-operators by 2015. Figure 1.7 in part 1 provides a graphic description of the anticipated Israeli desalination network.

In addition to this chain of five large coastal desalination plants, Mekorot (Israel's national water company) operates thirty-one small plants, mainly in the south of the country, and maintains an extensive desalination research program on seawater (Eilat, Ashdod), brackish water (Eilat, Kziot, Neve Zohar), and wastewater (Shafdan). The Mekorot facilities have a strong emphasis on tailoring the RO process to site-specific conditions and on best use of brackish water sources, which are limited but much cheaper to desalinate than seawater. Similarly, Mekorot is active in research on desalination of wastewater, which has a specific energy cost one-third to one-fourth that of seawater, but the technology is less mature and, obviously, faces cultural stigmas when it comes to household use.

Finally, while this is nowadays often couched, perhaps misleadingly, as a project designed to "save the Dead Sea," the Red-Dead canal megaproject, whose feasibility is now under review under World Bank sponsorship, was initially conceived as, and is still largely, a desalination project. The Harza Group pre-feasibility study of 1996 projected freshwater production of 850 mcm/yr, with the elevation difference being used to generate 550 MW (megawatts) of electricity, part of which would be used for the desalination plant and for pumping the water back up to consumers in Amman. This project will not be discussed here, nor will the additional important issue of the possibilities of, promises for, and fate of plans for sharing of desalinated water with the Palestinian Authority.

Environmental and Health Considerations in Israeli Desalination

Since the Mediterranean Sea is commonly regarded as oligotrophic (offering little support for life), some of the desalination impacts that might apply in other contexts (thermal impacts, for example) are seen to be less critical. At the same time, there are still large gaps in knowledge regarding this relatively new scale of operation of desalination technology, so caution is in order. Similarly, large-scale desalination for drinking water raises novel regulatory and human health issues both internationally (for example, the WHO) and in Israel (for the Ministry of Health and the Ministry of Environment). Additionally, initial results from Israeli experience with the use of desalinated water for agriculture have shown some surprising, negative results due to the altered elemental profile of water, with implications for water management and a revision of desalination standards (Yermiyahu et al. 2007). Some of these, as well as energy-related issues, are listed briefly below.

Energy Demands

Energy demands in desalination facilities are mostly for pushing water through the membranes. (In the Ashkelon plant, for example, there are thirty-two reverse-osmosis treatment trains, containing over 40,000 membrane elements.) This process constitutes 30%–40% of the water cost. The theoretical minimum amount of energy needed for RO desalination from seawater is around a kilowatt-hour per cubic meter, though even the most efficient actual plants do not drop below about four times this theoretical minimum. For example, the Ashkelon plant has a contractual specific energy of 3.9 kWh (kilowatt-hour)/m^3, and actual performance is 10%–15% below this. In Ashkelon, the facility is to be powered by two redundant sources: a natural, dedicated power plant fueled by natural gas, located adjacent to the desalination plant, and high-voltage linkage to the national electricity grid.

Boron Concentrations

While boron is found in very low levels in drinking water (on the order of 0.03 mg/l), it is present at much higher levels (more than two orders of magnitude greater) in seawater (4–7 mg/l). Since boron at these levels can cause reproductive and developmental toxicity in animals and also effects crops, additional boron removal processes must be added to desalination plants. Israel was forced to address this issue as a result of damage to sensitive crops when the Eilat plant went on line without boron removal. It was the first country to set a boron limit of 0.04 mg/l for the first generation of desalination plants, and stringent limits (lower than WHO standards) were written into the requirements for the current generation of plants recently tendered. At the Ashkelon plant, for example, the Boron Polishing System installed demands 10% of overall plant energy.

Overly Pure Produced Water

Desalinated water is remarkably pure H_2O. This is largely a boon, but may also be a hazard in some respects. Reverse osmosis lowers calcium and carbonate concentrations, which make the product water acidic enough to corrode the distribution system. This reduces the useful life of the system and can also introduce iron and other toxic metals (copper, lead, cadmium, zinc, nickel) into water. Post-treatment of desalinated water with lime or limestone corrects this problem. In addition, since the desalting process largely removes a range of ions normally found in drinking water, and which may have a supplementary dietary role, especially in certain high-risk populations, blending or chemical addition may be necessary (Cotruvo 2005). Additional consequences for agriculture of the altered chemical profile of desalinated water have also received wider attention for the first time due to research on Israeli experiences with water from the Ashkelon and Eilat facilities (Yermiyahu et al. 2007).

Purity of the Intake Water

Some toxic materials in source water, such as arsenic and small petroleum molecules, can pass through RO membranes. Others can be filtered but may compromise the efficiency of the desalination process. For example, during the first 15 months of operation of the Ashkelon plant, there was a summer deterioration in seawater quality, most likely from organic load (particularly sewage) from Gaza entering the plant inlet, causing reduction in production. In wastewater desalination, such as that conceived for the Shafdan facility, a broader suite of contaminants may be present, including metals, other chemicals, and pharmaceuticals (as mundane as caffeine and as worrying as endocrine disruptors).

Introduced Impurities and Brine Discharge

The RO process can introduce a variety of substances into the discharged water (backwash liquids containing chemicals used to prevent scaling, corrosion, and fouling of the filters as well as for pretreatment processes), in addition to the intrinsic production of saline brine that is two to three times saltier than seawater. In the Ashkelon plant, for example, the most notable effect observed so far is from ferric sulfate coagulant, which, even at levels of 28 ppm, adds about 450 tons of iron a year to the sea. Even when mixed with the cooling water of the Ashkelon power station, the discharge discolors the sea with a red plume, a situation now being monitored and presumably managed. It is unclear whether this is simply an aesthetic blight or will have more significant effects on the marine environment. While there is still too little known about the marine impacts of discharges from desalination plants, precautionary suggestions to reduce these include use of more environmentally friendly anti-scalants, reduction of iron content, pretreatment of brine for nitrogen so as to avoid eutrophication, and the release of organic cleaning solutions.

Microbes

Many microbial organisms, including bacteria, protozoa, and viruses in seawater, may be pathogenic. Not all of these are removed by the desalination process. Brominated and chlorinated organic byproducts of disinfection are additional concerns.

Social and Institutional Considerations in Israeli Desalination

Two of the more valuable aspects of desalination, in the Israeli-Palestinian context that is the subject of this volume, are the additional options and the loosening of constraint that it affords. Desalination can, at least temporarily, relieve what Professor Hillel Shuval has termed "hydro-hysteria," that is, a fearful inflexibility regarding territorial concessions and the future management of the West Bank because of its criticality as a source of Israeli drinking water. It also may help avoid irreversible overdrawing of aquifers or other consequential decisions made during a time of hydro-crisis. Thus, even the extra 15% of domestic water now being supplied by desalination is valuable for this buffering—both imaginative and actual.

At the same time, we must consider the lessening of options that desalination might entail. These stem from the fact that, for the foreseeable future, desalination plants will tend to be large and private and draw intensively on nonrenewable and possibly polluting energy sources. They will be large because the unit cost of water drops with the size of the plant and private because governments worldwide prefer "off budget" means of building new infrastructure. Drawing on the expertise of the private sector, the risk profile of desalination projects is well suited to the risk-sharing arrangements of private-public partnerships. Every large seawater RO plant in the world over the last 5 years involves some type of public-private partnership (see Pankratz 2005.) These plants are energy intensive because of the inherent demand of the negentropic desalination process, which can only be feasibly met by non-renewable sources in the short and medium term. Thus, desalination ties Israel's future more tightly into dependency on variability in the price of energy and to the incentive structures of the private sector.

Thus, ironically, in creating a stable source of pure water not subject to the climatic variations of the region, Israel has buffered itself from one source of vulnerability but exposed itself to several others. With desalination, Israel is increasingly dependent on water quality in the Mediterranean Sea, the terms of decade-long contracts, and, above all, energy price variability. To the extent that a larger portion of the cost of desalinated water is a variable cost dependent on rising energy costs, the relative advantage of desalination with respect to other forms of water source augmentation with lower variable costs, for the short run, can be expected to decline.

Desalination allows Israel to avoid hydrological constraints now, through a technological solution for meeting the inelastic demands for potable water; but it may introduce future energy constraints as the world enters an era where limitations in energy supply and carbon emissions reach the forefront of the policy agenda. In such an era, it is unclear whether alternative energy sources (Qiblawey and Banat 2008) will be able to meet the needs of a locked-in desalination-based water economy, making the nuclear-powered desalination plants a compelling option; there are certainly historical precedents for nuclear-powered desalination in the thinking of Israeli technologists and politicians.

While the public-private partnerships (PPP) at the core of all Israel's large and new desalination facilities offer many opportunities, they also can challenge those concerned with the best use of public monies and with the transfer of assets and public services from public to private hands. For example, while they can allocate financial risks to the sectors best able to accommodate them and harness expertise for the public good, BOT arrangements can also cloud accountability, avoid current crises by deferring liabilities to the future, and raise costs by introducing an additional layer of profit margins. The water community in Israel must consider these aspects of the shift toward desalination as well.

In short, desalination is changing the profile of Israel's water resources and perceptions of scarcity among government and business interests. Yet, this burgeoning technology must be considered systemically, with an eye to how it facilitates certain trajectories of development of an integrated energy-fiscal-hydrological system over the time horizon of decades.

REFERENCES

Cooley, H., P. Gleick, and G. Wolff. 2006. *Desalination with a grain of salt: A California perspective.* Oakland: Pacific Institute.

Cotruvo, J. 2005. Water desalination processes and associated health and environmental issues. *Water Conditioning and Purification* 47 (1): 13–17.

Dreizin, Y., A. Tenne, and D. Hoffman. 2008. Integrating large scale seawater desalination plants within Israel's water supply system. *Desalination* 220:132–149.

Pankratz, T. 2005. Global trends in public-private partnerships. Talk given at the Israeli Desalination Society Meetings, Tel Aviv.

Qiblawey, H. M., and F. Banat. 2008. Solar thermal desalination technologies. *Desalination* 220:633–644.

Safrai, I., and A. Zask. 2008. Reverse osmosis desalination plants—marine environmentalist regulator point of view. *Desalination* 220:72–84.

Tal, A. 2006. Seeking sustainability: Israel's evolving water management strategy. *Science* 313:1081–1084.

Yermiyahu, U., et al. 2007. Rethinking desalinated water quality and agriculture. *Science* 318:920–921.

Editors' Summary

Desalination has produced considerable optimism among water managers. Indeed, it removes some of the constraints in what was perceived as a "zero sum game" and offers negotiators much needed flexibility. Ultimately, desalination represents the possibility of forestalling the enormous shortages that have been projected for so long. Desalination serves to diffuse the explosive rhetoric put forward by the "hydro-hysterics" whose grim visions of a thirsty future do little to allow for rational discussion. Surely, the agricultural sector, which for some time has assumed that its freshwater supplies would only dwindle as domestic and industrial water demand grows, has reason for relief.

The private sector has proven to be a robust force in promoting this technology, even in the Gaza Strip, where the plants have been funded through private ventures. At the same time, even though the price for desalinated water has plummeted, for some time most farm operations will continue to see the cost as prohibitive. Palestinians in particular balk at the price of moving to desalination as the chief source of domestic water supply—even as a growing number pay far higher rates for bottled water whose quality is frequently inferior to the desalinated alternative.

Several concerns need to be addressed before desalination becomes a regional panacea for anticipated shortages. The first is technical. Palestinians are quick to point out that, unlike olive trees, desalination plants do not last forever. Like any factory, they require maintenance. For instance, if you stop running a desalination facility for a few days, the membranes in the plant can sustain irreversible damage. In Gaza, for example, fuel supply is unstable and the threat of violence can compromise water production (even as Israel has meticulously attempted to avoid water supply facilities in military actions). During the Intifada, chemicals became unavailable for key aspects of plant operation (e.g., chemical anti-scalants) and desalination facilities collapsed.

In the past, Israelis were surprised when Palestinian enthusiasm to receive water from desalination plants was not exceptional. In Gaza desalination is considered inevitable and a driver of hydro-independence. But proposals to pipe water directly to the West Bank from Israeli Mediterranean coastal plants still are perceived as inferior to the granting of control over groundwater resources over which Palestinian control was incontrovertible.

Environmental concerns are also raised and must be addressed. The copious quantities of electricity associated with the energy-intensive operation of desalination facilities translate into substantial greenhouse gases. For instance, the energy demands of the Ashkelon facility are comparable to those of a city with 45,000 residents.

Ultimately, desalination will play a critical role in relieving the pervasive water scarcity of the two sides. Yet, the water is costly and brings with it environmental costs. It is therefore important that the commitment to water efficiency and conservation in both entities is in no way attenuated as a result of present capabilities for producing freshwater far less expensively than in the past.

PART 11

THE JORDAN RIVER BASIN

The Jordan River Basin includes the tributaries to the Jordan River and Lake Kinneret (the Sea of Galilee). Even as the recent drop in rainfall in the watershed decreased dramatically, it remains the largest single freshwater resource in the area. Its administration and protection is central to long-term sustainable water management strategies for the parties in the area. Indeed, the steady decline in sea level in the Dead Sea is the direct result of present and past policies regarding the Jordan's waters in Israel, Jordan, and Syria. The Jordan River has been the subject of international negotiations and discussions since the 1950s, when U.S. president Dwight David Eisenhower sent businessman Eric Johnston as his personal emissary to arrange for a *modus vivendi* in regional water allocation. Although a comprehensive strategy for managing the Jordan River will ultimately require coordination with Lebanon, Syria, and Jordan, these two essays focus on Israeli and Palestinian perspectives on the Jordan River.

Managing the Jordan River Basin

A PALESTINIAN PERSPECTIVE

NANCY RUMMAN

From the Palestinian perspective, the Jordan River Basin is the most important surface water resource in the region. The river passes through five countries: it has its sources in Lebanon and Syria and flows through Israeli, Palestinian, and Jordanian lands, which are all legal riparians with legitimate rights. The West Bank (as part of Palestine) is therefore a watercourse state as its territory is part of an international watercourse. The climate in this part of the West Bank is characterized by hot and extremely dry summers because of the limited rainfall it receives and the very high evaporation rate that exceeds the rainfall throughout the year to a considerable extent.

Since 1967, Palestinians of the West Bank have not had access to the Jordan River waters. During this period, groundwater resources of the Mountain Aquifer (Western, Northeastern, and Eastern) have been utilized extensively by Israeli water managers for their development initiatives along the western side of the Jordan Valley. There are twenty-five Israeli settlements in the Lower Jordan River Valley, including the Dead Sea area. The total area of these settlements is 13 km², with a total population of 5,825. These 5,825 people have essentially stopped all Palestinian development in the Lower Jordan River Valley. These twenty-five Israeli settlements with 5,825 people use about 39 mcm yearly from thirty-five wells for domestic and agricultural purposes. The seemingly unlimited use of water for themselves—and the parallel Israeli restrictions on the Palestinians—has made socioeconomic development for the Palestinian majority living in the Jordan Valley nearly impossible.

Most of the Palestinian communities in the Jordan Valley suffer extremely from shortages of safe and reliable water supply for domestic, agricultural, and municipal purposes. The main water source supplying these communities is the limited groundwater which also provides the flow for local wells and springs. In recent years, the groundwater resources in many locations of the Jordan Valley have suffered from serious degradation, reflected in both a substantial decline in water levels and increasing salinity in several production wells. This constitutes a critical obstacle to local development.

The following factors and conditions form the general context for present hydrological conditions:

- due to climate change and reduced precipitation, the rates of recharges appear to be dropping;
- Israel continues to control most of water resources in the area;
- overpumping of wells in order to fulfill the high demand for water by agricultural and industrial activities is depleting the aquifer;
- the untreated wastewater of Israeli settlements exacerbates water quality problems;
- water quality in the Jordan River itself has continued to drop and makes much of the flow unusable.

To respond to these circumstances, greater efforts should be made and attention given to ensuring the reliable development and sustainable management of all water resources in this area. This essay gives a brief overview on the situation of the Jordan Valley area with respect to available water resources, development, management, and the Palestinian perspective on appropriate future policies.

Jordan Valley Water Resources

The Jordan River is not the only water resource that should be available to Palestinians in the Jordan Valley. There are a variety of sources that need to be considered within a comprehensive water management strategy for the area. The water resources in the area of the Jordan Valley are comprised of both groundwater resources (wells and springs) and surface water resources (Jordan River and floodwater). Groundwater is considered to be the greatest source of available water supply for Palestinians in the area, for extraction via the resulting wells or springs. Groundwater wells tap the quaternary aquifer in the Jordan Valley as well as shallow upper and lower aquifers of the hilly blocks. Some springs tap the upper aquifer while others tap the lower aquifer. Other surface water resources are restricted by the limited quantities of seasonal floodwater flowing in wadis and the unavailability of reasonable quality water from the Jordan River, which has been fully controlled in practice since Israeli occupation in 1967.

Groundwater Resources

AGRICULTURAL WELLS

Within the Jordan Valley area, there are more than 180 agricultural wells distributed across the valley, with a long-term average annual extraction rate of 9.0 mcm. The majority of these wells are clustered in the Jericho area, where there are more than 81 wells. Most of the existing wells in Jordan Valley were drilled before the year of 1967, and therefore should be considered as old wells, characterized by rundown physical conditions and operations, requiring urgent rehabilitation. Indeed, most of the agricultural wells were drilled between 1950 and 1966 with a total depth range from 50 to 200 m deep. Since 1967 very few new wells have been drilled or restored due to a number of constraints by Israeli authorities. It is reported that most wells have clogged screens with high silt accumulation at the bottom. The pumping rates vary from 40 to 80 m³/hr, with the pumps operating for about 10 to 12 hours per day.

SPRING WATER

Springs are the second major source of water supply in the Jordan Valley area. There are twenty-four springs in the Jordan Valley area with long-term average discharge of 45 mcm/yr. Most of these springs are used mainly for irrigation purposes through old open irrigation channels. Noticeable water losses take place through these channels with the drop estimated to range from 25% to 30%.

Surface Water

THE JORDAN RIVER

The historic natural flow of the river (excluding withdrawal for water supply purposes) is estimated to be about 1,470 to 1,670 mcm/yr. The headwaters of the Jordan River originate in Jabel Asheikh, where three tributaries—Al Hasbani, Dan, and Banias—join together in the Hula Valley. The Al Hasbani River originates in Lebanon and its average flow is 160 mcm/yr. The Banias River originates in Syria and its average flow is 160 mcm/yr. The Dan River's average flow is 260 mcm/yr. The Yarmouk River, which flows along the border between Syria and Jordan, also contributes to the Jordan River. The river ends its journey when it enters the Dead Sea.

The lower part of the Jordan River flows north to south, continuing along the Rift Valley until it reaches its final destination in the Dead Sea. The Jordan River also receives runoff water from wadis along both sides of the river. While the water of the Jordan River has been tapped to some degree for decades, recently, its natural flow has been almost completely diverted. The average estimated discharge of the Jordan River between 1977 and 1987 ranged from 422 to 435 mcm/yr. The current discharge of the Jordan River into the Dead Sea is estimated to be not more than 50 mcm/yr—less than 5% of its natural flow. In practice, the Palestinians do not have access to the surface water flowing into the Jordan River because of upstream diversions by Israel, Jordan, and Syria.

The total area of the Jordan River Basin covered by isohyets[1] of over 300 mm is 14,847 km². Of this area, 1,638 km² (11%) is within Palestinian territories. Israel is the greatest user of the Jordan River water, abstracting around 54% of the total flow. Israel transfers huge quantities of surface water through the National Water Carrier from Upper Jordan to Negev, equating to 440 mcm/yr. At the same time, Palestinians have been denied use of the Jordan River water due to the Israeli occupation since the 1967 war. In addition, Jordan uses 22% of the Jordan natural river flow, Syria uses 11%, and Lebanon uses around 0.3%.

In reviewing the different proposals and plans for developing and solving the water conflicts over the Jordan River, the 1956 Johnston Plan still seems the most important one. The plan was prepared by a special emissary of U.S. president Dwight Eisenhower, allocating what was deemed to be an equitable division of the stream to the different riparian areas. The Johnston Plan gives Palestinians rights to 270 mcm/yr of the water in the Jordan River Basin.

Since that time, development of the Jordan River has been, and will continue to be, a key factor for overall sustainable development and socioeconomic improvement in the region. Therefore, many plans and ideas have been proposed, trying to lay down or outline a permanent resolution of the water conflict concerning the waters of the Jordan River. Most of these ideas have failed due to geopolitical circumstances.

FLOODWATER

Floodwater has limited potential as a water resource in the West Bank. Part of this water (about 30 mcm/yr, on the average) flows through the major dry valley beds to the east, toward the Dead Sea. Because of the seasonal nature of the runoff, the modest duration of the runoff, and the topographic conditions, only a small portion of this runoff can be utilized to provide a dependable supply. Moreover, development costs to take advantage of these flows would be very high. Nonetheless, it has been estimated that a quantity of about 11 mcm/yr could be economically developed from these sources through the construction of small dams in some of the major valleys.

Future Water Resources Development and Management

A variety of development and research projects that are needed to provide for future Palestinian water needs in the Jordan Valley area have been identified (Aliewi and Assaf 2004). Storage dams or water retention structures on the main wadis of the western bank of the Lower Jordan River Valley should be constructed to help ensure an adequate reserve of water. Geological studies and engineering plans that will allow for the rehabilitation and development of major local springs, including civil works and storage reservoirs, should be carried out. Feasibility and technical studies for artificial recharge of the area's aquifers from seasonal runoff or from treated wastewater to enable either seasonal storage or a barrier to prevent saltwater intrusion should be done to provide an assessment of alternative water sources. These should include feasibility and technical studies about the use of winter runoff waters collected in flood plain areas, such as Marj Sanour of Jenin District.

Brackish water for agricultural and industrial uses may be another alternative source, and research and pilot studies should be carried out to investigate this potential. As well, brackish water desalination using renewable energy might prove to be a sustainable solution. Pilot projects that demonstrate the potential for artificial recharge and aquifer storage and for recovery of excess surface flows or treated wastewater should be implemented. Hydrological and meteorological surveillance networks, including establishing gauging, monitoring, and sampling systems with all necessary equipment and vehicles for water and soil monitoring of the area, are critical to tracking for assessment studies. Seismic and geophysical equipment for geological and water resource assessment studies are also needed.

The West Ghor Canal is yet another potential development project. It was proposed in the Johnston Plan of 1955 as a means to provide Palestinians with an equitable share of water from the Jordan River, where the Palestinian share was estimated at 240 mcm/yr to be used for the development of the Jordan Valley. In addition, pilot projects for the use of renewable energy (solar and wind) for water extraction and/or distribution have been proposed, along with public aware-ness campaigns.

There is an immediate need to begin the rehabilitation of existing wells and springs. The rehabilitation process for wells involves replacing or exchanging well pumps with related accessories, construction of guard and well facilities rooms, replacement of diesel engines with modern electrical ones, and the electrical and mechanical maintenance work.

The rehabilitation works required to attain optimal utilization of local springs involves cleaning the main sources of each spring; installing protection fencing; constructing delivery infrastructure, such as replacing the old conveyance system by piped ones and replacing the old irrigation networks; installing and supplying water tanks and chlorination units; and constructing catchment reservoirs to collect waters flowing from the spring.

There is also a pressing need to development new wells in the area. The Palestinian Water Authority (PWA) has plans to drill several new production wells near the Tubas and Baradala areas in the near future for domestic purposes. (The existing Tubas well is slowly drying up.) Table 11.1, based on research supported by a Japanese assistance program, presents future potential development of water resources in the Jordan Valley. For agricultural purposes, several substitute agricul-tural wells have already been drilled in Jericho area to replace the malfunctioning and abandoned wells.

The Red-Dead Sea Canal

The decline of the Dead Sea level to 417 m below sea level and the shrinking of the surface area of the Dead Sea to 500 km^2 are serious problems that need to be addressed. At the Johannesburg Environmental Summit in 2002, the Jordanian minister of water suggested the construction of a Red-Dead Sea Canal project (the Peace Canal) to protect the Dead Sea from disappearing, to desalinate some 850 mcm/yr of seawater, to generate 550 megawatts/yr of electricity, and to develop new tourism and industrial zones. Most importantly, the fact is that this project would provide an inflow into the Dead Sea to compensate for the "unnatural" reduction of its historic flow.[2]

Since the time of the proposal in Johannesburg, the projected total cost of this project has increased and is now estimated to be US$5 billion, with $1 billion given as a grant and the remaining amount as a loan. The project would probably take nearly 20 years to fully implement. The project would offer a new source of water and energy, provided that all of its phases are completed. A pre-feasibility study has

Table 11.1 Potential for future development of water resources in the Jordan Valley

		Available water volume			
Water resources	EXISTING 2005	PILOT TERM 2007–2009 (3 YEARS)	SHORT TERM 2010–2012 (3 YEARS)	MID TERM 2013–2015	LONG TERM AFTER 2016
(1) Existing water resources (mcm/yr)					
Existing springs	32.10	32.10	32.10	32.10	32.10
Existing wells	11.29	11.29	11.29	11.29	11.29
Mekorot	5.38	5.38	5.38	5.38	5.38
Subtotal (1)	48.77	48.77	48.77	48.77	48.77
(2) Future potential water resources (mcm/yr)					
Spring canal improvement			2.39	4.25	11.46
Well rehabilitation		0.49	3.53	7.05	10.8
New well development		0.76	0.76	0.76	0.76
Storm-water harvesting				0.50	5.50
Wastewater reuse		0.63	1.33	2.13	12.50
Subtotal (2)		1.88	8.01	14.69	41.02
Grand total (1) + (2)	48.77	50.65	56.78	63.46	89.79

Source: Japan International Cooperation Agency Study Team estimate.

Note: Further studies on storm-water harvesting are required after collecting sufficient data for analysis. Water resources of Jordan River flow are not included.

been prepared by the Jordanians, and a TOR (Terms of Reference) has been pre-pared by the World Bank and discussed many times. The study is now underway.

Palestine supports the proposed project of connecting the Red and Dead seas if and only if Palestine is considered as a full and historic partner and riparian, and without any impact on Palestinian water rights in the Mountain Aquifer basins and the Jordan River before its diversion. The proposed project of connecting the Red and Dead seas has long-term objectives which the Palestinians support as long as Palestinian water rights are secured, since Palestine is a full riparian within the Dead Sea Basin (30% of the Dead Sea is in Palestinian lands).

Palestine is ready to participate in regional projects that will benefit the countries in the region, but Palestinians will not give up their water rights in the Mountain Aquifer and in the Jordan River Basin itself. In other words, desalinated water from a Dead Sea desalination project will not be considered a substitute for the just water rights of the Palestinian people. Palestinian rights in the Dead Sea Basin should be secured as part of the Jordan River Basin, and Palestinian participation in this initia-tive should not undermine the Palestinian demand to secure its water rights.

Final Word

The Jordan River Basin is of critical importance to Palestine for economic, cultural, and environmental reasons. Palestine is a full riparian in the watershed and will continue to strive for its water rights in the basin. Ultimately, resolution of the present disagreements needs to be based on international law with the implementation of a comprehensive plan for the Jordan, ensuring equitable access to all parties.

NOTES

1. An *isohyet* is a contour of rainfall depth, in this case, total annual rainfall.

2. The primary reason for the shrinking of the Dead Sea and all the parallel environmental and resource ailments is transfer of waters out of the Jordan River Basin into the Negev through the Israeli National Water Carrier and diversion of waters by Jordan for irrigation.

REFERENCES

Aliewi, A. S., and K. Assaf. 2004. Brief overview and historical background of the proposed Red Sea–Dead Sea canal project. Proceedings of the International Conference on Regional Hydro-Political Challenges of Sustainable Management of Transbondary River Basin, October 26–27, Beirut, Lebanon.

House of Water and Environment. 2007a. The feasibility study on water resources development and management for Jordan River rift valley inventory survey for rehabilitations of wells. Ramallah, Palestine: HWE. http://www.hwe.org.ps/Projects/Research/Inventory%20 Survey%20Wells/Inventory%20Survey%20for%20Rehabilitations%2001%20Wells%20.pdf (accessed July 21, 2009).

———. 2007b. Inventory survey for improvement of spring water conveyance system for the feasibility study on water resources development and management for Jordan River rift valley. Ramallah, Palestine: HWE.

Managing the Jordan River Basin

AN ISRAELI PERSPECTIVE

RICHARD LASTER

DAN LIVNEY

The Jordan River begins in the northern part of Israel, the southern part of Lebanon, and the Golan Heights, where waters flows from springs, melting snow, and rain into the upper Jordan and from there into Lake Kinneret. The Yarmuk River flows through Syria and Jordan, joining the lower Jordan River a few kilometers south of the Kinneret. The river continues flowing south until the Dead Sea and is its major source of water.

The reduction in the water flows in the lower Jordan is a result of increasing extraction of water from the river's various sources over the past 50 years by the four riparian countries. Today the Lebanese remove some 50 mcm/yr from the Hatzbani and the Wazzani, tributaries of the upper Jordan; the Israelis remove some 400 mcm/yr from different points along the upper Jordan and Lake Kinneret; the Syrians remove an additional amount of about 400 mcm/yr; and the Jordanians remove some 600 mcm/yr. The lower Jordan is left with less than 100 mcm/yr, more than 1 billion m³ less than its normal natural flow.

The severe reduction in the flow of water down the Jordan has had a major impact on the Dead Sea. At one time there was an annual flow of over 1 billion m³ from the lower Jordan into the Dead Sea. Together with the flow from springs and winter runoff, this equaled the Dead Sea's evaporation rate, and thus the Dead Sea level remained stable. Reductions in the flow of water into the Dead Sea began in the 1960s, and today the level of the Dead Sea is falling at a rate of approximately 1 m/yr. Beyond the shrinkage of the sea, the falling sea level has resulted in other undesirable side effects. Outlet springs have shifted and are in danger of drying up completely. Over 2,000 sinkholes have opened up along the shoreline, endangering humans and wildlife alike. The receding shoreline has left waterfront tourist facilities far away from the sea, with mudflats separating them from the water.

The reduction in water quantity has been accompanied by a reduction in water quality. The continued reduction in freshwater flows causes progressively higher concentrations of pollutants. Partially treated sewage from Tiberias and the smaller settlements in the region is dumped into the river, along with saline spring water diverted around Lake Kinneret. Water quality tests taken in the area of the river between the Kinneret and the Yarmuk by the Ministry for Environmental

Protection have shown the water to be high in E. coli bacteria, nitrates, and chlorides, preventing usage of the river for fishing, swimming, or recreation of any kind. In general, the water quality improves slightly further downstream due to natural filtration processes.

How we reached this stage of serious reduction in water flow and water quality can be found in the story that is presented below, from a legal and administrative standpoint, rather than an ecological one.

Dreams of how to use of the Jordan River go back hundreds of years, but for the most part, these dreams followed an engineer's vision of using the Jordan to its fullest extent for agricultural and domestic use. The major legal interventions occurred at several stages, some during the British mandate period and others after the State of Israel was formed in 1948.

The need for international intervention is quite obvious. For over 100 years, the Middle East has been known for its tensions. Over the years, many have tried to make it a better and safer place to live by attempting, in varying degrees, to resolve the tensions by facilitating cooperation among the various riparian states. As Aaron Wolf quotes in his articles and Web site, "Water is often a bone of contention and conflict but it has rarely been the source of an outright military clash or war." This is true even in the Jordan River.

The Johnston Plan

Although there were spats of military intervention by Israel against Syria when Syria tried to divert portions of the upper Jordan, these spats never blew up into outright war. The region is volatile enough as it is, however, and the international community has always been keen on reducing tension in the area and preventing war by resolving conflicts. The most famous of these interventions and the one most quoted is that of Eric Johnston, who came to the region as an emissary of President Dwight David Eisenhower in 1953 to try to divide the water sources of the Jordan among the five riparian countries.

Johnston used a very unique method of negotiations. He came without political maps, but rather with hydrological ones. He pointed out on the maps where the sources of the water were located, the patterns of flow, and the quantities of water available to the riparians. He asked each riparian country what its basic water needs were, and they all presented a figure which he accepted and jotted down in his notebook as part of his famous water plan. The plan allocated 132 mcm/yr of water for Lebanon, 400 mcm/yr for Israel, 720 mcm/yr for Jordan, and 132 mcm/yr for Syria, each one to withdraw water from sources which were assigned by Johnston.

The plan was submitted to the Arab League and Israel for approval in 1955. Israel accepted the plan, and although some Arab governments expressed their support, the Arab League rejected it for the same reasons that the Arab League rejected numerous regional plans, including the United Nations 1947 Partition Plan that established an independent State of Israel. Any recognition of a plan would by definition recognize Israel's existence, and since this was anathema to the Arab League, there could be no approval of the plan. In spite of its formal rejection, the plan has served as a basis for withdrawals, and during the 1960s and '70s the number of withdrawals even corresponded to Eric Johnston's figures.

In fact, Israel and Jordan worked out their own arrangements for withdrawals even during the period when there were no diplomatic relations between the countries. These negotiations are known as the "Picnic Table Negotiations" because the representatives would meet near the Jordan River at a picnic table to resolve any serious conflicts over water extractions. Although this very pastoral scene of straw hampers and checkered tablecloths was good for reducing conflict, it was obviously bad for the Jordan River. Over time its entire contents were divided up so that as little water as possible reached the Dead Sea. The waters of the Dead Sea, which could not be divided up for agriculture or drinking water use, were therefore considered wasted water. Allowing water to reach the Dead Sea was considered almost sinful. The Jordan River was divided up between Israel and Jordan while Syria continued to withdraw water at a rate enumerated in the Johnston Plan.

Present Pumping Dynamics

Water conflicts continue to emerge along the Jordan River even today. For instance, the Lebanese began to withdraw 10 mcm/yr of water from the Wazzani River in 2002 without first consulting Israel. According to international law standards, this constituted improper behavior, and Israel notified several members of the international community. But the withdrawal was allowed because it was small and inconsequential and, of course, consistent with the Johnston Plan formula.

Now that the countries have successfully siphoned off all they could possibly withdraw from the Jordan, the Yarmuk, and the Kinneret, they are looking for other ways to capture and utilize more water. It would seem that today's decision makers can only see their own present uses and their own present needs and not the needs of future generations when it comes to taking natural assets. Although the environmental revolution began over 30 years ago with the Stockholm Declaration in 1972, few have internalized the essence of the declaration when it declared that man is a trustee for nature. It is not for man to reduce nature to its lowest common denominator but rather to use our assets wisely to protect them for future generations.

In fact, modern ecology talks about improving the quality of the environment for future generations, rather than detracting from it. This may sound appropriate in international conventions, but on the ground things are quite different. No country along the Jordan River has ever agreed to set a minimum basic amount of water necessary for life in and along the Jordan River. "Life" in this context refers to the ecological life of the river, its ecosystems, its attractive flow, and the quality of water. In addition, any decision made should take the future of the Dead Sea into consideration, seeing it as one of the real treasures on this earth with its extensive history, unusual location, huge depth, and inherently healthy quality of water.

The environmental section of the Israel-Jordan peace agreement of 1994 includes protection of natural resources, with specific paragraphs regarding the protection of the Jordan River and the Dead Sea. Its provisions include environmental protection of water resources, agricultural pollution control, nature reserves, and protected areas and ensure optimal water quality at reasonably usable standards. But no specifics or methods of implementation were included, leaving a nicely dressed document with no party to go to. Concerning water supply issues, however, the agreement is very specific, with the countries agreeing on reciprocal transfers of millions of cubic meters of water from one to the other. The treaty created a special commission, known as the Joint Water Committee, which has a mandate to cooperate in the protection of common water sources. Yet to date, Israel and Jordan have not been able to create a roundtable discussion for the protection of the southern Jordan River and the Dead Sea that includes all the relevant parties, and time does not seem to be working in favor of the river. Israel and Jordan have not set up a formal commission to control actions along the Jordan River and to punish violators for withdrawals that are illegal or illegal pollution.

Further exacerbating the situation is the attitude of both countries when it comes to water use. Jordan and many Israeli supporters want to dig a canal from the Red Sea to a desalination plant at the Dead Sea and pump the drinking water to Amman, the capital of Jordan. The reason for this project, in fact, is not to save the Dead Sea, which is the slogan used to sell the project, but to bring fresh water to Amman so that Jordan doesn't have to buy it from Turkey, Syria, or Israel. The proposed Red-Dead Peace Conduit needs to be carefully reviewed. It is a project of immense proportions which will have serious ecological effects not only on the Jordan River but on the Dead Sea as well. Jordan also has an extremely misguided agricultural policy, where huge amounts of water are used for irrigation in the Jordan Valley while people in Amman have little to drink.

Toward a Sustainable Orientation

This all leads to the conclusion that people are not looking at the problem from the correct standpoint. We must first look at the assets we have to use and then use them wisely. Second, let us begin thinking demographically. There has to be an end to overpopulation to allow us to enjoy what little is left of the natural assets available. How can a country continue to promote increasing populations when it has gone way beyond the carrying capacity of its water sources? This is true of Israel as well, which continues to promote large families and immigration from other countries. There has to be a realization that in order to enjoy natural assets, they must be preserved, and the continued denigration of our water sources will only lead to a continued devaluation in the quality of life not only for humans, but for all life forms. Human existence and quality of life depends on continued functioning of ecosystems.

What has the legal system done to improve the situation? Very little. The Johnston agreement was never signed, and while the Israel-Jordan agreement was signed, it was never fully implemented.

In addition to the above, one cannot conclude this essay without mentioning the Palestinian Authority and its desire to become an additional riparian of the

Jordan River. After the 1967 war, Israel captured territory that was once Jordanian but is now considered part of an entity entitled the Palestinian Authority. This Palestinian Authority is not yet a state in the sense that it is not yet a country recognized under the United Nations charter, but it is on the way to becoming a country and in the meantime is an authority with its own prime minister, parliament, and free elections. However, large portions of the Palestinian Authority are held under Israeli control.

The Palestinian Authority itself is divided into three regions, A and B, which are mainly under Palestinian control, and C, which is mostly under Israeli control. Huge portions of the areas adjacent to the Jordan River and the Dead Sea are currently under Israel's control, but in the future there will certainly be a great deal of Palestinian input. In addition, Palestinian cities and towns pollute large tributaries which flow into the Jordan River. One would expect a future peace agreement to include measures that will ensure that action is taken to prevent this situation.

Agreements known as the Oslo Accords were signed between Israel and the Palestinian Authority in 1993 through 1995. These agreements describe concepts of water use and misuse. The agreement also creates a Joint Water Commission and a Joint Technical Committee to manage the joint waters. Yet going beyond the agreement has become extremely difficult. Implementation seems to be a word which does not fit into the lexicon of Middle Eastern politics.

How can Israel and the Palestinian Authority improve the quality of the Jordan River? The starting point is opening the channels of communication, followed by creating basin-wide agreements to protect the quality of the streams and rivers flowing into the Jordan. Israel has taken the first step by creating basin authorities along its major streams, but the Palestinian Authority has not, nor do they have any intention of creating such authorities. Palestinian negotiators tend to look at water only from the standpoint of water use and not from the standpoint of natural assets. Therefore, they look at the facility use of water by setting up service companies, rather than natural water authorities, divided along political boundaries with little regard to the geography and watersheds.

For example, the present proposal on the table calls for the establishment of three water utilities in the West Bank (north, central, and south) and one in Gaza, divided along the present political boundaries of the governorates. In this situation there can be little agreement on the use of the natural flow of water, and therefore both sides seem to be talking, but neither side seems to be listening. Some of the major sources of pollution could easily be repaired by sewage purification works, and the water could then be reused in agriculture and then discharged into the Jordan. Yet this has not taken place at the proper rate. A peace agreement should build clear timetables for such measures.

This all leads to a similar conclusion that one would find along any international border with transboundary waters. Countries need to cooperate, to set up joint commissions, to look at water management from an integrated basin level, and to implement master plans and action plans for the major water bodies. As long as this does not happen, essays like this will continue to be written, criticism will be made, but little will be done because politicians like to have their coffee after a meeting about an agreement, but rarely like to question where the water for their coffee comes from.

REFERENCES

Geffen, M., and Y. Gal. 1992. *The Kinneret book*. Kiryat Ono, Israel: Kinneret Authority and the Ministry of Defense (in Hebrew).

Gvirtzman, H. 2002. *Israel water resources: Chapters in hydrology and environmental sciences*. Jerusalem: Yad Ben-Zvi Press.

Haddadin, M. 2001. *Diplomacy on the Jordan: International conflict and negotiated solution*. Boston and London: Kluwer Academic.

Hayes, J. B. 1948. *TVA on the Jordan: Proposals for irrigation and hydroelectric development in Palestine*. Washington, DC: Public Affairs Press.

Holtzman, R., U. Shavit, M. Segal-Rozenhaimer, I. Gavrieli, A. Marei, E. Farber, and A. Vengosh. 2004. Quantifying ground water inputs along the lower Jordan River. *Journal of Environmental Quality* 34:897–906.

Laster, R., and D. Livney. 2007. The Nahal Kidron/Wadi Nar governance institutions and legal structure: Israel and the Israeli-controlled West Bank. In *From conflict to collective action: Institutional change and management options to govern transboundary watercourses*. Jerusalem: BMBF Germany and Israel Ministry of Science.

Laster, R., D. Livney, and D. Holender. 2005. The sound of one hand clapping: Limitations to integrated resources water management in the Dead Sea Basin. *Pace Environmental Law Review* 22 (1): 123–149.

Lowdermilk, W. C. 1944. *Palestine: Land of promise*. New York: Harper.

Main, C. T. 1953. *The unified development of the water resources of the Jordan Valley region*. Prepared at the request of the United Nations under the direction of the Tennessee Valley Authority. Boston, MA: Charles T. Main.

Ministry for Environmental Protection and the Nature and Parks Authority. 2008. *Water and stream quality report for 2007*. Jerusalem: Ministry for Environmental Protection (in Hebrew).

Raz, E. 1993. *The Dead Sea book*. Jerusalem: Israel Nature Reserves Authority and Tamar Regional Council (in Hebrew).

The Transboundary Freshwater Dispute Database. N.d. Oregon State University, http://www.transboundarywaters.orst.edu/database/index.html (accessed November 2, 2009).

Wolf, A. T. 1995. *Hydropolitics along the Jordan River*. Tokyo: United Nations University Press.

Editors' Summary

More pages may have been written about the Jordan River than any other water resource in the world. Such keen interest internationally certainly has little to do with the size of the river, which for most of the year naturally is a modest stream. Rather, the historic, spiritual, and religious significance gives it a place in the world's imagination that has never been utilized from an economic point of view, nor protected ecologically.

Hence, future agreements over the Jordan have to clearly consider what its optimal role might be as a regional resource. Economically, rather than talking about adding trivial amounts of tomatoes to local farmers' yields, it makes more sense to pursue an ambitious tourist initiative that can bring the three riparians of the lower Jordan together. The economic potential of a peaceful Jordan River as a spiritual center, a resort center, or even a center for water sports is substantial. But to attract investment and visitors, the river will have to undergo a considerable makeover.

The first step toward the reclamation of the Jordan River needs to involve water quantity. The Jordan River's present environmental state is the result of default policy decisions of Israel, Jordan, and Syria, which have preferred transfer of water for agricultural or other objectives to preserving the integrity of the stream. This is a policy which can change, today, with the emergence of alternative water sources. At a time when the international community is seriously considering a multi-billion dollar project to bring water to the Dead Sea, surely the cost-effective advantages of returning the Jordan River's flow to its natural level should not be overlooked.

Even if a reasonable permanent flow in the river returns some of its basic aesthetic properties, development efforts will not be successful without substantial improvement of water quality. If baptisms, swimming, or participating in water sports endanger visitors' health due to water contamination, tourist initiatives will ultimately be unsuccessful.

Pollution into the Jordan comes from numerous sources and countries—and its abatement will require intervention in Jordan, Israel, Palestine, and Syria. Future management strategies for the stream should involve a basin-wide commission with all the riparian countries. Just as the "Nile Initiative" has been a locus for international involvement and support, so should a framework be created for the Jordan River that will readily allow for international agencies to provide funding for sustainable, peace-building initiatives. While this might not be possible with Syria at present, surely a Jordanian-Palestinian-Israeli agency to oversee flow, water quality, and tourism along the stream makes sense.

PART 12

GAZA'S WATER SITUATION

The extremely poor condition of Gaza Strip's groundwater resources has characterized its hydrological reality for some time. The massive salination of wells was well advanced during the period of Egyptian rule and has only grown worse over time. This part offers a joint assessment by leading Palestinian and Israeli hydrologists about the present state of affairs for Gaza and ideas for improving conditions.

The Gaza Water Crisis

YOUSEF ABU-MAYLA

EILON M. ADAR

Background

The Gaza Strip has a small area of about 365 km² in a semiarid region. It has one of the highest population densities in the world. One of the main issues facing the Gaza Strip today is a water crisis—the difficulty in obtaining safe and clean water where groundwater is the only water source. The water situation in the Gaza Strip has deteriorated in both quantitative and qualitative aspects. The problem has not been solved due to technical, social, and political constraints, according to the Palestinian Water Authority's plans. Groundwater reservoirs with adequate water quality are diminishing rapidly, and demand continually exceeds renewable supply. In addition, the Palestinian Water Authority lacks both the technical and financial resources to handle the water crisis on its own.

In the year 2007, the population living within the Gaza Strip reached about 1.45 million. Most models anticipate that the local population will double in the coming decade or in 15 years. Population growth requires more water to fulfill the needs for domestic activities and drinking as well as for local agriculture and industry. The annual groundwater abstraction is estimated at 165 mcm, where 85 mcm is used for domestic needs. Due to the low water-use efficiency following losses along the water distribution system (55%), consumption levels reach 80–90 l/day per capita. Water scarcity in terms of quality and quantity all over the Gaza Strip has severe negative impacts on the development of the Palestinian economy and on all aspects of people's lives. Steps must be taken immediately to address the water issues:

- New infrastructure must be developed for efficient municipal water distribution.
- New water sources must be introduced.
- Water conservation in the domestic and the agriculture sectors must be promoted.
- Remediated wastewater reuse should be introduced to the agricultural sector, associated with adequate dual water distribution network systems.
- Additional water resources by means of seawater and groundwater desalination must be established.
- Regional and international cooperation should be upgraded in water issues.

In other words, rehabilitation of distribution networks and establishment of water desalination plants and new wastewater treatment plants are the only feasible options open to Gaza Strip to address the current and the future water crisis.

Statement of Need

The Gaza Strip is densely populated, with an average of 2,500 inhabitants living within every square kilometer (in some areas even 4,300 inhabitants/km²). The shallow groundwater reservoir underneath Gaza and the southern coastal plain of Israel is a unified cross-border or transboundary hydrological unit, which is already heavily contaminated by anthropogenic impacts and depleted to the level which leads to massive seawater intrusion. The local Coastal Aquifer provides the entire water supply to Gaza. In other words, groundwater from the local shallow aquifer is currently the only source of water to both domestic and agricultural sectors. The quality of this groundwater has deteriorated over the years, and extensive numbers of wells are being shut down due to low water quality, which falls below the minimum standards. A supply of high-quality water and prevention of soil and groundwater contamination is the most fundamental problem in this semi-arid environment of the Gaza Strip.

Past use of groundwater has also affected the present water crisis. The fact that groundwater is available from only a few meters below the surface enabled almost every farmer to dig his own irrigation well. Local villages and the water authority dug relatively deep production wells for local municipalities for combined domestic and agricultural use, which resulted in a dramatic depletion of the water levels, even below sea level, enhancing seawater intrusion.

The rapid deterioration of groundwater quality in the extremely densely populated coastal plain of Gaza is due to uncontrolled pumping from the aquifer, intensive use of agrochemicals, irrigation with treated (and non-treated) effluents, and, in some areas, leaking sewage systems that are based on septic tanks or even "free flow" of domestic effluents in open channels or washes. The Gaza shallow aquifer is prone to contamination by the enormous number of septic tanks, infiltration of leaking sewage pipelines and deep percolation of soil-water loaded with fertilizers, pesticides, and herbicides from the intensively cultivated land.

The extremely dense population, whose mass family-unit housing covers the land with massive concrete and asphalt, eliminates much of the natural infiltration from rainfall, which decreases the amount of groundwater recharge below 50% of natural levels per urban unit area. Rainfall recharge of the aquifer amounts to about 20%–25% of the rainfall. This varies from 70 mm of rainfall recharge per year in the south to 125 mm in the north. Gaza's land is characterized by sandy soil which allows fast infiltration and groundwater recharge into the shallow phreatic aquifer. This natural aquifer replenishment is now blocked by concrete houses and asphalt, depriving the local groundwater reservoir of its annual freshwater replenishment. The combination of reduced groundwater recharge and massive percolation of polluted water and seawater intrusion has driven most of the Gaza aquifer far below the drinking level standards. In addition, natural replenishment of saline-brackish groundwater originating from the Eocene Aquitard, across the eastern border with Israel, elevates groundwater salinity along the eastern sections of the Gaza aquifer, precluding irrigation of various crops.

No constructive solution has yet been proposed to salvage the Gaza local water resources besides seawater and saline groundwater desalination. However, a sustainable development of local water resources cannot rely solely on desalination. The best long-term water storage in an arid climate is groundwater, which must be developed, treated, and protected just as any other precious natural resource would be. Due to groundwater contamination, the local water authority is looking for an "easy and simple" solution by producing "new water" by seawater desalination. Very little has been done so far in this area of local groundwater protection and remediation, and it has long been considered as a "lost" water resource.

One of the reasons for the current low groundwater storage capacity of this aquifer is because of the massive cover of concrete and asphalt that eliminates groundwater recharge from local rainfall. Subsurface storage of groundwater is by far the most sustainable long-term storage reservoir in arid lands. Therefore, the shallow aquifer of Gaza should not be neglected as a feasible source for future water supply, at least for agricultural and industry end users.

Water Resources in the Gaza Strip

The Coastal Aquifer of the Gaza Strip is part of a regional groundwater system that extends from the coastal areas of the northern Sinai in the south to Mount Carmel in the north. The Coastal Aquifer is generally 10 to 15 km wide, and its thickness ranges from mostly nonexistent in the east to about 200 m at the coastline. The approximate area of the entire aquifer is 2,200 km², with 365 km² beneath the Gaza region. The Coastal Aquifer consists primarily of Pleistocene Age Kurkar Group deposits, including calcareous and silty sandstones, silts, clays, unconsolidated sands, and conglomerates. Near the coast, the coastal clays extend about 2 to 5 km inland and divide the aquifer sequence into three or four subaquifer units, depending upon location (referred to as subaquifers A, B1, B2, and C). The confinement and the hydraulic separation among the subaquifers depend on the spatial continuity of the coastal clay layers. Toward the east, the clays pinch out and the aquifer is largely unconfined (phreatic).

Within the Gaza Strip, the total thickness of the Kurkar Group is about 100 m at the shore in the south and about 200 m near Gaza City. At the eastern Gaza border, the saturated thickness is about 60 to 70 m in the north and only a few meters in the south near Rafah. Local, perched water conditions exist throughout the Gaza Strip due to the presence of shallow clay layers.

A conceptual geological cross-section of the coastal plain geology is presented in figure 12.1. The base of the Coastal Aquifer is marked by the top of the Saqiya Group, a thick sequence of marls, clay-stones, and shales that slopes toward the sea. The Saqiya Group pinches out about 10 to 15 km from the shore, and in places the Coastal Aquifer rests directly on Eocene Age chalks and limestones. The aquifer's daily transmissivity values are in the range between 700 and 5,000 m²/day.

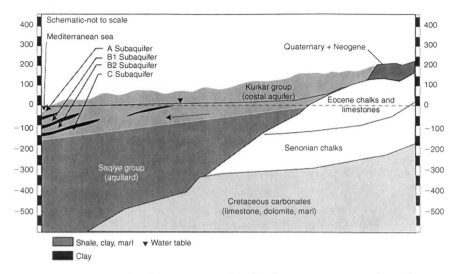

Figure 12.1 Generalized cross-section plain for the Gaza Strip Coastal Aquifer.

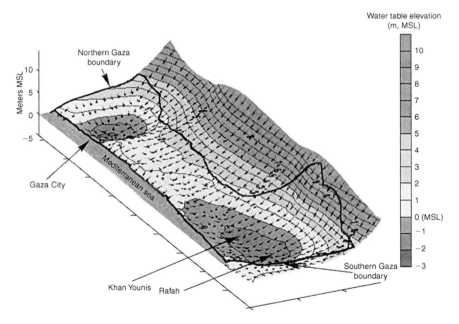

Figure 12.2 Groundwater flow directions in the Gaza Strip Coastal Aquifer (MSL = mean sea level).
From Palestinian Water Authority (PWA).

Groundwater Flow Regime

Under natural conditions, groundwater flow in the Gaza Strip runs toward the Mediterranean Sea. However, natural water flow patterns have been significantly disturbed by overpumping and artificial sources of recharge over the past 40 years.

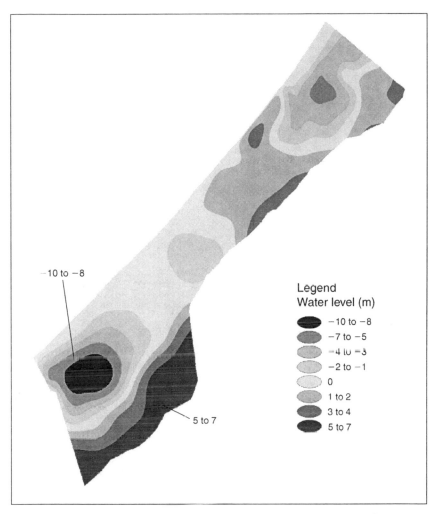

Figure 12.3 Groundwater level in the Gaza Strip Coastal Aquifer, 2005.
From Palestinian Water Authority (PWA).

Within the Gaza Strip, large cones of depression have formed over substantial areas in the north and south. Water levels are presently below mean sea level, inducing a hydraulic gradient from the Mediterranean toward the major pumping centers and municipal supply wells. Three-dimensional representation of water flow field is presented in figure 12.2.

Groundwater Level

In the year 2005 interpreted water-level maps for the Gaza Coastal Aquifer were developed (figure 12.3). In general, the groundwater level is continually decreasing, particularly during the past 10 years, where in areas like Rafah in the south of the Strip water level reaches more than 10 m below sea level, as shown in figure 12.4.

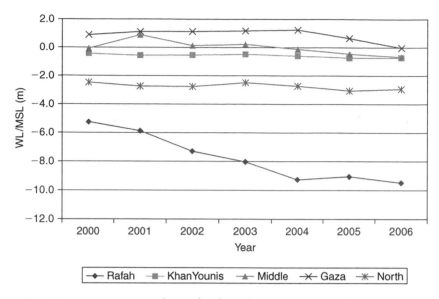

Figure 12.4 Average groundwater level in selected wells across the Gaza Strip.

Water Balance of the Gaza Coastal Aquifer

The water balance for the Gaza Coastal Aquifer was recently assessed. The calculations are based on the estimation of all water inputs and outputs to the regional aquifer system. The components of the current water balance of the Gaza Strip are as follows:

- outflows, which include total groundwater abstraction plus lateral outflow (including natural discharge to the sea), and
- inflows, which include effective recharge plus lateral inflow plus total return flows plus saltwater intrusion.

The 2007 Gaza Strip water balance has been simplified and displayed in table 12.1. The two main components of the water balance are municipal and agricultural well abstraction. The sum of both components exceeds the natural groundwater replenishment (rainfall recharge and lateral inflow from east/north). In other words, there was a deficit of about 70 to 75 mcm/yr in the year 2007, where the groundwater overpumping has a direct effect on the quality and the quantity of the groundwater. This deficit is expected to grow with the increasing of population in Gaza Strip.

Water Demand

Groundwater is the main resource for water in the Gaza Strip. The Strip relies mainly on groundwater to fulfill all local needs. As the natural safe yield of the aquifer is about 40 to 45 mcm/yr, present practices lead to a deficit of 40 to 45 mcm/yr of adequate water quality for domestic supply. In the event that all the returned water, from water and wastewater networks as well as from irrigation, is

Table 12.1 Water balance in the Gaza Strip, 2007

Inflows (mcm/yr)	Min	Max	Outflows (mcm/yr)	Min	Max
Effective rainfall recharge	40	45	Municipal abstraction	75	85
Lateral inflow from east/north	15	20	Agricultural abstraction	85	95
Deep percolation from water-system leaks	10	10			
Wastewater return flows	10	10			
Irrigation return flows	15	20			
Total	90	105		160	180
Net balance	−70	−75			

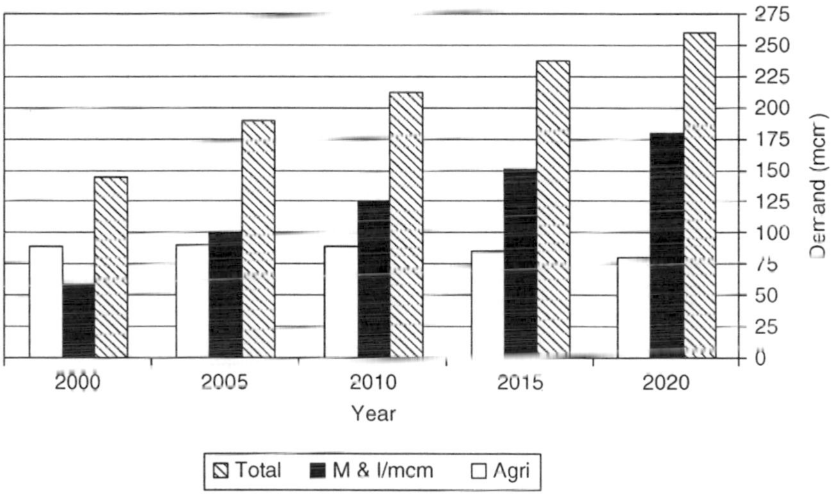

Figure 12.5 Present and future water demand for agricultural versus municipal and industrial use in the Gaza Strip.

considered (90 to 105 mcm/yr) in the water balance, total water deficit will still reach about 70 to 75 mcm/yr for both domestic and agricultural use.

Due to the population growth in the Gaza Strip, water demand is expected to increase to 260 mcm/yr by the year 2020 (figure 12.5). Taking into consideration all returned water, in spite of its quality, the total water input will be in the range of 90 to 105 mcm/yr. This will lead to a water deficit of 160–170 mcm/yr by the year 2020 if no management interventions are taken.

Groundwater Quality

Large parts of the Gaza Coastal Aquifer suffer from a continuous decline of water quality during the past decade. The deterioration is from pollution and increased

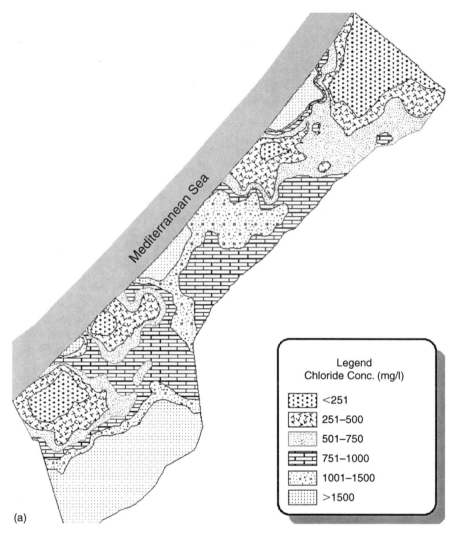

Figure 12.6 Chloride and nitrate concentrations in drinking wells.
Coastal Municipalities Water Utility (CMWU), Eng-Ashraf Mushtaha.

salinity. It is mainly due to overpumping, seepage of raw sewage, extensive use of fertilizers and pesticides in agriculture, solid waste dumps, and unchecked industrialization. The primary cause of concern is the unacceptable levels of salinity in the groundwater supply. Excessive and continuous mining of the subaquifer units has caused water tables to decline, with ensuing seawater intrusion from the Mediterranean. Seawater seepage extends several kilometers in different parts of the Gaza Strip aquifer; the fact that the aquifer slopes toward the sea does not help the situation. Furthermore, greater demand from the rapid population growth will further aggravate the problem. The amount of replenished water is decreasing, while the population is increasing.

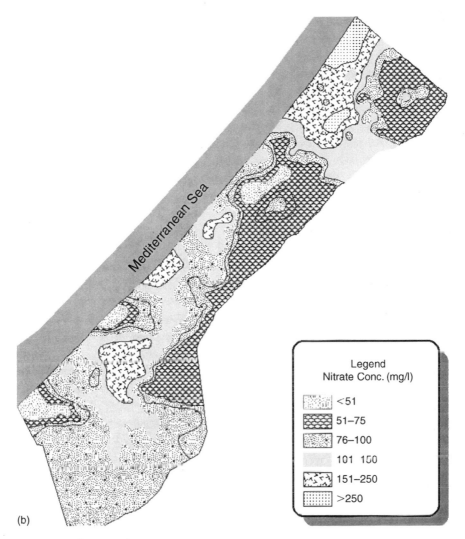

Legend
Nitrate Conc. (mg/l)

<51
51–75
76–100
101 150
151–250
>250

(b)

Figure 12.6 Continued

The quality of the municipal water supply is not acceptable, where the chloride content in most of these wells fluctuates from 300 to 700 mg/l, which is double the recommended value by the World Health Organization (WHO), which is 250 ppm.

Nitrate content in the well water is often used as a general indicator of pollution, especially when salinity is low. Nitrate levels in most of the wells are around 100–150 ppm (figure 12.6). This value is three times the recommended value of the World Health Organization, which sets maximum concentrations at only 50 ppm. When considering the other dissolved chemical constituents of domestic water, it can be concluded that most of the public supply wells are not suitable for drinking. The gap between the quality of domestic water in the Gaza Strip and the recommended values by the WHO will increase by time with the natural growth of population and its increasing water demand. Domestic water is also polluted by the leaching of wastewater into the groundwater system, with negative impacts on the health of the local residents, in general, and children, in particular. This is reflected in the disease profile that the Palestinians presently suffer, such as blue baby syndrome, renal failure, cancer, etc.

At present, nitrate concentrations have reached 600 ppm in some areas of the Strip, like Khanyounis, a city in the south. Chloride levels have exceeded 500 ppm, raised to 1,000–2,000 ppm in the east, mainly due to natural lateral seepage from the neighboring brackish Eocene aquifer that encompasses the northern Negev Desert. Data from the Palestinian Water Authority indicate that chloride concentrations have even hit 3,300 ppm in Deir-el-Balah. The pollution problem will only get worse, with chloride concentration increasing by 15 to 20 ppm annually. Besides eroding the availability of potable water, salinity levels have had a disastrous effect upon agriculture.

Strategies for the Future

There is a pressing need for a new strategy to solve the current and the future water crisis in the Gaza Strip. Priority must be given to domestic users, where water quality should be ensured to meet at least the minimum health requirements. Water conservation policy must be applied to achieve optimum resource use. This will include minimization of municipal leaks throughout sewage distribution networks through rehabilitation; enforcement of laws against illegal connections and illegal wells; proper metering of water; and tariff-system reform, which will lead to careful use of water and a more secure revenue base to help run and maintain the water supply system.

Reclaimed wastewater is of great potential and can be a major resource in solving the Strip's water problem. It has been estimated that more than half of the domestic water there can be reused when properly treated. The amount can even be elevated, providing that septic tanks are eliminated and centralized sewage systems are installed. New water resources, such as desalination of seawater and local salty groundwater, are also part of a broad and sustainable solution. Seawater desalination is more secure and may prove to be financially feasible in the light of improvement in the socioeconomic situation.

Another solution is to introduce new crop species that need less water and are less sensitive to water salinity than the existing crops. The new crops must be economically attractive to the farmers and have good market potential. As important, comprehensive runoff schemes should be developed in order to collect roof rainwater and catch most of the streets' runoff, which otherwise will be partly contaminated with sewage and/or be lost to the sea. The collected water can be used to artificially recharge the aquifer.

Critical to all of this, of course, are the intra-regional agreements and institutions for managing water, for sharing supplies, and for avoiding or mitigating quality problems.

Proposed Projects for Regional Cooperation

As the water issue has become a political matter, the development of a final status peace treaty and continued negotiation will contribute to a solution for the Gaza

Strip water crisis. Everyone in the region has the right to adequate quantity and quality of water, even as the specifics of such an arrangement have yet to be determined by the parties. The recognition of the rights to water and the fact that most water sources in the region are cross-border resources illuminate the ongoing need for coordinated water management strategy between all regional water authorities.

As water is a scarce commodity in the region and all parties already suffer from lack of sufficient and adequate quality of water for domestic and agriculture users, the most feasible and immediate solution for Gaza Strip is associated with the production of new water by means of desalination and treatment of effluents.

- Desalination Plants: Joint cooperation is needed in establishing seawater desalination plants with high capacity in the short (3 to 5 years) and long term (15 to 20 years).
- Wastewater Treatment Plants: Develop projects in the wastewater sector and establish reuse of treated wastewater by joint management between the two parties in operation and exchange of experience and information with bilateral and/or regional cooperation.
- Bilateral and Regional Cooperation: Cooperation and coordination are necessary in the management of water resources and projects through a common committee to mange the water sector (JWC).
- Cooperation and Exchange of Experience: There needs to be development and sharing of scientific, technical, and academic knowledge between the universities and research centers in order to develop common projects in the water sector, aiming on increasing research to present new recommendations.

Extending an invitation to the international community and neighboring countries such as Jordan and Egypt to participate in the infrastructure projects, such as desalination plants and/or wastewater treatment plants, will help in accelerating the production of additional water for Gaza. It will also strengthen the peace process, which may encourage donors to further support the water production and management sectors.

REFERENCES

CAMP. 2000. *Integrated aquifer management plan.* Coastal Aquifer Management Program, Metcalf and Eddy in cooperation with the Palestinian Water Authority (PWA). U.S. Agency for International Development, May.

Greitzer, D., J. Dan. 1967 The effect of soil landscape and quanternary geology on the distribution of saline and fresh water aquifers in the Coastal Plain of Israel, Water Planning for iIsrael Tel Aviv, Tahal, Ltd. June 1967.

Hadı, A. A. 1997. Gaza water crisis worsening. *The Palestine Report,* May 16, 2 (49).

Nasser, Y. 2003. Palestinian water needs and rights in the context of past and future development. In *Water in Palestine: Problems, politics, prospects,* ed. F. Daibes, 85–123. Jerusalem: Palestinian Academic Society for the Study of International Affairs (PASSIA).

Weinthal, E., A. Vengosh, A. Marei, A. Gutierrez, and W. Kloppmann. 2005. The water crisis in the Gaza Strip: Prospects for resolution. *Ground Water* 43 (5): 654.

Editors' Summary

The recent violence and military clash between Israel and the Gaza Strip is particularly unfortunate because this small, crowded, and indigent area is in desperate hydrological straights. The inevitable damage to infrastructure associated with full-scale war only exacerbated what was already a deplorable situation. Both the quantity and the quality of the available groundwater are unacceptable, and basic sanitation services are largely deficient. The impact on Palestinian public health and groundwater resources is severe. Even putting aside the humanitarian imperatives, the proximity of one of Israel's primary desalination facilities to the border with Gaza makes the steady discharges of raw Gazan sewage into the sea an Israeli problem as well as a Palestinian one. In short, there is a consensus that the severity of Gaza's water conditions makes it the top priority in international assistance for water in the area.

It is also clear what needs to be done, and this is set forward clearly by Yousef Abu-Mayla and Eilon Adar. Substantial infrastructure investment must begin with rebuilding a modern sewage collection and treatment system. As the Gaza Strip is ultimately a single metropolitan area, a highly efficient, comprehensive wastewater system, taking advantage of economies of scale, is essential. International commitment to investment in rebuilding Gaza after the recent conflict is substantial, and this creates an opportunity that should include ambitious sewage infrastructure. Regardless of the specific political dynamics at any given time, Israel must allow this project to take place and facilitate construction activities. It is, after all, in its own hydrological self-interest to do so.

Given the steady deterioration in the southern Coastal Aquifer, the future of Gaza's drinking water is in desalination. Reverse osmosis remains the most cost-effective option available. As most future peace plans contain a physical link between the West Bank and the Gaza Strip, Gaza will have the potential to "export" water to the Palestinian population in the West Bank through the planned land bridge or via other more efficient routes. With the Gaza population increasingly dependent on expensive bottled water (or exposed to unsafe tap water), desalination facilities should be expedited without delay.

Other proposed water management programs, such as an aggressive program for water conservation and efficiency, are crucial, starting with immediate work to plug the considerable leakages in the delivery system. But introducing physical and technology measures is not enough. Incentives must be put in place for water saving at the household and firm level. And there must be a regulatory system established that will control the illegal drilling of wells. The rainwater-harvesting program endorsed by the authors is the kind of low-cost investment in Gaza's hydrological future that should be seriously considered by funders. Time is of the essence. Given the grave hydrological circumstances, analysis cannot give way to paralysis and investment in change must be made without delay.

PART 13

CITIZEN INVOLVEMENT

Civil society organizations have begun to focus on building a "culture of peace" around water issues from the grassroots. Several organizations have taken up the challenge of working across the border over key transboundary issues such as pollution of groundwater and wells, wastewater management, cross-border streams, and the management of shared water resources. Given the differences in the political and social makeup between Israelis and Palestinians, civil society organizations focused on water necessarily have different priorities and means to be effective. While Palestinian NGOs necessarily focus on humanitarian and infrastructure development work, Israeli NGOs are more geared toward pollution prevention and habitat protection through advocacy-based and legal approaches. Though Palestinian NGOs have a strong focus on water conservation, surprisingly little attention is given to addressing water demand issues by the environmental movement in Israel. This part considers the range of organizations that are in a position to make important contributions toward developing creative and equitable solutions to regional environmental problems at a time when respective governments are mired in conflict and inaction.

The Role of Civil Society in Addressing Transboundary Water Issues in the Israeli-Palestinian Context

IYAD ABURDEINEH

GIDON BROMBERG

LUCY MICHAELS

NA'AMA TESCHNER

And we must show that water resources need not be a source of conflict. Instead, they can be a catalyst for cooperation.

—Kofi Annan, Secretary General of
the United Nations, 2005

In an area of conflict where governments have difficulty discussing civil issues of all kinds, it becomes the role of the civil society to become a voice for these concerns and proffer solutions. The urgency of the water crisis developing in the Middle East, which is inherently transboundary in nature, and the low level of negotiations between governments at this time necessarily bring civil society into the spotlight. The ongoing relationship between Israelis and Palestinians working in civil society on water issues can offer an invaluable alternative forum for addressing this crucial public health and environmental issue, where governments are failing.

This essay describes the activities of Palestinian and Israeli NGOs and grassroots initiatives focused on water issues. It explores where their activities in their respective societies differ and where they intercept. We specifically highlight examples of transboundary cooperation, its successes and failures, with a focus on Friends of the Earth Middle East (FOEME) and its Good Water Neighbors program. We also look at the future of the water conflict and the role of NGOs in formal decision making. This includes the importance of recognizing the cross-border NGOs as important players in resolving conflict and fostering solutions.

Water and Civil Society in the Palestinian Territories

The major NGOs focused on water in the Palestinian Territories are the Palestine Hydrology Group (PHG) and the Palestinian Agricultural Relief Committees (PARC), with offices all over the West Bank and Gaza. These organizations both preceded the establishment of the Palestinian Authority in 1994 and were established to do the essential work needed to provide water supply and infrastructure across the West Bank and Gaza Strip in the absence of an over-arching authority at the time. They are responsible for drilling wells and providing water for basic needs. Due to Israeli control over much of their water resources, these organizations must deal with Israeli officials on a regular basis.

Since these organizations are service providers with no ultimate decision-making authority, there is subsequently a close but tense relationship with the Palestinian Authority. For example, the Water Authority has at times applied for projects through the PHG. This tension is heightened by the fact that the Palestinian Authority has little capacity for enforcing regulation, especially in areas of the West Bank that are still under Israeli control. It is also heightened by the fact that both PARC and PHG are affiliated with left-wing groups and not Fatah.

The Palestinian Authority is also beholden to the international donors that fund many of the water infrastructure projects. In the aftermath of the Hamas election victory in 2006, the situation was complicated by the creation of parallel Fatah and Hamas ministries and the fact that international donors refused direct aid money to the Palestinian Authority, channeling it instead through NGOs. Fortunately, this situation has mostly been resolved.

The acute water scarcity in the Palestinian Territories means that the major work of environmental NGOs has to focus on emergency relief, humanitarian, and development issues. This is especially true of organizations that operate in Gaza, which also include the Environmental Protection and Research Institute and Palestinian Centre for Human Rights (PCHR) who have published reports on water issues in Gaza.

A significant problem in the Palestinian territories is the lack of trained experts and solid research on water availability. Work to rectify this is being carried out by organizations including the Land Research Centre and Applied Research Institute Jerusalem (ARIJ). ARIJ is also a research organization focused on water demand and supply issues as well some practical agricultural projects, including drilling wells. In terms of advocacy work, the House of Water and Environment, a scientific research organization based in Ramallah, has worked with Friends of the Earth Middle East to campaign for the protection of the Mountain Aquifer, highlighting pollution from olive mills, tanneries, and raw sewage. However, this is not an easy issue to resolve when polluters lack other means of disposing of their waste and the Palestinian Authority does not prioritize the enforcement of environmental regulations. In general, safeguarding water courses is considered to be the role of the authorities and not the responsibility of civil society.

While civil society organizations can lobby the Palestinian Authority to take action, there is little scope for NGOs to take legal action against either the Palestinian Authority or polluting companies, something that is increasingly common in Israel. Most Palestinian NGOs are unaware of this course of action, with considerable debate as to whether this is, in fact, technically possible. In any case, with no precedent, this would be an unlikely course of action for a Palestinian environmental NGO.

Water and Civil Society in Israel

Water has become a key issue for the environmental movement in Israel over the last decade. All the major environmental organizations include some activities focused on preventing pollution, restoring habitat, and raising public awareness about the health of Israel's water courses. This includes the Society for the Protection of Nature in Israel (SPNI), which campaigns against the continued degradation of Lake Kinneret; Adam Teva V'Din, which has taken legal action to prevent the pollution of the Kishon Stream and taken municipalities to court across the country for releasing sewage water into streams; and Sustainable Negev, which focuses on pollution in the Beersheva Stream. One organization, Zalul, founded in 1999, is solely devoted to protecting Israel's marine and freshwater environment.

Grassroots-led initiatives have also developed to address water issues, for example, the Citizens for the Environment in the Galilee, which promotes activity to prevent pollution of streams with sewage in Jewish and Arab towns in northern Israel. This work highlights the lack of infrastructure in Arab municipalities within Israel, especially in north and south of the country. The Galilee Society, which campaigns on environmental justice issues for Israel's Arab community, uses this platform to call for equal access to clean water and sewage treatment.

Israeli organizations primarily focus on the environmental and health affects of pollution of water courses, with far less energy targeted toward conservation measures. The exception to this is Israel's Green Party, which is launching a campaign on the municipal level on water conservation, water quality, and public health issues. Recently, the SPNI and an Israeli multinational engineering and water management company, TAHAL, won a tender from the Israeli Water Commission to run a campaign on water conservation, which is now in its pilot stages.

Almost all the organizations mentioned have focused their legal and advocacy efforts solely on pollution in Israel and Israeli polluters, with little analysis on transboundary water issues. The major mechanisms for action by Israeli NGOs have been both public awareness campaigns and use of legal means to sue the government for inaction. This approach was made possible with a change in the law in the mid-1990s and has been pioneered by Israeli lawyers working primarily through Adam Teva V'Din.

From the outline above, it is clear that Israeli and Palestinian NGOs working on water issues play a very different role in their respective political entities. While Israeli NGOs often find themselves both funded by and confronting the Israeli government through legal channels, Palestinian NGOs often find themselves simply replacing the government where service provision is lacking, and they are funded by international funding sources and development agencies.

Israeli-Palestinian Cooperation on Transboundary Water Issues

In the wake of the Oslo Accords, funding became available for joint work on environmental issues, including water. During this optimistic period, the idea of linking environment to peace-building and mutual tolerance as a rallying call for both Israelis and Palestinians became highly attractive. As a result, several joint organizations with both Israeli and Palestinian leadership developed in the immediate afterglow of Oslo focused on environmental issues, including some of the largest and best-funded NGOs in the Palestinian territories. Friends of the Earth Middle East, then known as EcoPeace, was established in 1994; the Palestinian-Israeli Environmental Secretariat (PIES) was formed in 1997 as a project of the Palestine Council on Health (PCH) and the Israel Economic Cooperation Forum, themselves both post-Oslo transition-era institutions. The focus of PIES included providing a forum for joint work, working with industry, and finding a means to transfer expertise and technical skills to the Palestinian environmental community from Israel.

Another joint initiative at this time came from a well-established organization, the Israeli-Palestinian Centre for Research and Information (IPCRI), which had been founded in 1988 in the worst days of the first Intifada. In 1992, IPCRI founded its Water and Environment program and hosted a series of joint discussions, "Our Shared Environment," bringing together experts from both Israel and the Palestinian territories for the first time. Consequently, this work led to small collaborative efforts on environmental issues funded by the International Development Research Centre (IDRC), a Canadian organization. A further initiative of IPCRI was the Joint Environmental Mediation Service (JEMS), designed to train Israelis and Palestinians in the technique of environmental mediation and, thereafter, to offer mediation to Israeli and Palestinian stakeholders in conflict over environmental issues. Other environmental organizations that began high-profile joint work at this time included Bird Life International.

The changing political climate in the wake of the assassination of Yitzhak Rabin, the election of a right-wing government in Israel, and, ultimately, the outbreak of the Second Intifada has threatened and somewhat diminished the enthusiasm for joint initiatives. While some joint organizations and projects fell afoul of the changing times, such as PIES, which collapsed completely within a year of the Intifada, many others are weathering the storm albeit in a more low-key way, and many of the connections developed in the preceding years have continued. In the current climate, however, it has become much harder to bring together Israelis and Palestinians simply to meet without encountering bureaucratic difficulties.

Indeed, in 2002, another cross-border NGO was founded, the Israeli-Palestinian Scientific Organization (IPSO), which has also focused on transboundary water issues. In 2006, IPSO participated in a UNESCO project to bring together six Israeli and Palestinian and other experts to establish a framework for joint projects focused on writing a common history for water management in the Middle East.

The major work of cross-border organizations with joint leadership, such as IPCRI and Friends of the Earth Middle East, has been to provide a bridge where relations between official bodies remain unresolved and problematic. As Robin Twite of IPCRI argues, part of the problem between official bodies in Israel and the Palestinian Authority is the imbalance of power between decision-makers on both sides.

While the Israeli Water Commission is well funded and resourced, the Palestinian Water Authority has to compete for funding from international donors and has to deal with the fact that it has limited authority over the West Bank. The Israeli Water Commission may be well meaning in its desire to see the Palestinians receive adequate water of an acceptable quality, but its superior situation and negotiating position can lead to it appearing over-confident and patronizing. Likewise, recognizing their position of weakness, Palestinian officials can appear over-critical, often repeating demands for the resolution of issues which they are well aware cannot be resolved by the Israeli Water Commissioner, such as the issue of water for the settlements.

Cross-border NGOs can provide a means of communication to enable the two sides to meet on more equitable terms. Further, they can contribute to a resolution of difficulties since they can be more flexible and are not directly involved in the political process.

Friends of the Earth Middle East (FOEME)—Good Water Neighbors Project

One of the cross-border organizations that has continued working throughout the Second Intifada is Friends of the Earth Middle East—the only joint Israeli-Palestinian organization engaged in work on transboundary issues from a peace-building perspective. The organization has produced numerous publications on transboundary water issues such as sewage water and the Mountain Aquifer. With a focus on problem solving and cooperative solutions, FOEME argues that water issues are an excellent bridge to promote cooperation between neighboring communities, especially in conflict areas, due to the interdependent nature of water resources.

Initiated in 2001, FOEME's Good Water Neighbors project works with neighboring communities in Israel, Jordan, and the Palestinian territories. It uses shared water resources as the basis for environmental education, water security, and peace-building. The project seeks to encourage dialogue and cooperation between the communities on the different realities of water availability and use in their communities as well as on how shared water resources can be managed sustainably. The project also seeks to directly address water scarcity issues through encouraging saving, reusing, and sustainable water practices within each community.

FOEME's work has ranged from developing low-tech water treatment methods and conservation projects at local schools and in public buildings to summer camps for kids, petitions, and awareness-raising posters. The project has also worked with local mayors and community leaders to build cooperation and lobbied at highest level to the European Parliament and the U.S. House of Representatives. By 2005, the project had established a cooperative work program between eighteen rural communities located on the borders of Israel, Jordan, and Palestine.

Beginning shortly after the outbreak of the Second Intifada, this project faced significant challenges: mistakes were made and the project had to be flexible enough to adapt to the constantly changing circumstances. Developing community involvement and trust was a slow process, with some participants being intimidated for taking part in activities and with a sense of outrage at the violence perpetrated on both sides of the conflict being a significant barrier. For this reason, the regional cooperation aspect of the project was initially kept at a low profile, with a focus on real investing in physical improvements in the communities and hiring locally respected workers. As trust developed over time, regional meetings became not only possible but "desirable," with the "other side" becoming a point of intrigue rather than a source for suspicion.

A powerful example of how these grassroots connections have developed through the Good Water Neighbors project, beyond simply the water connection, is the story of the West Bank village of Wadi Fuqin. Here, the villagers, with the vocal support of the FOEME and the neighboring Jewish community of Tsur Hadassah, have taken legal action to prevent the Separation Wall from being built beyond the Green Line, which would have affected the recharge area of the streams that flow into the village and cut villagers off from their olive trees. The court did not contest the petition and the wall has subsequently not been built there. These two communities are now developing a joint "development plan" for the area which includes environmental, economic, and social considerations as well as a sustainable tourism initiative. Meanwhile, joint initiatives in Emek Hefer and Tulkarem, between the Jordan River Valley mayors, and between Baka al Gharbia and Baka al Sharkia have yielded direct funding for cooperative projects, generating real solutions to ease the water and sewage problems of all residents.

In future years, funding is being made available by USAID and the European Union for more grassroots work based on this model of incorporating peacebuilding into development and community-assistance projects, such as water management. Such funding to develop more projects like these can only be of benefit to the region.

Joint Work from a Palestinian Perspective

Joint work is also not always relevant in the Palestinian context. Since the two political entities are at such different levels of socioeconomic development and civic education, it is understandable that there is not always "common ground" between Israeli and Palestinian NGOs. Priorities for one are likely to be discounted or ignored by the other. Besides, Palestinian organizations take accusations of "normalization" seriously—the implication being that by cooperating and working with Israeli organizations they are accepting the status quo of the Israeli occupation. Further, from a political perspective, it remains a fact that until the Palestinians receive full independence and a resolution over shared water resources with Israel, it will be a challenge for Palestinian organizations to engage in long-term planning for water management.

There is also, however, a widespread understanding that in the current context, water access and sanitation are basic humanitarian issues, and that some degree of cooperation with Israel is necessary due to the transboundary nature of the issue. Even the Hamas-led government in Gaza has indicated that they are open to discuss water management issues with Israel through a mediator. Therefore, some major Palestinian water-focused organizations, such as PHG and ARIJ, have worked on joint projects with academic institutions in Israel. Palestinian organizations, such as the German-government-funded GLOWA project, have also worked together in the context of large regional projects focused on the future of the Jordan River Valley.

Joint Work from an Israeli Perspective

With plenty of work to be done to protect water courses and prevent pollution from sources inside Israel and the disappointment of the collapse of the peace process, it is perhaps not surprising that for most Israeli environmental organizations, cross-boundary issues are not currently high on the agenda. In some cases this is organizational policy: for example, Adam Teva V'Din does not work over the Green Line, although it did take one case against the establishment of a landfill for Israeli waste being established in a settlement on the West Bank.

Notably, few Israeli peace organizations have comprehensively addressed water issues except for humanitarian efforts. For example, several years ago the Givat Haviva Institute of the Hashomer HaTzair youth movement provided tankers of water to provide relief for West Bank villages facing drought. Several Israeli human rights organizations do, however, address this issue. B'Tselem and Yesh Din both address the issue of Palestinian access to the shared water sources of the Jordan River and the Mountain Aquifer from a human-rights-based perspective.

In terms of joint research initiatives, the Arava Institute for Environmental Studies, based in southern Israel, continues to draw students from both Israel and the West Bank and has also carried out joint research on shared water resources, most notably a stream restoration project on the Alexander/Zumar River with students based both in Israel and the West Bank, supported by a Middle Eastern Research Council grant from USAID. Another USAID-funded project ran from 2001 to 2004 between Hebron University, the Technion in Israel, and the Royal Scientific Society in Jordan to reduce the environmental impact of olive-mill wastewater in the region, a major transboundary pollutant.

Since 2007, the Towns Association for Environmental Quality in Sakhnin, Israel, has worked in partnership with the Centre for Environmental Diplomacy in Ramallah to support Palestinian water engineers in establishing wastewater treatment facilities in their own communities, with support from the Adam Institute and the European Union. This work builds on a previous USAID-funded project to promote appropriate technology for wastewater treatment with project partners in Egypt, Israel (Sakhnin), and the Palestinian territories.

In 2008, an Israeli research institute, the Van Leer Institute, established the joint Israeli-Palestinian Study Group on Protection of the Environment in cooperation with the Palestinian Peace and Freedom Youth Forum. The aim is to further involve Israeli civil society in transboundary environmental issues, and it brings together students to study environmental issues and dilemmas of common interest, including water, solid waste, and the ecology of the Dead Sea.

Joint initiatives between academic institutions and NGOs and cross-border NGOs focused on transboundary environmental issues have clearly been invaluable in keeping discussions open and pushing toward a shared vision, especially at times when the conflict has been most fierce and official channels have been restricted and unconstructive. It is evident from the experience of the last 15 years, however, that such projects are vulnerable to the rapidly changing political situation, which sets the tone for how open and straight-forward or how complicated such cooperation can be.

The Role of Palestinian and Israeli Civil Society in Future Peace Agreements

NGOs working on transboundary water issues with many years of experience of joint work often have a far better grasp of the issues and the need for long-term equitable solutions than the officials designated to make decisions, who are mostly driven by short and expedient political thinking. This presents a challenge for NGOs attempting to become involved in the formal political process. Where they can most influence the agenda is through solid research and innovative thinking.

Examples of innovative thinking abound, such as the call by Friends of the Earth Middle East for the Dead Sea to be declared a UNESCO World Heritage site or for the foundation of a joint Israeli-Palestinian Water Committee to represent major stakeholders and function as an advisory board for both the Israeli Water Commission and the Palestinian Water Authority.

A further example is the water annex of the Geneva Accords: an attempt by civil society to draft a peace agreement acceptable to both Israelis and Palestinians in order to influence the peace process. However, this project has also highlighted several key points of disagreement both between participants and between a short- and long-term vision. Drafted by water experts David Brooks and Julie Trottier, the water annex has not yet been agreed on by other participants in the process, with the Israelis wanting minimal cooperation with a focus on hydrology and the Palestinians wanting hard numbers of how many million cubic meters of water they would receive in an agreement. The draft annex itself is much more holistic, highlighting "water for people," followed by "water for nature," and only then "water for agriculture." Neither Israeli nor Palestinian negotiators can agree, however, to prioritizing water for nature over water for agriculture, instead prioritizing economic needs above the needs of the environment and the vital ecosystem services it provides.

There is a general agreement among Palestinian NGOs that the Oslo Accords did not result in a just outcome on water issues. For this reason, water organizations have lobbied hard to be included in any new peace negotiations toward a final status agreement where water must be a component. In 2007, the Palestinian

Steering and Monitoring Committee, which led negotiations with Israel, invited civil groups, including NGOs, research organizations, and business organizations with an interest water issues, to be involved in discussions on the final status negotiations. Meanwhile, during the good years of the Oslo process, Friends of the Earth Middle East was informally invited as an observer to Joint Environment Committee meetings and asked to contribute ideas. In 2003, the Water Commission also became more open for dialogue on transboundary issues. While Friends of the Earth Middle East has always pushed the government to move forward on the peace process and prepared documents with creative ideas on how to resolve transboundary environmental issues, other Israeli organizations have shown less interest in being formally involved in the process.

A final way in which civil society can influence the peace process is through encouraging international involvement. This could include international mediation by a neutral third party—an idea suggested independently by both the World Water Council and Green Cross International. This could be invaluable if both sides were willing to accept that, left to themselves, they may have difficulty in reaching a mutually acceptable agreement.

Conclusion

In the light of population growth, existing water stress, and climate change, it would not be unreasonable to propose that without cooperation on water management between the Israelis and the Palestinians (and their neighbors) both sides face an uncertain future. Cooperation to improve water infrastructure, to share technologies for desalination and recycling effluent, to promote an ethic of water conservation and preservation of water resources, and to find a resolution to disputed transboundary water sources offers some hope of a sustainable future for the people living in the region and for the environment.

Civil society organizations, especially cross-border organizations, offer a way to move beyond the political crisis and address water issues without the heavy political baggage that surrounds the Israeli-Palestinian conflict. They can also offer innovative ways beyond the impasse, including engaging international civil society. Practical contributions by civil society organizations toward resolving the conflict include generating shared research as well as offering practical support through technology transfer and capacity building.

On a grassroots level, connections between neighboring communities forged by groups such as Friends of the Earth Middle East are invaluable in terms of raising awareness of the environmental justice issues. Perhaps the most important role of civil society toward resolving the transboundary water issues is, therefore, the personal connections and trust forged in communities and by environmentalists and scientists who have worked together on common concerns over the years. Such work has led to shared understandings and assumptions about these issues and has provided a forum for ongoing discussion, despite the changing political situation.

Areas of shared interest include the following:

- Avoiding damage to shared water sources (both streams and groundwater) through both sewage treatment and prevention of overpumping is important to both sides. Both Israeli and Palestinian NGOs are focused on preventing pollution. For Palestinians, this issue is framed in terms of creating the relevant infrastructure to avoid contamination, and for Israel this issue is framed in terms of protecting the environment and preserving open-air spaces.
- There are some forums for cooperation. Some Israeli and Palestinian NGOs recognize the value of building long-term and personal connections and creating "water and environment community" of experts, academics, and officials, and their members work together based on shared assumptions in spite of the political situation.
- Greater voice in the peace process is an area of shared interest for Palestinian NGOs keen to avoid another situation like the Oslo Accords, for joint Israeli and Palestinian organizations, and for Israeli NGO's focused on environmental justice and human rights issues.

Areas of disagreement include the following:

- Due to the drastically different socioeconomic situations in Israel and the Palestinian territories, NGOs from each respective political entity often have different priorities.
- Most Israeli environmental NGOs are not interested in addressing Palestinian water issues, apart from where they impinge on Israel. Most Palestinian environmental NGOs have no choice but to deal with transboundary water issues.
- Palestinian environmental NGOs are keen to influence the peace process based on a desire to achieve an equitable and reasonable agreement over transboundary water issues. In Israel, only human rights organizations and cross-border NGOs are interested in influencing the peace process.

REFERENCES

Friends of the Earth Middle East. 2005. *Good water neighbours: A model for community development programs in areas of conflict*. Bethlehem, Tel Aviv, and Amman: FOEME. http://www.foeme.org/index_images/dinamicas/publications/publ19_1.pdf (accessed July 21, 2009).

Twite, R. 2005. The role of NGOs in promoting regional cooperation over environmental and water issues in Israel and Palestine—successes and limitations. In *Palestinian and Israeli environmental narratives, proceedings of a conference held in association with the Middle East Environmental Futures project*, ed. S. Schoenfeld. Centre for International and Security Studies. Toronto: York University. www.yorku.ca/yciss//whatsnew/documents/Twitepaper.pdf.

Zwirn, M. 2001. Promise and failure: Environmental NGO's and Palestine-Israeli co-operation. *Middle East Review of International Affairs* 5:4.

Editors' Summary

Palestinian NGOs for many years essentially filled the vacuum created by the absence of local governance in the occupied territories, making Palestinian civil society unusually well developed, in general, and particularly impressive and professional in the water sphere. Israel's nongovernment sector has also flourished due to a combination of openness by the central government and court system, support from international Jewish philanthropy, and a highly engaged citizenry. This happy symmetry between Palestinian and Israeli civil societies has already been manifested in a litany of joint projects in the environmental and water spheres. Palestinian and Israeli academics have been especially involved in joint research and professional gatherings, responding positively to a variety of internationally funded programs encouraging academic cooperation.

Palestinian and Israeli water experts have been meeting and working together for years. The resulting collegiality and ability to articulate a common perspective should be exploited in regional efforts to resolve water conflicts. This can be done through the continuation and expansion of programs that encourage joint research, activism, and educational initiatives. Groups like Friends of the Earth Middle East and IPCRI have proven the potential of cooperative work. The broad network of national NGOs, especially in Israel, should be encouraged to become engaged regionally in these areas as well and compete for resources and support. But the contribution of the so-called third sector should go beyond the scope of the projects which have been undertaken to date.

The role of civil society worldwide has expanded over the years. There is no reason why Palestinian and Israeli NGOs should not be appointed as formal representatives to sit on the Joint Water Committee with full-membership authority—and not only with observer status. This would probably contribute to the reduction in the level of polarization and politicization in deliberations. Funds should be made available to ensure the quality and integrity of NGO participation. Public interest groups can play an essential role in monitoring and generating data as well as disseminating information to the public.

There is no need for NGOs to lose their independent "watch dog" status as they are integrated into a regional water management system. The peace process needs civil society's forthright ability to speak plainly and to set environmental and hydrological considerations above political constraints. It would seem that the Palestinian and Israeli nongovernmental communities are ready for this new and expanded challenge.

PART 14

THE ROLE OF THIRD PARTIES IN CONFLICT RESOLUTION

In order for the Palestinian state to develop and maintain its water resources sustainably for the foreseeable future, foreign assistance will play a critical role. Retired diplomat Robin Twite has been involved as a mediating force in the field for over 15 years and is widely accepted as an objective authority by both Israelis and Palestinians. This part offers his insights about how the international community can play an effective role in expediting programs and projects that will contribute to resolving water conflict in the area.

The Role of Third Parties in Helping to Resolve the Conflicts over Water Issues in Israel and Palestine

ROBIN TWITE

It is by now almost axiomatic that third parties have a key role to play in resolving the conflict between Israelis and Palestinians. Since 1948 the two peoples have struggled to resolve their differences but with little success. Again and again outright conflict has been succeeded by an uneasy truce, but there has been no real resolution of the issues of concern to both parties. Unhappily, this still remains true. Over the whole of the period since the establishment of the State of Israel third parties, individual states, and international organizations have attempted to intervene constructively but with only limited success. NGOs and academic institutions in the region can, in some sense, be classed as "third parties" since they strive to play a constructive role in alleviating the conflict and have made use of international funding. Their efforts have also had marginal impact.

It is the purpose of this essay to look at the role of third parties in relation to disputes of water resources between Israelis and Palestinians since 1994. Water is in short supply in both Israel and Palestine, and it is inevitable that there will be disputes as to how it can best be managed. These have been exacerbated by the fact that since 1967 Israel has been largely able to control the way in which water is distributed in the region.

Over the years since 1948 there have been two principal ways in which the international community has sought to resolve conflict over water. The first has been the active intervention at the international level in water disputes; and the second, particularly in evidence since the early 1990s, is the provision of aid to assist in the development of water resources and their effective management.

International Initiatives

On the international level, interventions that have had an impact on the water situation since the establishment of the State of Israel have included the negotiations surrounding the Johnson Plan in the late 1950s, put forward by U.S. president Dwight Eisenhower's special envoy, Eric Johnston, after whom the initiative was named. In retrospect, this was considered to be successful, even though the plan was never formally accepted by all parties. The framework it created had a definite impact on the way water issues were handled in the Jordan basin from the late 1950s onwards. It was this type of initiative which representatives of the international community had in mind when they included water issues in the Oslo Accords in 1993 and 1994.

The Oslo Accords are the most important contribution to resolving issues related to water that the international community has made in recent years. Their most significant features were the clear recognition of Palestinian water rights, agreements on water pumping by Palestinians from the Mountain Aquifer, and provision for the setting up of the Joint Water Committee, on which senior officials and experts from both sides sit and discuss water issues. Also of use, particularly during the 1990s, was the work of the Multi-lateral Committee on water resources, established as part of the effort to resolve the conflict between Israel and Palestine immediately after the Madrid Conference in 1993. This working group (like the other five multi-lateral negotiating committees on other key issues, including the environment) was intended as a forum in which Israelis and Palestinians could meet in peace with representatives of countries interested in assisting the development of the region so that they could together work out agreed policies. In practice they achieved much less than had been hoped for.

The Provision of Aid to the Water Sector

These efforts to provide a framework for mitigating and, hopefully, in the long term, resolving the conflict over water in the region were supplemented shortly after the establishment of the Palestinian Authority, when the international community, backed by individual foundations and NGOs, undertook a major effort to assist in the development of water resources in the Palestinian Authority areas.

This effort was designed both to improve the quality of life of the people of the region by providing additional water resources and, in the long term, to promote understanding and a peaceful resolution of conflicts over water. The aid programs that resulted were almost all designed to assist the Palestinian Authority directly. As Israel's economy was successful and its GNP relatively high, the great majority of countries and international organizations declined to provide funding for projects which were, even in part, within its borders. However, in addition to funds for the Palestinians, some limited funding was made available to universities and institutions of higher education for projects which enabled Israelis and Palestinians to work together on research related to water issues within a scientific and academic context, as well as to NGOs which promoted mutual understanding and compromise over water and environmental concerns.

It is the main focus of this essay to look at what the international communities' well-meant efforts achieved when seeking to resolve conflicts in the water sector, in particular, what degree of success resulted from providing aid to the sector over the 15 years since 1994. This will mean making a brief assessment of these efforts and, in particular, looking at what factors have limited their impact. The essay also will suggest what can be done to help the international community make a more effective contribution, using aid as its instrument, to the development of the water sector in the future.

What Motivates Third-Party Intervention?

It may be worthwhile at this point to look at the factors which govern the attitudes of third parties in long-running conflicts, such as that between the Israelis and Palestinians. Motivations for involvement in conflicts which have deep roots are always mixed. It is possible to distinguish here between three types of aid providers—individual states providing bilateral assistance, international organizations distributing funds on behalf of the international community, and private foundations.

Where individual states are concerned, economic self-interest undoubtedly plays a part; aid programs almost always have a recognizable economic dimension. International assistance has often been given with all manner of conditions, leaving the recipient of aid little choice but to use the donor's equipment and hire its experts. Where the Israeli-Palestinian dispute over water is concerned, such economic motivation has not been paramount. It is true that individual bilateral donors have used consultancy companies based in their home countries and that, in some cases, pumps and other equipment have been provided by the donors using their own countries' resources, thus providing work for the firms producing them. But these considerations have not been central. The region is small and the economic benefits to be derived from aid to the environment and water sector are not economically significant.

The wish to play a part on the world stage, which is also an aspect of national self-interest, undoubtedly influences some players. When the Multinational Committees on water resources and the environment were established in 1994, their efficacy at first was diminished by the fact that a number of states signed up as partners in the various committee, though they had little experience in the region and lacked the resources to be of real assistance. They wanted to be part of the program and to be seen as active. While it might seem reasonable to involve as many potential partners as possible in the aid process, the participation of countries with nothing to contribute slowed up the process.

While economic considerations and a desire to play an international role evidently provide some part of the motivation for aid programs in the region, there are others. Some part of the motivation of donors lies in fear. A dispute such as that in Israel and Palestine threatens the peace of the Middle East and can, like a small fire, spread uncontrollably. Enlightened self-interest is undoubtedly a factor. Also important in some cases are the influence of particular national groups within the donor-states' own society (notable instances of this being the influence of the Jewish community or of the Christian right in the United States) and a wish on the part of individual statesmen and administrations to be seen as helping resolve conflict so as to gain political credit at home.

However, altruism and idealism also have a role. These considerations influence particularly NGOs, but they also motivate many staff members working in aid programs who become genuinely concerned about the impact of their programs. So far as international bodies (such as the various UN agencies or the World Bank) are concerned, more idealistic motivations are at work (though it would be a mistake to regard such agencies as removed from the influence of member states upon their policies). The same is true of major private foundations working in the region, where a wish to improve the quality of life of the people and to promote peace combine to motivate their efforts.

Limitations on Progress after the Oslo Accords

In 1994, when the Oslo Accords were signed and recognized as the template which could provide a basis for long-term settlement, it was clear that funding would be available for substantial projects in the water sector. All parties shared a perception that they were entering a new era in which cooperation was recognized as important and resources existed to support positive development.

Today, 15 years later, things look less promising than had been anticipated. In this respect, activities related to water are not different from others. The outbreak of the Second Intifada in 2000 and political developments in the region since then have had an adverse effect on relations between Israelis and Palestinians at all levels.

The Joint Water Committee still meets, but the Multilateral Committee on Water Resources, like the parallel committees, has not met for some years. (Certain initiatives which were undertaken under its auspices still survive—among them EXACT, a database on Middle Eastern water resources and Middle Eastern center for work on desalination in Oman. These, though useful in themselves, are not of major significance.) Both Israelis and Palestinians were discouraged by the limited results of the committee, and it appears to have died simply through inanition.

So far as aid is concerned, in the last 15 years large sums have been provided, major works undertaken, a variety of research studies completed, but many important projects, though planned, have never been realized. As a result, a sense of deprivation persists among Palestinians who return again and again to the question of "water rights," while for their part, Israeli officials and experts view what is happening in Palestine with a mixture of irritation and condescension. They are particularly critical of the failure of the Palestinians to deal with the treatment of wastewater, which they ascribe to Palestinian incompetence.

Professor Marwan Haddad, for over a decade a prominent exponent of cooperation between Israelis and Palestinians in the field of water, expressed the Palestinian sense of frustration in a recent article where he stated that discussing with Israelis only water needs and quantities separately from water rights will end by making the Palestinians having no control over their water supply or quality. He goes on to say that "Palestinians fear that accepting such an approach will end in separating them from their land and their resources."

For their part Israeli officials never tire of pointing to the fact that while the international community has been willing and able to pay for the construction of wastewater treatment plants in the West Bank and Gaza, only about 5% of

Palestinian wastewater is being treated and the flow of untreated sewage in the ground threatens the integrity of the Mountain Aquifer, which is a key resource for both Israelis and Palestinians.

How is it that in spite of the reasonable sense of optimism that both parties felt in 1994 and the genuine wish of the international community to assist them reach a long-term settlement of outstanding issues over water, genuine agreement has proved so far to be unattainable? The disappointment was apparent even before the outbreak of violence in 2000 did such damage to Israeli-Palestinian relations.

The question is especially salient because there were successes. For example, deep and important new wells were dug in the West Bank using American and other aid funds. These wells substantially increased the amount of freshwater available in Hebron and elsewhere. In addition, distribution systems in the West Bank were extended, more communities received piped water, and monitoring of existing resources improved. At a different level, a number of significant research projects involving Israeli and Palestinian scientists and academics took place; and the efforts of NGOs such as Friends of the Earth Middle East and the Israel Palestine Center for Research and Information (IPCRI) were instrumental in bringing together officials, academics, and professionals in a variety of contexts, including seminars, conferences, and on-the-ground projects. The cumulative effect was the formation of a community of individuals involved professionally in the water field whose desire to cooperate is evident.

But in spite of these positive features, the general picture is somewhat gloomy. A great part of the responsibility for the failure to resolve conflict over water must, of course, be attributed to the political situation. It was not to be expected that water issues could be separated from other controversies and that peace would prevail over the division of water resources when violence and mutual suspicion dominated elsewhere. At the same time, there is still room for considering what has diminished the ability of the international community to help resolve the water issue.

Why Was Progress toward a Solution so Limited?

Looking at the over-all situation, it is possible to discern certain factors which would have made effective resolution of the problem difficult even had a better atmosphere prevailed. Among them is the fact that Israel had the controlling interest from the outset. It is difficult to achieve parity when one party in a conflict is so evidently weaker. Israelis negotiated from a position of strength, Palestinians from one of weakness. This simple and inescapable fact had adverse effects. For example, it damaged the effectiveness of the Joint Water Committee. From verbal accounts of what happened at the many meetings of the committee (the minutes are not in the public domain), it is evident that while most members of the committee worked well together at a personal level, the Palestinian representatives felt themselves to be in the position of junior partners. Palestinians had to ask permission of the Israeli authorities for relatively minor matters and were in no position to challenge Israeli decisions about the use of water within Israel proper, even though it might impinge on the water situation in the West Bank and Gaza. So difficult did meetings become that a prominent official in USAID said, off the record, in an interview in 1999 that without active pressure from his government, the Joint Water Committee might well have ceased to function.

At a different level, the fact that the Palestinian administration generally was not always effective clearly impeded successful implementation of projects. Water management was no different in this respect than other areas of concern. Nor was this a surprise. The civil administration the Israelis created in the West Bank and Gaza worked well with Palestinian local authorities and other professionals until about 1977. From that point on, relations deteriorated and Israel dominated all important decisions about water management, much as it controlled most other aspects of life of the Palestinians until the signing of the Madrid agreements.

In the 20 years subsequent to the Six Day War in 1967. Palestinian administrators and staff had limited responsibilities and worked mainly on local issues in their town or rural area. In 1994 Palestine was a state in the making and the norms of the civil service and the many agencies working in the area had to be established. Moreover, the human resources available to the Palestinian Authority were not comparable with those available to Israel. There were within the Palestinian Water Authority, in local government and in academic institutions, men and women with excellent qualifications, but they were relatively few. The Israeli Water Commission could draw on the expertise and knowledge of thousands of experts in its own ranks, in other professional organizations such as Mekorot, in universities, and in research institutes, while the number of experts in Palestine was only hundreds.

In retrospect, it seems clear that aid agencies, anxious to show results, did not make sufficient allowance for the inadequacies in the human capacity among the recipients of aid. Training programs for staff in the water sector were undertaken by donors, but they were not coordinated and those trained were not always able to use their newfound skills in the existing bureaucratic structures. As late as 2004 USAID was proposing to spend $20 million over 5 years on training technical staff for the water sector. This constituted a sign that it recognized the need to strengthen the capabilities of the Palestinians involved. (This program was ultimately cancelled after Hamas took control of the Palestinian Authority in 2006.)

On the whole it can be said that aid agencies in their water programs took too little cognizance of the weakness of the Palestinian state. Though they provided expert advisors, some of whom wrote excellent reports, the existence of these individuals had a limited impact. Most worked for a relatively short period (between 2 and 4 years) and were replaced by others who had to learn the local situation afresh. This is, of course, a usual hazard of aid work, but in the case of Palestine it had a particularly negative effect because of the relative inefficiency of the Palestinian ministries and agencies. More direct involvement was perhaps necessary on the lines of the arrangements made in Amman, where the office of GTZ, a German aid agency which has given much help to Jordan in developing its water resources, is housed in the same building as the relevant ministry and firmly implanted there.

A particularly striking and instructive case relates to the World Bank's efforts to improve solid waste disposal by building sanitary landfill sites in the West Bank. This involves the water sector indirectly, since solid waste disposal's effects on the water quality of the adjacent aquifers are well known. In this case, plans were made in the late 1990s for the establishment of two state-of-the-art disposal sites: one in Jenin in the north of the West Bank and one in the south in the Hebron area. The plan for Jenin was, in fact, implemented, though it is not yet fully operational for logistic reasons. The selection of a site for the Hebron region was stymied by the attitude of the Hebron local authority, which refused to cooperate unless the site it preferred was selected. This site was within the municipal borders of Hebron. Other potential users of the site, such as the town of Bethlehem, objected, and no decision was taken on the selection of a site. No effective mechanism existed for over-riding these obstructive positions. Only recently has work begun again to resolve this problem.

While cases such as this reflect directly on the ability of the Palestinian Authority to respond adequately to donor initiatives which it had initiated itself, other efforts to assist were frustrated by wider political considerations. Perhaps most notable in the water field was the fact that while donor funding existed for the construction of a wastewater treatment plant in East Jerusalem, such a plant was never built. The difficulty, which has yet to be resolved, lay in the reluctance of the Palestinian Authority to agree that wastewater from Jewish settlements should be treated at the plant as well as that from East Jerusalem and Bethlehem. In the view of the Palestinian Authority this constituted de facto recognition of the settlements' legitimacy and was a step on the way to normalization of their existence. Partly as a result of considerations of this type, over a decade after the Oslo Accords less than 10% of wastewater in Palestine undergoes any kind of treatment.

In yet another case when good intentions fell victim to the impact of violence, a desalination plant in Gaza (for which USAID was providing funds and development was well advanced and included a distribution system) was halted in 2003 when three U.S. government employees were murdered and their murderers were not brought to justice. It has never been resumed.

The work of international agencies has also been impeded by reluctance to acknowledge the validity of criticism. A striking example of the latter was provided by the fate of a desk study, "The Environment in the Occupied Territories," which UNEP undertook in 2004 and which contained a large number of recommendations as to how the situation could be improved. Many of the concrete suggestions related to water management. The desk study was widely circulated but its recommendations had little impact. Both the Israeli Ministry of the Environment and the Palestinian Environmental Quality Agency appeared to feel that they were the target of criticism and were unwilling to respond effectively.

Factors such as these outlined above weakened the impact of the efforts of the international community to assist the Palestinian Authority to make better use of the water it has and so contribute to a climate in which both Israelis and Palestinians could look at water issues in a more relaxed and hopeful atmosphere.

Nongovernmental Initiatives

For many years—from 1967 to the early '90s—assistance from international agencies, overseas governments, and private foundations reached Palestinian society through institutions of higher education and NGOs, where practical and research work on water issues was being undertaken. NGOs such as the Palestinian Hydrology Group, based in Ramallah, Anera, and the Applied Research Institute, based in Bethlehem, were particularly successful in attracting funding from the Arab world and international donors for work on water issues. Their work, particularly in rural areas and in the preparation of reports on the situation, has had a positive impact. But their reach was limited and they did not enjoy the authority of power. With the creation of the Palestinian Authority their role somewhat diminished, but they are still important players within the West Bank itself and attract some international funding.

It is not easy to assess the impact of nongovernmental initiatives in a cross-border context. Recently, IPCRI made an effort to draw together information about joint projects relating to water undertaken by Israeli and Palestinian institutions of higher education and by NGOs seeking to promote Israeli and Palestinian cooperation since 1994. Information was collected about over fifty such projects. Some addressed problems such as the management of the Mountain Aquifer, which lies under Israel and Palestine, or the future of the Dead Sea; others explored questions relating to water quality, while yet others aimed to provide a framework within which Israelis, Palestinians, and international experts could share their knowledge. The aggregate total amount of funding directed by donors to these initiatives was tiny compared with the amounts given by official aid agencies to the Palestinian Authority.

Some projects resulted in valuable reports, program evaluations, and publications, but it was hard to find any concrete information about many others as to what was achieved. In general, evaluation of such projects left much to be desired, though some left important publications as their legacy. There is, however, a consensus among those who participated in the survey that the work has contributed to the creation of a "water community" of experts from Israel and Palestine who are personally acquainted, who understand one another's concerns, and who can work together when required.

Conclusions—the Way Forward

It appears that in spite of the genuine wish of donors to help mediate the conflict over water and improve the management of water resources in the region, social and political factors have in no small measure frustrated their efforts. Much effort has gone into promoting projects, preparing reports, and debating the water problems of the region. But the issues are far from resolved.

The question then arises, What can be done to improve matters in the event that the general political situation improves? Assuming there is a genuine wish on the part of third parties to assist, how should they proceed once the current impasse is resolved and a degree of normalcy returns to the region. When negotiations over water are resumed, it seems that the international community will need to take a lead role as it has tried to do earlier. Large sums are needed to fully exploit the water resources available to Palestinians and add to the total amount of water available through desalination and the treatment of wastewater. Neither the Israeli authorities nor the Palestinian authorities are likely to change their basic attitudes in the near future, and the work of third parties has to be directed to creating efficient mechanisms for cooperation, the distribution of aid, and the implementation of projects. This is especially true because so many of the solutions to the conflict involve investment in infrastructure, something that the funding associated with a final agreement should be able to provide.

The work the Joint Water Committee, valuable as it is, needs to be made more transparent and allow for more involvement of major donors in its work. USAID is already closely linked to the committee; other aid agencies should be also.

It would also be valuable to provide a way in which a mechanism could be established for resolving individual and local disputes over water, using techniques for environmental-dispute resolution developed over the last two decades in North America and Europe. Thanks to the work of NGOs, notably IPCRI, there is already some familiarity with these techniques in the region, and a new initiative designed to create such a body might bring positive results.

It might also be worth considering the establishment of a water council containing Israeli and Palestinian experts which could act as a semi-official forum for the airing of concerns. This could be managed by an appropriate international agency or an NGO. Such ideas have already been floated in a variety of forums, but lack of political will prevented their implementation.

In an effort to create a better atmosphere, the international agencies and national donors would be well advised to make more of an effort to involve the Israeli ministries and the Water Authority in their work. Many donors have their offices in the West Bank (a notable exception is USAID, which has its offices in Tel Aviv) and have little or no contact with the Israeli authorities. This is a pity since ideally their work should benefit both parties. If it is possible to permit aid to go to Israel in specific cases where the water problem is cross-border, this would be a great advantage for all concerned.

As far as work on the ground goes, donors should keep professional staff at their local posts for as long as possible, certainly not less than 4 years, to ensure continuity in their work. The need for cooperation among donors is self evident, and efforts have been made to secure more effective sharing of plans and information. A committee of representatives of donors to the Palestinian Authority exists and should continue to meet. Donors tend to be competitive, with some proposed projects simply more attractive than others. It is up to the recipients of aid to discern where there is overlap and inform potential donors so that resource utilization can be maximized and the consequences of "competition" are not serious. This is particularly true in the realm of procurement, where incompatible hardware or other equipment presented by different donors can cause serious problems.

Donors should also consider extending more funding to the academic institutions and NGOs which are working to bridge the gap between the two sides. Such funding should also provide adequately for the overheads of the recipient organizations, many of which have little by way of endowment funds to cover their basic expenses. Funding for such NGO activities can benefit all parties. NGOs by their nature are able to promote community involvement (as Friends of the Earth has done), provide training for professionals from both communities (as the Arava Institute has done), and help to establish a professional community (as IPCRI has done). Universities and research institutes can establish long-term cooperative research programs, the results of which can benefit all parties.

But if more funds are provided for NGOs and academic institutions, the international donors should also monitor more closely the results of such efforts. More effective monitoring, including specification of clearer performance indicators and timetables, should be an integral part of the whole process. A mechanism is needed to coordinate the efforts of NGOs and academic institutions—perhaps the provision of a special fund to which a number of key donors contribute.

All this will only be possible if there is an adequate degree of flexibility on the part of those involved. The structures of decision-making within Israel and in the Palestinian Authority areas are not always such as to promote cooperation. Besides the actual water authorities on both sides, many other government ministries, from defense to health, feel they need to participate in decision-making about water. Only direction at a high level, from senior members of the governments of both sides, can change such negative dynamics.

The representatives of the donor community, working through national governments and international agencies, will need to influence senior political decision-makers and convince them, through persuasion and with funding, that cooperation pays. To do this effectively, individual officials will need to have a keen and personal interest in the work they are doing and its results. They will not be able to sit in their offices and "administer" but will have to go out and familiarize themselves with people with whom they are working and their daily considerations. They will have to care for the welfare of the communities in which they work at both an official level and more personally. Such effort to humanize aid will pay dividends in the long run.

Cooperation pays and third parties can help to promote it. They need to be vigorously involved both at a policy level and through the distribution of aid and the promotion of joint projects. Without such efforts the water problems in the region can never be dealt with effectively.

REFERENCES

Fisher, F. M., and A. H. Lee. 2005. *Liquid assets: An economic approach for water management and conflict resolution in the Middle East and beyond*. Washington, DC: Resources for the Future.

Haddad, M. 2007. Politics and water management: A Palestinian perspective. In *Water resources in the Middle East*, ed. H. Shuval and H. Dweik, 41. Berlin: Springer.

Husary, S., T. Najjar, and A. Aliewi. 1995. *Analysis of secondary source rainfall data from the northern West Bank*. Jerusalem: University of Newcastle and the Palestinian Hydrology Group.

Husseini, H. 2007. Palestinian Water Authority: Development and challenges—legal framework and capacity. In *Water resources in the Middle East*, ed. H. Shuval and H. Dweik, 301. Berlin: Springer.

Keidar, J., and F. Kawash. 2005. Regional water data banks project multilateral working group on water resources. In *Food security under water scarcity in the Middle East: Problems and solutions*, ed. A. Hamdy and R. Monti, 213–215. Bari:CIHEAM-IAMB.

Oka, H. 2002. Activities of the multilateral environmental working group. In *Security and environment in the Mediterranean*, ed. H. G. Brauch, P. H. Liotta, A. Marquina, P. F. Rogers, and S. M. El-Sayed, 573. Berlin: Springer.

Seby, I. 2003. Joint mismanagement: Reappraising the Oslo water regime. In *Water resources in the Middle East*, ed. H. Shuval and H. Dweik, 203–212. Berlin: Springer.

Sofer, A. 1994. The relevance of the Johnston Plan to the reality of 1993 and beyond. In *Water resources in the Middle East*, ed. H. Shuval and H. Dweik, 107. Berlin: Springer.

Sogge, D. 2002. *Give and take: What's the matter with foreign aid*. London: Zed Books.

Twite, R. 2005. The role of NGOs in promoting regional cooperation over environmental and water issues in Israel and Palestine—successes and limitations. In *Palestinian and Israeli environmental narratives, proceedings of a conference held in association with the Middle East Environmental Futures project*, ed. S. Schoenfeld. Toronto: Centre for International and Security Studies, York University. www.yorku.ca/yciss//whatsnew/documents/Twitepaper.pdf (accessed November 8, 2009).

United Nations Environmental Program. 2003. *Desk study on the environment in the occupied Palestinian Territories*. Geneva: UNEP.

West Bank Water Department. 2004. Institutional reform towards national bulk supply utility. In *Food security under water scarcity in the Middle East: Problems and solutions*, ed. A. Hamdy and R. Monti, 123. Paris: CIHEAM-IAMB.

Editors' Summary

If the past 15 years have made anything clear, it is that leaving Israelis and Palestinians to resolve their differences will have limited results. Quantum leaps forward in the region became possible due to interventions of third parties. The United States has been particularly active in this realm, from the work of special presidential envoy Eric Johnston during the 1950s to the work of the Clinton administration during the 1990s. The increasing status of the "quartet"—the negotiating consortium comprised of the United States, Russia, the EU, and the UN—creates a broad international umbrella for facilitating hydrological progress. This is a positive development that should be welcomed by both sides. Water constitutes a particularly promising area where this influence can find positive expression.

Robin Twite's presentation offers a frank assessment of what has and what has not been achieved by the international community's involvement in the water realm to date. The disappointing results in no way mean that third parties should find better areas on which to focus their assistance. Rather, aid should be given more strategically, prescriptively, and resolutely, with third-party involvement going beyond financial support. Twite's overall suggestions are widely accepted by both Palestinian and Israeli experts alike.

Accordingly, it is extremely important that once third parties decide to get involved, they remain involved and their staffs have the professional skills as well as the requisite attention spans and tours of duty to get beyond superficial familiarity. Given the anticipated strategic role of aid in Palestinian in improving conditions, there is room for participation of experts in the joint administrative bodies, like the Joint Water Committee. Indeed, the success of similar bilateral bodies, such as the International Boundary and Water Commission established under the Treaty between the United States of America and Mexico regarding Utilization of Waters of the Colorado and Tijuana Rivers and of the Rio Grande Rivers, was due to professional membership. This commission, for over half a century, has shown that joint management works when decisions are made by experts and engineers rather than by diplomats and politicians. Israelis and Palestinians are generally supportive of expanding the local Joint Water Committee to formalize input from the international donor community.

Any peace accord that is ultimately reached by Israel and Palestine will be fragile. The new equilibrium will only become more robust when the emergence of real benefits to the two parties becomes apparent. Israel's benefits will largely be diplomatic and associated with its enhanced security and status within the Middle Eastern community. Palestinians must see a transformation not only in

308

their political freedom but also in their quality of life. Water is a critical component of this change. International assistance will be crucial for upgrading the pressing sewage, water delivery, and desalination infrastructure investments that can both improve the lives of the Palestinians and stabilize existence for all residents of the region.

PART 15

COOPERATIVE WATER MANAGEMENT STRATEGIES

Ultimately, innovative institutional frameworks will need to be created for "joint" Palestinian-Israeli management of water resources to be effective. Marwan Haddad and Eran Feitelson have collaborated in numerous publications on this subject, providing numerous ideas for possible models. This part offers their latest thinking on the subject.

Joint Aquifer Management

INSTITUTIONAL OPTIONS

MARWAN HADDAD

ERAN FEITELSON

The Mountain Aquifer, composed of three sub-basins, supplies approximately a third of the Israeli water consumption and is the source of almost all the water supplied to the Palestinians in the West Bank. Due to the properties of this aquifer, it has long been suggested that it should be managed jointly. If the two parties do indeed intend to manage this shared resource judiciously, it is likely they will need to come up with innovative management structures. A series of options has been proposed in the past for such a structure (Feitelson and Haddad 1998). In practice, a coordinated management structure was established in the interim agreements (Oslo B) signed in September 1995. This structure is composed of a joint water committee (JWC) and joint supervision and enforcement teams (JSETs). Early experience with this structure led to arguments that it is insufficient and that there exists a need to move to more sophisticated structures (Nasseredin 2001). Practical steps to this end were also proposed in lieu of the permanent status negotiations that were expected at the time (Haddad et al. 1999).

This essay considers possible frameworks for joint management structures between the two parties. It begins by briefly reviewing the set of options identified in prior work. Then, the implications of a complete breakdown in relations, resulting in separate management, are reviewed. A discussion of these implications shows that there are still options that may be worth pursuing. Some steps for advancing such options are raised in the conclusion.

The Options: A Brief Review

There are four basic options for managing a shared aquifer: separately, in a coordinated manner, jointly, or by delegating responsibility to an outside body. Under separate management each party sets its own policies, drills its own wells, determines its own extraction rates, and sets its own standards. Coordinated management implies that each party manages the aquifer within its own territory but coordinates its actions with the other party. This is, in essence, the type of structure established under the Oslo B agreement. Joint management is the situation whereby a single institutional structure is established to carry out certain tasks viewed by the parties as the most crucial for adequate management of the aquifer.

Delegated responsibility involves assigning responsibility for the aquifer, or for some management tasks, to an external body. This could be a regional or international body or a privately owned corporation.

In practice, the sustainable management of any aquifer requires that many actions be undertaken (Haddad, Arlosoroff, and Feitelson 2001). These include determination of pumpage regimes and rates, drought policies, protection measures, monitoring, enforcement of restrictions on pumpage and land use, recharge enhancement projects, wastewater treatment standards and reuse policies, and crisis management measures. In addition, coordination of research as well as monitoring and sharing of data, models, and expertise facilitate a more effective management regime. Thus, any structure for managing a shared aquifer can potentially address multiple issues. The extent to which it does so is a function of the terms of reference set for the structure. Therefore, there are many options for transboundary bodies, ranging from bodies that coordinate a single activity to bodies that manage the aquifer comprehensively.

In previous work, a flexible-sequential framework for the management of shared aquifers was proposed (Feitelson and Haddad 1998). It suggests that, initially, a limited number of activities be undertaken jointly. These could serve as the basis for cooperative management structures. Additional activities would then be added to the purview of the structures over time. The added activities could lead to one of five basic orientations, according to the rationale chosen. Alternatively, from the second stage onward, activities could be added so as to expand the scope of the structure to include additional orientations. The five possible orientations identified were resource protection, whereby the activities are geared toward the protection of the aquifer; crisis management, whereby the focus is on managing crisis situations, as in such situations the most contentious circumstances arise; efficient water use, whereby the focus of the structure is assuring the efficient use of water, most commonly through a trading system; effective water supply, where the management of the extraction of the water and its distribution to consumers, and perhaps also the collection and treatment of sewage, are entrusted to a third private company; and comprehensive-integrative management, whereby an attempt is made from the outset to manage all aspects of the aquifer. This is the direction suggested in the Bellagio draft treaty (Hayton and Utton 1989).

We suggest that as resource protection and crisis management constitute the most imminent concerns, it might be most appropriate to focus on them during the early stages of implementation. Establishing transboundary markets or franchises was seen as more problematic, given the complete inexperience locally with such structures. A comprehensive-integrative approach is also seen as an unlikely early structure, given the inherent complexity and lack of confidence between the governments.

Issues Raised by Separate Management

As the transaction costs associated with establishing cooperative management regimes escalate, the likelihood that the aquifers will ultimately be managed

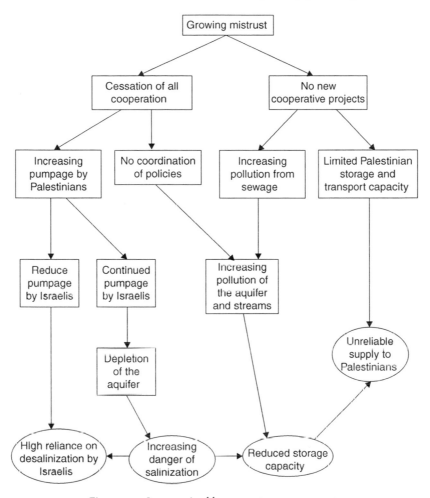

Figure 15.1 Issues raised by separate management.

separately increases. If a separation regime can endure, it is indeed unlikely in the foreseeable future that a cooperative structure will replace it, given the loss of confidence between the parties since September 2000. To assess whether there is a chance that a separate management regime will endure, it is necessary to identify and assess the issues such a regime raises. These are outlined in figure 15.1.

Under separate management each side will determine its own pumpage regime. The Palestinians are likely in this case to increase their extractions, given the current shortages and their desire to reduce their dependence on Israel. Israel can respond to this likely development in one of two ways (Tal 2001). It can reduce its pumpage so as to assure a sustainable yield or continue to extract all it extracts currently. While the first option may lead to confidence-building and thus possibly to better results in the long term, it is counter-intuitive and contradicts much of the current Israeli thinking. Hence, it is more likely that the result will be a race to the bottom, as the aquifer will increasingly be overpumped. The full implications of such massive

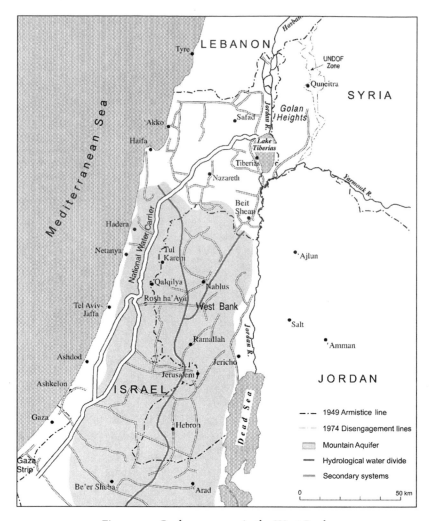

Figure 15.2 Recharge zones in the West Bank.

overpumping are not fully known, due to the uncertainty regarding underground saline water bodies. Still, it is clear that the threat of salination of the aquifer will rise and that water levels will drop, consequently raising extraction costs.

A second issue that is likely to arise is that of pollution. This includes both pollution from landfills and other point sources and wastewater collection, treatment, and reuse. As most of the recharge zones are in the West Bank (see figure 15.2), it is likely that the Palestinians will have a disproportionate effect on this issue. The degree to which there will be point source pollution will be a function of solid and hazardous waste handling in the Palestinian entity and land-use regulations therein. Given the multiple challenges that face the Palestinians, regardless of their exact boundaries, it is unlikely these issues will receive much attention, at least in the upcoming years. Thus, we can expect both point and nonpoint pollution to worsen as a function of population growth, economic growth, and changes in economic activities.

Currently, most of the wastewater generated in the West Bank flows untreated over the aquifer recharge areas. Some initial steps have been undertaken to build new wastewater collection and treatment plants on the West Bank with external funding. However, much of the West Bank is not yet connected to sewer systems, and almost none of the wastewater is treated to a secondary level. Even with external funding, it is likely that it will take considerable time before these problems are addressed. Moreover, the success of wastewater treatment is a function of the level of maintenance. Therefore, the mere construction of treatment plants does not assure that the wastewater will indeed be treated properly.

The wastewater treatment and reuse problem becomes even more difficult when the wastewater crosses boundaries. This issue has been tested in the Tulkarem region. In the Zomar/Alexander watershed, a local-level agreement between the municipality and the bordering Israeli regional council was reached. Thanks to intervention and funding from the German government, primary treatment was established in Tul Karem, and effluent levels were upgraded when the discharges reached the Yad Hana plant inside Israel. As a result, the Alexander River conditions have also improved. In a study of the options for managing the sewage of the Jerusalem region, Eran Feitelson and Qasem Abdul-Jaber show that separate management is the most costly and least effective option, and they suggest that third-party involvement by privatization should be explored. If the levels of distrust preclude any cooperation, then it is quite obvious that pollution from raw sewage is likely to remain an unresolved problem.

Water supply to the Palestinians in the West Bank will continue to be a problematic issue if the systems are totally separated, especially in drought situations. Given the lack of storage capacity in the Palestinian territories and the absence of conveyance systems in a north-south direction, except for the Israeli national water carrier, the Palestinians will find it difficult to balance the temporal and spatial variations in supply and demand. Hence, the Palestinians will face significant difficulties in assuring reliable water supply without Israeli assistance in conveyance and augmentation. Thus, even if Palestinians increase their extractions from the aquifers, the population, especially in the cities along the national water divide, may still suffer supply problems, especially in summer and drought years.

Assessing the Effects of Separate Management

If, indeed, the Mountain Aquifer is to be managed separately, none of the issues noted in the previous section will likely be addressed, especially if any attempt to address them will be perceived as providing the other side with a free rider option. Moreover, even if attempts are made to address some of these issues by one of the parties, the costs associated with such solutions will be considerably higher than in any cooperative mode.

Cooperation between the two parties has two potential benefits. First, any cooperative agreement will impose external obligations on the two parties that may induce them to undertake actions that they may not do otherwise. For example, if the water-for-wastewater exchange idea is adopted (Feitelson 2001), Israel will be required to augment Palestinian supplies, particularly in drought situations (Fischhendler 2003). At the same time Palestinians will be obliged to treat their wastewater to a pre-specified level (probably advanced secondary). Secondly, cooperation may facilitate greater cost-effectiveness. It will allow for exploitation of economies of scale, better use of resources, and more effective data generation and use.

From a long-term perspective, it is obvious that separation is an inferior option. This is particularly true, subsequent to the introduction of large-scale desalination in Israel, and will continue to be so—for as long as desalination will remain more costly than pumpage from the aquifer. As long as this condition holds true, the deterioration of the aquifer and the subsequent rise in the cost of supplying clean potable water from it will continue to imply an increase in the overall cost of water supply.

Over time the deleterious effects of separation are likely to become increasingly apparent. However, groundwater issues are generally less perceptible than other issues (including surface water issues), and the ability to rectify the damage to groundwater is limited and costly (Gvirtzman 2002). Thus, it is likely that by the time the damage is apparent enough to trigger action, it may be very late and much of the damage could be irreparable.

All of the adverse results of separation are well known to both parties, or at least to the experts on both sides. The problem with the establishment of cooperative regimes is largely an outcome of what Miriam Lowi (1993) termed "upper politics." As she correctly pointed out, no agreement on water is likely unless it conforms to the outlines of interests framed by the upper politics. At the same time, all international negotiations are constrained by domestic politics, as all such agreements have to be ratified domestically.

In the context of "upper politics" it is important to note that 8 years after the breakdown of the peace process of the 1990s, neither party advocates a return to the pre-Oslo "no recognition" stance. Rather, both sides publicly state that eventually they would like to reach an agreement. Despite the violence, there are ongoing discussions between the parties on various issues. The relative invisibility of water, particularly groundwater, and the anticipated tangible benefits, especially a better and more reliable supply to the Palestinians and less pollution to the coastal streams in Israel, mean that specific proposals for joint management of aquifers should reemerge. Moreover, if the confidence-building measures within the water field, advanced by Marwan Haddad, Eran Feitelson, Shaul Arlosoroff, and Taher Nasseredin (2001) prior to the breakdown in negotiations, are implemented, the transaction costs of cooperation may be somewhat reduced again.

A final status agreement that goes beyond separate or coordinated management approaches will have to address several thorny questions. For instance, it must resolve how differences will be adjudicated in a transboundary context and what will happen when certain customers default. Moreover, what will be the legal basis for such structures in transboundary situations, how are capital costs to be recovered, and how is the oversight of the franchise in the third-party option to be structured? Furthermore, it is necessary to understand what is likely to happen when a two-party situation turns into a three-party situation, as will happen when an international firm or other third party assumes responsibility for any part of the shared water system. That is, the likelihood that Israelis and Palestinians will cooperate vis-à-vis the international firm (so as to get the best deal and level of services) has to be compared to the likelihood that the international firm will play the two sides against each other, thereby worsening the distrust among them.

Conclusions

The current trend in the management of the shared Israeli-Palestinian aquifers is toward separation. However, due to the close interrelationship between the water sectors of the two parties and the attributes of the aquifers, this option is probably the worst from a resource management perspective. In the long term it seems, therefore, that some form of cooperative management will be needed, as was recognized already in the Oslo B agreement. Yet by the time the damages of separate management become apparent, much damage may be done to the detriment of both parties. Moreover, the greater the damage, the greater the cooperation will be needed to mitigate it. Actually, even the coordinated management structure established in the interim agreement was arguably insufficient. Thus, the two parties will probably need to discuss cooperation options again, regardless of the current impasse.

The main obstacle to greater cooperation is the loss of trust between the two parties. This loss pertains both to the existing coordination structure and to the good intentions and commitment of the other party to peaceful resolution of differences. At the same time, if and when the two parties do seek an area where agreements are feasible, which can be acceptable to wide domestic audiences, water may stand out as such an area. Thus, it seems likely that negotiations over water issues will resume at some point. However, they will be overshadowed by the loss of trust.

To overcome this impediment, it is suggested that the confidence-building measures identified by Haddad, Feitelson, Arlosoroff, and Nasseredin (2001) be implemented. These include changes in the way the institutions function and an augmentation of Palestinian water supply. However, such steps are likely to be insufficient. In particular, there will be a need to seek concurrently the cooperative structures that may be most appropriate for the current situation and that may be conducive for further agreements. It is suggested that structures based on third-party involvement may be particularly suitable for this purpose. In addition to their purported effectiveness, benefits may turn a two-party situation, where the two parties are highly suspicious of each other, into a three-party game, where the two parties share interests vis-à-vis the third party. However, to implement this type of structure, substantial preparatory work is needed.

REFERENCES

Feitelson, E. 2001. Water rights within a water cycle framework. In *Management of shared groundwater resources: The Israeli-Palestinian case with an international perspective*, ed. E. Feitelson and M. Haddad, 395–405. Boston/Dordrecht/London: Kluwer.

Feitelson, E., and Q. Abdul-Jaber. 1997. *Prospects for Israeli-Palestinian cooperation in wastewater treatment and re-use in the Jerusalem region*. Jerusalem: Jerusalem Institute for Israel Studies and the Palestinian Hydrology Group.

Feitelson E., and M. Haddad. 1998. A stepwise open-ended approach to the identification of joint management structures for shared aquifers. *Water International* 23:227–237.

——. 2001. A sequential flexible approach to the management of shared aquifers. In *Management of shared groundwater resources: The Israeli-Palestinian case with an international perspective*, ed. E. Feitelson and M. Haddad, 455–473. Boston/Dordrecht/London: Kluwer.

Fischhendler, I. 2003. Legal and institutional adaptation to climate uncertainty: A study of international rivers. Unpublished manuscript.

Gvirtzman, H. 2002. *Israel water resources*. Jerusalem: Yad Ben-Zvi (in Hebrew).

Haddad, M., S. Arlosoroff, and E. Feitelson. 2001. The management of shared aquifers: Principles and challenges. In *Management of shared groundwater resources: The Israeli-Palestinian case with an international perspective*, ed. E. Feitelson and M. Haddad, 455–473. Boston/Dordrecht/London: Kluwer.

Haddad, M., E. Feitelson, and S. Arlosoroff. 2001. The management of shared aquifers. In *Management of shared groundwater resources: The Israeli-Palestinian case with an international perspective*, ed. E. Feitelson and M. Haddad, 3–23. Boston/Dordrecht/London: Kluwer.

Haddad, M., E. Feitelson, S. Arlosoroff, and T. Nasseredin. 1999. *Joint management of shared aquifers: An implementation oriented agenda*. Final Report Phase II. Jerusalem: Palestine Consultancy Group and Harry S Truman Institute for the Advancement of Peace.

——. 2001. A proposed agenda for joint Israeli-Palestinian management of shared groundwater. In *Management of shared groundwater resources: The Israeli-Palestinian case with an international perspective*, ed. E. Feitelson and M. Haddad, 476. Boston/Dordrecht/London: Kluwer.

Harpaz, Y., M. Haddad, and S. Arlosoroff. 2001. Overview of the mountain aquifer: A shared Israeli-Palestinian resource. In *Management of shared groundwater resources: The Israeli-Palestinian case with an international perspective*, ed. E. Feitelson and M. Haddad, 43–56. Boston/Dordrecht/London: Kluwer.

Hayton, R., and A. Utton. 1989. Transboundary groundwaters: The Bellagio Draft Treaty. *Natural Resources Journal* 29:664–720.

Lowi, M. 1993. *Water and power: The politics of scarce resource in the Jordan River Basin*. Cambridge: Cambridge University Press.

Nasseredin, T. 2001. Legal and administrative responsibility of domestic water supply to the Palestinians. In *Management of shared groundwater resources: The Israeli-Palestinian case with an international perspective*, ed. E. Feitelson and M. Haddad, 107–114. Boston/Dordrecht/London: Kluwer.

Palestinian Economic Council for Development and Reconstruction. 2001. *Palestinian water strategic planning study*. Technical Assistance and Training Department, PECDAR.

Tal, G. 2001. Management of shared water resources in a situation without cooperation: The Mountain Aquifer case. Department of Geography, Hebrew University of Jerusalem (unpublished seminar, in Hebrew).

United Nations Environmental Programme. 2003. *Desk study on the environment in the occupied Palestinian Territories*. UNEP.

Editors' Summary

This part's underlying assumption is ultimately embraced by all of the book's participating authors: joint management of water resources between Israel and Palestine is inevitable. If the management system if designed wisely and equitably, this cooperation will also be more environmentally sound and economically efficient than unilateral actions which would inevitably lead to a tragedy of the commons dynamics—or what the authors refer to as a "race to the bottom."

The authors identify "trust" as a crucial dwindling resource that will need to be replenished as part of the establishment of an effective joint management strategy. The presence of third parties in a joint management framework can help provide some glue until personal ties become more solid. But trust will probably not constitute a problem for the water experts working on a joint committee, who presumably will be working together on practical solutions. Rather, political leaders who have a "bigger picture" to consider, in which water is but one element, will need to overcome the distrust accrued during past disappointing outcomes in order to move beyond earlier reconciliation attempts in other spheres. But nothing builds trust like achieving something concrete together, and water management surely can do that.

Joint management, indeed, is not an "all or nothing" proposition. A gradual and modular approach, as suggested in this part, appears to be the most promising and practical approach at present. If sufficient baby steps are undertaken, then the resulting momentum will lead to longer strides without either side noticing the magnitude of the change. What is particularly important is that decisions made jointly produce tangible benefits and that these are better communicated to the sides to create support for steadily increasing the level of joint management decisions and actions.

It is also important to focus energies at the present stage. The proposal that the joint water management process prioritize resource protection and crisis management in its future work makes sense in this context. These topics enjoy the greatest potential for "win-win" dynamics with the opportunity of showing the public and decision-makers the benefits of cooperation. Managing water resources together takes longer and is guaranteed to be more frustrating than unilateral policies and actions. But it also offers the hope of not only increasing the sustainability of the resulting decisions, but helping this troubled region move toward a new culture of cooperation.

Contributors

ZIAD ABDEEN is an expert in health sciences and has held several senior positions, including dean of research at Al-Quds University in Palestine. He is presently based at the university's Nutrition and Health Research Institute, and his research involves topics as diverse as risk assessment, air pollution monitoring, and treatment of leishmaniasis.

ALFRED ABED RABBO is an associate professor in the Department of Chemistry at Bethlehem University. He is the founding director of the university's Water and Soil Environmental Research Unit. He has been involved in dozens of research initiatives involving assessment of surface and groundwater quality.

YOUSEF ABU-MAYLA is the director of the Water Research Center at Al-Azhar University in Gaza. His research has involved rainwater harvesting, drinking-water quality, and groundwater hydrology. Dr. Abu-Mayla has been involved in numerous water-management planning projects and has consulted for NGOs and international agencies.

IYAD ABURDEINEH has a master's degree in environmental science and policy from George Mason University. He currently is on the staff of the Palestine Water and Environmental Development Organization (WEDO) as well as Friends of the Earth Middle East (FOEME) in Bethlehem. Previously, he worked with several Palestinian environmental NGOs.

EILON M. ADAR, director of the Zuckerberg Institute for Water Research at Ben-Gurion University, is a hydrologist and expert in water management. His research explores a novel transient-mixing-cell model approach, utilizing hydrochemistry and environmental isotopes, coupled with a non-steady flow model for quantitative assessment of groundwater flow systems.

AMJAD ALIEWI is the director-general of House of Water and Environment, a leading Palestinian environmental NGO. He holds a PhD in groundwater resources modeling from the University of Newcastle upon Tyne. His research has focused on water resources development, management, and planning, with emphasis on groundwater flow and pollution modeling.

KAREN ASSAF is a hydrologist presently affiliated with the Arab Scientific Institute for Research and Transfer of Technology in Ramallah and Arrabeh/Jenin, West Bank, Palestine. She has served as head of planning for the Palestinian Water Authority and published widely in the field of groundwater management in Palestine.

SAID A. ASSAF is director of the Arab Scientific Institute for Research and Transfer of Technology in Ramallah and Arrabeh/Jenin, West Bank, and is a leading Palestinian agricultural researcher. He previously served on the faculty of the University of Kansas. He still enjoys running his family farm.

DROR AVISAR is the head of the hydrochemistry laboratory at Tel Aviv University. He has worked as a lecturer at the University of California, Santa Barbara. Dr. Avisar's research focuses on understanding the physical-chemical processes associated with the occurrence and transport of pharmaceutical contaminants within the aquatic environment.

ALON BEN-GAL is a senior researcher in the Department of Environmental Physics and Irrigation, Institute of Soil, Water, and Environmental Sciences, the Agricultural Research Organization, Gilat Research Center, Israel. His research assesses irrigation of crops, utilization of saline and recycled wastewater, and plant response to environmental stress conditions.

GIDON BROMBERG is the Israeli director of EcoPeace/Friends of the Earth Middle East. He completed a 2007 World Fellowship at Yale University on global leadership and received *Time* magazine's Environmental Hero award. In early 2009 he was awarded the prestigious Skoll Prize for Social Entrepreneurship.

ERAN FEITELSON currently heads the Federmann School of Public Policy and Government at the Hebrew University, Jerusalem. In 1999 he was appointed chair of Israel's Nature Reserves and National Parks Board. He has served on several national and regional planning teams and has published widely on planning, water policy, and transport policy issues.

YAAKOV GARB is a lecturer at the Blaustein Institutes for Desert Research at Ben Gurion University and a visiting assistant professor at Brown University. Dr. Garb draws on interdisciplinary social analysis and science and technology studies (STS) to examine the environmental impacts and social contexts of technologies, projects, and trends.

AVITAL GASITH is a professor at Tel Aviv University's Faculty of Life Sciences and is considered to be Israel's leading authority on stream restoration. He has published widely in the field and served as an advisor to the Israeli government on stream restoration and biological monitoring.

MARCIA GELPE is Professor Emerita, William Mitchell College of Law, Minnesota, as well as Professor Emerita and director of the Center for Environmental Law, Netanya Academic College, Israel. She was on the original staff of the U.S. EPA and has published widely about environmental law in the United States and Israel.

NAHED GHBN received his doctorate in water and environmental engineering from Warsaw University in Poland. He has prepared and implemented numerous technical and economic studies involving infrastructure projects. He has conducted a range of research, training, and educational programs in the Palestinian planning, water, and environmental sectors.

MARWAN HADDAD is a professor of hydrological engineering at Al Najah University in Nablus, West Bank. He has published and consulted extensively on issues involving water management and water quality. Dr. Haddad was co-editor of the influential book *Management of Shared Groundwater: The Israeli-Palestinian Case with an International Perspective.*

RAMY HALPERIN is a consulting engineer for environment and health. He served as chief engineer and head of the Environmental Health Department at Israel's Ministry of Health, where he oversaw drinking-water quality. He served as coordinator of two official government committees that updated drinking-water quality regulations in Israel.

YARON HERSHKOVITZ is completing his doctorate at Tel Aviv University in the area of stream monitoring. He has been involved in numerous research initiatives monitoring stream conditions in Israel.

HIBA I. HUSSEINI is a managing partner with Husseini and Husseini, Attorneys and Counselors at Law. She has served as a consultant to the Palestinian Water Authority, participating in negotiations with Israel. In addition she has been a consultant to international organizations operating in the water and environmental sector in Palestine.

YOSSI INBAR is the director-general of Israel's Ministry of Environmental Protection. In his past position as deputy director-general for infrastructure at the Environmental Ministry, he chaired an inter-ministerial committee that established new wastewater treatment standards for Israel. Dr.Inbar has been an adjunct faculty member in environmental management at Hebrew University.

ANAN JAYOUSI is an associate professor in hydrology at An Najah University. He received his PhD in civil and environmental engineering from Utah State University. He conducts a variety of research in the fields of water resources planning and management and serves as an international consultant about water resources.

DORIT KERRET is a lecturer in the Department of Public Policy, Tel Aviv University. Her research focuses on environmental management, enforcement, and policy. She completed her doctorate at Tel Aviv University and post-doctoral studies at the Harvard School of Public Health.

NADER EL-KHATEEB is director of the Palestine Water and Development Organization (WEDO) in Bethlehem. With a background in engineering and water management, he has led research in the area of stream water-monitoring, management, and wastewater treatment. He is also the Palestinian director of Friends of the Earth Middle East.

RICHARD LASTER teaches environmental law and policy at Hebrew University's Faculty of Law, School of Environmental Sciences, and the Geography Department. Since 1980 he is the senior partner of a private law practice specializing in environmental law. Prior to this he was the first legal advisor at Israel's Environmental Protection Service.

CLIVE LIPCHIN is the director of research at the Arava Institute for Environmental Studies, Israel. He teaches courses in sustainable development, water management, and cultural and environmental interactions. Dr. Lipchin oversees research projects, workshops, and conferences about transboundary environmental problems facing Israel, Jordan, and the Palestinian Authority, recently focusing on the Dead Sea.

DAN LIVNEY is a lawyer in the law firm of Laster and Gouldman. His work focuses mainly on environmental law research on both the national and international level. He is also an olive farmer on Kibbutz Gezer.

LUCY MICHAELS is a doctoral researcher at the Albert Katz School for Desert Studies at Ben Gurion University of the Negev. She has worked extensively with peace, environment, and social justice organizations in Israel, Palestine, and the United Kingdom. Recently, she completed a Fulbright Fellowship at Yale University.

NANCY RUMMAN is a hydrologist who works as a senior staffer at the House of Water and Environment in Ramallah, Palestine. With a background in water engineering, she has researched and consulted widely in the area of water management and has been affiliated with research projects at Newcastle University.

ALON TAL is based at the Blaustein Institutes for Desert Research at Ben Gurion University. He is the author of *Pollution in a Promised Land* and *Speaking of Earth*. In 2008 he won a life achievement award for his public interest work from Israel's Ministry of Environmental Protection.

NA'AMA TESCHNER completed her master's degree at Ben Gurion University in 2007. She is presently enrolled in a PhD program at the School of Geography, the University of Leeds, United Kingdom. Her research focuses on the interplay between water, energy, and climate change in dry lands.

KHALIL TUBAIL is an associate professor of soil science and the acting dean of the faculty of agriculture at Al Azhar University in Gaza, and he runs the Arab Association for Quality Development and Improvement. He conducts research in the fields of saline water management and wastewater reuse in agriculture.

ROBIN TWITE is a retired British diplomat who founded the Environmental Department at the Israel Palestine Center for Research and Information. He has initiated numerous conferences and research on issues involving water management and has taught conflict resolution in various academic institutions throughout the region.

Index

Adam Teva V'Din, 285, 289
Adin Committee, 164, 165
aerobic ponds, 184
agriculture: early Jewish, 211; in Israel, 71–72, 76, 183, 211–222; local farming, 224; in Palestine, 39, 69, 76, 155, 177; subsistence farming, 154; sustainable, 193; use of treated wastewater in, 175, 179–180, 203; water consumption in, 219; Zionist attitude towards, 71–72, 193, 211. *See also* desalination; rain-fed agriculture
aid programs, 299–300, 301, 308
Alexander River, 130, 317
Amman, 241, 261
anaerobic stabilization ponds, 184
anti-scalants, 243
Applied Research Institute Jerusalem (ARIJ), 284, 289
aquatic organisms, 143
aquifers: deterioration of Palestinian, 21; recharge of, 175, 180, 181, 189, 314; shared management of, 313–320. *See also* Mountain Aquifer
Arab League, rejection of Johnston Plan, 259
Arava Institute for Environmental Studies, 131, 289, 305
Arava Valley, 217
arson, Carmel forests, 74
Ashdod desalination plant, 241; "Deal of the Year" (2007), 238
Ashkelon desalination plant, 240, 241, 242; "Desalination Plant of the Year" (2006), 238

bacteria, pathogenic, 164
Barak, Ehud, 72
barley, 201
beef production. *See* cattle
Bellagio draft treaty, 314
Ben Gurion, David, 33, 239
benzene, 31
Besor Reserve, 142
biodiversity, in rivers, Israel, 142
biological oxygen demand (BOD), 143, 171, 177, 184, 185
blue baby syndrome, 22, 276
blue water, 113

boron, 242
bottled water, 168, 170–171, 230, 278
brackish water: use of in Israel, 72, 215–217, 220, 254; use of in Palestine 53, 57, 112, 114. *See also* desalination
brine discharge, 233, 235, 243
British Mandate, 81, 195
Brooks, David, 290

Cabinet of Ministers, Palestine, 83–84
Canaanites, 195
canals: cement, 204; dirt, 204; West Ghor Canal, 255
cash crops, Palestine, 196
cattle and livestock, 214, 224
Centre for Environmental Diplomacy, Ramallah, 289
cesspool systems: Israel, 184; Palestine, 5, 168, 176
chloride concentrations in water: Gaza, 275; Israel, 162; Palestine, 21–22, 158, 232
cholera. *See* water-borne diseases
Citizens for the Environment in the Galilee, 285
citrus cultivation, 177, 179, 185, 196, 198–201, 213; Gaza, 229
climate change, 110–111, 251, 291
Clinton, President Bill, 308
Coastal Aquifer, 27, 29–31; area of, 269; contamination of, 30–31, 168; exploitation of, 159; Gaza, 3, 23–24, 104, 154, 229, 268–278; Israel, 162; overpumping, 31,104; pollution of, 119; recharge of, 179–181, 272; salinization of, 162. *See also* Gaza
Coastal Water Utility, Palestine, 86
conservation, of water, Palestine, 60
consumption, of water, 120; in Gaza, 229, 267; in Israel, 139, 215; in Palestine, 17–18, 24, 37, 154–155. *See also* agriculture
contamination, of water, 151; biological, 158
crops: Gaza, 276; industrial, 111; Israel, 187; Palestine, 134, 196–198. *See also* field crops
cropping patterns: Palestine, 111, 197, 208
crop subsides, Israel, 71
cryptosporidium. *See* parasites
culture, water: in Israel, 71–75; in Palestine, 67–70

dairy products. *See* cattle

dams, storage, 254

Dan Region Wastewater Reclamation Project (Shafdan), 32–33

Dan River, 253

data and information sharing, 46

Dead Sea, 3, 117, 127, 290, 304; decline, 72, 249, 255, 258; evaporation rate, 258; protection in Israel, 96, 261; UNESCO World Heritage site, 290

Degania dam, 127

desalination, 3–5, 123, 291, 318; agriculture, 221–222; environmental impacts of, 4, 235–236; in Gaza, 4, 229–237, 269, 277, 303; Hadera, 53, 241; history in Israel, 239–241; in Israel, 33–34, 77, 168, 215, 238–244; in Palestine, 114; Palmachim, 240; private sector, 246; pure water, 242; pre-treatment, 233; seawater, 230, 232; small scale systems, 230; use of brackish water, 203, 230–232. *See also* Eilat; reverse osmosis; technologies

desertification, 111

disinfection, of water: Israel, 165, kits, 170; Palestine, 180; UV, 181

distillation. *See* technologies, desalination

drinking water quality: Gaza, 158; Israel, 163–165; Palestine, 156–158

drinking water resources: Israel, 162–169; Palestine, 153–155, 156, 232

drinking water standards, 151–171; chemical, 164, 165; EC, 163; Israel, 163–165; microbial, 164, 165; Palestine, 153–161, 171; WHO, 163. *See also* World Health Organization

drip irrigation: Israel, 34, 77, 214, 220

drought-resistant crops, 3, 111

droughts: Israel, 1, 33, 37, 72, 74 123, 145, 217, 221, 239; Palestine, 111, 112, 289

dye industry, 129

dysentery. *See* water-borne diseases

Eastern Aquifer, 111

Eastern Groundwater Basin, 104

ecology, modern, 260

EcoPeace. *See* Friends of the Earth Middle East

education, 170, 287

effluent: disposal and reuse, Israel, 185–187, 217, 291; management concept, Palestine, 179; standards, Palestine, 177–178

Eilat, desalination, 239, 240, 241

Eisenhower, President Dwight David, 249, 254, 259, 295

electric conductivity, 158

electrodialysis. *See* technologies, desalination

emergency relief, 284

environmental infrastructure, 38

Environmental Protection and Research Institute, 284

Environmental Quality Authority, Palestine, 84–85, 87–88

environmental situation, Gaza, 175

Eocene Aquifer, 153, 269, 276

European Community, 163, 288

European Parliament, 287

eutrophication, 29

evapotranspiration, 139

farmers: in Israel, 221; in Palestine, 196. *See also* agriculture

farming. *See* agriculture

Fatah, 284

fecal coliform concentrations, 177, 178, 180

Feitelson, Eran, 311

fellahin (subsistence farmers), 69

ferric chloride, 236

ferric sulfate, 243

fertilizers, 108, 109, 157, 158, 159, 162, 219, 221, 268, 274

field crops, 224; in Israel, 214; in Palestine 199–201, 205

floods, 112, 131

flowers, cultivation in Israel, 213–214

fluoride, 23

fluvial systems, Israel, 137

Freedom of Information Law, 100

freshwater resources, 27–28

Friends of the Earth Middle East, 132, 149, 283, 284, 286, 290–291, 292, 301, 305

fruit cultivation, 196, 199–201, 205, 213

Galilee Society, 285

Gaza: area of, 267; Coastal Aquifer, 272–277; geology of, 269–272; groundwater flow regime, 269–270; new water resources, 276; population, 267, 268, 273, 274; regional cooperation, 276–277; sources of water, 267; water crisis, 267–269; 72–273; water deficit, 273; water quality, 268, 276. *See also* desalination

Gaza regional north-south water carrier, 234

Geneva Accords, 290

geological studies, 111

geopolitical changes, 121

giardia. *See* parasites

Good Water Neighbors Project, 132–133, 283, 287–288

Gordon, A.D, 71

grassroot water initiatives, 283, 285, 288, 291

gray-water, 112; recycling, 132

Green Cross International, 291

greenhouses, 203, 205–206, 213, 224

Green Line, 184, 288, 289

Green Party, Israel, 285

green water, 113
groundwater, 5; banking, 112; contamination
of, 6, 157, 318; deterioration of, 233; Gazan
resources, 267–271; Israeli resources,
117–121; Palestinian resources, 103–108,
protection of in Israel, 96; recharge, 112;
shared resources, 103–123, 292; West Bank
resources, 21
groundwater management, Palestine, 108–110

Haddad, Professor Marwan, 300, 311
Hamas, 53, 58–59, 284, 289
Harza Group, 241
health, Gaza, 276. *See also* illnesses; water-
borne diseases
heavy metals, 162, 177–178, 185–187
Hebron University, 289
Helsinki Rules, 3
herbicides, 221, 268
House of Water and Environment,
Ramallah, 284
"hydro-hysteria," 243, 244
hydrological sustainability, 37

illnesses, linked to unsafe drinking water,
229. *See also* water-borne diseases
industrial discharge, 112
industrial solvents, 189
infiltration ponds, 179
infrastructure, of water distribution, 170,
292; in Gaza, 267, 278; impact of IDF,
68–69; in Israel, 71–72, 225; in Palestine,
67, 109, 129, 155
Integrated Aquifer Management Plan, 231
Inter-Ministerial Committee (Inbar
Committee), 185
International Development Research Centre
(IDRC), 286
intifada, 68, 76, 225, 246; first, 286; second,
286, 287, 288, 300
irrigation, use of recycled wastewater in, 173,
175–177, 179, 180
Israeli-Arab War (1967), 195
Israeli-Palestinian-American Committee, 45
Israeli-Palestinian Centre for Research and
Information (IPCRI), 286, 293, 301, 304,
305, 306
Israeli-Palestinian Scientific Organization
(IPSO), 286
Israeli-Palestinian Study Group on
Protection of the Environment, 289
Israel River Rehabilitation Administration,
143–144
Israel Water Authority, 26, 287, 290, 305

Jenin project, 47
Jewish Agency, 212

Jewish National Fund, 144
Johannesburg Environmental Summit
(2002), 255
Johnston, Eric, 249, 259, 295, 308
Johnston Plan, 254, 259–260, 261, 295
Joint Environmental Mediation Service
(JEMS), 286
joint projects, 45
Joint Supervision and Enforcement Teams
(JSETs), 51, 56, 59, 313
Joint Technical Committee, 262
Joint Water Committee (JWC), 6–7, 43, 45,
208, 293, 305, 308; establishment of, 44–45
81, 261, 262, 298, 313; failures of, 63, 148, 301,
302; role of, 46–47, 51, 277, 300; successes
of, 58–59, 63
jojoba oil production, 201, 207
Jordan River, 3, 19, 53, 104, 112, 127, 137, 195,
204; Palestinian Authority, 261–262;
pollution, 264; protection of, 261; pumping
dynamics, 260–261; sources of, 251, 253, 255;
spiritual centre, 264; tributaries of, 249;
water conflict, 254, 259–260; water quality,
251, 262–263; water quantity, 258–259, 264.
See also recreation
Jordan Valley, 21–22, 104, 111, 117, 137, 196,
289; agricultural wells, 251; floodwater,
254; groundwater resources, 251–252;
spring water, 252; surface water, 253–254
Judean desert, 143

kibbutz, as agricultural settlement, 211
Kidron Stream, 127
Kurker Group, 269

Lake Kinneret (Sea of Galilee), 27, 28–29, 53,
119, 137, 139, 258, 285; disinfection of, 165;
ozonation of, 165
land confiscation, Palestine, 197
landfill, 289, 303
Land Research Centre, 284
land use, Palestine, 197
legislation, water, 79, 98; in Israel, 90–97;
in Palestine, 81–89; licensing
arrangements, 99
low-volume irrigation systems, 219. *See also*
drip irrigation

"making the desert bloom," 211
management strategies, Israel, 31–34
marine life, effect of desalination on, 235
Mediterranean Sea, 127, 241, 244,
270–271, 274
Mediterranean water shortages, 50
Mekorot Company, 52–53, 57, 155, 156,
170, 241
membranes. *See* technologies, desalination

metering, of water, 220
methemoglobinemia. *See* blue baby syndrome
Mexico, 5, 6, 99, 308
microbes, 243
micro-sprinklers, 219
Middle East Research and Cooperation initiative (MERC), 133
military occupation, Palestine, 196; land use before and after, 198–201
Military Order (MO), 81–82
minerals, 221
Ministers Committee for Economics, Israel, 185
Ministry of Agriculture: Israel, 212, 217; Palestine, 83, 203
Ministry of Energy and Natural Resources, Palestine, 83
Ministry of Finance, Israel, 239
Ministry of Health: Israel, 163, 164, 184, 185, 241; Palestine, 83–85, 87, 88
Ministry of Local Government, Palestine, 84, 85, 88
Ministry of Planning and International Cooperation (MOPIC), 84
Ministry of the Environment, Israel, 33, 96, 187, 241, 303
moshav, as agricultural settlement, 211, 213
mosquitoes, 129, 133, 189
Mountain Aquifer, 3, 27, 29, 101, 128–129, 155, 251, 287, 298, 304; catchment area, 117, 313; finite resource, 110; geology of, 117–118; historic rights to, 122; Jewish settlement above, 119; management of, 314–319; overpumping of, 315–316; Palestinian rights to, 256; pollution, 119, 301; protection of, 284, 314; recharge of, 117, 316–317; salination of, 316; source of drinking water, 156, 158, 162
Mount Scopus Group, 118–119
mudflats, 258
Multi-lateral Committee, 298, 300

Nahr-El-Auja-Tamaseeh Basin. *See* Western Groundwater Basin
nationalization, 225
National Master Plan 34B, 240
National Planning Council, Israel, 93
National Water Carrier, 32, 71, 165, 215, 239; taste of water, 168
National Water Council, Palestine, 83, 88
National Water Plan, Palestine, 86; methods of implementation, 87–88
natural water resources, 49
Nature and Parks Authority, Israel, 144
Negev, 143, 217, 218, 239, 276, 285
Neighbors Paths, Peace Park, 149

NGOs, 47, 88–89, 95, 97, 100, 295, 298, 299, 305, 306; in agriculture, 204; cross-border, 287, 290; Israeli, 281, 283–285, 293; Palestinian, 281, 283–285, 290, 292, 293, 304
"Nile Initiative," 264
nitrate concentration in water: Gaza, 275, 276; Israel, 171; Palestine, 22–24, 157, 180–181, 232
nitrogen, 181, 184
Northeastern Groundwater Basin, 104

olive cultivation, 130 177, 196, 199, 284
Oslo Accords, 14, 81, 129, 262, 286, 290–291, 292, 298, 313; background, 43, 300, 318; cooperation, 45, 47–48, 50–51, 56; failures of, 62–63, 303; implementation of, 45–48, 51; Israeli perception of, 49–50; lessons learned from 48, 60; obstacles, 48; Palestinian expectations of, 43–45; successes, 62–63
Ottomans, 81, 195
overpopulation, 261
overpumping: Gaza, 268, 269, 272; Israel, 189, 239–240; Palestine, 156; water depression as a result of, 56. *See also* Mountain Aquifer
ownership of water, Israel, 90

Palestine Hydrology Group (PHG), 284, 289, 304. *See also* NGOs
Palestine Water and Environmental Development Organization, 130–131
Palestinian Agricultural Relief Committees (PARC). *See also* NGOs
Palestinian Authority, 262, 284, 298, 303, 305
Palestinian Centre for Human Rights (PCHR), 284
Palestinian Environmental Quality Agency, 303
Palestinian-Israeli Environmental Secretariat (PIES), 286
Palestinian Negotiation Support Unit (NSU), 52
Palestinian Peace and Freedom Youth Forum, 290
Palestinian Steering and Monitoring Committee, 291
Palestinian Water Authority (PWA), 15, 21, 46, 54–55, 59, 68, 132, 287, 290, 302; establishment of, 81–83, 155–156; Jordan River, 255; role of, 82–85, 87, 159, 171, 267
Palmachim beach, 34
parasites, water, 164
parks, riparian. *See* recreation
Partition Plan, United Nations (1947), 259
Pasternak, Dov, 205
peace agreement, Israel-Jordan (1994), 260

peace process, 121, 122, 290, 318
per capita water consumption. *See* consumption of water
Permanent Status Agreement, 49, 52; lack of, 57; problems affecting implementation, 57–58
pesticides, 109, 159, 221, 268, 274
piping system: in Gaza, 268; in Palestine, 155
Planning and Building Law (1965), 73
plastic tunnels, 204. *See also* greenhouses
polio. *See* water-borne diseases
polishing reservoirs. *See* reservoirs
political instability, 48
pollution, water: drinking water, 156; penalties in Israel, 95–96; penalties in Palestine, 87–88; prevention of, 50, 285, 289; sea, 91–92; sources of in West Bank, 25; transboundary, 142–143, 317
population growth, 121, 173, 291, 317; Gaza, 267, 273, 274; Israel, 136, 139; Palestine, 109, 114, 149, 199. *See also* overpopulation
poultry, 214
precipitation: in Israel, 26, 136, 251; in Palestine, 110, 157
pricing, of water, 224–225; in Israel, 34, 74, 90, 211, 220; in Palestine, 69
privatization, 171
public education programs, 8
Public Health Ordinance, Israel, 91, 96
public-private partnerships (PPP), 244

Rabin, Yitzhak, 286
Rafah, 269, 271
rain-fed agriculture: in Israel 214; in Palestine, 195–198, 201, 224
rainwater: harvesting, 21, 68, 279; infiltration, 158, 268; in Palestine, 104, 132, 157
recreation, 179; in Jordan River, 259, 264; riparian parks, 149–150
Red-Dead canal, 53, 75, 241, 255–256, 261; cost of, 255–256
refugee population, Palestine, 199, 229
reservoirs: in Gaza, 267, 269; polishing, 184; seasonal, 184
reverse osmosis, 220, 231–233, 242–244, 278; desalination plants, 233–236; home systems, 230
river restoration, 8
Roman rule, Palestine, 195

salinity: of drinking water, 157; of groundwater in Palestine, 21–22, 104, 108, 156, 175; of soil, 134, 190
Saqiya Group, 269
sanitation, 289
Sea of Galilee. *See* Lake Kinneret

seasonal reservoirs. *See* reservoirs
Separation Wall, 197, 288
septic tanks, 170, 268, 276
sewage: to grow crops, 128; untreated, 21, 50
sewage treatment, 173–191; in Gaza, 175–181; infrastructure, 183, 189; Memorandum of Understanding (MOU), 54; Palestine, 53–55, 122–123, 179–181; projects pending, 45–46; Ramallah, 55; recycling, 32; upgrading, 5, 170, 173
Shafdan plant, 217, 243
Sharif, Nabil, 53
Sharon, Ariel, 72
sheep production, 201
Shuval, Hillel, 243. *See also* "hydro-hysteria"
sinkholes, 258
Six Day War (1967), 302
slaughterhouses, 129
Society for the Protection of Nature in Israel (SPNI), 285
sodium, 187; concentration in water, 158
soil, 183, 185, 211
solid waste, 129
springs: rehabilitation of, 254; West Bank, 67
stream contamination, transboundary, 127–128
stream health assessment, Israel, 141–142
stream reclamation, Israel, 144
stream rehabilitation, Israel, 136–137, 144–145
stream restoration, 125–150; bilateral cooperation in research, 131; Israel, 143–144, 145; Palestine, 130–131, 134, 148
streams: Mediterranean climate streams, 137–138; multiple stressed stream ecosystems, 139–141; in Palestinian culture, 128; transboundary, 134, 149
stream-supplied irrigation, in Palestine, 69
Stockholm Declaration (1972), 260
subsidies, Israel, 74, 212
sulfate, in West Bank, 22
surface water, 128–129; monitoring and modelling, 133–134; sources of pollution in Palestine, 129–120
sustainable agriculture. *See* agriculture
sustainable tourism, 288
sustainable water management, Palestine, 108–109, 112

TAHAL, 239, 285
Tal, Shimon, 53
tankers, water, 157
technologies: desalination, 230–232; distillation, 230; membrane, 231, 238
theft of water, 55–56
toluene, 31
total dissolved solids, 22, 54, 143, 177, 184, 185, 235

Towns Association for Environmental
    Quality, Sakhnin, 289
transboundary water issues, 283, 285–287,
    289–291, 318–319
transboundary water resources, 103, 133, 262,
    281; in Gaza, 268
trees, 111
Trottier, Julie, 290
turbidity, water, 164–165, 232
Twite, Robin, 287, 295

unauthorized drilling, 56
UNESCO, 286, 290
United Nations, 6, 300, 303
United Nations International Panel on
    Climate Change (IPCC), 123
United States, 5, 6, 99, 131, 308
untreated wastewater, 127
USAID, 233, 234, 288, 289, 302, 303, 305
U.S. House of Representatives, 287
UV disinfection. See disinfection, UV

Van Leer Institute, 289

wadis: Gaza, 229; Jordan River, 254;
    Palestine, 158, 175
wastewater, treated: use of in agriculture
    175, 179, 180
wastewater disposal, Palestine, 158
wastewater recycling, 173, 217–218
wastewater reuse, 3, 226, 314, 317; Israel,
    32–33, 73, 96, 99, 131, 183–188; Palestine, 112,
    131, 134, 177–178, 187
wastewater treatment plants: Gaza, 277,
    300–301; Israel, 33, 184–185; Palestine,
    175–177, 179, 180–181, 190; West Bank, 317
water allocation, 98; in Israel, 67; in Palestine
    50, 60, 67
Water and Soil Environmental Research
    Unit (WSERU), Bethlehem, 156, 157
Water Authority, Israel, 90
water-borne diseases, 151, 163, 189
Water Commission, 291
"water for peace" strategy, 204
Water Law, Israel, 74, 90–94, 136;
    enforcement of, 95, 98–100
Water Law, Palestine, 82–85; enforcement
    of, 87–88, 98–100
water loss, delivery systems, 67–68
water management: framework in
    Palestinian authority, 82–84; 108–110, 113;
    nature's right, 145
water market: bilateral, 4; multilateral, 4:
    regional, 4
Water Master Plan, 231

water needs, in Palestine, 15–21, 25, 238
water quality: coordination of standards,
    7, 98; drinking water, 76; Gaza coastal
    aquifer, 23–24: protection of, 5; protection
    of in Israel, 91–96; public participation,
    7–8, 111; West Bank, 21–23
water resources, 288, 297; development of in
    Israel, 52–53; development of in Palestine,
    20; freshwater, 27–28; in Israel, 26–35, 37;
    in Palestine, 13–25, 37–38, 103–108; in West
    Bank, 13–18
water retention structures, 254
water rights, 2–3; agreements between
    Palestine and Israel, 1–2; disagreements, 2;
    Palestinian, 18, 25, 38, 57, 225, 300
watersheds: in Israel, 136; Jordan River
    Basin, 257; transboundary, 131–132, 136,
    145, 150
water shortages, 1; in Israel, 183; in Palestine,
    45, 68
water sources: developing new, 40–50
water supply: in Israel, 91; to Palestinian
    homes, 60; Palestinian shortfall, 45
water usage cycle, 109–110
Wazzani River, Lebanon, 260
weather stations, 133
wells, 190, 281, 284, 313; in Gaza, 265, 268,
    272, 275; Jenin project, 47; Jordan River
    Basin, 251, 255; in Palestine, 14, 21, 179, 203,
    255, 284; in West Bank, 301
West Bank Water Department (WBWD),
    14–15
Western Aquifer Basin, 104
Western Groundwater Basin, 103–104
West Ghor Canal. See canals
wetlands, as treatment plants, 132, 145
Wolf, Aaron, 259
World Bank, 241, 300, 303; Red-Dead
    canal, 256
World Health Organization (WHO), 24, 154,
    157, 241; drinking water standards, 163, 229,
    234, 242, 275; effluent reuse guidelines,
    178–179, 180–181
World War II, 195
World Water Council, 291

Yarkoun-Taninim Basin, 117, 119. See also
    Western Groundwater Basin
Yarmouk River, 253, 258, 260

Zaslavsky, Dan, 74
"zero sum game," 3, 37, 246
Zionist, resettlement in Palestine, 211.
    See also agriculture
Zomar-Alexander Stream, 130, 133, 317